CANADIAN POLITICS

A Comparative Reader

Edited by
Ronald G. Landes
Saint Mary's University

Prentice-Hall Canada Inc., Scarborough, Ontario

For my identical twin brother Don:
a most admirable comparative
reference point in life.

Canadian Cataloguing in Publication Data

Main entry under title:

Canadian politics : a comparative reader

Includes index.
ISBN 0-13-113861-8

1. Canada - Politics and government.   I. Landes,
Ronald G., 1945-

JL65 1985.C36 1985   320.971   C84-099463-X

46,132

© 1985 by Prentice-Hall Canada Inc.

Prentice-Hall Inc., Englewood Cliffs, New Jersey
Prentice-Hall International, Inc., London
Prentice-Hall of Australia, Pty., Sydney
Prentice-Hall of India Pvt., Ltd., New Delhi
Prentice-Hall of Japan, Inc., Tokyo
Prentice-Hall of Southeast Asia (Pte.) Ltd., Singapore
Editora Prentice-Hall do Brasil Ltda., Rio de Janeiro
Prentice-Hall Hispanoamericana, S.A., Mexico

ISBN 0-13-113861-8

Design: Lisa Guthro/Robert Garbutt Productions
Copy Editor: Deborah Burrett
Production Editor: Charles Macli
Production: Alan Terakawa
Typesetting: Howarth and Smith

Printed and bound in Canada by Imprimerie Gagné
1 2 3 4 IG 88 87 86 85

Contents

iii

Preface for Teachers

The possible justifications for a collection of articles on politics are as numerous as the various approaches to the discipline itself. The assumption on which this book is based is that Canadian politics can be understood best in a comparative framework. Therefore, our specific rationale is to provide an interesting series of readings on Canadian politics which contains as much explicitly comparative material as possible—hence our title, *Canadian Politics: A Comparative Reader*. As a result, this compilation is the only one available which seeks to locate the study of Canadian politics within the broader tradition of comparative political analysis.

To that end, *Canadian Politics: A Comparative Reader* might be used in conjunction with several other paperbacks (in lieu of a reader which focuses only on Canada) or as a companion volume with *The Canadian Polity: A Comparative Introduction*, whose broad structure it follows. The countries which form the bases of the comparative readings are Canada, Britain and the United States, although all three are not necessarily dealt with in every selection. Some articles focus only on Canada, while others deal with broader themes of comparing political systems (to which the Canadian experience can be profitably and easily integrated).

The criteria for article selection were fourfold. First, each analysis had to be written in a style and format suitable for use by undergraduate university students. Second, as many readings as possible had to compare Canada with other countries. While a number of articles might look only at Canada, these would be of such a nature as to allow comparisons to be easily made by the student. Third, some studies of a broad comparative focus also had to be included. Fourth, although the selections had been published previously, none of those chosen would be available in any other collection of readings.

In compiling this text an extensive search of the social science periodicals and recent political science literature was conducted which resulted in a variety of sources being utilized. As an example of the diversity and range of articles considered, the following list of journals from which we have reprinted articles should be instructive: *The Canadian Journal of Political Science, Parliamentary Affairs, Policy Options, The Canadian Historical Review, The Parliamentarian, Journal of Commonwealth and Comparative Politics, The American Review of Canadian Studies, Canadian Public Administration, Public Opinion, Canadian Parliamentary Review, Political Studies, International Political Science Review,* and the *Manitoba Law Journal.* Several excerpts from books as well as three articles from newspapers (*The Globe and Mail, Financial Times of Canada*) have also been included.

The thirty-five readings are organized into two main sections—Part One: Political Institutions and Structures and Part Two: Political Processes and Political Behaviour. Part One is composed of subsections on the constitution, federalism and each of the three branches of government, while Part Two is structured around the topics of political culture, political parties and electoral behaviour. Within the two main sections, each subsection is preceded by an introduction to the topic which briefly summarizes the main themes of each article and establishes continuity between readings through its analytical commentary. A further aid to integrating the selections is provided by the subject index which allows cross-referencing of major topics and concepts.

The editor would be most appreciative of any comments that readers or colleagues might have. In particular, suggestions regarding articles for future editions would be welcomed. Please send your views to the editor at the following address: Political Science Department, Saint Mary's University, Halifax, Nova Scotia, Canada, B3H 3C3.

Preface for Students

A typical approach to the study of politics at the beginning university level is to focus on the governmental and political processes of one's own country. While such a perspective is indeed important, the rationale for this book is somewhat broader, namely, that Canadian politics can be more easily understood and explained in a comparative context. The student of Canadian politics can learn much from the political processes and practices of other countries.

In that light, we have selected thirty-five readings on particular aspects of Canadian and/or comparative politics. While some focus only on Canada, others concentrate on either broad issues and topics important for comparative analysis or on more specific comparisons among the liberal democratic polities of Canada, Britain and the United States. The book is divided into two main sections: Part One focuses on political institutions and structures, with particular reference to the constitution and the three branches of government; Part Two concentrates on political processes and political behaviour, with subsections on political culture, political parties and electoral behaviour.

At the beginning of every unit a brief summary of each article's main themes is presented to help guide the student. In addition, the subject index at the end of the book is useful in cross-referencing important themes and concepts in the various selections.

Since this work is designed as a pedagogical tool for students, any reaction from you would be most welcomed by the editor. Your views and suggestions for improvements in future editions of this text can be sent to the editor at the following address: Political Science Department, Saint Mary's University, Halifax, Nova Scotia, Canada, B3H 3C3.

Acknowledgments

While the editor, of course, assumes responsibility for any errors in or criticisms of this volume, any credit must first of all go to the individual authors whose work and cooperation have made this volume possible. A grateful word of thanks is also most deserved by the journal editors and publishers of the articles reprinted here.

Saint Mary's University provided a congenial atmosphere in which to work. Gratitude is certainly owed to Ms. Laurie Jonah, political science departmental secretary, for her typing and, especially, for the extensive correspondence involved in a project such as this. Finally, the encouragement of several friends and colleagues is most happily and sincerely recorded, in particular, that of Dr. Peter Dale, Professor Edward J. McBride, and Professor Fred Crooks.

The editorial and production staffs of Prentice-Hall Canada have, once again, been superb: efficient, courteous, productive and on schedule. A most appreciative thank you is hereby given to Cliff Newman, Marta Tomins, and Tim McCleary.

Political Structures and Political Institutions

Few observers of the nature of government in Canada would likely disagree with the suggestion that "A Canadian is a person who has a dream, which he wants financed by government."[1] The magnitude of government is one of the most visible traits which strikes foreign commentators about Canadian politics.

In 1850, for example, a young Henry David Thoreau made an 1100 mile trek through pre-Confederation Canada. While his observations in *A Yankee in Canada* reveal some of the typical shortcomings of an expert having visited the place he writes about at least once, Thoreau recorded some interesting, comparative comments about the mid-nineteenth century role of government in Canada and the United States. Thoreau describes English government—and by implication, Canadian government as well—as a "government. . .that cannot afford to be forgotten. . . ." He adds that the principal advantage which, in his opinion, makes the American system more tolerable "is the fact that there is so much less of government with us." Thoreau concluded that "in Canada you are reminded of the government every day. It parades itself before you. It is not content to be the servant, but will be the master; and everyday it goes out. . .and exhibits itself and its tools."[2]

The important and extensive role of government in Canada has certainly not declined since Thoreau's day. Even though mankind may very well make "a poorer performance of government than of almost any other human activity,"[3] governments still provide the context within which basic individual and societal choices are made.

> Governments set the frames of our lives. They establish policies and make decisions that limit our freedoms, affect our economic well-being, and contribute greatly to our happiness and to our discontents.[4]

Governments carry out such functions, in part, by providing specific institutional contexts within which the battles for influence and power in the polity take place. Institutions such as the executive, legislative and judicial branches of government establish both the parameters of the political process and the basic rules of the political game. Governmental institutions are the "recognized and accepted arrangement of ultimate power in a country."[5] However, although political institutions and structures heavily influence the outcome of the political contest, they do not entirely predestine the result.

> Our political institutions, our history and contemporary circumstances, create restraints upon and offer opportunities for initiative

2

and innovation by our political leaders. But institutions, history, and circumstances are their chamber pots of fortune.[6]

Institutional arrangements vary significantly between different types of systems; for example, democratic as compared to totalitarian polities, presidential as compared to parliamentary systems. Even within a particular grouping, such as democratic parliamentary systems, institutions show elements of uniqueness. For example, the British and Canadian patterns of cabinet government are fraternal, not identical, twins. Thus, the nature of political institutions, their development and composition, and their interrelationships have often formed a focal point for comparative political investigations: "any analysis of government is, in the deepest reality, either implicitly or explicitly comparative."[7]

Constitutional and institutional comparisons have played a significant part in the field of comparative politics because the "purpose of a constitution is simply to lay down the rules for the operation of the organs of government in relation to one another and in relation to the citizen."[8] In Part One, the readings analyze the nature of constitutions as well as significant aspects of each of the three branches of government.

NOTES

1. "All Canadian Air Farce," C.B.C. Radio, April 24, 1983.

2. HENRY DAVID THOREAU, *A Yankee in Canada* (Montreal: Harvest House, 1961), pp. 105-6.

3. BARBARA TUCHMAN, *The March of Folly: From Troy to Vietnam* (New York: Alfred A. Knopf, 1984), p. 4.

4. CARL COHEN, *Four Systems* (New York: Random House, 1982), p. vii.

5. JOHN H. REDEKOP, "Canadian Political Institutions," in Redekop (ed.), *Approaches to Canadian Politics*, 2nd ed. (Scarborough, Ontario: Prentice-Hall Canada, 1983), p. 149.

6. ROBERT CRAIG BROWN, "Fishwives, Plutocrats, Sirens and Other Curious Creatures: Some Questions About Political Leadership in Canada," in R. Kenneth Carty and W. Peter Ward (eds.), *Entering the Eighties: Canada in Crisis* (Toronto: Oxford University Press, 1980), p. 159.

7. JEAN BLONDEL, *Comparing Political Systems* (New York: Praeger, 1972), p. 5.

8. J.R. MALLORY, *The Structure of Canadian Government*, rev. ed. (Toronto: Gage, 1984), p. 3.

The Constitution and Federalism

In democratic political systems constitutions are usually key elements in restraining and restricting the potential abuses and misuses of political power. As a result, such constitutions help to foster a pattern of constitutional government: "the most ancient, the most persistent, and the most lasting of the essentials of true constitutionalism still remains what it has been almost from the beginning, the limitation of government by law."[1]

To produce a system of constitutionalism is a difficult task indeed, for most constitutions in the modern era have neither created constitutional government nor lasted very long.

> Duration is not the only political virtue, but it is a virtue. Constitutions, by their name and function, can be deemed successes only if they last long enough to give stability to the political life of the society they are supposed to serve.[2]

In that regard the Canadian, British and American constitutional experiences are significant exceptions to the general pattern. Even the constitutional drama of 1980 to 1982 in Canada, which culminated in the passage of the Constitution Act of 1982, did not fundamentally alter the Canadian pattern of "constitutional conservatism":

> The major lesson to be drawn from recent Canadian constitutional experience, then, is the truly impressive capacity of the existing constitutional system to survive, to outlast its detractors, and to frustrate those who seek its fundamental transformation.[3]

In successfully preparing any constitutional document, a series of important questions must be answered: first, what type of politi-

4

cal system is desired (e.g., democratic, authoritarian, totalitarian); second, what type of governmental structure will be selected (e.g., presidential or parliamentary); third, what basic political principles will be incorporated into that structure (e.g., federalism); and fourth, what specific mechanisms will be used to achieve the decisions taken in answer to questions one through three (e.g., a Charter of Rights, judicial review, a competitive party system). No matter what answers are chosen, the drafting of the ensuing document presents a range of problems and pitfalls.

Having made a comparative study of constitutions, Edward McWhinney, in reading number one ("Some Rules of Constitutional-prudence for Contemporary Constitution-makers"), specifies a compendium of valuable guidelines for composing a successful constitutional document. As McWhinney emphasizes, a constitution is not merely a legal document, but a political one as well. Moreover, while a constitution may reflect a society's political ideas at a particular moment in time, if it is to endure, it must not be tied too closely to any one specific ideology or party. Finally, societies change, as do the various extra-constitutional rules such as the electoral system. To survive and to carry out its basic functions, a constitution must be flexible enough to adapt to that changing environment. On the basis of this list, an interesting comparative assessment could be made of the Canadian and American Constitutions. Moreover, these rules might serve as a guide in evaluating the constitutional reform process in Canada between 1980 and 1982 and the resulting Constitution Act of 1982.

In designing the Canadian polity, the Fathers of Confederation selected two basic principles of political organization: federalism and parliamentary sovereignty. Federalism, the division of power between levels of government, is an attempt to structure the political system to achieve both unity (i.e., a national government) and diversity (i.e., provincial governments). The federal principle has been a key point of controversy throughout Confederation and during periods of constitutional reform. In reading number two ("Comparing Federal Systems"), Herman Bakvis analyzes some of the issues involved in comparing federal and non-federal systems and suggests that Canada has much to learn from the "federal experiences" of other countries.

The second basic principle of Canadian government, the supremacy of parliament (the unrestricted ability to pass legislation), is an idea that does not easily mesh well with that of federalism. In reading number three ("Reconciling Parliamentary Supremacy and Federalism in Canada"), Douglas Verney traces the relationship between these two principles of government during the evolution of Confederation. Canada, it is concluded, has moved from a pattern of imperial federalism based on Britain, to one of constitutional federalism, based on the American experience. Finally, the new Constitution Act of 1982 also embodies both principles, thus continuing in Canada a hybrid polity based on both federalism and parliamentary supremacy.

The problem of political change and, in particular, the impact of the United States on the pattern of Canadian government and the adaptation of the various political principles within a single political structure, is the concern of reading number four by C.E.S. Franks ("Borrowing from the United States: Is the Canadian Parliamentary System Moving Towards the Congressional Model?"). Professor Franks' assessment is centred on three important constitutional principles: separation of powers, a dual executive and federalism. In contrast to much conventional wisdom, Professor Franks concludes that, while recent institutional changes in Canada have been based on the American model, the end product has often embodied a move in the opposite direction.

NOTES

1. CHARLES HOWARD McILWAIN, *Constitutionalism: Ancient and Modern*, rev. ed. (Ithaca, New York: Great Seal Books, Cornell University Press, 1958), p. 22.

2. D.W. BROGAN, *Politics in America* (New York: Anchor Books, Doubleday and Company, 1960), pp. 1-2.

3. ALAN C. CAIRNS, "The Politics of Constitutional Conservatism," in Keith Banting and Richard Simeon (eds.), *And No One Cheered: Federalism, Democracy and the Constitution Act* (Toronto: Methuen, 1983), p. 31.

Some Rules of Constitutional-prudence for Contemporary Constitution-makers

EDWARD McWHINNEY

The celebrated constitutionalist of the French Revolution, a priest with the developed political skills of survival in dangerous times, is known for his constitutional aphorisms, or general canons of wisdom for those charged by political leaders with the task of drafting a new constitutional charter. The Abbé Sieyès generalized against a background of his own personal, unusually rich and varied experience in constitution-making and constitutional drafting over the first decade of the Revolution, which produced four distinct and different constitutional charters, each intellectually well conceived and elaborated, in only eight years. The Abbé Sieyès' aphorisms were the product of direct, firsthand, trial-and-error experience. While that learning was certainly French, it was also eclectic since drawing very fully on the writers and philosophers—Montesquieu and Rousseau for example—and on foreign examples thought to be especially relevant in the French Revolutionary context of the 1790s—the American Declaration of Independence of 1776, the original Articles of Confederation of 1779, and, finally, the Constitution of the United States of 1787, adopted only two years before the outbreak of the French Revolution itself.

The canons of constitutional-prudence that follow are linked, by direct ties of consanguinity, to the Abbé Sieyès' aphorisms, but try to update and extend these in the light of all the empirical experience since the time of the French Revolution and in many seemingly disparate legal systems.

Rule 1   Keep the constitutional charter short. A constitution is neither a municipal ordinance on sewers and drains, nor a master planner's detailed blueprint for a new community welfare programme.

Reprinted from Edward McWhinney, *Constitution-making: Principles, Process, Practice*, pp. 133-6, by permission of University of Toronto Press. © University of Toronto Press 1981.

Rule 2 Keep the language of the charter clear and non-technical. The charter is intended to be read and understood by ordinary citizens, and not simply by constitutional specialists and supreme court judges.

Rule 3 Avoid flights of oratory in the constitutional charter. A constitution should not be made an excuse for a party *pronunciamento*, or, for that matter, for honorific gestures and "complimentary expressions."

Rule 4 Keep the charter neutral, or at least open-ended in political-ideological terms (particularly in bill of rights provisions). Otherwise the charter may become too closely identified with the transient fortunes of a particular political party or pressure group, and rise and fall with them.

Rule 5 Do not try to solve too many and too specific, purely temporary and short-range, problems in the charter. A constitution is not a railway excursion ticket, good for one journey only, on one particular day and to one particular place; but is intended to endure, if not for the ages then at least for a certain term of years.

Rule 6 Actual constitutional drafting is, in the end, a professional legal exercise. If the constitutional draughtsman does not himself have a direct political mandate—coming, for example, from his own direct popular election as a member of a constituent assembly—then he should be clear, always, as to the limits of his professional drafting mandate and, if necessary, seek fresh political instructions from the political arm of government. Constitution-making is not an excuse or licence for the constitutional drafter to go on a personal ego trip: he should respect his technical mandate and its political limits.

Rule 7 A pre-condition for any politically viable exercise in constitution-making is a prior political consensus—on the part of the society for which the constitutional charter is intended, or at least its dominant political élite—as to the main goal values and policies of that society for the future. If that prior societal consensus does not exist, the constitution-maker may have to exercise self-restraint and return his brief to the political decision-makers.

Rule 8 Where a sufficient, but not a substantial or comprehensive societal consensus exists—a tolerable accommodation or coexistence of the rival forces within the society—the constitution-maker may feel justified in going ahead nevertheless. In that case, he should resist all the temptations to try to draft the "Sermon on the Mount," but, instead, make an ally of time and operate modestly and limit himself to those constitutional areas where significant societal consensus does exist. This would suggest less a single constitutional charter, adopted in one blow, than a series of specific, and limited, organic acts adopted successively, and over a period of years, as the opportunity presents itself.

Rule 9 A constitutional charter should never try to act in vain or to legislate the politically or socially impossible. Do not make the constitutional charter so rigid or difficult to change by the ordinary modes of constitutional amendment that you invite people to try to change it by extra-constitutional means and direct action, or else to ignore it altogether.

Rule 10 Law cannot exist in isolation from society. The text of a constitutional charter should have a lapidarian quality, or in-built element of generality that facilitates its continuingly creative adaptation, through time (by judicial interpretation and executive-administrative application—apart from formal amendment), to changing societal needs and expectations.

Rule 11 Be cautious in your borrowings from other constitutional systems, developed for other societies. Remember the principle of the non-transferability of constitutional institutions. What works beautifully in another society may turn out very badly, or at least quite differently and unexpectedly, when translated to your own society, since the underlying political, social and economic conditions may be quite different between that other society and your own.

Rule 12 Even seemingly limited, piecemeal constitutional change may have far-reaching and unexpected consequences within a constitutional system. Remember the principle of the interdependence of constitutional institutions. Transform any one institution and you have to expect reciprocal effects and interactions upon the other institutions of government and the system of constitutional checks and balances generally.

Rule 13 Don't forget the *extra*-constitutional rules that effectively condition or limit the application of a constitutional charter. Change in a society's basic electoral system and electoral laws may be at least as important as change in any of the key governmental institutions (executive, legislature, or judiciary) in building or maintaining democratic constitutionalism. It may also, according to the principle of the "digestibility" of proposals for constitutional change, be more than enough for any society that is already a going concern to absorb fully and successfully into its existing constitutional system at any one time.

Rule 14 Do not place too great a "Trust for Salvation" in constitutional drafters. No constitutional charter can save a sick society! Always take into account the human element in constitutional decision-making and application. Drafting a new constitutional charter can never be a substitute for wise political action—the exercise of the ordinary skills of political compromise, and respect for the constitutional "rules of the game."

Rule 15 Where, as in the case of a newly independent, developing country or a one-party state, political exigencies may dictate the adoption of a didactic, programmatic constitutional charter, it would seem prudent to separate the postulation of ideological objectives, which are normally either quickly achieved or else quickly overtaken by events and historically dated, from the establishment of the institutional machinery and processes and procedures of government which, in contrast, are likely to have more long-range operation and utility. This can sensibly be achieved by enacting the general principles or programme in their own special statute, separate and distinct from the charter defining the politically more neutral, machinery provisions of the constitution.

Comparing Federal Systems

HERMAN BAKVIS

What can we as Canadians learn from the experience of other countries? One major reason for looking at Canadian problems in a comparative context is to examine some of the alternatives and how they might operate in Canada. However, we have to be care-

Adapted from Herman Bakvis, *Federalism and the Organization of Political Life: Canada in Comparative Perspective* (Kingston, Ontario: Institute of Intergovernmental Relations, Queen's University, 1981), pp. 1-13. By permission of the author.

ful: institutions and practices borrowed from abroad may have quite a different effect when placed in the Canadian setting. But here, too, the comparative experience can help us. The second reason for examining other nations is to help us understand the important political forces and processes in Canada. For example, the experience of countries like Belgium, Ireland, Spain, India and Nigeria, may help pinpoint the causes involved in the rise of ethnic conflict. We can then use this understanding to assess the adequacy of proposals concerning representation of the two major linguistic communities in Canada or to help decide what kind of official recognition should be given to ethnic communities which are neither English nor French.

Why Make Cross-national Comparisons?

Many would argue that the amount of useful information we can acquire through cross-national comparison is limited. Some years ago Kenneth McRae stated that Canada is unique and therefore difficult to compare with other nations on an overall basis.[1] No country has the same social, economic and cultural make-up combined with a federal system of government as Canada; no other nation stands in the same relation to a much larger neighbour. Countries which are linguistically or culturally divided tend to be much smaller. Countries comparable in terms of geography are either much less developed, for example India, or have a vastly different political system, for example, the Soviet Union. McRae's sentiments are shared by many: most academics studying Canadian politics do not think in comparative terms and neither do the vast majority of Canadians.

Is there anything at all which can be learned from looking at other federal systems, or even non-federal systems? The rejection or neglect of comparative analysis frequently rests on mistaken assumptions about what the comparative method involves. Much of the work done in the social sciences, and by most people in everyday life, involves making comparisons, if only implicitly. For example the statement that Canada is unique implies comparison; it begs the question, unique with respect to which countries? An answer to this question requires specifying the characteristics of other countries in order to show how Canada differs. Thus, the problem of comparison in large part is one of definition. If we define the units of comparison as unique then comparison is impossible. The task becomes easier, however, if we admit that all systems contain within them common characteristics or factors: it is the combination and the number of these characteristics which differ from system to system.

The aim is to understand how the Canadian federal system operates and what the consequences might be if we were to change elements within the system, or the relationships between them, for example by altering the role of the supreme court vis-à-vis the powers held by parliament or introducing proportional representation for the House of Commons. Such a new or revised combination of elements may well exist in some other context and may offer valuable lessons as to the probable consequences of this new arrangement if it were implemented in Canada. For example, some economists have argued for changes in the current Canadian fiscal equalization arrangement. At the moment, the federal government plays an important role in redistributing some of the federal tax revenues to the governments of the "have-not" provinces, thereby ensuring a roughly comparable standard of provincial government services across the country. It has been suggested that equalization should be left to the provinces; one such scheme would have the richer provinces contribute money to a pool and then the richer provinces, or all ten provinces, would decide amongst themselves how to allocate these moneys to the different provincial governments. What might be the consequences? In West Germany, there is a limited form of such an arrangement called "second round" sharing where the Laender (the equivalent of Canadian provinces) decide amongst themselves how to divide up a revenue pool. Experience indicates that invariably the money is shared on an equal per capita basis. Unlike the current Canadian system very little *re*distribution takes place in West Germany.

There would, of course, be several aspects to any equalization scheme run by the provinces, such as reduction of provincial dependency on the federal government; but the West German experience can help in judging the probable consequences of such a new system, at least in certain areas, and ultimately aid in evaluating its overall viability. However, such a comparison between West Germany and Canada involves admitting that there are at least certain common characteristics between the two countries, their so-called uniqueness notwithstanding. The latter point is especially important; frequently people will raise objections to cross-national comparisons by invoking the "unique" qualities of systems, qualities which in reality may have very little bearing on the problem at hand. Medical scientists, when they discover that the rate of a particular type of cancer is much higher in one country than in another, rarely say that there is something unique about each of these countries. They begin collecting data about variables which, on the basis of previous research, have been linked to this type of cancer. There may be several characteristics of these countries which make them quite different from one another; but most of them will not be in any way relevant to explaining the nature of the particular phenomena under investigation, whether it be cancer or, in our political science example, the way in which revenue equalization is handled.

In the social and political world, relationships are often more complicated and the boundaries between different variables are not as clear-cut. Nevertheless, there is much to be gained from minimizing differences between systems, selecting countries on the basis of interesting problems and de-emphasizing their unique and different nature. By this means, we can generate common cases from several countries. Since many of the more interesting countries differ radically from Canada in terms of epoch or state of development, I would like to discuss briefly some of the misgivings people may have in transcending these dimensions.

Comparisons Across Time

The most frequent comparisons made in the study of Canadian federalism, and Canadian politics generally, involve comparing the present with the past: powers held by the federal government presently are compared with the powers which were held during the second World War; the era of co-operative federalism is compared with the current era of competitive federalism. Many of the comparisons made are not very explicit, and often are used only for descriptive purposes. In many cases, explanations are implied when authors refer to changes in the underpinnings of Canadian federalism. It should also be emphasized that nation-building, province-building and nation-breaking are processes which occur over time. For this reason, if we wish to corroborate our suspicions about what may be unfolding in Canada, it is possible to look at past trends and developments elsewhere. Thus, the creation of the Irish Republic, and the subsequent pattern of relations between Britain and Ireland, may offer lessons as to what relations might be like between a separate Quebec and the rest of Canada.

The time dimension is important in another way. When we think of comparisons, we usually think in terms of contemporary political systems. However, there were political systems in the nineteenth century and earlier in the twentieth whose experiences may well be relevant to understanding the Canadian situation. The case of Ireland and its separation from Britain in 1920 is one obvious example. Less obvious might be the Austro-Hungarian Empire and pre-war Czechoslovakia.

The time dimension, thus, has two aspects. We can compare two systems over time, and compare systems drawn from different historical epochs. Both types of comparison can yield valuable information. The former is a type many people engage in automatically, though not on a very systematic basis, whereas the latter is something many people shy away from. However, if the limiting conditions are properly identified and controlled, the number of cases available for examination will be greatly increased.

Comparing Western with Non-Western Systems

During the 1950s and early 1960s, a common theme in the literature on political development was that there was a category of nations which could be called developed and another category of so-called undeveloped nations. The latter referred mainly to the newly emerging nations in Africa and Asia, as well as to the older but still undeveloped nations in South and Central America. Since then, the very distinction between developed and undeveloped nations has come under attack.[2]

There are important differences to be sure: third world countries are characterized as having been under colonial rule, being relatively non-aligned, and seeking to industrialize as quickly as possible. They are also seen as having problems in integrating different groups and regions, in providing stable government, and in keeping conflict within manageable bounds. In particular, it is argued that many of these new societies are constantly threatened with incipient civil war as a result of competition between leaders of the different communal groupings; it is claimed that these leaders can find no common ground, perceiving all conflicts as a zero-sum game. This is contrasted with the allegedly more moderate politics of the first world. But with the passage of only a few years, this distinction is also being questioned. Communal conflict, often discussed under the rubric of ethnonationalism, has reared its head in a number of the more advanced industrial societies. The current conflict in Northern Ireland is just as intractable as many of those in the non-Western world. Nationalist movements having regional bases within nations have sprung up in Britain, France, Italy, Spain, Yugoslavia and Canada. The black power movement in the United States can also be put in this category, although it lacks a territorial base. In this dimension, therefore, it appears that Western countries share at least certain characteristics with non-Western nations.

What makes ethnic conflict in the third world particularly relevant is that several of these countries adopted federalism as a method of satisfying ethnic group demands for autonomy. Furthermore, over time countries like India and Nigeria have adjusted their federal arrangements to account for new ethnic demands. India re-adjusted state boundaries and created new states in 1956 to ensure as much as possible the internal homogeneity of states in terms of language and ethnicity. The aim was to avoid the overlapping of state and linguistic boundaries, which had resulted in linguistic minorities within several of the states, many of whom felt aggrieved by the treatment they received at the hands of majorities. In Nigeria, the problem was how to reduce the dominance of the Northern Hausa ethnic group. This group was essentially bounded by one of the four states; however, it constituted over fifty percent of the population, with the result that the Northern People's Party dominated the central government. The tragedy of civil war over Biafra's attempted secession may be attributed in part to this situation. The military authorities who have ruled Nigeria since the end of the civil war have introduced an administrative system involving 12 states; and the new constitution has 19 states. The basic strategy was to fragment the dominance of the largest ethnic group through the creation of individual states, thereby creating a more balanced federal arrangement. Thus, here we have two third world countries employing different strategies to deal with ethnic conflict within federal arrangements. They may well offer lessons for Canada.

As well, descriptions of the relationship between the Canadian West and Central Canada (i.e., the manufacturing and financial centres of Ontario and Quebec) often bear a resemblance to the literature on colonialism.[3] This suggests that the experience of new nations may not be so far removed as we think. At a minimum, an examination of third world countries will indicate whether or not it is legitimate to use terms like "quasi-colonial status" in the Canadian context. We can learn other things as well. Of prime importance to many third world countries is rapid economic growth and industrialization. Having the examples of the industrial and post-industrial revolutions before them, the prime goals of virtually all new nations is to speed up the process of economic development as much as possible. A variety of strategies have been developed by the different countries to achieve this goal: five-year plans, emphasis on the rapid development of heavy industry, such as steel plants, the introduction of labour intensive industries and so on. Unfortunately, many of these strategies have failed to produce results. Their failure, however, may well be illustrative of what can go wrong. Of major concern currently in Canada is regional economic development. In the early post-war period, the emphasis in Canada was on developing the national economy, while scant attention was paid to regional disparities. Since the early 1960s, however, serious attempts have been made to disperse economic growth more widely. The strategies employed by both the federal and the provincial governments, as well as a number of the resulting failures, bear some resemblance to the efforts of third world countries.[4] Furthermore, Canada, unlike the United States, Japan and many West European countries, is highly dependent on foreign investment, branch plants and the export of raw materials to other countries.[5] This places Canada closer to many third world countries.

In comparing third world countries with Canada on the dimension of economic development, one might want to look at the specific strategies employed. Further questions one might want to explore include: to what extent are local governments involved in the planning and development stages? Does the initiative come from the centre or do elites on the periphery play an important role? What effect do federal structures have? Do they determine the degree of decentralization of patterns of growth? Does the centre attempt to by-pass or co-opt local governments? With regard to the industrialization projects themselves, to what extent are deprived regions exploited by external agents (e.g., multinationals) who become involved in such projects? Does the existence of autonomous institutions coinciding with deprived regions lead to competition between regions to the detriment of all concerned?

Many of the new nations have adopted federal systems, and some like India deliberately examined the Canadian case in order to avoid certain of the pitfalls into which the Canadian system had fallen. Perhaps it is time for us to look at the newer federations to see whether they, in fact, have avoided our pitfalls. We may well profit from their experiences.

Comparing Federal with Non-Federal Systems

The distinction between federal and non-federal systems is not clear-cut. It is very difficult to find a purely federal state which meets all the criteria concerning the independent and co-ordinate status of governments as originally specified by K.C. Wheare.[6] At the same time, it would be unusual to find a system which can be called a purely unitary state. Most polities are decentralized in some form, even if it is only at the administrative level, as in France. Federal arrangements are unique, however, in that they do give institutional expression and a degree of autonomy to territorially-based interests. These territorially-based interests need not be unusually strong, although institutions do tend to render the territorial cleavage more politically salient than might otherwise be the case. Societies like Germany which have a federal arrangement may be quite homogeneous in terms of culture, economic interests and other matters. On the other hand, societies having a unitary system may be highly pluralistic and fragmented: Belgium is an example. Thus, it should be kept in mind that both federal and non-federal systems can be either homogeneous or pluralistic in their societal make-up.

Under what circumstances do we compare federal with non-federal societies? And what type of non-federal systems do we examine in undertaking comparisons of this sort? Since social science is concerned with the relationships between variables, the only way one can tell if there is a relationship is if there is variation in the variables of interest. Thus, frequently the only way we can evaluate whether or not federalism has an effect on policy-making, for example, is to point to examples which are similar in most respects but are not federal systems. In some instances, therefore, it may well be worthwhile to compare a country like France with Canada. The former is a highly centralized unitary state, while the latter is not. A comparison of this sort can highlight the impact of federalism on economic planning. National economic policy may well be much more coherent in France. But the Canadian political system may be much more responsive when it comes to dealing with local needs than is France. Thus, it is important to look at non-federal systems in order to provide a basis for comparison.

There are also more pragmatic reasons for looking at non-federal systems. In many instances, the kind of examples we are looking for are not in evidence in other federations. Very few federations have linguistic divisions similar to Canada's. Switzerland has three linguistic groupings and the linguistic cleavage is further complicated by the religious cleavage. Yugoslavia, a federal society, has four linguistic groups. Belgium, a unitary state, has two. In spite of its unitary character—albeit becoming federal—it is similar to Canada in certain respects. One of the interesting aspects of societies with two language groups is that institutional divisions tend to generate more than one minority. Within Canada as a whole, French-Canadians are in a minority. However, within the province of Quebec there is an English-language minority. And one can find significant French-language minorities in the provinces of Ontario and New Brunswick. The interests of these three French-language communities are often contradictory. This makes it difficult to develop language legislation which will meet with the approval of the different minorities. In Belgium as a whole, the two language groups are in relative balance. In Brussels, however, the Flemish are in a distinct minority position. But again the interests of the Flemish community in Brussels are frequently at variance with those of the Flemish living outside of Brussels. In the spring of 1980, the Belgian government fell because proposals for constitutional change, though acceptable to the two main language groups, proved to be unacceptable to the Flemish minority in Brussels. It drives home the point that proposals for constitutional change in countries like Belgium and Canada must take into account the interests of more than one minority, even though these minorities may speak the same language.

Examination of relatively homogeneous unitary systems also has its uses, particularly in the area of constitutional engineering. In the case of West Germany, a new federal constitution, the Basic Law, was imposed on a war-torn society.[7] This provides us with one example of constitutional engineering in a federal society. However, it is difficult to evaluate in what way the Basic Law has contributed to the stability of post-war German society. A great many other variables, such as economic growth, reactions to the horrors of war and the experience of a totalitarian regime, may also account for this stability. In France, by contrast, the transition from the Fourth Republic to the Fifth occurred within a very short period of time. In this case, therefore, it is possible to pinpoint with greater certainty the effects of constitutional change. Many of the basic social and economic forces in French society remained constant. The influence of these forces on political life, however, was altered largely because of institutional changes: the legislature in the Fifth Republic became much less important, and many interest groups which previously had access to government through parliamentary deputies found that their influence had declined considerably. In terms of learning what might be achieved through constitutional engineering, the French example is instructive.

As noted at the beginning of this section, there are forms of decentralization other than the federal model. It is possible, for example, to decentralize government authority to groups in society which do not have a territorial base. In the Netherlands, for example, socio-religious subcultures have a great deal of autonomy not only in the cultural sphere but also in economic life.[8] All the major blocs in Dutch society are represented on major decision-making bodies in areas like national economic policy. The socio-religious blocs in the Netherlands, though lacking a territorial base, gained considerably in importance because of changes in the early part of the twentieth century in the manner of disbursing state funds in education, culture and welfare. One reason for wanting to look at decentralized non-federal systems is to see if they offer a model which we might want to adopt as an example for Canadian political development. It has been argued that in Canada we should try to promote class-based, as opposed to provincially-based, communities[9] or, alternatively, that we should structure our political institutions on the basis of the two linguistic communities. In all instances, we would want to examine non-federal societies in order to obtain some idea as to what kind of polity would develop if we were to try to encourage the growth of non-territorially-defined communities.

Thus, there are a number of reasons why we should want to look at non-federal societies. They provide us with a basis for comparison and models for Canadian political development. As well, they add to the number of cases available for analysis, particularly in studies of constitutional engineering, non-territorial forms of decentralization and ethnic/linguistic pluralism.

NOTES

1. K.D. McRAE, "Empire, Language and Nation: The Canadian Case," in S. Rokkan and S. Eisenstadt (eds.) *Building States and Nations* (Beverly Hills: Sage, 1973).

2. R.S. MILNE, "The Overdeveloped Study of Political Development," *Canadian Journal of Political Science* 5 (1972): 560-68.

3. C.B. MACPHERSON, *Democracy in Alberta: Social Credit and the Party System* (Toronto: University of Toronto Press, 1953).

4. P. MATHIAS, *Forced Growth* (Toronto: Lewis and Samuel, 1971).

5. J. HUTCHESON, *Dominance and Dependency: Liberalism and National Policies in the North Atlantic Triangle* (Toronto: McClelland and Stewart, 1978).

6. K.C. WHEARE, *Federal Government* (Oxford: Clarendon Press, 1946).

7. E. McWHINNEY, *Federal Constitution-Making for a Multi-national World* (Leyden: Sijthoff, 1966).

8. A. LIJPHART, *The Politics of Accommodation: Pluralism and Democracy in the Netherlands*, 2nd ed. (Berkeley: University of California Press, 1975).

9. G. HOROWITZ, *Canadian Labour in Politics* (Toronto: University of Toronto Press, 1968); and J. Porter, *The Vertical Mosaic* (Toronto: University of Toronto Press, 1965).

Reconciling Parliamentary Supremacy and Federalism in Canada

DOUGLAS V. VERNEY

Confederation did not see the establishment of the Westminster system in all its aspects. A basic assumption of that tradition was the supremacy of Parliament. In Canada Parliament was limited in two vital ways. First, the British North America Act specifically exempted certain fields from the Canadian Parliament's jurisdiction

Adapted from Douglas V. Verney, "The 'Reconciliation' of Parliamentary Supremacy and Federalism in Canada," *The Journal of Commonwealth and Comparative Politics* Vol. XXI, No. 1 (March, 1983), pp. 22-44. By permission of Frank Cass and Company Limited.

by entrusting them to the provinces. Secondly, the general power to amend the act remained in the hands of the British Parliament. In law, at least, Confederation established what we shall call imperial federalism—not parliamentary supremacy.

Over the years, imperial federalism was modified by the Canadian Parliament. On the one hand, Parliament used its numerous powers to establish its paramountcy over the provinces. On the other, it persuaded the Parliament of the United Kingdom that its role in the amendment process was largely formal. For all practical purposes it was the Parliament of Canada, and not the Parliament at Westminster, which was "supreme."

Even so, the Canadian Parliament never claimed to be legally supreme in the omnicompetent sense associated with the British Parliament. In Britain there was no BNA Act restraining Parliament, and, of course, nothing like a Section 92 had even been contemplated for, say, Scotland, Ireland and Wales. Nor was there any other legislative body claiming to exercise even the most formal control over Parliament itself. Parliament, and Parliament alone, was sovereign and could never be charged by the courts with acting *ultra vires*, i.e. beyond its competence.

Canada's parliamentary federalism did not, then, mean parliamentary supremacy in the British sense of complete parliamentary sovereignty. It simply meant that Westminster was the model, a model to be adapted to Canadian conditions. Among these conditions was the country's federal structure.

In law, the United Kingdom Parliament was supreme. Yet much depended on the nature of the conventions surrounding the exercise of this power, particularly in the light of the Statute of Westminster and the negotiations preceding its passage. After the 1949 amendment to the BNA Act, however, the Government and Parliament of Canada assumed that for most practical purposes the Parliament of Canada, and even the House of Commons alone, was supreme.

But the Westminster doctrine of parliamentary supremacy, as Dicey noted, was quite clear: it meant not only supremacy for all practical purposes but supremacy in law. The Parliament of Canada was not supreme in law.

In Canada, the notion of parliamentary supremacy depended to a great extent on convention, since, as far as the law went, it was the British Parliament that was supreme. Federalism, on the other hand, depended on the legal distribution of powers specified in the Constitution. It was to be the federal principle, dependent on law, that was to challenge the parliamentary principle, dependent on conventions. These conventions were assumed to be the same, whether in Westminster, Ottawa or the provincial capitals. In fact there came to be much disagreement over their precise nature. This was to raise the question whether a practice, such as the Canadian procedure for proposing amendments to the BNA Act, could be treated as a convention unless there was widespread agreement as to its nature.

The "Reconciliation" of Parliamentary Supremacy and Federalism

If, then, the Canadian Parliament was not supreme, just what institution was? One possibility is that the question was wrongly put: that no single institution exercised supremacy. Perhaps power was divided between the Parliament of Canada and the Westminster Parliament.

In a sense this was true. Power *was* divided. Although the British Parliament was supreme in law, by convention the power was exercised in practice by the Canadian Parliament. This Parliament alone requested amendments to the Constitution, requests always granted by Westminster. And although by convention the Canadian Parliament enjoyed sole power to make recommendations for changes in the BNA Act, after 1907 it became increasingly common for Ottawa to consult the provinces on matters directly affecting their interests.

But if power was divided between the Canadian Parliament and the provincial legislatures, then there was an obvious alternative to the principle of parliamentary supremacy: the Constitution. In a federal system the principle of constitutional supremacy ensured that each government remained within its assigned limits. Certainly, in the United States, whose Supreme Court gradually became the Canadian model, the Constitution was regarded as supreme. The American Supreme Court interpreted the Constitution and exercised authority as an umpire through what Americans called the principle of "judicial review."

When the Canadian Supreme Court replaced the Judicial Committee of the Privy Council as final court of appeal, it came to be assumed that the principle of judicial review, a term rarely used in earlier times, had a place in the Canadian political system. Analo-

gies were frequently drawn with the US Supreme Court's celebrated case of *Marbury v. Madison* in which Chief Justice Marshall,
with masterful logic-chopping, had established the principle of judicial review. Canadian courts, it was argued, had always practised
judicial review.

Before 1949, however, the Judicial Committee could not properly be described as having exercised the principle of judicial review on the American model. It was, after all, an imperial tribunal:
it acted on behalf of the Crown: and it was subject to the ultimate
authority of the British Parliament—in conformity with the doctrine of parliamentary supremacy. It practised the same judicial
interpretation that ordinary English courts adopted in dealing with
the question whether local governments were acting *ultra vires* (i.e.,
beyond the powers or legal authority of). In its judgments, the Judicial Committee did not declare acts of Canadian legislatures to
be unconstitutional: it merely said that they were *ultra vires,* that is
to say, outside the limits set by the British Parliament. The Judicial
Committee might appear to Canada to be an umpire *ab extra* (i.e.,
from outside), but looked at from within the British political system it was very much an umpire *ab intra* (i.e., from within), without
any independent legal authority.

After 1949, when the Judicial Committee ceased to be final court
of appeal, it was often suggested in Canada that the Supreme
Court should now model itself not on the Judicial Committee, with
its often narrow interpretation, but on the American Supreme
Court with its broad powers of judicial review.[1] But there was
nothing in Canada corresponding to the American Constitution,
the authority for Marshall's claim that the Supreme Court should
exercise the power of judicial review. Moreover, in the United
States the Constitution was revered as the creation of the American people through their representatives gathered in a Constitutional Convention in Philadelphia. Hence the opening words of
the Preamble: "We, the people of the United States . . . ."

Chief Justice Marshall was able to argue his case supported by
two doctrines: the supremacy of the Constitution and the sovereignty of the American people. He lived in a new country that had
vigorously opposed British parliamentary supremacy and the pre-
rogatives of the Crown. It was therefore doubly difficult for his opponents to challenge the logic of his argument.

By British standards the American Constitution was a remarkably novel document. It separated the executive, legislative, and judicial branches through separate institutions (although it blended

their powers). Through the first ten amendments (the Bill of Rights), it prohibited the government from encroaching on certain rights which the Constitution declared henceforth belonged to individual citizens or to the states. Most important of all, for our purposes, the Constitution distributed power between the federal government and the states. Neither the separation of institutions within government, nor the passage of the Bill of Rights, was essential to the federal structure of the United States. What was essential was the distribution of power between the federal government and the states. It was this federal distribution of power that the British government could never accept for Ireland within the United Kingdom itself, for the simple reason that it would end the supremacy of Parliament. Yet this same distribution of power principle was granted to Canada. Canada, however, was different from Ireland. Federalism was possible in Canada because the British Parliament necessarily remained supreme, and supreme in Canada over both orders of government. Canada's federalism, as established in 1867, can perhaps be described as a form of "imperial federalism."

With the passage of time and the emancipation of Canada from imperial control, it was increasingly regarded, in both the United Kingdom and Canada, as anachronistic for Canada's federation to be considered fundamentally one of imperial federalism.[2] Yet little attention seems to have been given to the need to replace imperial federalism by another principle, for example, by what we may call "constitutional federalism." Instead, as we have seen, the British Parliament retained its crucial role in the amending process. Yet this was considered, even by the British Ministers, as simply a formality.[3] The Judicial Committee came to be regarded as a useful institution of Canadian federalism and not an instrument of British imperialism.[4] Its successor, the Supreme Court of Canada, was encouraged by some Canadian constitutional lawyers to transform its role from that of judicial interpretation of the BNA Act into judicial review of the Constitution.

But if the principle of judicial review, with its connotation of a broad interpretation of the Constitution, came to be generally accepted, what would happen to the old principle of parliamentary supremacy? Canadian jurists were able to convince themselves that the two principles could be reconciled—and indeed that they had been reconciled from the outset. They did so by stating that, whereas in the United States there were areas of individual rights on which no legislature could trespass, in Canada there were no such areas. Just as Parliament in the United Kingdom was supreme, so in Canada the legislatures, Parliament and the provincial assemblies together, were supreme.

In other words, they took one of the features of the Canadian political system which distinguished it from the American (the absence of a constitutional Bill of Rights), and contrasted it with one aspect of parliamentary supremacy—legislative supremacy over the courts. But we have already seen that the feature they chose, the absence in Canada of a Bill of Rights entrenched in the Constitution, had nothing whatsoever to do with the federal principle. And of course they virtually ignored the "formal" role of the UK Parliament.

In sum, Canadians were asked to believe that the very distribution of legislative power which was fundamental to federalism in both Canada and the United States, and which created the contradiction between federalism and parliamentary supremacy, had actually resolved the problem. For example, in September 1981, when the Supreme Court reviewed—and reviewed broadly—the proposed Constitution Act, it reiterated what had come to be the conventional wisdom, stating:

> There is also an internal contradiction in speaking of federalism in the light of the invariable principle of British parliamentary supremacy. Of course [sic], the resolution of this contradiction lies in the scheme of distribution of legislative power.[5]

The Court did not address itself to the fundamental problem facing Canada, once the British Parliament ceased to be supreme, of reconciling the doctrine of parliamentary supremacy with a federal system. For the adjudication of disputes between the two orders of government in a federation required an umpire generally regarded to be *ab extra*, and the amendment of the Constitution, either by the people themselves, or by both orders of government.

So long as the term "parliamentary supremacy" referred to the British Parliament, and so long as the Judicial Committee served as umpire *ab extra*, the contradiction between the two principles created no problem. Admittedly, the British Parliament rarely had to act. But the fact that it dealt with few issues was irrelevant. What mattered was that those issues that were fundamental *were* legally the responsibility of that Parliament alone.

When Canada became virtually independent between 1926 and 1949, there was little awareness that here was a theoretical decision that ought not to be avoided. Instead, Canadians assumed that the system had operated satisfactorily throughout Canada's long period of gradual emancipation: it would surely continue to operate as before.

In other words, the reconciliation of the two principles was not thought to present an insuperable problem. The Fathers of Confederation were, after all, pragmatists: "Pragmatic in their approach to politics, they were not impressed by lofty statements of principles and goals."[6] Nor did later generations of Canadians go in for grand theory: for all practical purposes the system worked well. Canada had succeeded in evolving from the colonial (or imperial) federalism of 1867 (in which the imperial authorities retained ultimate supremacy through the Governor-General, the Westminster Parliament, and the Privy Council), to a system of federalism that after 1949 began to take on a resemblance to the constitutional federalism practised in the United States.

The Emergence of Judicial Review

Before 1949 it seems to have been general Canadian practice to consider the recommendations of the Judicial Committee to be matters of "judicial interpretation," following British usage. This was, of course, correct nomenclature since the Privy Council was in fact interpreting such imperial statutes as the BNA Act, and doing so in accordance with English law.

After 1949 the term "judicial review" became increasingly popular, just as the preferred term for the BNA Act became "the Constitution of Canada." Barry Strayer entitled his book *Judicial Review of Legislation in Canada*; Edward McWhinney's book, called *Judicial Review*, went through several editions; and, as we have seen, the term was freely employed by such authorities as Peter Hogg, Peter Russell, and Donald Smiley.

Clearly it was easy for English-Canadian observers who believed in the unfettered national legislative powers of the Parliament of Canada to forget that the Privy Council laboured under severe constraints. It had no alternative, as an imperial tribunal, but to treat the BNA Act as an ordinary statute of the British Parliament. So long as it accepted both the supremacy of the British Parliament and the federal character of Canada, it could hardly contribute to making the Parliament of Canada supreme. In treating both orders of government in Canada as comparable to English local governments, and therefore capable of acting *ultra vires* but not unconstitutionally, the Judicial Committee was conforming to the rules of imperial federalism whereby both orders of government in Canada were subordinate to the imperial Parliament.

The Judicial Committee displayed its Executive character in its day-to-day deliberations. It did not meet as a court, the judges wearing robes, but as a committee, its members meeting informally as committees do, wearing lounge suits. Business was conducted informally. As an advisory body to the Sovereign, the Committee itself published no reports and revealed no dissenting opinions. Its advice was tendered to the Crown and was then published, like other Executive orders, by Order-in-Council in the Sovereign's name. It was not surprising that the Irish resented having to appeal to this Committee as their highest tribunal.

In sum, we need to remind ourselves that the Judicial Committee of the Privy Council did not play a role comparable to that of the American Supreme Court. It did not engage in judicial review of the Constitution. It did not enjoy the legitimacy of a written Constitution emanating from the people, but depended on the prerogative power. Its status was not even that of ordinary English courts: it was part of the Executive branch. Its function was not that of broad review but of careful interpretation in conformity with the doctrine of parliamentary supremacy, the supremacy of the British Parliament. Finally, the Judicial Committee did not really interpret a Constitution but an Act of the British Parliament which by English law had to be treated as an ordinary statute.

By adopting the American language of discourse, Canadians may have hoped that they could convince themselves that Canada could evolve from British imperial to American constitutional federalism—replacing one civilisation by another—by simply adopting American practices as they seemed convenient, and dropping British traditions no longer appropriate. This would, of course, have been in conformity with the notion of the Canadian political personality as one with a preference for "real issues" and "avoidance of unnecessary theoretical decisions." Canadian intellectuals could continue to enjoy the luxury of "philosophical federalism." After all, it was a cardinal English-Canadian assumption that the American principle of constitutional federalism had successfully been grafted on to the British principle of parliamentary democracy. Whatever might be their theoretical incompatibility, the two principles worked together in practice as "parliamentary federalism." But when questions of theory, and in particular of the legitimacy of the Supreme Court, began to emerge after 1960, the limitations of parliamentary federalism became apparent. Difficult constitutional problems could no longer be avoided.

Canada had not yet faced a crisis of legitimacy. "Parliamentary federalism" had apparently been successful, and it was conveniently overlooked that in law it was the Parliament of the United Kingdom which was supreme. "Federalism" appeared to be compatible after all with parliamentary supremacy, and it was forgotten that Canada's federalism had been imperial, not constitutional: that it was the Judicial Committee that adjudicated.

Once the Parliament of Canada assumed the sovereign legislative role of the British parliament, as it seemed intent on doing by the 1949 amendment of the BNA Act, and once the Supreme Court modelled itself on the American Supreme Court and began to undertake genuine judicial review of the Constitution, then the contradictions between the British tradition of parliamentary supremacy and the logic of constitutional federalism stood exposed.

For in making the analogy between Canadian and American federalism and assuming that the Courts in each country played a similar role, Canadians were encouraged to forget that any further development in the direction of constitutional federalism by Canada would be fraught with difficulty. In the first place, whereas the American Constitution was established *de novo* by the States, any new Constitution would have to take into account an already existing federal government in Canada. Furthermore, a new Constitution was more than likely to be introduced by the federal government itself, not by the provinces.

Only if the federal government's initiative in drafting a new Constitution restructuring the political system completely failed and only if a constitutional convention were then called, would Canada be in a position at all similar to that of the United States. Such a convention is conceivable even in Canada, and might have to be called in order to find out just what type of political system a majority of the people of Quebec really wanted. For a Constitution proposed solely by the federal government could always be said by the *Parti Québécois* to represent only the federalists in Canada. On the other hand, the federal government could argue that the people of Quebec elected not only the *Parti Québécois* but also the federalist Liberal Party of Canada, and by an overwhelming majority in 1980. Were the Quebec electors compelled to elect delegates to a constitutional convention, they would have to choose between federalism and separatism: they would no longer be able to have it both ways—to elect separatists to Quebec City and federalists to Ottawa.

Canada: A New Hybrid?

During the long period of negotiations before the passage of the Constitution Act 1982, many who proposed change, especially those committed to an entrenched Charter of Rights, were willing to replace legislative supremacy by the principle of judicial review. On the other hand, because of the determination of several provincial premiers to retain the principle of legislative supremacy, it seemed for a while that the Constitution would not be modernised.

The agreement finally reached is interesting because it appears to establish a system in which both principles have a place. It is true that some observers suspect that in the course of time one or other will triumph. Theoretically, the decision to incorporate both conflicting principles is inherently unsatisfactory in comparison with the clear assumptions underlying British and American government. But it is quite possible that both principles will be incorporated into Canada's parliamentary federalism. Canada may well have established a new "hybrid" system.

Canada is not alone in its disinclination to opt for one system or the other. The Indian political system, which moved earlier than Canada in the direction of constitutional federalism, remains fundamentally one of parliamentary federalism. For nearly two decades it has been oscillating between the two principles of parliamentary supremacy and judicial review. In other words, while it may not be possible to reconcile two contradictory principles in theory, in practice a number of important political systems manage somehow to combine them. Parliamentary federalism may well be a distinct genre, one that has to be examined on its own merits.

Indeed, one of the most extraordinary developments in the modern world has been the emergence of new political systems—in India, in Canada, in France, in Germany and the European Community, to name a few—which are not based on one of the "pure" theories of government. Their success suggests the need for a new approach to the analysis of political systems which accepts hybrid political systems as a separate category.[7]

This conclusion does not mean that political theory has limited value in such comparative political analysis. What it does suggest is that the study of political theory and the study of political institutions are two distinct enterprises. The attempt to combine them through "empirical theory" has its limitations.

NOTES

This article is drawn from my forthcoming book, *Three Civilizations, Two Nations, One State: Canada's Political Traditions.*

1. EDWARD McWHINNEY, *Judicial Review* (Toronto, 1969), pp. 74-5.

2. See, for example, House of Commons, *First Report from the Foreign Affairs Committee*, Session 1980-81: *British North America Acts: The Role of Parliament*, Volume I, ix, Also *Minutes of Evidence*, 87, 105 (London, 1980-81).

3. Statement by Dr G. Marshall, *Minutes of Evidence*, 85ff.

4. P.H. RUSSELL, *Leading Constitutional Decisions: Cases on the British North America Act* (Toronto, 1965), pp. xi-xii.

5. Supreme Court of Canada: Judgment, 28 September 1981.

6. R.I. CHEFFINS AND R.N. TUCKER, *The Constitutional Process in Canada* (Toronto, 1969), p. 8.

7. My study of Swedish parliamentary government in the 1950s led me to undertake *The Analysis of Political Systems* (London, 1961). My study of the Canadian political tradition, one which is more complex than either the British or the American, has persuaded me of the need for a comparative study involving hybrid systems. This I shall probably call "The Adaptability of Political Systems."

Borrowing from the United States: Is the Canadian Parliamentary System Moving Towards the Congressional Model?

C.E.S. FRANKS

In the development of its political institutions Canada has been, placed as it is between the United States and Britain, more like the ham in the sandwich than the link between the two. Our political structure and processes are based on the examples of both other countries. This paper will examine the extent to which the basic parliamentary Westminster model, which Canada has adopted, has borrowed intentionally or otherwise from the example of the American congressional system. The questions of the differences between the two systems, their respective advantages and disadvantages, what Canada has borrowed, ought to borrow, or ought not to borrow, are at least as old as Canada, and are still continuing. They, and their ramifications, are keys to major problems in Canadian politics.

In the Westminster system, the key part of Parliament is the elected House of Commons. The House is divided into government and opposition sides. The government enjoys the support of a majority. The electorate votes more on the basis of party and party leaders than on the merit of the opposing candidates in constituencies. The leader of the largest party is appointed Prime Minister. He selects his cabinet ministers from among the Members of Parliament in his party. Ministers are the administrative and political heads of departments. All ministers, including the Prime Minister, sit in Parliament where they answer questions, propose legislation and defend their departments against opposition attacks. It is a system of "responsible" government. Ministers

Reprinted from C.E.S. Franks, "Borrowing from the United States: Is the Canadian Parliamentary System Moving Towards the Congressional Model?" *The American Review of Canadian Studies*, Vol. XIII, No. 3 (Autumn, 1983): 201-214. By permission of the publisher.

are responsible *to* Parliament *for* administration and policy. A government retains power until it is defeated, either in an election or in a vote of confidence in the House. Unless it is a minority, holding less than half the seats, a government is never defeated in the House because party discipline is rigid. The government in effect controls Parliament. Thus on most major points the Canadian parliamentary system is quite different from the American Congressional-Presidential model.

One of the earliest comparisons of the two systems is contained in Walter Bagehot's *The English Constitution*, first published in 1867, the year of Confederation, when Canada was created by an Act of the British Parliament. As Bagehot noted, the prime feature of the Westminster model is that it is based not on the separation but on "the close union, the nearly complete fusion, of the executive and legislative powers."[1] The body in which these powers are fused is the cabinet, which heads the executive, is composed of elected members of the House of Commons, and controls the majority in Parliament, and, consequently, the processes of Parliament itself. This centralization of power is not, like the American, built upon a system of checks and balances. To quote Bagehot again: "The English Constitution, in a word, is framed on the principle of choosing a single sovereign authority, and making it good; the American, upon the principle of having many sovereign authorities, and hoping that their multitude may atone for their inferiority."[2]

A second characteristic of the British system, according to Bagehot, was that it was divided into two parts: ". . . first, those which excite and preserve the reverence of the population—the *dignified* parts, if I may so call them; and next, the *efficient* parts—those by which it, in fact, works and rules."[3] The dignified parts included the monarch and the House of Lords; the efficient segment was the cabinet. In comparison, in the United States, where the functions of chief of state and head of government are combined, the dignified and efficient institutions are one and the same.

The most important constitutional feature which Canada has borrowed from the United States is the federal structure: authority is divided between two levels of government, each with its own autonomous legislative and executive institutions. In both countries the reason for this structure is the same, that they occupy huge and diverse land masses, that their culture and people are diverse, and that there is a need, in government, both for sensitivity and responsiveness to local and regional issues, and for national integration and national government. In all federal systems there is a constant tension between regional and national interests and issues. These tensions have been especially prominent in Canada in recent decades, and many Canadian experts, both academics and politicians, have cast envious eyes towards the United States, where the problems seem to be handled much better, and the processes of regional co-ordination and integration seem to work more smoothly.

These three questions—whether power is becoming dispersed rather than fused at the federal level in Canada; whether the dignified and efficient parts are melding together; and whether Canada is moving towards an American model for handling federalism—will be considered below. There is no doubt that our parliamentary system is changing, and there is no doubt that the prominence of the American example influences these changes. What the real impact of these changes is, and whether they move Canada closer to a congressional model, are the focus of this paper.

The Separation of Powers

The dominance of the cabinet over both the executive and legislative branches of government is the fundamental fact of the Canadian parliamentary system.[4] The instrument of dominance is the party. The major Canadian political parties are centered around, and find their raison d'être in, their parliamentary representation. The federal Parliament has been dominated by the Liberal Party for this century, and provincial legislatures similarly have been marked by long periods of one-party dominance. Dominant parties at both the federal and provincial levels, as long as they retain power, hang together and are not defeated or even threatened by loss of support of their elected representatives. In fact, party discipline is far more rigid in Canada than in Britain, where governments are frequently defeated, on non-confidence issues, in Parliament. No government in Canada has been defeated in the House by withdrawal of support by its elected members.

There are immense benefits to a governing party in this coherence and dominance. The parliamentary system operates on the winner-take-all principle, so that appointments, contracting, advertising, engaging counsel, etc. are all totally within the control of the cabinet, with no review or check by the legislature. Similarly,

the drafting of legislation, the preparing of budgets, the administration of government and the exercise of discretionary authority
are also within the control of the cabinet. With these tremendous
perquisites of power, it is not surprising that successful Canadian
political parties are power- rather than ideology-oriented, and that
there is no desire for the Government to share power with other
parties. The ten elections since 1957 have produced six minority
governments. In not one of these did the Government enter into a
coalition with other parties. Successful minority Governments retained power by policy concessions to the third and fourth parties,
which ensured their support. This has not generally been hard to
ensure, because these smaller parties have most to lose through
frequent elections. The official opposition has been left out of
power, without even these minor sops to gain its support.

A result of this situation has been weak parliamentary control of
the executive. When Bagehot wrote, governments in Britain were
regularly defeated in Parliament, and often changed without elections. He could with some justification call the cabinet a board of
control chosen by the House, and held responsible and accountable to it. The growing rigidity of party discipline in both Britain
and Canada have made this inter-election control largely ineffective, leaving the ultimate sanction with the electorate. In Canada,
where the tradition of one-party dominance is so strong, even this
sanction is normally lacking and the system is not only one of fused
power, but of uncontrolled power as well.

Political parties are not part of the formal constitution of Canada, any more than they are of the United States. But they are, at
least when speaking of long-standing governing parties, like the
federal Liberals and the Ontario Progressive Conservatives, the
most powerful of the political institutions, with this power centered
in the cabinet.

This domination by the executive not only leaves little room for
Parliament as an institution, but also leaves little autonomy for the
individual M.P. as well. In recent years there has been an effort to
reform the procedures and structures of Parliament, in particular
the House of Commons, so as to redress this imbalance. The Liberal Government of Prime Minister Trudeau, to give it credit, has
taken the leadership in these reform efforts, and has done more to
improve the House than any previous Government. The resources
available to both individual members and parties have been enhanced so that a Canadian Member of Parliament now has far better staff and research resources than his British counterpart.[5]

These moves have been consciously intended to give the Canadian M.P. some of the benefits of his American counterpart, who must surely be the best housed, staffed, and provided for legislator in the world.

The second major reform of the House of Commons, like the previous one, has also been a borrowing from American practice. In 1969 the committee system of the House was reformed to create a series of specialized standing committees to which bills would be referred after second reading, and which would examine the estimates of departments and make inquiries into policy and administrative issues. Backbench M.P.s on both sides hoped to gain a stronger role in the legislative process through these reforms; the Government hoped to be able to process more business through the House by increasing the number of channels for handling business.[6] To a modest extent, both these hopes have been realized. Private members often find satisfaction through committee work, and the House can handle more business. However, there is still intense dissatisfaction for both cabinet and private members: for the Government, an inability to get legislation through Parliament; for the M.P.s, lack of influence. Hopes for more independent Members of Parliament, and more autonomous parliamentary committees, proved illusory as the Government retained control over committees through its majority on them, its appointment of chairmen, and its control of committee resources and agenda.

Dissatisfaction with the system in 1982 caused the "bell-ringing" episode which prevented Parliament from doing business for fifteen days, and one of the prices the Government paid for the resumption of business was the creation of a new committee, composed largely of backbenchers and outside Government control, to examine procedures. It has recommended, and the House has adopted, changes to make the committees smaller, less under Government control, and more cohesive.[7] It has also recommended that the function of considering Government legislation be taken away from the specialized standing committees and given to ad hoc legislative committees to consider each bill following second reading.[8] Thus one of the prices the committees will pay to be more autonomous is that they will no longer be responsible for what was their most important function. Interested members from the specialist standing committees will doubtless serve on the legislative committees, but there is no doubt that these committees will be controlled by the Government.

These moves are away from the American model, and more in line with Britain, where for a long time there has been a series of "standing" committees handling government legislation. Only recently, however, has the British House of Commons established a series of specialized committees. Even so, the British committees have more autonomy than the Canadian, and some of their chairmen are, unlike the Canadian, appointed from the opposition. In the past fifteen years Canada moved first towards the congressional style of committee, but has since retreated and become more like the British. But parliamentary procedures in Canada remain even more rigidly dominated by party discipline than the British.

A second sort of borrowing from the American example has been less recognized as such, partly because it has been mixed with indigenous Canadian factors. This is the centralization of policy-making within the Prime Minister's Office and the Privy Council Office (or Cabinet Secretariat). Since 1968 these two bodies have been dramatically strengthened at the expense of individual ministers (except the Prime Minister), the departments and agencies of government, and their clientele and interests they serve. The arguments for this growth have been to co-ordinate government activities, to control a growing bureaucracy, and to rationalize policies so that they form part of a coherent framework of goals and functions for Government.[9] The Canadian sources for these changes were a reaction against the muddled and often messy policy-making of the previous Diefenbaker and Pearson Governments, coupled with a sense of Cartesian order and logic derived in part from the *collège classique* training of many of the new ministers. Canadian politics, at least for the major parties, are not ideology or programme oriented; rationality, in the sense of establishing an orderly framework of goals and priorities for government, and an orderly process for policy-making, appeared to offer a way of coming up with coherent policies in the absence of a philosophical base for the governing party.

The American sources for the changes can be found in two places: first, in the technology of economic analysis and programme management—cost/benefit analysis, PPBS (Planning Programming Budgeting System), etc.—which the United States has developed in the post-war years; and secondly, in the efforts to strengthen the office of the President, and presidential control over the executive branch and the legislative output of Congress.

What Canadian reformers failed to realize, or at least did not articulate, was that in the United States these tools were not only a scientific technology to improve government, but also instruments of political power. Emphasis on economic analysis shifted power to those doing the analyses, in particular those in central agencies, and were part of the effort towards centralization in a system that was then, is now, and always has been far more decentralized and unco-ordinated than the Canadian.

The result of the changes in Canada has been to put even more power into the hands of a cabinet structure which was in the beginning the most powerful part of the political system. What was desirable to redress excessive decentralization in the United States was not necessarily desirable in the quite different Canadian situation. In Canada pressure groups are not so strong as in the United States, nor do they find such easy access to influencing budgets and other decisions. Central control of the budgetary processes through the Treasury Board and the Department of Finance was already stronger than in the United States, as was policy control through cabinet. There is no Canadian counterpart to the powerful union in the United States of interest groups, Congressional committees and bureaucracy. In Canada, pressure groups, departments and outside influences over financial and policy processes in general have been arguably weakened by the growth of central agencies. Although the centralizing and rationalizing of policy-making have to some degree reduced the autonomy and independence of ministers and departments, they have done so at a cost of excessive centralization. This borrowing from the American model has not moved the Canadian system closer to the checks and balances of the American system, but away from them, towards an even greater fusion of powers.

In spite of the generally negative conclusions reached here about reforms of Parliament and policy-making, it would be wrong to conclude that Parliament itself has been weakened. Quite the reverse, with its improved committee system and staff resources Parliament is more active and influential now than before 1968. The turnover of the House of Commons, which historically has averaged 40 to 60 percent at each election, appears to be diminishing and more experienced members will mean a more influential Parliament. Nevertheless, party discipline in Canada is still much too rigid, and all parties in Parliament suffer from severe intellectual constipation. The remedy for these ills, however, does not lie in institutional reform but in political action, participation and commitment by more of the populace. Failing that, Canada is condemned like other countries to the most unhappy of fates: it has the government it deserves.

The Dignified and Efficient Branches

To Bagehot the monarch and, to a lesser extent, the House of Lords, were the dignified branches of government. With little admiration for the political awareness of the common man, Bagehot noted:

> The elements which excite the most easy reverence will be the *theatrical* elements—those which appeal to the senses, which claim to be embodiments of the greatest human ideas, which boast in some cases of far more than human origin. That which is mystic in its claims, that which is occult in its mode of action; that which is brilliant to the eye; that which is seen vividly for a moment, and then is seen no more; that which is hidden and unhidden; that which is specious, and yet interesting, palpable in its seeming, and yet professing to be more than palpable in its results; this, howsoever its form may change, or however we may define it or describe it, is the sort of thing —the only sort—which yet comes home to the mass of men.[10]

To no institution in modern Canadian politics does this description apply more aptly than to Prime Minister Trudeau. His maddening, elusive, brilliant figure is far and away the brightest star in the political skies. He is the senior head of government in the western world. Since Trudeau was first elected in 1968 the United States has had five presidents.

Several analysts have argued that under Prime Minister Trudeau Canada has shifted away from cabinet government to prime ministerial government in which power is centered in the Prime Minister.[11] A different viewpoint was argued in the previous section: that power has indeed shifted, but not to the Prime Minister personally so much as to the central agencies, the Prime Minister's Office and the Privy Council Office. The Prime Minister himself is not more powerful than before but his staff is; the individual minister has lost power, but the collective cabinet and its secretariat have gained.*

The change that has affected the office of the Prime Minister itself is that it has become the central element of the *dignified* rather than the *efficient* branch of government. The cost of this has been the debasement of the other elements of the constitution. As in the

---

*The predictions made and conclusions drawn in this section clearly must be read in the context of subsequent political developments. While Prime Minister Trudeau has now been succeeded in office by John Turner and Brian Mulroney, the changes which he wrought in these matters will likely remain.

United States, in his office are now united the symbolically important functions of chief of state and head of government. He personifies government and has, in Richard Gwyn's words, become our "single combat champion."

Two other elements of the constitution have suffered in their creation of an imperial Prime Minister. First, the crown has become vestigial, invisible and insignificant. The Governor General is the representative of the monarch in Canada. The office has always been weaker than the monarchy in Britain, in part because the incumbents hold the position for only a few years, and in part because the less hierarchical Canadian society is a less comfortable natural home for a hereditary monarch. Nevertheless, until recently the crown was a living and significant part of the constitution: it was a visual symbol of government on mail trucks, government letterheads, publications, and buildings; the Governor General opened and closed sessions of Parliament, and gave the speeches from the throne at the beginning of sessions; he visibly and actively toured Canada and made state visits abroad.[12] The role of the Governor General has gradually diminished until the present incumbent is all but invisible. The Prime Minister makes state visits and receives dignitaries. There has been no opening of Parliament since 1980, and no speech from the throne. The crown as a symbol has long since disappeared from documents, buildings and elsewhere. Some of this de-emphasis has been consciously intended to appease French-Canadian hostility. Some was the unfortunate result of a stroke suffered early in his term by Governor General Jules Leger, and some by a successor who does not appear to relish the dignified function. Media coverage of the office is minimal. Much of the decline is the result of increasing public focus on the office and person of the Prime Minister, a change which, to say the least, Prime Minister Trudeau has done nothing to discourage.

The denigration of the crown leaves a gap in Canadian political consciousness and imagery. The crown historically represents a national will and interest as opposed to warring factions, passing governments, self-interested political parties and pressure groups. It is above party and personality. Administration and justice are carried out in the crown's name, not the party's or the Prime Minister's. With the passing of the crown, this sense of a beneficent, impartial body with an overriding long-term concern for the well-being of the nation has also gone. Perhaps this point is best illustrated by a comparison with the United States, where the Constitution and the position of the President fulfill this mystical dignified symbolic function. The Constitution is the source of civic and political ideals. If it were to disappear, or fall into disrespect, all the national focus that would be left to idealize would be the office and person of the President. This would be a loss.

The second institution whose symbolic role has been weakened is Parliament. Increasingly in recent years, major policy announcements have been made outside Parliament. Prime Minister Trudeau only speaks there on rare occasions—often a year or more has gone by without his addressing Parliament apart from brief answers during question period. The traditional dignified occasions of opening the session and throne speech, as has been noted, no longer occur yearly. All of these changes contribute to making Parliament uninteresting and irrelevant. The squabbling, fractious, conflict-oriented aspects of Parliament are emphasized. It is not so much that the Government is disrespectful of Parliament (Prime Minister Trudeau's unfortunate comment in 1969 that M.P.s are "nobodies" outside the House was an unusual lapse) as that the Government ignores Parliament and when possible by-passes it.

One example of this should suffice. In 1977, after much parliamentary and media discussion, a Commission of Inquiry was formed to examine improprieties and worse in the security service of the RCMP. The Commission's report, released in 1980,[13] found that there had indeed been wrong-doings and recommended that a new civilian security service be created, a new act be passed to govern the activities of the service, and that parliamentary control over the security service be strengthened by, among other measures, consultation by the Prime Minister with the Leader of the Opposition on the appointment of the head of the security service. The Government's first public action on the report was to appoint a head for a new civilian service without consulting the Leader of the Opposition. The report has not been tabled in Parliament, nor has it been debated there or referred to a committee. The Government, in May 1983, introduced a bill to create a civilian security agency. It was greeted with intense hostility by the opposition, the press, and provincial governments. To a large extent the bill was modelled on proposals contained in the Commission's report. If the report had previously been studied by a parliamentary committee, or even discussed in some detail in Parliament, the proposals for unusual powers for the agency would not have been greeted with such surprised shock and hostility. The bill will have a difficult time getting through Parliament; some of this difficulty could have been alleviated if the Government had treated Parliament with more respect, and involved it earlier in discussion. Opposition obstruction has caused some of this desire to ignore and by-pass Parliament, but the neglect is overdone, and the consequences unfortunate in both the short and the long run. An essential step in the mobilization of consent is for the Government to undergo the obstacle course of parliamentary scrutiny. The Government acts as though it does not appreciate the symbolic importance of parliamentary combat.

A third fundamental alteration by the Trudeau Government is the creation of a new Canadian Constitution. Before 1982 the major written constitutional documents were the British North America Act, a workmanlike mid-nineteenth century British statute setting up the terms of Confederation, and its subsequent amendments. Constitutional jurisprudence was largely a series of uninspiring cases dealing with the division of powers between the federal and provincial levels. The BNA Act required an act of the British Parliament to amend it. One of the most persistent drives of the Trudeau Government has been to replace the BNA Act with a new Constitution, including an amending formula and a bill of rights. There was strong objection from various provincial governments. In spite of this, in 1982 Canada had a new constitution.[14] Quebec still opposed the change. The end product, though in general intent based on and borrowed from the American example, is peculiarly Canadian: it has an amending formula which is not an amending formula because provinces can opt out of amendments, and an entrenched bill of rights which is not entrenched because governments can again opt out by taking advantage of a "notwithstanding" clause.

However, the question that must be considered here is not the merits or faults of the new constitution as a legal document, but its symbolic power. Some aspects of it are weak as symbols: the language, though an improvement on earlier proposals, reads in parts more like a legal instrument than a statement of civic and political ideals; the Province of Quebec has taken advantage of the "notwithstanding" clause to exempt every provincial statute from the constitutional bill of rights. Nevertheless, nine provinces and the federal Government agreed to the final product, which is no mean achievement, and is evidence of strong support for this sort of public statement of commitment to ideals. And though many experts were initially pessimistic about the usefulness of the bill of rights in light of previous judicial reluctance to overrule Parliament and governments, the first year of the new constitution's existence has produced strong evidence of judicial activism and boldness, and at present over 500 cases are before the courts which involve the charter of human rights. It is quite likely that the charter will have a real and useful impact on citizens and governments. If it does, it could, in time, have a symbolic and dignified role in Canada comparable to the Constitution in the United States. On the other hand, the separatist government of Quebec might succeed in making it a symbol of what is wrong with Canada.

My impression is that the role, function, nature and identity of the symbolic, dignified parts of all systems are being transformed by the mass media, and that this is causing an alteration on the efficient side as well. More specifically, the institutions which get strong media attention are becoming the significant symbols of authority. This enhances their power. Modern media also tend to personalize power and governance. Consequently, the apparent "presidentialization" of the Prime Minister's office in Canada might well be a convergence of the two systems rather than a borrowing. This, however, is very speculative. Perhaps Bagehot was correct, and there will inevitably be a separation between the dignified and efficient parts: to the extent that Prime Minister or President appears as the symbolic focus of power, the office has moved from being efficient to being dignified, and real power is being exercised elsewhere. That is certainly my impression of how, except for matters like the constitution where Trudeau has a strong personal concern, the system has changed in Canada. The PMO and the PCO, largely hidden from public view, have gained what others have lost. I suspect that the Office of the President, and other central agencies in the United States, are gaining power in the same way. The media are perhaps unwittingly restructuring our political system.

Federalism

If the strength of the cabinet is one of the dominant realities of Canadian government, then the other dominant reality must be the importance of the federal structure. Virtually every problem of government has a federal-provincial aspect, and the federal-provincial contest often seems to dominate politics.[15] Whether federal discussions are with one provincial government, as in energy policy, or with many, as in constitutional reform, the mode of interaction is negotiation between governments, and more particularly between cabinets. There are four reasons for the prominence of this executive federalism in Canada: first, with only ten provinces, each individual province is more prominent than any single state in the United States; second, the provincial level of government has more responsibilities and functions than the state level; third, the French fact in Canada, and the representation of French Canada by Quebec, with over a quarter of the people of Canada, gives an emphasis on provincial autonomy which other provinces take advantage of; and fourth, the dominance of the cabinet makes interaction between governments rather than conflict resolution within the federal Parliament an appropriate mode of action.

Federal-provincial relations are as much a claim for identity and autonomy of the government as they are modes for expressions of legitimate regional diversity. They are also executive-oriented and exclude many legitimate interests.[16] For example, as Canada is now ruefully discovering, negotiations on energy policy between Alberta and the federal government left out the oil industry. Federal-provincial relations are also divisive, as they pit government against government, and area against area. They are conflict-oriented, and confrontational by nature. Separatist sentiment in Quebec is being echoed by separatist sentiment in the West. There is a real danger that Canada might fall apart.

Faced with these problems, Canadian politicians and academics look elsewhere for guidance from happier federal states. The United States and Germany are the two most admired, and in particular the upper chambers of these two countries appear to offer examples of how regional interests can be harmoniously accommodated within a federal legislature rather than through confrontation which encourages separatism.

The Senate in Canada is not an important body. The hopes of its creators were not high, and they have not been met. In spite of, or more properly because of, its insignificance, the Canadian Senate has been the subject of more proposals for reform than any other part of the central government—and, it should be noted, these proposals have produced fewer changes than any other efforts at reform. In recent years proposals have centered upon methods of transferring much of what now takes place in federal-provincial confrontation to a new upper chamber.[17] It would be appointed or elected so as to represent more authentically provincial and regional interests. It would have strong influence over the resolution of federal-provincial problems. It would ensure that regional interests be recognized in major appointments to central government institutions. The intention of borrowing from the American model is pervasive in these on-going discussions.

None of these reforms to the upper chamber in Canada has yet been implemented. I am skeptical whether they will be, as there are two problems in them in relation to Canadian political practice which have not been adequately considered, but which are crucial for success. First, for the new upper chamber to function as reformers would wish, there will have to be a profound change in party discipline and the meaning of party at the federal level. This would have repercussions on the lower chamber that have not, as yet, been imagined. Second, the decision rule of Parliament is a simple majority of members present. This decision rule does not give an adequate voice or veto to provincial and minority interests. For the reformed Senate to have legitimacy, this rule would have to be changed, and change would put the Senate into conflict with the cabinet and the House of Commons. I doubt whether this sort of change would be accepted by provincial governments or by the cabinet and House. They would be in the invidious position of losing salience but not responsibility.

The cabinet is supposed to exercise power on behalf of all the people of Canada, and it is responsible to an elected chamber which already represents everyone in the country. Surely it makes more sense to improve the processes of policy-making and accountability so that the cabinet does fulfill its functions and is shown to do so through established parliamentary institutions than to add new institutions to an already complex system. The constitution debate showed that a parliamentary committee (established in spite of a reluctant government) could mobilize consent for reform against the wishes of nine provincial governments. In the battle for public support, which is mostly what federal-provincial confrontation is about, existing parliamentary processes are powerful: in this instance more powerful than nine provincial governments. Federal-provincial politics, so Joe Clark claimed as Leader of the Opposition, do not need to be confrontation-oriented. He did not stay in power long enough as Prime Minister to prove his argument. Nevertheless, I still wonder whether he might well have been correct, and whether a restructuring of federal-provincial relations, with less emphasis on the battle of the single combat champions, might not be more useful than Senate reform. Perhaps these attempts to borrow from the United States are the pursuit of a mirage.

The Direction of Change

Most of the changes to the institutional structure of the Canadian parliamentary-cabinet system have made us more like the Americans, and most have also been conscious borrowings from the American model. The structure and aspirations for our system of parliamentary committees, the strengthening of central agencies, the changes to the processes of policy-making, the adoption of a written constitution with a charter of human rights, are all largely American in origin. The fusion of the dignified and efficient elements through the enhancement of the role of the Prime Minister was not so much intentional as a logical outcome of other actions. Nevertheless, it too would not likely have happened without constant reinforcement of the American model through the barrage of American news, television and other information that Canadians are exposed to. It is not far off the mark to say that most Canadians *expect* their political system to operate like the American, and are confused when it does not. These common perceptions reinforce the pressures towards, and ease of, making changes in the direction of the congressional-presidential model. Proposals for Senate reform, borrowing greatly from the American model, I have suggested, find much of their attractiveness in this pervasive understanding and acceptance of the United States system.

But even though the specific institutional changes have been in the direction of the presidential-congressional system, the end product of these reforms has not been change in the same direction. In spite of a structure of active specialist committees Parliament has not become a strong check on the executive. The conflict between the need for government control of parliamentary business and the desire for committee autonomy led, thirteen years after the initial reforms, to a retreat away from the American towards the British model. Government domination of Parliament was not reduced. Improvement to parliamentary control over the executive will not come from borrowing from the U.S.A. Strengthening of central agencies and rational policy-making increased the fusion of power, leading away from the checks and balances and separation of powers. The enhancement of the symbolic role of the Prime Minister had a similar result. The result is retention of the dominance of the cabinet, a disenchantment with reforms, and disillusion with the institutions and processes of government in Canada.

I have tried to show in this paper how difficult it is to borrow from another system. Canadian reformers thought they understood how congressional committees operated, and what reforms to policy-making could accomplish, but the context of parliamentary-cabinet government is so different from congressional that the results have been quite contrary to expectations. I have also suggested that Canadians do not, generally, understand their institutions of parliamentary-cabinet government. Their perceptions of how government operates are based in large part on impressions of the American system, and these lead to misunderstanding of and dissatisfaction with the Canadian system which, in turn, lead to misguided reform. The changes to the processes and institutions of Canadian government have been great in the last fifteen years. It has been an age of reform. Two positive, and one negative, conclusions can be made: first, the efforts towards reform, and the fact that changes have been made, are proof of a laudable desire to make government work better; second, the processes of reform, and their failures as well as their successes, focus attention on the parliamentary-cabinet system and help improve understanding of it; and third, and more negative, the ease with which massive changes have been made suggests that understanding, acceptance and support for the parliamentary tradition are not widespread or deep. Otherwise there would have been more resistance to many of the changes.

One final question needs to be considered: whether any of this matters and what the outcome of different institutional structures and changes really is. There are important differences between Canada and the United States. In Canada, government has a more dominant role; it is more actively involved in the economy, culture and society. Canadian government is more welfare-oriented, with universal medical care, hospital care, unemployment insurance and old age pensions, to mention only a few. Conventional explanations attribute these differences to differences in political culture: Canada has a corporatist tradition in both the conservative and socialist ends of the spectrum, whereas politics in the United States is more liberal and individualistic. This is perhaps true, but perhaps it is at least equally significant that the parliamentary system, with the dominant role it gives the cabinet, enables the executive to express a public interest beyond party and interest group, and gives it a strong motive to govern so that it appeals to a general rather than particular interest, and that this institutional feature has permitted Canadian governments to be more activist and welfare-oriented than American. If this is so, then proposals to move towards the American model in Senate reform must be viewed with caution. Even if reforms were to improve national integration and reduce the salience of federal-provincial conflict (and I have expressed my doubts above about success for this), then they would at the same time open up the political processes to every organized special interest in Canada. A feature of Canadian politics is that mass institutions, whether parties or pressure groups, are weak, while special interests, both government and economic, are strong. Experiences with tax reform in the early seventies proved that interest groups could use parliamentary committees very effectively to mobilize opinion in favour of their particular interests and away from reform. A Senate copied from the Americans might well entrench and reinforce this particularism and make the national government less able to act in a general public interest. The unanticipated consequences of Senate reform could be unfortunate. It is puzzling that the policy successes of our parliamentary system are attributed to political culture rather than to institutions, while solutions for our problems in integration are sought in institutional reform rather than in political action which could alter political culture.

NOTES

1. WALTER BAGEHOT, *The English Constitution*, The Fontana Library Edition (London: Collins, 1963).

2. *Ibid.*, p. 220.

3. *Ibid.*, p. 61.

4. Useful studies of the role of the executive in Canadian politics are: AUDREY D. DOERR, *The Machinery of Government in Canada* (Toronto: Methuen, 1981); and THOMAS A. HOCKIN (ed.), *Apex of Power: The Prime Minister and Political Leadership in Canada*, 2nd ed. (Scarborough, Ontario: Prentice-Hall of Canada, 1977).

5. See ALISTAIR FRASER, "Legislators and their Staffs," in Harold D. Clarke et al. (eds.), *Parliament, Policy and Representation* (Toronto: Methuen, 1980).

6. See C.E.S. FRANKS, "The Dilemma of the Standing Committees of the Canadian House of Commons," *Canadian Journal of Political Science* IV, 4 (December 1971).

7. Canada, House of Commons, Special Committee on Standing Orders and Procedure, *Third Report*, December 1982.

8. *Sixth Report*, April 1983.

9. Among the useful discussions of this topic are: RICHARD D. FRENCH, *How Ottawa Decides: Planning and Industrial Policy-Making 1968-1980.* (Toronto: Lorimer, 1980); JAMES GILLIES, *Where Business Fails* (Montreal: The Institute for Research on Public Policy, 1981); and CHRISTINA McCALL-NEWMAN,

Grits: An Intimate Portrait of the Liberal Party (Toronto: Macmillan, 1982), Part 4, "Michael Pitfield and the Politics of Mismanagement: the Liberal Party, 1977-1979."

10. BAGEHOT, *op. cit.*, p. 64.

11. See DENIS SMITH, "President and Parliament: the Transformation of Parliamentary Government in Canada," in Hockin, *Apex of Power.* A contrary view is offered in Richard Schultz, "Prime Ministerial Government, Central Agencies and Operating Departments: Towards a More Realistic Analysis," *ibid.* Richard Crossman's introduction to the edition of Bagehot cited above first introduced the argument for "prime-ministerial" government. Richard Gwyn's *The Northern Magus: Pierre Trudeau and Canadians* (Toronto: McClelland and Stewart, 1980) is also useful.

12. A good discussion of the position of the Governor General can be found in Jacques Monet (ed.), *Jules Leger, Governor General of Canada, 1974-1979: A Selection of his Writings on Canada* (Montreal: Les Editions La Presse, 1982), in particular the introduction by Monet, and "A Pause for Reflection" by Leger.

13. Commission of Inquiry Concerning Certain Activities of the Royal Canadian Mounted Police, *Second* and *Third Reports* (Ottawa: Minister of Supply and Services, August 1981).

14. See ROBERT SHEPPARD AND MICHAEL VALPY, *The National Deal: The Fight for a Canadian Constitution* (Toronto: Fleet Books, 1982); and David Milne, *The New Canadian Constitution* (Toronto: Lorimer, 1982).

15. See: DONALD V. SMILEY, *Canada in Question: Federalism in the Eighties*, 3rd ed. (Toronto: McGraw-Hill Ryerson, 1980); ROGER GIBBINS, *Regionalism: Territorial Politics in Canada and the United States* (Toronto: Butterworths, 1982); and RICHARD SIMEON, *Federal-Provincial Diplomacy: The Making of Recent Policy in Canada* (Toronto: University of Toronto Press, 1972).

16. For example, DOUGLAS BROWN AND JULIA EASTMAN with IAN ROBINSON, *The Limits of Consultation: A Debate Among Ottawa, the Provinces and the Private Sector on An Industrial Strategy* (Ottawa: Science Council of Canada, 1981).

17. Important recent proposals include: The Special Joint Committee of the Senate and the House of Commons on the Constitution of Canada, *Final Report*, 1972; Government of Canada, Federal-Provincial Relations Office, *The House of the Federation* (Ottawa, 1978); Ontario Advisory Committee on Confederation, *A New Second Chamber* (Toronto, 1978); The Task Force on Canadian Unity, *A Future Together* (Ottawa, 1979), (The Pepin-Robarts Report); Canada, Senate Standing Committee on Legal and Constitutional Affairs, *Report on Certain Aspects of the Canadian Constitution*, 1980.

The Executive Branch of Government

With few historical exceptions, governments have been dominated by the executive branch, while the bureaucracy has been a key player in the political process. This section examines, from a number of perspectives, the structure of the executive branch and the relationship between it and the bureaucracy.

The rapid expansion of government in recent decades has been executive-centred and controlled. This general trend is evident in both presidential and parliamentary systems. However, in the single executive, American presidential pattern, the growth of government has been most noticeable around the Office of the President. In the dual executive, Canadian parliamentary structure, that growth has been focused on the political executive (i.e., the prime minister and cabinet), not on the formal executive.

The political executive has emerged as the repository of power and influence, while the formal executive increasingly has been restricted to a symbolic role: "The cabinet, dominated by the Prime Minister, stands at the apex of the parliamentary system of government in Canada."[1] However, such developments have not necessarily meant the demise of the "dignified element" of executive authority. Significantly, the formal executive retains important powers, even if they are rarely invoked: "The Offices of Governor General and Lieutenant-Governor are constitutional fire extinguishers with a potent mixture of powers for use in great emergencies."[2] As Eugene Forsey argues in reading number five ("The Role and Position of the Monarch in Canada"), the formal executive's job remains more than a symbolic one, even after the passage of the Constitution Act of 1982.

In contrast to the formal executives in Canada and Britain, political executives face the possibility of not only electoral and parliamentary defeats, but also the potential removal from office by their own party during the interelection period. On being chosen British Prime Minister in 1868, Benjamin Disraeli proclaimed that he had "climbed to the top of the greasy pole." Making it to the top and staying there are not always as easy as it might appear.

In reading number six ("The Vulnerability of Prime Ministers in Canada and Britain"), Patrick Weller compares the factors which contribute to the potential political demise of the political executives in Canada and Britain. While removal of a prime minister from office may be rare, electoral decline, scandals, or poor public opinion polls always raise the spectre of such a possibility: "Indeed there may be something of an 'iron law' of unavoidable prime-ministerial failure: every Prime Minister will have an Achilles' heel on which critics can focus. . . ."[3] Although Joe Clark was in opposition at the time of his removal in June, 1983 and Prime Minister Pierre Trudeau voluntarily resigned and was replaced by John Turner in June of 1984, many of the factors analyzed by Weller could be used in explaining the reasons for the recent changes in the leadership of the Conservative and Liberal parties of Canada.

In addition to the prime minister, the cabinet is the second key element of the political executive: "The unchallenged centre of power in the government of Canada is the Cabinet."[4] While powerful, the internal structure and functioning of the cabinet has often been ad hoc and dependent on the views of the prime minister or influential departmental ministers.

> When Mackenzie King was prime minister the cabinet had no agenda, no minutes were kept, decisions were not formally recorded, and senior civil servants were seldom present. The ministers simply got together and talked about whatever King and his mother thought was important that day.[5]

The major role of the cabinet is the determination of public policy for the nation. Under Pierre Trudeau the fluid pattern of cabinet decision-making became "rationalized," because the Prime Minister believed that "Government policy-making should not be haphazard; it should be planned."[6] In reading number seven ("The Canadian Cabinet: Priorities and Priority Setting in the Trudeau Era"), G. Bruce Doern surveys the role of the cabinet in the policy-making process. After a brief historical overview of priorities from 1867 to the present, Doern examines the policies of the

Trudeau era in detail through an investigation of throne speeches and budget speeches. Doern's analysis illustrates both the complicated pattern of cabinet decision-making and the continual intermingling and alteration of economic and political priorities. The final section of reading number seven discusses some of the limitations on rational decision-making in Canada.

Because of the cabinet's key role in setting public policy, its composition can tell us much about not only how decisions are made, but also about emerging trends in the political agenda of the nation. In reading number eight ("The Canadian Cabinet in Comparative Perspective"), William Lammers and Joseph Nyomarkay analyze the career patterns of Canada's political elite in comparison to those in France, Great Britain and the United States. In particular, the authors are concerned with the connection between recruitment patterns and the growth of technologically-oriented societies. They examine this relationship from the perspective of three modern developments: specialization, nationalization, and bureaucratization. Their conclusions about the effects of each of these developments on the make-up of contemporary cabinets are important for understanding the content and pattern of public policy in Canada.

While the prime minister and cabinet make many of the major decisions regarding the political agenda of the polity, they cannot, by themselves, implement such policy. That task is carried out by the bureaucracy or civil service. In reading number nine ("The Development, Role and Control of the Bureaucracy"), S.E. Finer traces the evolution of the bureaucracy and the rise of the modern state in Europe. One of the major themes of Finer's analysis is that the more the bureaucracy is controlled the less able it is to be innovative and creative. Even though the dividing line between politics and administration has rarely been precise, politicians generally seek to control their bureaucracies.

One method of controlling the civil service in Canada has been through the use of deputy ministers who are, in effect, the "non-partisan, civil servant" leaders of each government department. However, because deputy ministers are appointed by the government and because they have become key players in the policy process, their role has become increasingly politicized (i.e., the line dividing politics from administration has become blurred). The resulting dilemma created for deputy ministers in Canada is analyzed by Ted Hodgetts in reading number ten ("The Deputy Ministers' Dilemma").

A second method of exerting some influence over the bureaucracy is through the patronage powers retained by the political executive. Control and direction is possible because a party's own workers infiltrate the bureaucracy; a patronage appointee's loyalty is likely to be to his party, not to the bureaucracy. In reading number eleven ("The Politics of Patronage: James Gardiner and Federal Appointments in the West, 1935-57"), Norman Ward provides a fascinating historical example of how this process worked in Western Canada. While some of the specific patterns of the Gardiner example no longer apply, patronage remains a significant mechanism in Canada for not only building party support, but also for controlling the bureaucracy.

NOTES

1. W.A. MATHESON, *The Prime Minister and the Cabinet* (Toronto: Methuen, 1976), p. 1.

2. FRANK MACKINNON, *The Crown in Canada* (Calgary: McClelland and Stewart West, 1976), p. 122.

3. R.M. PUNNET, *The Prime Minister in Canadian Government and Politics* (Toronto: Macmillan of Canada, 1977), p. 28.

4. J.R. MALLORY, *The Structure of Canadian Government*, rev. ed. (Toronto: Methuen, 1976), p. 76.

The Role and Position of the Monarch in Canada

EUGENE FORSEY

The Monarchy and the Constitution

Under the British North America Act, 1867, section 9, "the executive government and authority of and over Canada is hereby declared to continue and be vested in the Queen." By section 15, the command-in-chief of all military and naval forces is likewise declared to "continue and be vested in the Queen." This still holds.

The Canada Act, 1982, the final United Kingdom Act relating to Canada, provided (section I) that the Constitution Act, 1982, should come into force on proclamation by the Queen. That took place on 17 April 1982. The Constitution Act, 1982, provides (sections 50 and 53(I)) that the British North America Act, 1867 (henceforth to be known as the Constitution Act, 1867), with the deletion of section 20, section 91, head I, and section 92, head I (which are now covered by sections of the 1982 Act), and the addition of a new section 92A (giving the provinces limited additional powers over natural resources), remains part of the constitution of Canada.

So the Queen's position is unchanged.

What is more, it is now entrenched. Section 41(a) of the Constitution Act, 1982, provides that any constitutional amendment relating to "the office of the Queen, the Governor-General and the Lieutenant-Governor of a province" must have the consent of all the provincial legislatures. This is a marked exception to the general amending formula, which requires the consent of only two-thirds of the provinces with at least half the population of the ten.

It is also a far cry from the Constitution Bill, 1978, which would have vested the command-in-chief in the Governor-General and "the executive power" in the Governor-General "in the name of the Queen"; would not have "precluded" the Queen from exercis-

Adapted from Eugene Forsey, "The Role and Position of the Monarch in Canada," *The Parliamentarian* Vol. LXIV, No. 1 (January, 1983): pp. 6-11. By permission of publisher and author.

ing the powers of the Governor-General; would have made Parliament consist not of the Queen and the two Houses but of the Governor-General and the two Houses; would have struck out "in the Queen's name" from the Governor-General's summoning of Parliament; would no longer have required Members of Parliament or of the provincial legislatures to take the oath of allegiance set out in the fifth schedule to the Act of 1867; and would have made all these changes by Act of the Dominion Parliament alone, without any reference to the provinces.

The Constitution Act, 1867, section 3, provided that the federated provinces were to "form and be one Dominion under the name of Canada." The Fathers of Confederation, so Lord Carnarvon informed the Queen, intended "the new title" to be "a tribute to the monarchical principle, which they earnestly desire to uphold." The Constitution Bill, 1978, would have deleted section 3 of the Act of 1867, and substituted for "Dominion" "the Canadian federation." The Constitution Act, 1982, leaves section 3 of the Act of 1867 intact. So "Dominion," that "tribute to the monarchical principle," remains the legal constitutional designation of Canada.

The 1982 Constitution Act's triple reaffirmation of the monarchy is not mere inadvertence. The 1978 Bill's proposals on the subject evoked a storm of protest. The Dominion government's own 1980 proposals would have required, for any constitutional amendment "in relation to the office of the Queen, the Governor-General and the Lieutenant-Governor of a province," not the consent of all the provincial legislatures, but only of those of Ontario, Quebec, two of the four Atlantic provinces with at least half the population of the four, and two of the four western provinces with at least half the population of the four. The proposals presented to the Senate and the House of Commons in February 1981, again, would not have required unanimous consent of the provincial legislatures, but only of those of Ontario, Quebec, two Atlantic provinces, and two western provinces with half the population of the four (or the electorate of such provinces, in a referendum). The changes finally embodied in the Constitution Act, 1982, must have been insisted on by the governments of the nine provinces which adhered to the "accord" which led to the passage of that Act.

Plainly, then, republicanism is not a political force in Canada. Equally plainly, belief in the monarchy is, and a formidable one.

Powers of the Governor-General—real and otherwise

The vitality of this belief has been demonstrated, in rather eccentric fashion, by some rather curious recent notions about what real power the Queen's representative has, or should have.

Fifty years ago, the conventional wisdom was that he had, and should have, almost none; that the "reserve power" to act against the advice of his Ministers in very exceptional circumstances had become little more than a constitutional Cheshire Cat: nothing remained but the smile. Lord Byng's right to refuse a dissolution of Parliament to Mr Mackenzie King (in very exceptional circumstances—indeed, in one respect, utterly unprecedented circumstances: a vote of censure was under debate) had been fiercely contested. The leading academic constitutional authority of those days, Professor MacGregor Dawson, in his book, *Constitutional Issues in Canada, 1900-1931*, headed the chapter on the Governor-General with another figure from *Alice in Wonderland*, the Mock Turtle: " 'Once,' said the Mock Turtle at last with a deep sigh, 'I was a real turtle.' "

Gradually, the existence of the reserve power became acknowledged in academic circles and officially by the government which, in its constitutional proposals of 1969, said that the Governor-General should "retain" the right "to select a Prime Minister and to decline advice to dissolve Parliament," and in 1978 would have given him, explicitly, the right to refuse a dissolution.

So far, so good. But in the last three or four years there has been a tendency to go to the other extreme, and to attribute to, or advocate for, the Governor-General (whose powers, whatever they are, flow solely from the fact that he is the representative of the Queen) powers which no reputable constitutional authority, hitherto, would have admitted. There has even been one proposal to give him, explicitly, absolutely new and very important constitutional powers and functions. More and more people seem to feel that if anything is amiss in the body politic, the Governor-General is (to borrow a phrase from Sir Pelham (P.G.) Wodehouse) "the chap to kiss the place and make it well."

This tendency manifested itself as early as 1972. Preliminary results of the general election of that year indicated that no party would have a clear majority but that the Conservatives, under Hon. Robert Stanfield, would have 109 seats to the 107 for the Liberals, under Rt Hon. Pierre Trudeau. Immediately, some people declared that it was the Governor-General's right (or duty) to dismiss Mr Trudeau and call on Mr Stanfield to form a government. This heresy (which, of course, amounts to contempt of the House of Commons) has cropped up several times since, and will probably reappear next time an election gives an opposition a plurality of seats. Fortunately, it is hard to imagine any Governor-General ignorant enough, foolish enough, or rash enough to adopt it, unless, of course, the incumbent Prime Minister asked for a fresh dissolution before Parliament could meet, or failed to advise the summoning of Parliament within a reasonable time.

Patriation confrontation

The vicissitudes preceding the passing of the Canada Act and the Constitution Act of 1982 led to a remarkable suggestion that the Governor-General might possess even wider reserve power than anyone hitherto had contemplated. The Dominion government, having failed to secure the agreement of the provinces, had proposed to ask the Parliament of the United Kingdom for the necessary legislation with the support only of the two Houses of the Dominion Parliament and of two provincial governments, and in the teeth of furious protests by the other eight provinces.

The Supreme Court of Canada ruled that this proposed request, though legal, would be constitutionally improper: that by constitutional convention a "substantial degree of provincial consent" was necessary for constitutional amendments of the kinds proposed. An eleventh-hour conference of the eleven governments produced an "accord" from which only Quebec dissented: "substantial" provincial consent had been achieved. After the event, on 21 January 1982, the Governor-General, Rt Hon. Edward Schreyer, in a press interview, said that if the final conference had broken down, and there had been "an absolute absence of willingness to discuss anything any further . . . the only way out . . . would have been to cause an election to be held and the Canadian people asked to decide."

There would, of course, have been only two ways the Governor-General could have "caused an election to be held." He might have persuaded Mr Trudeau to tender the necessary advice (there can be no question of his right to persuade a Prime Minister to take, or refrain from taking, any action whatever). But if this had failed, he could have attained his object only by dismissing Mr Trudeau and calling on Rt Hon. Joe Clark, the Leader of the Opposition, to take office for the purpose of advising an immediate election.

The idea of letting the Canadian people decide looks "fit, and fair, and simple, and sufficient." But is it?

In the first place, if there really was a convention requiring the consent of a "substantial" (undefined) number of *provincial governments*, a *Dominion* general *election* could settle nothing, unless it induced some (how many?) provincial governments to change their minds, which they might well decline to do.

But, it may be objected, surely "the people" are the political sovereign? Surely a decision by "the people" would override any convention?

But whose "decision"? Parliament's? Or the electorate's? An election could easily produce a majority of seats in the House of Commons for one side and a majority of the popular vote for the other. (Only twice since 1917 has any Canadian party got a majority of the popular vote.) Besides, one side could get a majority of seats, or of votes, or both, Canada-wide, while the electorates of several provinces gave a majority of seats, or of votes, to the other. What then becomes of even the spirit of the Supreme Court's "substantial" provincial consent convention?

The specific problem, of course, never arose, and the formulas for constitutional amendment are now laid down in black and white in the Constitution Act, 1982. But the assertion of a reserve power in the Governor-General to solve problems of Dominion-provincial relations by forcing a Dominion general election could open a Pandora's box.

Proposals for a more political role

More recently still, we have had two proposals (this time from the pen of a former Governor-General, the late Jules Léger) which would really transform the office of Governor-General into something strange, if not rich.

First, on the Speech from the Throne at the opening of Parliament: "I would hope that, in future, it might be possible for the Governor-General to express his own personal ideas on relevant subjects, such as, for example, energy, ecology, or the lot of the native peoples."

Note the word "relevant." Who would decide which subjects were "relevant"? Note the "for example." Note the three chosen examples, all of which might be the subject of lively partisan controversy.

Note also that in the same passage Mr Léger compares our Speech from the Throne, unfavourably, with the American President's Speech to Congress on the State of the Union.

The whole proposal indicates a total misconception of the two very different systems of government and, specifically, of the two offices of President and Governor-General. The President is supposed, and expected, to be partisan; the Governor-General is supposed, and expected, to be non-partisan.

Secondly, Mr Léger asks: "Why could not [the Governor-General] be appointed Chairman of a renovated Senate?"

The answer to that is that it would be a colossal waste (worse, misuse) of his time. Instead of doing his proper work, he would be largely occupied in merely sitting, listening, putting motions, and deciding occasional points of order; unless, of course, he was given the right to speak in debate and/or to vote, which would plunge him into the maelstrom of partisan politics.

Mr Léger suggested also that the Governor-General, here, might preside over meetings of the Privy Council, as the Governor-General of Australia presides over meetings of the Australian Executive Council.

In at least the first fifteen years after Confederation, formal meetings of the Canadian Privy Council (actually, of two or more Ministers, with the Governor-General present) were commonplace. In Australia, there are prescribed rules for the meetings of the Executive Council, and the Governor-General has a well understood role in the proceedings. Whether, in the formal meetings of the Canadian Privy Council a century and more ago, the Governor-General ever played more than a formal part is doubtful. Certainly any such meetings have long since become very rare. Whether, as Mr Léger suggests, they could be revived "without difficulty" is also doubtful. Mr Léger says that, with such a procedure, "the Governor-General could follow more closely some of the government's decisions and more easily fulfil his duty as guardian of the constitution." Yes, but cabinets might not be much enamoured of this, and would be, I should think, pretty certain to jib at it.

In connexion with his suggestion that the Governor-General could preside over a "renovated Senate," Mr Léger observes, "The constitution of the Federal Republic of Germany may perhaps offer a kind of model for us." I leave to experts on the German constitution the possible implications of this. But it is another indication of how some Canadians hanker after a more active, positive, Governor-Generalship, and of how they are prepared to jettison established British (and Canadian) constitutional practices in favour of alien importations.

Another manifestation of the same hankering appears in Professor Edward McWhinney's recent book, *Canada and the Constitution, 1979-1982*. He asks, "Why should not a Canadian Governor-General . . . exercise the reserve, discretionary, prerogative powers conferred upon him by the BNA Act (sections 50 and 54-7)? . . . if the need for the exercise of his legal powers should arise in his own, proper constitutional judgment. . . . Would some of the currently fashionable proposals for election, at least indirect election, of the Governor-General as head of state change and magnify that office by conferring upon it its own constitutional mandate?" (They would indeed; fortunately or unfortunately, they could be brought about only with the unanimous consent of the provincial legislatures.)

Is change necessary?

The Canadian Governor-General already has the acknowledged reserve power to refuse a dissolution of Parliament in certain circumstances, and even, in very special circumstances, power to dismiss a government; even the then former Prime Minister, Mr Mackenzie King, in 1926, recognized this.[1] He has also the power, in certain circumstances, to choose the Prime Minister, and here his power is really greater than the Queen's in the United Kingdom. In the United Kingdom, if a Conservative Prime Minister dies, or resigns for personal reasons, his party has formal machinery for electing a new leader forthwith and the Queen calls on him (or her) to form a government. The same holds for the Labour party. In Canada, party leaders are chosen by national conventions which take months to organize. So, if a Canadian Prime Minister dies, or resigns for personal reasons, the Governor-General, after taking soundings among leading figures of the government party, must choose a Prime Minister to hold office till the party, in convention, can elect a new leader.

But a Governor-General's exercise of "his own, proper constitutional judgement" in respect to the powers conferred by sections 50, 54, 55 and 57 of the Constitution Act, 1867, is something else again. (Section 56 is not really relevant. It confers on the Gover-

nor-General no power whatever. It merely imposes on him the duty of sending all Canadian Acts to "one of Her Majesty's principal Secretaries of State," and provides that "the Queen-in-Council" (United Kingdom) may disallow any Act within two years and that the Governor-General must then signify such disallowance by proclamation or by speech or message to both Houses of the Canadian Parliament.)

Section 50, in effect, empowers the Governor-General to dissolve Parliament.

Section 54 makes it "unlawful" for the House of Commons "to adopt or pass any vote, resolution, address, or Bill for appropriation of any part of the public revenue, or of any tax or impost that has not been recommended to the House by message of the Governor-General."

Section 55 empowers the Governor-General to refuse assent to Bills or to reserve them for the signification of the Queen's pleasure.

Section 57 provides that a reserved Bill shall have no force unless, within two years, the Governor-General signifies by proclamation, or by speech or message, to both Houses of the Canadian Parliament that it has received the assent of the Queen-in-Council (U.K.).

If the Governor-General exercised his legal powers under sections 50, 54 and 55, "in his own, proper constitutional judgement," he could dissolve Parliament, *proprio motu* (would he have to find a Prime Minister to assume responsibility?); he could prevent a government from introducing any expenditure he disapproved of; he could veto any Bill he disapproved of; he could send any Bill to London in a state of suspended animation and it would not come into force unless assented to within two years by the Queen-in-Council. Even then, under section 57, he could prevent its coming into force by simply refraining from making the proclamation or speech, or from sending the message required by that section.

The (Imperial) Conference on the Operation of Dominion Legislation, 1929, formally declared reservation of Dominion Bills and disallowance of Dominion Acts constitutionally obsolete, and said they would be abrogated if the Dominion asked for it. It is scarcely conceivable that their exercise could be revived now. Indeed, it is almost incredible that the Constitution Act, 1982, leaves them intact.

But if the Governor-General exercised his legal right to dissolve Parliament, or to refuse to recommend an expenditure, or to refuse to assent to a Bill, or to reserve a Bill for the Queen's pleasure, responsible government would disappear.

That such ideas as Mr Léger's or Professor McWhinney's (or even Mr Schreyer's) should have appeared at all is explicable perhaps partly by the attractions (for some) of the American presidency, or (for others) of the French or German, but chiefly by widespread popular dissatisfaction with the working of the Canadian electoral system.

In the last few elections, it has become clear that the Conservatives can get almost no seats in Quebec and the Liberals almost none in the West (and that the New Democratic Party has only the slenderest chance of getting enough seats to form even the official opposition); so that a government of either major party is likely to face serious feelings of alienation in one or the other region. But that giving the Governor-General a massive increase in personal, discretionary power would provide a remedy is, to say the least, far from clear, and the remedy might well prove far worse than the disease. The proper remedy for defects in the electoral system is change in the electoral system. If plumbing does not work properly, we do not tear off the roof.

Conclusion

The role of the monarch herself in Canada is now in some respects less than it used to be, in some respects greater.

The 1947 Letters Patent empowered the Governor-General to exercise all the powers of the Queen. Till 1978, however, some, such as declaration of war, ratification of treaties, appointment of ambassadors, were exercised by the Queen herself, acting, of course, on the advice of her Canadian Ministers. In 1978, this ended: the Governor-General now performs these functions, again, of course, on the advice of the Queen's Canadian Ministers. But the Queen herself, on the advice of her Canadian Prime Minister, appoints the Governor-General.

On the other hand, the Queen was directly consulted on the changes in her position proposed by the Constitution Bill, 1978, and on the changes noted just above; she was kept in touch, directly, by her Canadian Prime Minister and other of her Canadian Ministers, with all the developments leading up to the passage of the Canada Act, 1982, and the Constitution Act, 1982; and it was she herself who brought the latter Act into force, by proclamation,

in Ottawa, in the notable ceremony of 17 April 1982. Furthermore, she personally opened the Canadian Parliament in 1957 and
1977 (her father had personally assented to Bills in 1939); she
opened the Olympic Games in 1976 and the Commonwealth
Games in 1978; she has been present at formal meetings of her Canadian Privy Council; and her personal prestige and popularity
throughout Canada (except in Quebec) are amply attested by the
size and enthusiasm of the crowds that welcome her on her increasingly numerous visits. The marked success of the visits of
other members of the Royal Family, the avidity with which Canadians watched the wedding of the Prince and Princess of Wales, and
the huge sales of books on the Royal Family are further evidence
of the abiding faith of most Canadians in the oldest and most stable of their political institutions.

NOTES

1. See also R. MACGREGOR DAWSON AND NORMAN WARD, *The Government of
Canada*, 5th ed. (Toronto: University of Toronto Press, 1970), p. 162.

The Vulnerability of Prime Ministers in Canada and Britain

PATRICK WELLER

Prime ministers hold their position by virtue of their party leadership; they had to have the support of party members to be elected
in the first place. But what is the relationship thereafter? Prime
ministers, it is argued, have become so powerful through a variety
of constitutional, conventional and political factors that they have

Adapted from Patrick Weller, "The Vulnerability of Prime Ministers: A Comparative Perspective," *Parliamentary Affairs* Vol. 36, No. 1 (Winter, 1983): 96-117. By
permission of publisher and author.

developed a capacity to act almost independently of their parties. So can prime ministers be called to account by their parties? Can they be held answerable to their supporters? Answerability implies sanctions. Do the parties have any sanctions that can be applied against prime ministers or do they in practice have to wait for electoral defeat to undermine the leader's position?

These questions can be posed in much blunter fashion. In extreme circumstances can prime ministers be sacked by their own supporters? It is important to be clear about the meanings of the terms. Some prime ministers retire of their own free will. Others may be persuaded that their continued presence will be detrimental to their reputation, their party or their nation; reluctantly, but with a degree of consent, they stand down. To talk of prime ministers being sacked suggests that they have been removed, against their will, by their own supporters, and not defeated in parliament or in an election. To examine whether they can be sacked, it is necessary to ask *to whom* prime ministers are answerable—to the party in parliament, or to the party as a broader organisation? And *how* they may be called to account? In other words, and more generally, are prime ministers vulnerable to party revolt?

The question of the vulnerability of prime ministers has been heightened by the political changes of the last forty years. The media now concentrates on prime ministers, to the partial exclusion of their ministerial colleagues. Governments are identified by their leaders' names; the government's projection of a sense of competence is often judged by the prime minister's own performance. As a result the reputation of the prime minister has become seen almost as a prerequisite for a party's electoral success. When prime ministers can manipulate and dominate the media—Macmillan around 1958, Trudeau in the early years of Trudeaumania—their position is unchallengeable. But the reverse of this development is that if prime ministers are unpopular, or in policy terms out of sympathy with many of their supporters, then the pressure for their removal is likely to be all the greater. The removal of a leader in office may be a traumatic experience; but if party members feel it can save office or a party's identity, it might be considered an acceptable risk. If, that is, the prime minister is vulnerable.

The conditions that may create that vulnerability are therefore important in any discussion of prime ministerial authority. So too are the implications that might spring from those different levels of vulnerability. If prime ministers can only be removed with great difficulty, their direct answerability to their party must be limited.

But if they can be easily removed, such a situation might lead to a lack of stability.

In much of the debate on prime ministerial powers, people assume that prime ministers have become secure from internal challenge. J.P. Mackintosh certainly believed so. After asking rhetorically whether prime ministers could be sacked, he concluded that they could not be. Referring exclusively to Britain, the only instance he recalled in the twentieth century when a leader was *forced* to resign because of the withdrawal of party support was Neville Chamberlain; and he argued that even then the final blow was cast by the Labour party's refusal to serve in a coalition under Chamberlain.[1]

The historical record of the last fifty years (i.e. since 1932) seems to support Mackintosh's point. The reasons for prime ministers leaving office can be categorised in four ways: electoral or parliamentary defeat, death or willing retirement, reluctant retirement and sacking. On that basis, six British prime ministers have been defeated at the polls, four retired voluntarily, one was pushed, while two, Eden and Macmillan, are placed between the "willing" and "reluctant" retirements by different commentators.[2] None were actually sacked by their parties. To take two contrasts, in Canada five prime ministers were defeated at the polls and two retired at the time of their own choosing; no prime minister was persuaded to retire or sacked.[3]

If the analysis is taken to include former prime ministers, the point can be extended. Obviously it is likely to be easier to remove leaders of the opposition than prime ministers; they have less resources, less prestige and less patronage; they do not have the same national stature as prime ministers and their removal is likely to have less ramifications because it will not lead to divisions within a government. Yet the procedures to remove an opposition leader must be a prerequisite to the removal of a prime minister. In practice in Britain three former prime ministers retired (how willingly is less certain) and one was sacked; in Canada two retired willingly, one was sacked.[4]

But vulnerability cannot be assessed on the basis only of the number of leaders who have been deposed. Success alone is too crude an indicator. First, because it is possible to imagine a system where prime ministers are always vulnerable but where they have never been sacked because, aware that they are liable to challenge, they take precautions; whereas in another system, where prime ministers are institutionally more secure, the occasional successful revolt might occur. Second, because there is, in all countries, a trend towards making prime ministers more answerable to their parties. In the Conservative party more than elsewhere, it was assumed that a leader, once selected, had the right and responsibility to lead. Leaders were not expected to be directly answerable to the party. More recently the attitude of many of its members is epitomised by the question raised by one of Heath's critics: was the leadership to be regarded as a freehold or a leasehold? Parties want leaders to be answerable. The record of the past may therefore only provide a limited guide to the new pressures that are now developing.

What is important, therefore, is to examine the problem of prime ministerial vulnerability systematically, to consider the institutional factors which may allow challenges to be made and the implications of these methods for the general behaviour of prime ministers. These "rules of the game" will never explain all the pressures on prime ministers, but they may make it easier to assess and explain the degree of vulnerability that they must face.

Obviously prime ministers do not always receive the uncritical support of their party colleagues. The reasons for which they lose favour are many: policy flexibility or inflexibility; action or inaction; a declining public image or personal characteristics. Each may create new problems or exacerbate old ones. The list of factors, or combinations of them, is almost infinite. Several consequences may result. The most likely is the fear that the government will lose the next election under the existing leadership. Or there may be a growing feeling that a change in policy direction is needed for the ideological security of the party. Whether any of these factors is later turned into a desire for action may depend on a range of other factors such as the proximity of an election or the availability of an ideologically sound alternative, or on the internal structure of the parties, that is, on the degree of ideological division or the existence of organised factions. Dissatisfaction or unpopularity does not of itself lead to a challenge, but it is a necessary condition. However, apart from the appreciation that the reasons for a challenge to the leadership may be disparate, it is not necessarily important for the purpose of this article to discover why prime ministers lose the support of their party colleagues. What matters is the degree to which those prime ministers are then vulnerable.

Within any one system it may be difficult to isolate the circumstances that lead to more or less prime ministerial vulnerability.

Personal and temporal factors may loom so large that institutional factors receive less attention than they should. If, on the other hand, comparisons are made in two countries—each with a similar parliamentary system, similar constitutional assumptions, similar cabinet principles and prime ministers with similar (but, as in the other categories, not identical) powers—then it becomes easier to see how procedures and institutions contribute to degrees of vulnerability.

For that reason two countries of the Old Commonwealth—Britain and Canada—have been chosen as examples. This selection is made for two main reasons; first, the structure and principles of government have developed from the same Westminster model. The role of the prime minister is never directly spelt out in constitutional doctrine; nor are the methods of electing them. Yet the perception of the prime ministers' roles is similar; as is the relationship with their head of state. In later constitutions much less is left to chance or an understanding of how the system ought to work.

The second reason is that, in practice if not at first sight in name (and with the exception of the British wartime coalition), the governments are formed by single parties. In Britain and Canada prime ministers have headed minority governments, but they have not been forced to share office in coalitions. Coalition governments undoubtedly alter the situation. Prime ministers there may fall because their partners decide to leave the coalition, or because they will stay only if the party providing the prime minister changes its leader. Or a coalition may prevent the change of prime minister because the partners refuse to serve under anyone else. On occasion intra-party machinations may lead to arrangements with coalition parties to demand a restructuring of the coalition under new leadership. Thus any multi-party system that leads to a necessity for coalition government adds an additional problem to assessing the causes of vulnerability. There are many European precedents for this type of change. The complications are reduced by looking at countries where the decision to sack prime ministers will be entirely in the hands of the parties they lead.

It is worth remembering that each of the systems of leadership election and dismissal discussed here are compatible with parliamentary democracy and collective cabinet government, even though the impacts they may have will differ. None are somehow constitutionally correct or incorrect. Nor is it the purpose of the article to determine which is preferable. The objective is only to identify what it is in institutional terms that may make prime ministers vulnerable.

Britain

In Britain, from 1965 to 1980, the methods of electing party leaders were similar; more often they were different. Before 1965 Conservative leaders "emerged," chosen by a process of consultation among the party elites. In practice that meant selecting the person who was most acceptable as prime minister, because between 1922 and 1965 no one was first elected leader of the party while in opposition. Leaders usually left when they saw fit; the persistence with which Churchill hung on to the prime ministership, despite the almost unanimous view of his cabinet colleagues that he should retire, shows how much the decision lay in the prime minister's hands.[5] Since 1965 the Conservative leader has been elected by the Conservative members of the House of Commons. Both Heath and Thatcher were chosen by similar methods and both while the party was out of office. In the first ballot the leading candidate had not only to gain a majority, but to get 15 per cent more votes than the next highest candidate; the purpose was to ensure that the leader reflected some consensus in the party. If this was not achieved a second ballot was held for which new nominations were called. Thus compromise candidates could enter.

Although Heath did not win by the required percentage, he did get a simple majority. The other candidates then withdrew and there was no need for a second ballot. But, having elected him, there was no available mechanism for removing him, or formally challenging his hold on the leadership. While he was prime minister there was no hint of a move to unseat him. But after he had lost the two elections of 1974, demands for his removal swelled. The electoral defeats were only one of the reasons for the desire for change. His relations with his backbenchers had often been difficult and strained; and there were feelings that new policy directions might be required too. This dissatisfaction culminated in a meeting of the 1922 Committee of Conservative backbenchers which almost unanimously demanded that Heath put his position to a vote. This was the occasion when one member asked whether the leadership was freehold or leasehold.[6] Heath thought it should in practice be the former; the 1922 Committee and his critics demanded the second.

Forced to act by party demand, Heath commissioned a committee headed by Sir Alec Douglas-Home to establish a procedure by which a party could elect—or re-elect—a leader. The committee adopted similar procedures to those used in 1965, allowing for three ballots, the last of which would decide the issue by a process of preference distribution. In the first ballot Thatcher headed Heath, who then retired from the contest. In the second she gained a clear majority over the four candidates who entered the race after Heath withdrew.

These two contests were fought while the party was in opposition, but they set important precedents. The rules devised by Douglas-Home also included the provision for the leader, whether or not prime minister, to face a ballot within six to nine months of the opening of a new parliament, or within 28 days of the beginning of each new session if there was a challenger to the incumbent. No such challenger has yet emerged, but there is now a formal process by which the leader can be opposed.

However, it appears there is no mechanism to challenge a prime minister at any other time. Conservative ministers do not meet with backbenchers in regular party meetings; at times they may be invited to address the 1922 Committee, but they are not members of that committee, nor are any formal votes taken there. It therefore appears that if a substantial part of the Conservative parliamentary party do want to change their leader at any except the prescribed time, there are no procedures to allow it. If there is no challenge then, the prime minister is "constitutionally" safe for another year.

The leader of the Labour Party was initially elected by the members of the parliamentary party by a process of exhaustive ballot. After each ballot the candidate with the lowest number of votes was dropped and a further ballot held on a later date until one person received an overall majority of votes; the elections of Attlee, Gaitskell, Wilson, Callaghan and Foot were all conducted by these means; only one of those ballots was directly electing a prime minister. While the party was in opposition the leader had to be re-elected on an annual basis and his position could be challenged. When the party had a parliamentary majority, the leader had to be re-elected at the beginning of each parliament—a procedure that was largely a formality since the leader would have just won a general election. In 1945 Morrison did argue that Attlee should not accept a commission to form a government until his position as leader had been confirmed by a meeting of the parliamentary party. Attlee ignored the suggestion, which was based on Morrison's hope that he might be elected instead of Attlee to head the Labour government.[7] Nor, in later cases, did Wilson seek to confirm his position before forming a government.

Since the 1979 election the process of leadership election has changed drastically. The most important decision was to require that the leader of the party be elected annually by a national conference. Initially the electoral system, accepted by the Wembley conference of January 1981, gave unions 40 per cent of the votes and the constituency parties and the parliamentary party 30 per cent each—in the latter case considerably less than most of the parliamentary party wanted. The system was used for the first time in the election of the deputy leader in September 1981 when Denis Healey narrowly defeated Tony Benn.

The reasons for the change were complex. Much of the extra-parliamentary left wanted to ensure that the parliamentary members were more responsive to their wishes and would adhere more closely to their policies; both Wilson and Callaghan had shown at times an impatience with the demands of the party organisation. Further, there was an argument, espoused particularly by Tony Benn, that the prime minister was far too powerful and that whereas he may be able to dominate the parliamentary party he would not be able to control the conferences.[8] The move was therefore designed to make the prime minister more amenable to the party wishes by making him more directly answerable.

Yet, in the debate over the methods that should be used to elect leaders, little attention was given to means that could be used to remove him at other times. Some members of the left did make suggestions; for instance, Benn's supporter, Michael Meacher, wanted a Labour prime minister to submit his record to conference for approval between 18 and 36 months from the date of the preceding election.[9] But no such suggestions were taken up. The resolution finally adopted at Wembley did include a clause that, as Mostyn Evans, general secretary of the Transport and General Workers Union, argued, "gave the necessary stability to a Labour prime minister because when the party was in office there could be an election [for the leadership] only if a motion to that effect was carried at annual conference."[10]

It seems to be rather a strange definition of stability, but it might mean that Labour prime ministers are secure from revolt within the parliamentary party but could be forced to face a ballot by a vote of annual conference. However, if conference were to dismiss a prime minister who retained the support of the parliamentary party, the tensions so created would be vast. It would mean imposing a prime minister on a reluctant party. Obviously the process would be theoretically possible, but it would seem unlikely to happen in practice unless the party was ideologically divided in an irreconcilable way. If the move were made because electoral defeat was looming, it is unlikely that a prime minister would still retain the majority support of the parliamentary party.

Tony Benn has suggested that there are still mechanisms available at other times. He has argued that if a prime minister grossly abused his or her power, he or she "would be overthrown by his or her Cabinet colleagues through a collective resignation or by Labour MPs through a withdrawal of support in the Commons. Either of these events would precipitate a change of leader, or a general election."[11] But such a suggestion raises several questions. First, it is worth asking how the Labour conference would react if *its* duly elected leader was then removed at the initiative of precisely those groups from which the power to elect leaders has been so bitterly wrested. Indeed, it is perhaps surprising that Benn, the advocate of outside election, should rely on such traditional methods to control a prime minister. Second, if a prime minister did resign, how would he be replaced—by the parliamentary party or by a conference that would take time to convene?

Obviously the threats of cabinet or parliamentary revolt are potent weapons that may create restraints on a prime minister; every prime minister needs cooperation and consent. Yet it is questionable whether they could be utilised; they certainly have not been in the last fifty years. At times the Callaghan government was defeated in the House of Commons, but his opponents within his own party always supported the government on votes which it declared to be a vote of confidence. Nor is it likely that a collective resignation in a cabinet selected by a prime minister can be easily orchestrated. Most prime ministers are likely to retain some loyalty among those they choose. It may be true that these methods are effective because in the past they have acted as a deterrent and have not had to be used. But the evidence could equally be interpreted to suggest that they are no longer valid in practice.

Indeed, both these proposed methods of removing prime ministers are alien to twentieth century precedents. It may be true that some prime ministers have been "persuaded" to retire voluntarily, but this moral pressure, in Britain at least, was exerted in the days when leaders emerged rather than were selected. It is less certain, although still not impossible, that similar tactics could be adopted now. A prime minister that wants to hang on to his or her position could with justification point to the fact that there were existing mechanisms and invite the critics to use them. It does not mean that prime ministers who made a spectacular blunder or major error might not be persuaded to resign; but that is different from saying they are being forcibly removed. As one observer has commented: "Those who live by the vote must be killed by the vote."[12] The existence of formal mechanisms will make traditional pressures more difficult to use on a stubborn leader. When these mechanisms have been deliberately ceded to a broader section of the party, traditional pressures become even more difficult to use.

Canada

In Canada the leaders of the major parties have been elected by a convention of delegates for the past fifty years and that process is now well established. It serves to ensure that all sections and regions are represented in the choice of the national leader—an important factor in a country where the major parties often have few or no representatives elected from some of the provinces. The numbers involved are large. The Liberal convention of 1968 had 2472 delegates; 1584 of them were elected by constituency organisations, the others were members of parliament (130), university student delegates (130) or ex-officio delegates (including Liberal candidates defeated at the previous election, provincial leaders and the representatives of various party organisations and subordinate bodies). The Progressive Conservative Party convention had 2411 delegates, 1320 of whom were constituency delegates, 95 were MPs, 116 were university student representatives, 428 were ex-officio and the remaining 452 were appointed as delegates-at-large (they consisted of leading members of the party not otherwise selected or eligible to attend the convention).[13]

Leadership conventions are held when the leadership is vacant. Thus the Liberal party, which has governed Canada for the majority of the last sixty years, has only held four leadership conventions —in 1919, 1948, 1959 and 1968. Two of those conventions were almost foregone conclusions as there was no real doubt that St. Laurent would win in 1948 and Pearson in 1958; indeed, in 1948 Mackenzie King carefully manipulated the convention process to ensure the outcome he wanted.[14] In both 1948 and 1968, the convention was, in choosing the leader, also choosing the prime minister.

But prior to 1966 there was no mechanism available for convening a convention unless the leadership was vacant. So, when asked if a Liberal leader could be deposed, Lester Pearson could state in the early 1960s: "There is no institutional way . . . we haven't had to dispose of leaders. We've had very few leaders. As you know, I'm the fourth . . . The leader deposes himself. I don't know what other arrangements there could be."[15]

The difficulties that could emerge when a prime minister lost the confidence of his colleagues were shown by the divisions that occurred in the Progressive Conservative cabinet of John Diefenbaker. In 1963 several ministers decided to move against him in cabinet in an attempt to replace him. Diefenbaker heard of their plans, hastily convened a meeting of the parliamentary party before the cabinet met, and received a vote of confidence there. The cabinet rebels thus were unable to depose him. Therefore the constitutional and party consequences of such a cabinet revolt remain speculation; no one can be certain whether cabinet *can* remove a prime minister. Diefenbaker then called a general election at which his minority government was defeated. The divisions in the party thus led to Diefenbaker's loss of the prime ministership, though not the party leadership. After the 1963 election the Progressive-Conservative Party was split in a bitter internecine fight until 1966 when its annual meeting voted for the convening of a leadership convention, with the intention of deposing Diefenbaker. Throughout the period Diefenbaker retained the support of the majority of the parliamentary party; at the last minute at the convention he announced that he would again be a candidate but was resoundingly defeated. The events that led to his fall illustrated that support from caucus alone was not enough; the leader had to maintain the support of the extra-parliamentary wing of the party too.[16]

Around 1966 both major parties accepted that to leave the timing of an unsuccessful leader's resignation entirely to his personal judgement could create problems. At the national meeting of the Liberal Party in 1966 the party debated how leaders could be controlled. One delegate, now a senior minister, argued that "the party must have its check reins to keep the leader close to the party" and wanted automatic conventions within two years of each election. Eventually the conference accepted that a resolution calling for a leadership convention would be placed on the agenda of the first biennial conference to be held after each general election. If the resolution was adopted after a secret ballot, a leadership convention would be called within a year. Thus once during the life of each parliament the biennial conference could in effect pass judgement on a Liberal prime minister by deciding whether he should face reelection. Trudeau, the only leader the Liberal Party has had since then, has never been threatened by that process. Rather, after his electoral defeat in 1979, he had agreed to stand down when the defeat of the Clark government interrupted his retirement plans and catapulted him back into office.

In 1969 the Progressive Conservatives formally moved in the same direction, but they distinguished between the times the party might be in government or in opposition. When the party was in opposition, and if it had failed to increase its standing in the House by 20 per cent at the previous election, the first post-election general meeting would vote in a secret ballot on a motion calling for a convention. If the party was in government, no resolution could be put to a general meeting unless it had received formal notice that the prime minister had lost a vote of confidence in caucus. In other words, to depose an unwilling Progressive Conservative prime minister it first required a vote of no confidence to be passed in caucus, then for a motion calling a leadership convention to be passed by the annual meeting and then for a contest. The whole process would most likely take a year and would almost inevitably be totally destructive to a ruling party that tried to utilise it, even if it is unlikely that a prime minister who has lost the confidence of both parliamentary and extra-parliamentary parties would still want to appeal to the wider audiences of the convention. In practice none of these mechanisms have been used to convene a leadership convention.

By the standards of Britain these mechanisms seem very complex; and so they are. But they are a move, albeit a small one, in the direction of answerability. They restrict to a degree the right of a leader to hold office as long as he wants, but they probably would only be used against a leader of the opposition. The impact on a government of trying to remove a prime minister would be too great.[17]

Factors Affecting Vulnerability

From these brief institutional and political surveys some lessons can be drawn about the factors that make prime ministers more or less vulnerable to internal party revolt in the type of parliamentary system examined here.

Constituency. The first, and most obvious, lesson is that prime ministers are answerable to those who elected them as party leader. Therefore the broader the constituency, the more difficult it is to call together and the less vulnerable the prime minister is likely to be. For instance, Mackenzie King, leader of the Canadian Liberal Party from 1919 to 1948 and prime minister for much of that period, "placed great stock in the fact that he was selected by a democratic convention and not by the parliamentary caucus." Diefenbaker similarly argued in 1967 that "only a party convention had the right to undo what a similar convention had done eleven years before."[18] Canadian prime ministers have always had a dual responsibility—to the parliamentary caucus with which they must work on a regular basis and to the broad party that elected them. To lack the full confidence of the former may indeed make life difficult for a Canadian leader, but it need not be immediately fatal.

Further, there are always logistic and political reasons that make it difficult for a broad constituency to assert its authority, however unquestioned it may be. It takes time to organise a leadership convention and considerable pressures to have one convened. The results are likely to be unpredictable as the prime minister could conceivably use the considerable resources available to seek for votes. Indeed, the costs in terms of public division were regarded as high enough for the Liberals in 1968 when several cabinet ministers were competing for a leadership that was voluntarily vacated. A campaign against a fighting incumbent could only be destructive.

Contrast the Canadian situation with the British. In the British Conservative Party the process may be easier because the constituency is defined. Even though in 1974 there may have been no formal mechanism to remove Heath, the fact that the 1922 Committee was *part* of a defined group and, with its executive newly elected in October, could be seen to represent that part, gave its demands a certain legitimacy. Presumably, when the party is in government, it could act again, though doubtless with less weight, against an incumbent prime minister. With the Labour Party, the extension of the electoral suffrage to the party conference will probably make it more difficult to challenge a prime minister at any but the official opportunity.

Influencing the Constituency. An important question raised by the limited size of the numbers involved is the degree of control over that constituency that the prime minister may exert. The federal structure of a party has important implications because it creates a number of power centres, not all of which can the prime minister control. The implication is that it becomes possible for individuals to maintain a strong power base in a province and to develop their own reputation. This is particularly true in the Canadian Progressive Conservative Party whose leaders have been provincial premiers. Politicians with a strong regional base can exist independently of the prime minister's patronage.

In the British Conservative Party the central party machinery is under the direct control of the party leader. Members of parliament are not regularly threatened in their renomination and the prime minister is exclusively responsible for the selection and dismissal of ministers. The focus is therefore more likely to be on parliamentary than on extra-parliamentary pressures and prime ministerial patronage remains influential.

When the constituency is wider than the party in parliament, prime-ministerial influence is far harder to exert. In Canada federal party organisation is often ephemeral, particularly in those provinces where the ruling federal party may be weak. The prime minister's influence over many delegates to the convention is likely to be more through his reputation than his patronage, particularly in those regions where his personal identification is low. In the British Labour Party, where the new methods of election have been designed in part to reduce the leader's influence, the capacity to influence the constituency will depend more on factional links than direct patronage.

Federalism fractures the party organisation in Canada. It creates more party groupings which can exert pressure. It makes it more difficult for the central organisation (itself usually weak) or for the prime minister to influence parliamentarians if the party in parliament is the arena in which a leader is to be threatened. The size of the constituency has to be coupled with the accessibility of that constituency to prime ministerial pressure in assessing vulnerability.

Formal Opportunity.   Even if the constituency is clearly prescribed, that in itself need not make the prime minister vulnerable. What is also required is a consideration of the formal occasions at which challenges can be launched, or at least a set of rules that allow that opportunity to be created. In Canada prime ministers and their cabinet meet with backbenchers in party meetings on a regular basis. Those meetings discuss legislation that ministers propose to introduce into parliament and provide a regular forum for free-ranging criticism of ministers' proposals in an atmosphere that is generally hidden from public view, but they are not a forum in which challenges can be made. In the British Conservative Party, the rules do not provide for regular or formal ministerial-back-bench meetings.

Instead there is a formal occasion or set of occasions, at the beginning of each parliament or each session, when a prime minister can officially be challenged. The existence of prescribed occasions has two effects. First, it is highly unlikely that a prime minister who has won or retained office will have his or her leadership challenged. Second, it presumably increases the difficulty of mounting pressure at any other time. If there are no rules determining when a prime minister's position should be reviewed, it is in a sense always under review. But once proposals are codified, they can be appealed to as a means of staving off dissatisfaction at other times; grumblers can be told to wait.

Prescribed times for challenge have other impacts that help protect a prime minister. Changing the leader is a traumatic exercise; it is always a last resort, considered probably because party members can see no other way of avoiding an electoral defeat or because there may be no other way of ensuring that the leader adheres to party policy. It would be suggested when other methods, such as cabinet pressure and persuasion, may have failed. On only a few occasions, under any system, will a party be so divided, a prime minister's reputation so poor and fears of defeat or misdirection so paramount that a challenge will be considered. Such challenges will generally have to be made when all these factors come to the boil. But it is unlikely that the right moment will often, if ever, coincide with the moment when the formal review takes place. Further, if this is true of a parliamentary party which elects a leader, the chance of an outside body exercising its formal rights is likely to be even more limited; the political reverberations that would be created by an extra-parliamentary body removing, or seeking to remove, a prime minister would be too great. The time involved is just too long.

An Alternative Prime Minister.   The fourth important criteria for assessing the vulnerability of prime ministers is the need for an alternative. Whether or not the possible methods of deposing prime ministers seem practical, no leader can be replaced by a vacuum. An alternative person has to be promoted, even if he or she is not actually a candidate.

However, under some sets of rules an alternative candidate is a
sine qua non of a challenge. The position of a British Conservative
prime minister is put to a ballot *if* there is an alternative candidate.
That means that some leading figure must be prepared to take on
an incumbent prime minister in face-to-face battle. Few people
have the prestige or perceived ability at the best of times; even
fewer of those may be willing to face charges of divisiveness and
disloyalty. To challenge a prime minister may put a career at risk.
If the candidate does badly, his or her reputation might be harmed
irreparably. It is one thing to stand without any expectation of winning when the party leadership is vacant, as a means of indicating a
future interest; it is quite another to take on an active prime minister. The rules therefore protect a prime minister. Further, many
prime ministers will try to ensure that there is no obvious alternative around whom support can coalesce. Harold Wilson commented that he "never had less than three or four [crown princes]
and at one time had . . . six."[19] Rivals are discouraged, watched
and, if necessary, cut down to size.

Whatever the system, alternative candidates have to be prepared
to get involved. If they refuse to be considered, the exercise is futile. Discussions of replacing Attlee with Bevin ended abruptly
when Bevin was not interested.[20] A challenge to Thatcher needs a
distinguished figure around whom to coalesce; who will play that
role?

The need for a clear alternative may be less obvious when extra-
parliamentary bodies assess the leadership. In Canada to call for a
leadership convention in theory opens the gates to anyone. Even
so, if the prime minister is fighting against his deposition, it would
be difficult for ministers to challenge his leadership, probably criti-
cise his policies and stay in cabinet. The degree of difficulty in articulating an alternative is thus heightened now that formal procedures for removing the leadership have been established.

However it seems that Canadian prime ministers have been less
concerned about the development of powerful ministers, perhaps
because they do not see them as rivals. The great difficulty involved in removing leaders gives them security; and the need for
ministers to oversee much of the patronage in their own provinces
gives them an independent, but not necessarily threatening,
power-base. The traditional role of the Quebec lieutenants like St.
Laurent, the strength of individual ministers like C.D. Howe and
Walter Gordon who in some ways were more dominant than their
prime ministers, illustrates that Canadian leaders do not seem to
feel threatened. Yet that conflict of personality seems endemic in

Britain. The explanation must partly be that in Canada ministers may be regarded as potential leaders—when the job is vacant; in Britain they are considered more readily as immediate rivals.

The Implications: Accountability or Stability?

The model discussed here has been limited to two parliamentary systems with majority parties. There vulnerability can therefore be seen to depend on four factors: the constituency, the influence that can be exerted on that constituency, the opportunity and the existence of an alternative. The narrower the constituency, the less easy it is to control; the more frequent the opportunity and the less the need for a specific alternative, then the more vulnerable the prime minister is.

The institutional arrangements can be summarised neatly.

FACTORS OF VULNERABILITY

	Party	Constituency	PM's Influence	Opportunity	Need for Alternative
Britain	Lab.	Broad	Low	Annual	Yes
	Cons.	Narrow	High	Annual	Yes
Canada	Lib.	Broad	Low	Rare	No
	Cons.	Broad	Low	Rare	No

Of course, institutional factors are not the only ones that may determine the vulnerability of leaders. Some leaders may be regarded as tougher than others; opponents will be more wary of taking them on. Poor health may provide extra opportunities; so might circumstances beyond the government's control. Nor are the existing institutional constraints immutable. New rules cause new politics. If, for instance, Tony Benn's proposals to remove some of a British Labour prime minister's resources are adopted, so that, for instance, he no longer chooses his ministers, his position will be weakened. Further, any faction which has control of the party may, for ideological or electoral reasons, seek to change the rules. If coalition governments become necessary, that too may alter the situation. Yet these other factors, important though they may be, will operate within a party framework and must abide by some "rules of the game." Institutional constraints will structure the role of the prime ministers.

The choice of methods can also be understood along a spectrum where the choices at either end are between stability and answerability. A vulnerable prime minister is, and feels, immediately answerable to his parliamentary party. While non-vulnerable prime ministers obviously do not ignore the cabinet and parliamentary colleagues with whom they must work, they are less in danger of immediate challenge.

There are some important implications. A vulnerable prime minister must pay constant attention to his backbenches and to his public image. If his party fears he may lose the next election, it may take preventive action. If the policies of his government are considered ill-advised, the supporters might start considering alternatives. His reputation is being constantly assessed, often in comparison with potential alternatives. He can ill afford to sack popular senior ministers in case they act as the centre of an internal party opposition. Rumours can be a deadly device as party opponents try to destabilise the situation and cast doubt on their leaders' ability. Therefore, if a vulnerable prime minister is doing badly, it creates the conditions for constant plotting and intrigue; while the uncertainty lasts, all his attention will be directed toward survival; governing must wait. On the other hand vulnerability does create answerability. The prime minister must listen to the party, must heed the views of influential colleagues and must keep an open door. However dominant he may be personally, he can not afford to ignore his power base.

A non-vulnerable prime minister can, to an extent, remain immune from these immediate threats. That immunity is comparative only; no leader can afford to have too rebellious backbenches or too fractious a cabinet. However, if the prime minister is not answerable, there may be more open criticism, more grumbling, and a greater feeling of frustration among backbenchers who feel that they have been ignored too much or merely taken for granted. Prime-ministerial arrogance or intolerance may be less dangerous to a non-vulnerable leader. On the other hand such a government may have greater stability. Intrigue may be less as the party has, except for prescribed moments, delegated responsibility to the prime minister without demanding so much input. Leaders are less worried about their backs or about factions within the party. Seen from another angle, this stability may be regarded as an unfortunate inability of the party to influence an ineffective prime minister.

Both answerability and stability in the terms discussed here have their advantages and disadvantages. Nevertheless, the differences that they create, emerging in part from the degree of vulnerability of prime ministers, are substantial. There is no doubt that, in the last two decades, the trend has been towards greater answerability. It is necessary to be aware of the costs and benefits of that process. Prime ministers will never be regularly removed by internal revolt; they have too many political resources for that. But the mechanisms for change have important implications in themselves. They are also essentially manipulable; it is possible to move from one to another within bounds that are consistent with parliamentary government. It is therefore important, in discussing methods of electing prime ministers, to ask what other institutional and political outcomes these procedures might have.

NOTES

I would like to thank Michael Lee and John Warhurst for their comments on an earlier draft.

1. *The Government and Politics of Great Britain* (London, 1974); see ch. 8, "Can the Prime Minister be Sacked?" for a summary of his views.
2. Defeated at polls: Churchill (1945), Attlee, Douglas-Home, Wilson (1970), Heath, Callaghan. Retired: MacDonald, Baldwin, Churchill (1954), Wilson (1976). Pushed: Chamberlain.
3. Defeated at polls: Bennett, St. Laurent, Diefenbaker, Trudeau (1979), Clark. Retired: MacKenzie King, Pearson.
4. In Britain Attlee retired at his own volition; Douglas-Home and Callaghan were persuaded to retire, Heath was sacked. In Canada Bennett and St. Laurent retired; Diefenbaker was sacked. After June, 1983 another name must be added to the list, that of former Prime Minister Joe Clark; see note 17—Ed.
5. A. SELDON, *Churchill's Indian Summer: The Conservative Government, 1951-55* (London, 1981), pp. 40-54.
6. P. COSGROVE, *Margaret Thatcher: Prime Minister* (London, 1979), p. 56.
7. See B. DONOGHUE AND G.W. JONES, *Herbert Morrison: Portrait of a Politician* (London, 1973), pp. 338-43.
8. "The Case for a Constitutional Premiership" in *Arguments for Democracy* (London, 1981), pp. 22-30.
9. *The Times*, 21 March 1980.
10. *The Times*, 26 January 1981.
11. *Op. cit.*, p. 39.
12. *New Statesman*, 16 October 1981.
13. Figures from J.C. COURTNEY, *The Selection of National Party Leaders in Canada* (Toronto, 1973), pp. 120-3.

14. See R. WHITTAKER, *The Government Party: Organising and Financing the Liberal Party of Canada 1930-58* (Toronto, 1977), pp. 171-8.

15. Cit. F.C. ENGELMAN AND M.A. SCHWARTZ, *Canadian Political Parties: Origin, Character, Impact* (Toronto, 1976), p. 243.

16. G.C. PERLIN, *The Tory Syndrome: Leadership Politics in the Progressive Conservative Party* (Montreal, 1980), pp. 24-8.

17. The removal of Joe Clark as Conservative leader in June 1983 does not alter the argument because first, he was not the prime minister but the former prime minister and second, he was not forced to call a leadership convention. At the January 1983 Progressive Conservative meeting, the resolution calling for a leadership review was defeated by a 2 to 1 margin. However, to clear the air in time for the next general election, Clark resigned and called a leadership convention anyway, which he contested and lost to Brian Mulroney. It is interesting that the rules for convening a leadership review process were made more difficult to use in the future, once Clark had been ousted. For an analysis of this process, see PATRICK MARTIN, ALLAN GREGG AND GEORGE PERLIN, *Contenders: The Tory Quest for Power* (Scarborough, Ontario, 1983).

18. COURTNEY, *op. cit.*, pp. 128-9.

19. HAROLD WILSON, *The Governance of Britain* (London, 1976), pp. 51-2.

20. See G. BROWN, *In my Way: Memoirs* (London, 1971), p. 50.

The Canadian Cabinet: Priorities and Priority Setting in the Trudeau Era

G. BRUCE DOERN

The federal Cabinet has several major occasions when it attempts to inform Canadian citizens about priorities and about what it stands for. These include Speeches from the Throne, Budget Speeches, speeches on the tabling of expenditure estimates, and

Adapted from G. Bruce Doern, "Priorities and Priority Setting in the Trudeau Era: The Political Problems of Doing First Things First," in Doern (ed.), *How Ottawa Spends 1983: The Liberals, the Opposition and Federal Priorities* (Toronto: James Lorimer and Company, 1983). By permission of author and School of Public Administration, Carleton University.

crisis speeches by the Prime Minister. From time to time political party conventions and the electoral hustings provide additional vehicles for this essential act of political communication and policy-making.

The purpose of this article is to critically review priorities and priority setting. This is done by taking two portraits of priorities over two time periods. The first portrait is historical and encompasses Canada's history since 1867. The second view focuses on a shorter period, the Trudeau era from 1968 to the early 1980s, and includes an analysis of the formal expression of priorities in Throne Speeches and Budget Speeches.

With these two portraits in mind we then briefly examine a number of fundamental political factors which have made it difficult for governments to do first things first, and to take a long-term concerted view of their priorities. These include the ebb and flow of the dominant economic and social ideas and beliefs, the inexorable ticking of the electoral clock and the partisan political survival instincts it encourages, the constant demands from agencies, groups, classes and regions dissatisfied with the status quo or the current view of priorities, the limits of resources and knowledge, the partly media-induced need to be constantly *seen* doing "something," and the practical need to put old policy wine in new bottles.

Despite these difficulties, governments and political leaders must attempt to set priorities. These priorities, even when short- or medium-term in nature, affect the fate of particular individual policy fields. It therefore follows that one cannot understand or explain the drift or evolution of a single policy field, except in relation to the broader cluster of priorities present in any given time period. Some policy fields are persistently high on the priority list (e.g., inflation, unemployment) while others bob up and down like pistons on an engine (e.g., policies for research and development). Still others manage to squeeze their way onto the agenda but only to its outer fringes (e.g., occupational health, or policies for Native Peoples).

An Historical View of Priorities

Priorities always look clearer in the past than in the future. Hindsight has its much advertised advantages. The main reason for reviewing priorities in an historical perspective is that political systems have memories. Both policy successes and failures become a part of political institutions, partisan allegiances, regional identities and the overall collective political and social composition of Canada. While certain decades may have been dominated by one or more overall priority concerns, they also communally produce an historical list of grievances and perceptions of grievances which affect the priorities of subsequent decades. Some of these unresolved grievances persist to the present day. A second reason for taking an historical perspective is that the early 1980s seem increasingly to be a major historical watershed, beginning in a period of virtual economic depression and massive technological change. In this section we briefly review national priorities in six time periods, 1867 to 1914, 1914 to 1929, 1930 to 1945, 1945 to 1957, 1957 to 1970, and 1970 to the 1980s. Needless to say, these dates are somewhat arbitrary since history can rarely be chopped up quite this conveniently. For our limited purposes, however, the periods help us highlight major events and trends.

1867 to 1914: The National Policy

This period may be characterized as being dominated by Sir John A. Macdonald's National Policy.[1] The National Policy was in fact an array of policies intended to create an industrial base in Ontario and Quebec under a protective tariff, unite the country from sea to sea by building the Canadian Pacific Railway, and settle the West both to develop its resources and to supply the eastern industrial heartland but also to head off encroaching American interests anxious to exploit the Canadian frontier. The National Policy was national and regional policy rolled into one. It was an act of defiance against the "efficiency" of the north-south axis of North America. It embraced tariff policy, transportation policy and immigration policy. It was achieved through an English-French Canadian political alliance within the Conservative Party that survived, initially at least, both financial scandal and the hanging of Louis Riel.

Though challenged by the Laurier government and a brief flirtation with free trade, the National Policy essentially survived intact. It helped create the modern Canadian industrial structure, centred in Ontario and Quebec, but truncated in shape in the sense of having to serve a small Canadian market with limited export potential for manufactured goods. It was also a resource-based policy dependent on the resources of the hinterland, both to serve the industrial heartland and to export resources abroad.

1914 to 1929: The Attack on the National Policy

Those Canadians who increasingly saw themselves regionally, and even in terms of economic classes, as the victims of the National Policy, made some political headway in the 1914 to 1929 period. The period can therefore be seen as a period of attack against the National Policy. Aided by the massive changes induced by World War I, including the Conscription Crisis and the continuing rapid settlement of the West, the period produced major challenges to the previous national consensus.[2] Prairie populism rose in opposition to eastern financial and industrial power. Provincial governments, thought initially to be minor appendages to a centralized federal government, began to exercise influence because of the need to build and finance the social, economic and educational infrastructure of an increasingly industrialized, urbanized and less agricultural and rural population. Hydro facilities, schools and highways had to be built, and minimum social insurance programs had to be created to assist those who were the casualties of the market. Increased labour militancy resulted as well from a struggle for basic recognition of labour's rights—rights which were, in the main, not achieved until World War II.

1930 to 1945: Depression and War

Depression and World War II traumatized this period of Canadian and global political life. It emblazoned on the consciousness of post-World War II political leaders a desire to avoid future wars and depressions, but did not produce results in the specific period between 1930 to 1945. It was essentially war itself that ended the depression and put labour, capital and land back to productive use.[3] Though made infinitely worse by the depression, the period was nonetheless initially a continuation of the pattern of challenge to the National Policy by those who were not its beneficiaries. It produced yet another wave of prairie populism and eventually yielded the agrarian and labour alliance that later became the Cooperative Commonwealth Federation, the predecessor to the New Democratic Party (NDP). In the midst of World War II, the political left enjoyed its greatest electoral success until that time, forming a government in Saskatchewan and the official opposition in Ontario.

Despite the growing protest against the status quo there was, in the 1930s, no equivalent level of national leadership or reformist social philosophy in Canada to that of Roosevelt's New Deal in the United States. Canada's national politics continued to be influenced by the inevitable delicacy of English-French relations, relations which soured badly in the midst of another Conscription Crisis in World War II.

World War II resurrected and greatly expanded Canada's industrial base but left it centred in Ontario and Quebec. Canada's natural resources again became valuable to a Western alliance desperately in need of an expanded and secure resource supply base. Since the co-operation of labour would be essential to the war production effort, the period saw the first extensive national recognition of labour's right to bargain collectively and to strike.

1945 to 1957: Keynesianism and the Second National Policy

This period is often viewed to be one in which a Second National Policy was assembled to dominate federal priorities in the post-war decade. Such a policy was forged, it is often suggested, by the Keynesian doctrine which created an acceptable economic and social rationale in a capitalist economy for increased intervention by the state.[4] Thus, governments had to construct both a permanent infrastructure of programs that would stabilize the economy in the post-war era, and also strategically alter aggregate taxing and spending activities to ensure that economic investment and consumer demand were maintained. While Keynesianism helped legitimize the idea of this kind of macro intervention it was not the only philosophical basis for intervention in Canada. The post-World War II reconstruction program was also influenced by the strength of populist and left wing political pressure, by the pre-war and wartime use of public enterprises, and by the general social welfare concepts articulated in the United Kingdom by the Beveridge Report and its Canadian equivalents.

It is probably fair to characterize this period in terms of the emergence of a Second National Policy but it is an error to associate it fully with Keynesian economics. Keynesian fiscal policy has never been fully practised in Canada, and certainly not in this period. Moreover, other than the new array of social welfare programs launched in the post-World War II period (family allowances, expanded old age security programs, etc.), the core of Canada's economic policies during this period were not forged by a Keynesian

Department of Finance but rather by a Department of Reconstruction, Defence Production and later Trade and Commerce headed by C.D. Howe.[5] Howe's policies were essentially to use tariff and tax policies to encourage foreign equity investment in Canada. The result was to produce continued prosperity until the late 1950s and also to reinforce the age old pattern of Canada's truncated industrial structure first put in place by Macdonald's National Policy.[6] But by the end of the 1950s, it was now dominated by foreign ownership.

The period was also characterized by Liberal Party dominance and by the dominance of the federal government over the provincial governments.[7] The latter was reflected in the tight post-war tax agreements which centralized fiscal control in Ottawa. Liberal Party dominance was assured by the renewed English-French accommodation, evident in the King-Lapointe, King-St. Laurent, and St. Laurent-Howe-Pearson leadership alliances within successive Liberal Cabinets, and by the Liberals' successful portrayal of the Tories as the anti-Quebec party.

1957 to 1970: The Heyday of Social Programs

In general we characterize this as the heyday of social policy. This was first reflected in the *regional* definition of social policy and other grievances which led to the election of the Diefenbaker government. The quasi-populist basis of the Diefenbaker appeal was reflected in the spurt of reforms in 1957 and 1958 which included agricultural and rural development programs, hospitalization grants, and old age pension increases. It was evident in the loosening of the federal fiscal reigns through more generous tax agreements with, and equalization payments to, the provinces.[8]

The second round of change occurred in the mid-1960s when the Pearson government launched several major social policy initiatives including the Canada Pension Plan, Medicare, further old age security increases, the Canada Assistance Plan and federal assistance to higher education and manpower training.[9] Much of this was accompanied by buoyant expectations about a growing economy. The economy was buoyed by the expansionary consumer demand of the post-war baby boom as well as extensive immigration in the 1950s and 1960s. The growing economy would produce increased revenues even without the need for massive tax increases and hence the social programs were affordable, both those launched by Ottawa, and still others launched by increasingly expansionary and aggressive provincial governments.

The early Trudeau years promised more of the same, albeit sold under the label of "The Just Society." Where the Pearson Liberals offered a quantum jump in social welfare, Trudeau offered a qualitative leap promising a renewed effort to reduce regional disparities and to improve linguistic, cultural, environmental and individual rights.[10]

1970 to the 1980s: The Slow Rediscovery of Scarcity

The period from the early 1970s to the present is perhaps best characterized as one in which there was a grudging and belated rediscovery of scarcity. As declining economic growth and high inflation rates exerted their deadly double influence, politics, policy and the allocation of resources became increasingly a "zero-sum" game. Gains for one group, region or class increasingly became a visible loss for another group, region or class. The Organization of Petroleum Exporting Countries (OPEC) oil crisis and the continuing pressure of the environmental movement initially taught Canadians more about scarcity in its even broader ecological dimensions. By the early 1980s, social policy programs were under attack as beleagured debt-ridden governments sought to redeploy scarce tax dollars to shore up the industrial base of the economy or to reduce huge deficits.

We will have much more to say later about the specific priorities of the last two periods, especially in the Trudeau era, and thus we have treated them briefly here. In terms of the six periods, however, it is possible to see the dominant concerns of each era. Depending upon one's metaphorical preference, they show a different ebb and flow, or a different phase in the swing of the pendulum between different aspects of public policy, politics and ideas: in short, between creating economic wealth and redistributing it regionally and among income groups, between economic policy and social policy, between national policy and regional equity and sensitivity, between the centralization and decentralization of federalism, and between those who benefit from technological and other kinds of change and those who attempt to stabilize and protect their lives from the adverse effects of such changes.

Hindsight allows us to see priorities with greater clarity. But the priorities of the past have also been forged in vastly different political times. For example, the role of mass communication, especially television, is only a recent phenomenon. The early decades were not characterized by democratic mass suffrage and by democratic methods of choosing leaders. For these and other reasons, not the least of which is that it is part of Canada's more recent political memory, we need to have a second portrait of priorities, one in which all of the general modern conditions of democratic politics are present.

Priorities in the Trudeau Era: A More Detailed Look

The priorities of the several Trudeau governments should be ultimately viewed in the context of the broad historical priorities sketched above. But they are also noteworthy because they were devised by governments headed by a Prime Minister who had openly enunciated a philosophy whose intent was to make public policy processes more rational. When he first came to power Trudeau was very critical of what he perceived to be the disorganized nature of the previous Pearson government. The Trudeau philosophy was not always internally coherent or logical but it was quite clearly pronounced and even given considerable fanfare. That the philosophy and subsequent practice have not been the same is quite evident, a fact which happily lends credence to the view that politics has a rationality of its own and that it is consequently difficult to take the "politics" out of politics. Nonetheless, the Trudeau era in Canada, in concert with parallel developments in other countries, witnessed the most exhaustive and serious attempt to rationalize and manage policy processes.

We review the Trudeau priorities and the priority-setting process in a dual way. We survey them chronologically in each of his periods in office, but in each period we also compare selected Throne Speeches and Budget Speeches, particularly to illustrate the continuous difficulty in meshing general priorities with economic priorities. Even though we have properly referred to the period since 1968 as the Trudeau era, we also refer to the Clark government's priorities and priority-setting machinery.[11]

When comparing the general internal documents on priorities with Throne Speeches and Budget Speeches it is essential to remember that we are not comparing totally analogous documents or policy occasions. They also often deal with different time periods. The internal priorities exercise and the documents it produces is centred in the Priorities and Planning Committee of the Cabinet, chaired by the Prime Minister. It is intended to drive the *internal* decision and resource allocation process and operates annually. The Speech from the Throne is a *public* document intended to convey the government's overall legislative and policy plans to Parliament as well as communicate a general view of priorities to Canadians. Throne Speeches are not necessarily given on an annual basis but rather to open a new session of Parliament. The Budget Speech presents the Minister of Finance's (and the government's) view of the state of the economy and the fiscal and other policy measures needed to manage the economy effectively. Budget Speeches are prepared in relative secrecy even within the Cabinet. They usually occur annually but in some years there have been two Budget Speeches per year. We refer here only to selected major developments since 1968. It is sufficient to stress, however, that our brief chronological review of the Trudeau years shows the difficulty of co-ordinating the priorities reflected in these several priority-setting documents and time frames.

1968 to 1972

In 1968-69 and 1969-70, the internal priority-setting exercise was characterized by the development of a short list of general but tough priorities including language policies and the removal of regional disparities. Most other programs were held constant in budgetary terms. The priorities reflected the initial flowering of the Trudeau "rational" priority-setting process and were aided by the newness and hence the power of the 1968 Trudeau mandate. The toughness and shortness of the priority list were also aided by the 1969 fight against inflation which included an effort to curtail government-expenditure growth. The 1968-69 effort included, among other things, the development of an X budget of so-called expendable programs, and resulted in the cancellation of programs such as the Winter Works employment scheme (albeit soon to be resurrected in a new form a few years later when unemployment was perceived as the main problem).[12]

By 1970, however, both the general political environment and the pressure of ministers and bureaucratic departments made the priority exercise less formally "rational" in the abstract sense of that word, but quite politically rational. Thus the October Crisis of

1970 converted the internal priority-setting exercise into a vague search for programs that would aid "national unity." In addition, the pressure from ministers and departments that had been "ranked" low for two or three years in a row increased greatly. They increasingly demanded fairer treatment and equity in the budgetary and the priority-setting process. These internal arguments and the need to maintain bureaucratic and ministerial peace and tranquility were aided by and reflected in the declining political strength of the Trudeau government in 1971-72, and by growing unemployment. By the 1972 election, the priority-setting process generated a veritable "wish-list" of priorities.

Table 1 (Trudeau Era Government Priorities) illustrates the evolution of the priorities as expressed publicly in Throne Speeches. In 1968 the priorities were packaged as "The Just Society" and corresponded to the internal list enunciated above. Given expenditure restraint, many of the key priorities did not, at the outset at least, involve heavy expenditure commitments. By 1970, in a Throne Speech which pre-dated the Quebec October Crisis, the priorities were expressed in terms of the "new age of the 1970s." The major priorities were generally social in nature. By 1972, as Table 1 shows, the priority list had become decidedly economic in emphasis, with the more social issues relegated to a low priority status. The 1972 pre-election Throne Speech was couched, nonetheless, in the somewhat vague theme of the need to "remove the barriers that create isolation."

Selected Budget Speeches during this period, as shown in Table 2 highlight the initial effort at securing expenditure restraint in 1968-69 as a major part of the priority concern about inflation. The 1968 Budget Speech also highlighted the promised post-Carter Commission tax reform process. The Commission had focused on the need for a simpler, more egalitarian tax system based on the concept that a "dollar is a dollar" and that all forms of income should be taxed on a fair progressive basis. Meanwhile, the 1968 Budget and subsequent budgets continued to tax and confer tax benefits on an incremental basis in response to ongoing political and fiscal needs. The 1970 Budget Speech continued to stress the need to fight inflation with specific targeted measures but also revealed the need to ameliorate the regional impacts of the otherwise blunt macro fiscal and monetary policy levers.

TABLE 1

Trudeau Government Priorities as Reflected in Throne Speeches in Selected Years

Year	Main Theme	Major Priorities Stressed	Lower Priority Items
1968 (Sept. 12)	— "The Just Society"	— Foreign policy and Defence — Constitutional Reform — Official Languages Act — Expenditure Restraint — Parliamentary Reform — Regional needs and opportunities	— "Careful planning and hard reviews" — Information Services to be Improved (Information Canada) — National Parks & Monuments — International Development Centre
1970 (Oct. 8)	— No major theme — Opened with views of "New Age of the 1970s," and Canada on the "Threshold of Greatness"	— Urban problems — Law reform (debate on abortion and non-medical use of drugs) — Improved Unemployment Benefits — Tax reform — Pollution control	— Grain export sales — Adjustment of textile industry — Inflation — Unemployment in some regions
1972 (Feb. 17)	— "The need to remove the barriers that create isolation"	— Unemployment and economic security — Industrial Strategy and Science and Technology — Trade policy — Competition policy — Farmers and fishermen income and price stabilization	— New Canada Labour Code — Equality of women — Family Income Security Plan — Non-medical use of drugs — Protection of privacy — Extension of CBC services to cover 98% of Canadians

TABLE 1 (continued)

1973 (Jan. 4)	— No overall theme but stress on priority for economic and social policy	— Strengthening trade ties with Europe — Job creation — Reformed social security system — Housing and Urban Assistance	— Competition policy — Airport security — Fitness and amateur sport — Tightening immigration rules — Conference on Western Economic Opportunities
1974 (Sept. 30)	— Serious international economic situation improve economic supply	— Inflation — Increase the supply of goods and services — Protect those least able to protect themselves — Soften the impact of soaring oil prices — Expenditure restraint	— Consultative processes with business, labour, provinces, professions and farmers — Transportation services to — Preventative health care — Social security review — Equal status of women
1976 (Oct. 12)	— No overall theme	— National unity • Language policy — Equality of opportunity • Inflation • Fiscal restraint • Reduction in public service • Small business incentives • Job creation targeted to areas of high unemployment • Less adversarial labour relations	— Competition policy — Oil and gas conservation — 200 mile limit over waters — Resume indexing of family allowances

	— Individual freedom
	  • Freedom of information legislation
	  • Human rights
	— Role of Governments
	— A middle road between laissez faire and growing intervention	

1978 (Oct. 1)	— Strengthening the economy and the renewal of the federation	— Expenditure restraint ($2 billion reduction in projected spending)
		— Wage restraint in public sector
		— Transfer dollars to:
		  • Industrial expansion
		  • Job creation
		  • Assistance to the needy
		— Revised Constitution Bill
		— Publication of "A Time for Action" proposal for constitutional renewal
		— Increased training for young people
		— Reduce costs of unemployment insurance
		— Child benefits system
		— Make Post Office a crown corp.
		— Consultation with business, labour and other groups

1980 (Apr. 14)	— Canadians want more effective government not less government	— Expand Petro-Canada — 50% ownership of petroleum industry — Mandatory fuel efficiency standards — Strengthening of Foreign Investment Review Agency — $35 per month increase in Guaranteed Income Supplement — National Trading Company — Employment programs for women — Efficiency in government

SOURCE: Throne Speeches, Various Years.

TABLE 2

Trudeau Government Priorities as Reflected in Budget Speeches in Selected Years

Year	Main Theme	Major Priorities Stressed	Major Tax Changes
1968 (Oct. 22)	— Prosperity with problems	— Control of public expenditures, especially federal-provincial social programs — Resisting inflation — Tax reform consultative process to discuss Carter Commission reforms	— Exemptions for estate & gift taxes — Changes in tax on life insurance companies — 2% Social Development Tax to maximum of $120
1970 (Mar. 12)	— Need to fight entrenched inflation	— Fight inflation — Ameliorating the regional impacts of macro fiscal and monetary policies — Expenditure restraint — Credit control powers — Measures to control inflation in construction industry	— None
1972 (May)	— Economic expansion to reduce unemployment	— Promote greater social justice by easing financial burden borne by pensioners, blind, disabled, veterans & students — Reinforce competitive position of manufacturing and processing	— Two year capital cost allowance provision

industries, especially in light of uncertainty created by recent international monetary crisis

1973 (Feb. 19)	— Reduction of unemployment	— Reduce unemployment — Increase old age pensions — Reduce inflation without controls	— Two year capital cost allowance provision to be accompanied by review mechanism to ensure jobs are created — Indexation of tax system to begin in 1974 — Reduction of basic federal tax by 5%
1974 (May 6) (Pre-election Turner Budget defeated) Basically reintroduced in Nov. 18, 1974 Budget after Liberal majority restored	— Attack inflation by encouraging increased supply of goods & services — Inflation traceable primarily to international forces including high energy & food prices	— Encourage supply — Act directly against high prices where practical — Alleviate adverse impact of rising prices, particularly low income Canadians — Reduction of budgetary deficit compared to previous year (from $1 billion to $450 million) — In reintroduced Budget of Nov. 18, 1974, emphasis placed on cooperative consultative effort to achieve consensus to slow price increases	— Non-deductibility of provincial royalties & taxes on mining & petroleum corporations — 10% surtax on corporate income tax — Increased excise taxes on high energy consuming vehicles — 12% federal sales tax removed on clothing & footwear — Registered Home Ownership Savings Plan introduced

TABLE 2 (continued)

| 1976 (May 25) | — Anti-inflation, but need to attack the underlying structural problems of economy in consultation with major groups | — Reinforced the priority for wage & price controls introduced Oct. 15, 1975
— Structural policies
  • Conserving energy
  • More efficient pricing of govt. services through user fees
  • Productivity
  • Employment & labour force
  • Expenditures to be kept to no higher than trend in GNP
  • Gradually lower rate of monetary expansion | — Two year tax write-off on equipment enabling companies to use industrial waste as fuel source
— Increased small business tax incentives
— Doubling of deductions for expenses of child care |
| 1978 (Nov. 16) | — Laying the basis for future growth | — Gradually reduced rate of monetary expansion
— Expenditures to be kept below rate of growth of GNP
— Reduced rate of growth in transfers to provinces
— Need for improved consultation
— "skeptical about the search for a single grand industrial strategy"
— Reallocation of $300 million to assist industry | — Reduction in UIC payments by employees & employers
— Doubling of employment expense deduction
— Refundable child tax credit
— Increase investment tax credit with higher rates for depressed regions
— Doubling of R&D investment tax credit |

1980 (Oct. 28)	— The National Energy Program	— Energy self-sufficiency, opportunities for Canadians & fairness in pricing — Need to reduce the deficit — Monetary restraint — Major shift of energy incentives from tax incentives to direct grants — Western Canada Fund	— Major new energy revenue taxes & charges — 8% surtax on net oil & gas production — Natural gas & gas liquids tax — Petroleum compensation charge levied on refineries to produce blended price of oil — Elimination of oil & gas depletion allowances
1982 (June 28)	— How to get the economy growing again by bringing down inflation & increasing productivity "The Six Percent Society"	— Controls on federal Public Service wages to 6% in 1983 & 5% in 1984, & "temporary" elimination of collective bargaining — Limitation of federal administered prices to 6 & 5% objectives — Limitation of indexation of taxes and selected social benefits to 6% and 5% rather than at full inflation rate — $300 million housing incentive; $3000 grant to purchasers of new houses — Relaxation of FIRA foreign investment rules	— Proposal for creation of new investment instruments to tax only real investment income & capital gains — Postponement & alteration to controversial Nov. 1981 Budget effort to close off tax loopholes

SOURCE: Budget Speeches, Various Years.

The pre-election Budget of May 1972 and the post-election Budget of February 1973 saw priorities shift to a concern for unemployment and social justice. This represented a response to genuine problems plus the electoral imperatives of a government in political trouble. The international monetary crisis and the Nixon economic shocks of 1971 also prompted the government to offer a new round of special capital cost allowances to enable Canadian manufacturers to compete and create jobs.[13] The 1972 election campaign was highlighted by NDP Leader David Lewis' campaign against "corporate welfare bums." This led the minority Trudeau government in the 1973 Budget Speech to promise a published review of the capital cost allowance program to ensure that it was producing the economic benefits claimed by the government.

1972 to 1974

Between 1972 and the election of 1974, during a time of minority government, the internal priority-setting process was virtually indistinguishable from the processes of parliamentary survival. Thus, during this time the Priorities and Planning Committee and the Legislation and House Planning Committee of the Cabinet had to work closely together. Despite the changed political circumstances and the criticism by the Liberal caucus of the growing power of the central agencies, the formal internal priorities exercises continued to be processed by the Privy Council Office (PCO) in much the same way as before 1972. The terminology to describe the process changed, however. Thus priorities were expressed as "major objectives" and "policy thrusts." The process also changed through the initiation of "Cabinet planning studies." These were new names given to what in the early period had been referred to as the identification of "priority problems." These were not the same as the priorities themselves, but rather were issues requiring analysis and possible future action. By 1974 there were studies underway in a host of areas including mineral policy, demographic objectives, decentralization of the public service and education to name only a few. As Richard French points out, the net effect of these cosmetic changes was that the paper flow did not fundamentally change.[14] The sobering results of the 1972 election did, however, lead central agency officials to ponder why the line departments were not responding to the policy signals emanating from the top. In short, there was concern that the bureaucratic troops were not marching on cue and that the government's priorities were not well understood by the Canadian people.

The substantive priorities in this period articulated in the Throne Speech of 1973 displayed a more balanced economic and social list. This is perhaps indicative of the government's tactical effort to secure the support of the NDP in the minority House of Commons situation, through an emphasis on direct job creation and a reformed social security system. It is important to note that the 1973 Throne Speech pre-dates, and thus does not even mention, the OPEC oil crisis or energy policy. This crisis, coupled with Tory and NDP criticism of energy policy, resulted in Prime Minister Trudeau's speech in December 1973 outlining federal energy policy.[15] It included a commitment to cushion oil prices for eastern consumers and to establish Petro-Canada as a state-owned company.

The Budget Speeches in this minority government era revealed a primary concern first for unemployment in the second Turner Budget of February 1973 and then inflation in 1974. The basic provisions of the 1973 Budget were described [in Table 2]. Of particular interest was the introduction of indexation of the tax system and of selected social programs. This was a direct response to Conservative Opposition Leader Robert Stanfield's criticism of the way in which the government was profiting from inflation from increased revenue which it was able to collect without having to impose increased taxes.

The May 6, 1974 Budget Speech, which was defeated in the House of Commons, gave clear emphasis to anti-inflation measures. The government traced the main cause of inflation to international factors, including the OPEC oil cartel's price increase. The Budget stressed the need to increase the supply of goods and services. The Budget was the first in the 1970s to bring energy policy and federal-provincial conflict over resource control and resource revenue shares to a head. This arose when the Turner Budget made provincial royalties and taxes on mining and petroleum companies non-deductible for federal tax purposes.

1974 to 1979

As with most experiments in human organization, people charged with responsibility for the priority-setting process tried to learn from their early experience. Following the return to a majority Trudeau government in 1974, efforts were made to enhance both the legitimacy of the priority-setting process among ministers and their officials, and the follow-up exercise. This included more elaborate ministerial meetings as well as the submission from departments of their plans regarding how they would contribute to and implement the priorities. An effort was also made in the mid-1970s to make the priority list more explicit and detailed. The crux of the problem was highlighted in an internal Cabinet report dated January 30, 1975.[16]

As a result, the new priority exercise of 1974-75 involved a small group of PCO and Prime Minister's Office officials interviewing each minister. As Richard French points out, these interviews revolved around two questions posed to each minister in the newly elected Cabinet: "What does the government have to do during its mandate to win the next election?" and "what do you want to be remembered for having done, should the government lose the next election?"[17] This produced a list of priorities. Departments were then asked to indicate how they could contribute to these priorities. After each area on the list was discussed in detail with departmental officials, an overall Memorandum was prepared and discussed at the Cabinet's Meach Lake retreat. This document identified five themes and sixteen priority policy areas as follows:

1. A more just, tolerant, Canadian society, including:
   • social security
   • native rights
   • law reform
   • bilingualism
   • labour-management relations

2. With a greater balance in the distribution of people and the creation and distribution of wealth between and within regions including:
   • demographic and growth patterns
   • transportation
   • national industrial and regional development

3. Which makes more rational use of resources and is sensitive to the natural and human environment including:
   • conserving our natural resources, particularly energy resources
   • maximizing the use of Canada's agricultural and fisheries resources
   • diversity of life styles and mental and physical health

4. Accepting new international responsibilities particularly with regard to assisting developing countries including:
   • sharing of resources
   • alleviating international crises

5. With an evolving federal state capable of effective national policy as well as sensitive, responsive and competent government at all levels including:

- federal-provincial relations
- communications
- parliamentary reform[18]

It is instructive to note that nowhere in this document was the growing concern for inflation and unemployment reflected. By the fall of 1975 the priority exercise had disintegrated, replaced by the wage and price control program and a "law and order" package devised by a handful of officials and ministers in Finance, the PCO and the Prime Minister's Office.[19]

The content and process of the 1975 priority-setting exercise is all the more remarkable because the previous Throne Speech of September 30, 1974 did stress the serious international economic situation. As Table 1 again shows, the priorities were inflation and restraint, ameliorated by the need to soften the impact of soaring oil prices.

While the income control program was being put in place late in 1975 and early in 1976, priorities lurched in yet another direction. By the October 12, 1976 Throne Speech, the priority item was national unity and language policy, a priority precipitated by the air traffic control strike and the bitter dispute over language policy and air safety.[20] The dispute resulted in Prime Minister Trudeau's national television address prior to the Olympic Games which described the crisis as being equal to the Conscription Crisis of World War II.

The 1976 Throne Speech also reflected the growing influence of neo-conservative criticism of the growth of government. While leaning to the right, the Liberals portrayed themselves as having a middle-of-the-road view of the role of government. This was also reflected in the publication of two philosophical position papers, *The Way Ahead* and *Agenda For Cooperation*, both of which addressed issues regarding the "post-incomes control" society, and the need to fundamentally restructure the economy.[21]

By the fall of 1978 and the new Throne Speech of October 1st, the major themes of the 1976 Speech were even more entrenched. The election of the separatist Parti-Québecois government in Quebec resulted in a new round of proposals for Constitutional Renewal. The growing popularity of the Progressive Conservatives under Joe Clark, expressed in both polls and by-elections, strengthened the neo-conservative emphasis in Liberal priorities (e.g., expenditure restraint, public sector wage restraint, and industrial expansion). This included a sudden "$2 billion expenditure cut" exercise ordered by Trudeau in August 1978.[22] This exercise was carried out through processes entirely separate from the

"normal" priority-setting routine. It was a Prime Ministerial "light-
ning bolt" which hit while most ministers were on their August va-
cations.

The economic policy emphasis on anti-inflation policy is evident
in the two 1974 Budgets of John Turner and the 1976 Budget of
Donald Macdonald. The content, however, is quite different.
Turner opposed controls and promoted priorities and policies
which would encourage the supply of new goods and services. Following the 1974 election which returned the Liberals on an anti-
controls mandate, Turner attempted an elaborate but unsuccessful
consultative process with business and labour to bring down
prices.[23] When the Macdonald Budget was brought down following Turner's resignation, wage and price controls were a fait ac-
compli. The Macdonald Budget focused on the need for major underlying structural policies including energy conservation,
expenditure growth less than the growth of the Gross National
Product, and gradual reductions in the rate of monetary expansion.

The Chrétien Budget of November 1978, the last Budget prior
to the 1979 election that saw the defeat of the Liberals, witnessed a
continuation of the 1976 themes about structural reform of the
economy but couched the budgetary priorities in terms of "laying
the basis for future growth." It contained a pre-election mixture of
neo-conservative restraint with social measures such as the Child
Tax Credit as well as investment tax credits with higher rates ear-
marked for economically depressed regions. Even though the
Budget Speech had been preceded by the August budget cuts exercise and the formation of the Board of Economic Development
Ministers to co-ordinate and devise an industrial strategy, Mr.
Chrétien pointedly expressed his skepticism in the Budget Speech
about the search for a single grand industrial strategy.

The 1980s

The Liberal Throne Speech of April 1980 gave testimony to the
Liberals' new aggressive post-election position. Reacting against
the Clark government's "community of communities" and neo-
conservative view of Canada, the Liberal Throne Speech asserted
that Canadians wanted more effective government not less government, and that they wanted someone to speak for Canada. It
promised constitutional renewal, an expanded Petro-Canada, steps
to achieve 50 percent ownership of the petroleum industry, and a

strengthened mandate to enable the Foreign Investment Review Agency to review foreign investment more vigorously.

The 1980 Throne Speech did not, however, reveal the degree of aggressiveness and initial coherence of the overall *internal* strategy devised by senior ministers, advisors and officials.[24] The basis of the strategy can be summarized briefly.

— There was a fundamental belief among senior Liberals that the national government could not restrict itself to acting merely as a referee between competing interests of the Canadian "communities." They profoundly rejected the short-lived Clark government's "community of communities" concept of Canada.

— The Trudeau Liberals concluded that their plans and policies had to be designed, wherever feasible, to reassert federal presence and visibility. Such a presence and identity was to be fostered by actions and decisions in which the federal government dealt *directly* with individual persons, businesses, and other social institutions rather than channelling its support *through* the provincial governments.

— Federal ministers were increasingly tired of reacting to the initiatives of provincial governments and of being perceived as a mismanaged, debt-ridden and remote government, while the provincial governments basked for most of the 1970s in the political glory of balanced budgets, perceived competence, and sensitivity and closeness to "their" people.

— With the Quebec referendum "settled," the Liberals turned their attention westward to try to forge some kind of a new political coalition that would strengthen their representation, legitimacy, and power in the West. This search was premised on a strategic political view that they would have their best electoral prospects if they tried to woo the left-of-centre NDP voter. They would also have to latch on to the western resource boom, influence its direction, and be *seen* to be influencing it in significant ways.

The federal identity approach or the "new nationalism" was centred in the Constitution with its Charter of Rights and the National Energy Program. In addition to these high risk initiatives, the 1980 plan envisioned three other large aggressive initiatives—an industrial strategy, a Western Canada Fund to help build Liberal support in the otherwise barren Liberal electoral territory, and major changes in social programs, especially the federal-provincial arrangements for financing health and education. The nationalism and federal identity focus, carried out on several policy fronts concurrently, was intended to be conflict oriented and to assert federal jurisdiction.

In terms of resource allocation the Liberal expenditure plans gave a clear indication, if carried out, that economic development and energy expenditures would receive the top priority and social expenditures would be given a low priority. The Trudeau Liberals retained the full scale envelope system begun by the Clark government, including the publication of five-year expenditure plans. This system was intended to bring the priority-setting machinery closer to a possible resolution of the problems identified earlier in the 1970s, namely, the need to link policy choices directly to resource allocation and the need to link new expenditures to ongoing or "base" expenditures. The Prime Minister, however, abandoned the Clark experiment with an Inner Cabinet because of the obvious tensions it had created among Clark ministers excluded from the inner group.

The Budget Speeches of the early 1980s reflected the usual range of coherence and incoherence with overall priorities. Finance Minister Allan MacEachen's first Budget in the fall of 1980 was the National Energy Program Budget. It contained radical changes to the structure of oil and gas industry incentives, from tax incentives to direct grants favouring Canadian firms. The second MacEachen Budget of November 1981 diverged from overall priorities in some respects. On the one hand, it asserted the need to fight inflation, reduce the deficit, and to stick to a tough monetary policy and high interest rates. On the other hand, it experimented with a quasi-social policy of closing off loopholes or tax expenditures and reducing the highest marginal tax rates. The 1981 Budget, however, did not redistribute the additional revenues obtained to low income Canadians, but rather shuffled them around to other middle and higher income Canadians. The Budget produced a political disaster in an economy sinking into depression. It was widely perceived to be one which produced neither good economic or social policy.[25]

The June 1982 Budget was designed to recover from the previous budgetary debacle. It was produced by yet another aberration from the overall priority-setting process, a small ad hoc group of ministers. The Budget produced the plan for the "Six Percent Society." The focus was on an anti-inflation attack anchored on a policy of statutory control of public service wages. All three MacEachen Budgets contained some underlying continuity of concerns over inflation and the deficit but in other respects they revealed the normal political need to respond to often contradictory short- and medium-term realities and perceptions of realities.

The Political Imperatives and Problems of Doing First Things First

We have taken two portraits of priorities, one capturing a 115-year period and the other a decade and a half of the Trudeau regime. When looking at whole decades in the distant past, priorities seem clearer. When priorities deal with the future, politics and uncertainty are the constant companions. Governments are caught between a rock and a hard place. If they try to stick to a medium-term view they may be guilty of arrogant rigidity and of being insensitive to present needs. If they engage in too many ad hoc short-term responses, they are accused of failing to plan or failing to create a "climate for investment." Neither rationality nor incrementalism is good enough.

Throne Speeches in the Trudeau era have evolved from quite philosophical documents in the early years to somewhat more prosaic ones in the later period. All, however, contain the veritable wish list of "priorities" for different constituencies and regions, an act of essential political communication. The trends in substantive priorities show the Liberal tendency for continuous movement across the middle of the political stage, a "to-ing and fro-ing" between a relative focus on social priorities (1968, 1970) and economic priorities (1972, 1974), between left (1980) and right (1978). Despite this tendency, certain subjects are persistently at or near the top of the priority list (inflation, national unity), while others move on and off the list (competition policy, immigration, women's issues) on the fringes of politics.

The expression of general public priorities is partly an act of political theatre. This does not necessarily make it unreal or a meaningless charade. We have seen, however, how public priorities expressed in Throne Speeches do not usually equate well with internal resource allocation processes, including those expressed in Budget Speeches. The analysis shows how the machinery had to be constantly changed to get a better fit between internally expressed priorities and actual resource decisions. Various ways have been tried, including the special exercises of 1974, the creation of the Board of Economic Development Ministers in 1978 and the envelope system of 1979. Indeed, there have been several occasions when the Prime Minister and his senior advisors deemed it necessary to concoct special priority-setting devices. The October Crisis of 1970, the wage and price controls priority of 1975, the August Budget Cuts of 1978, the National Energy Policy of 1980, and the "Six Percent Society" initiatives early in 1982, all emerged from special machinery which disobeyed the normal priority-setting rules. Indeed it can be said that there are as many abnormal priority-setting procedures as normal ones in the Trudeau era.

Budget Speeches also reveal the varied and episodic links between nominally economic priorities and the broader Throne Speeches. They raise the oldest "chicken versus the egg" question about priorities. Should the economic framework and fiscal posture largely set the scene for overall political priorities or should it be vice-versa? A review of several Budget Speeches shows the obvious economic tone of Budget Speeches but reveals them to be profoundly political documents as well. There are a number of factors which contribute to this revolving door pattern of priorities. Most of them cannot be attributed to the personality of Prime Minister Trudeau but rather reflect larger forces. Each of these are examined briefly.

Undoubtedly the strongest incentive against the rational setting of, and adherence to, priorities is found in the inexorable ticking of the electoral clock. A political party without power cannot make policy. Therefore, at best, the ideal political planning cycle extends only to about three years since electoral preparations are likely to neutralize the fourth year.

There is of course a paradox here because there is inherent in democracy a view that a general form of rational behaviour is occurring. That is, it is assumed that a particular political party is elected with a mandate and that it will "keep" (implement) its major election promises. Even when the general public is aware of the inflated bidding war inherent in electoral promises, it seems to expect that at least the major promises and priorities will be implemented.

But this quasi-rational expectation about a government's priorities is confounded by two other equally powerful forces—the need to survive politically and the obligation of the government to *govern*—and hence to reach decisions and set priorities in relation to the host of domestic and international demands and situations which impact on it *between* elections. There can be little doubt that political survival is a powerful instinct. Most politicians would prefer to be in power rather than in the opposition. The accoutrements of public office—salary, prestige, status and influence—are valued and coveted. To retain them, political parties in power are often prepared to change priorities to help sustain the coalition of voter support that will preserve them in office. These self-interest motivations, however, are rarely totally separate from the need to govern and hence to deal with the dominant political ideas. Thus self-interest and purposeful *governing* responsibilities are inextricably linked.

Priorities are also difficult to sustain because of the inevitable limits of information and knowledge. Many policies fail because we lack theory (that is, a knowledge of causal relations) and we lack knowledge about what is required to change human behaviour in desired ways. Interests do not always want to "behave" properly. Policies rarely fail merely because we lack clear objectives. Because of the limits of knowledge, governments must constantly adjust priorities and policies. In short, they must constantly try to *learn* and at the same time adjust to the power of other institutions.

A scarcity of resources also accounts for shifting priorities. Many priority concerns and policy fields are under-resourced in terms of time, money, personnel and political will. Some are over-resourced. There is therefore a constant pressure to change priorities to increase the resource support for neglected areas.

In this context it is also necessary to appreciate the source and intensity of policy initiatives and demands. There are obviously external as well as internal demands and pressures, both for change and to sustain the status quo. External demands can emanate from other countries (foreign policy concerns), other levels of government in Canada, as well as from interest groups and opposition political parties. Internal demands can come from ministers themselves, political advisors and staff, senior bureaucrats, policy and planning branches, and from line departments equally anxious both to expand empires and to do "good things."

The relative predominance of these sources of initiative and demand not only affect and change priorities but they also raise democratic concern about where the power to initiate *should* rest. Are some outside interests too powerful? Are ministers controlled by bureaucrats? Is the policy and priority-setting process a "top-down" one or a "bottom-up" one, the latter implying an inordinate influence by line ministers and departments rather than by the Prime Minister and central agencies or, alternatively, of excessive influence by bureaucrats over ministers.

To this confusing tug and pull of "interests," institutions and ideas one must add a further factor, namely the largely media-induced tendency of politicians to believe that they must "be seen doing something." The media's attention span *is* short. They thrive on new announcements and on personalities, and on who is "win-

ning" and "losing." They criticize priorities but never have to allocate resources. They thrive on the latest reactions to the monthly
ritual of unemployment and cost of living statistics and to Gallup
polls. This adds a further dimension of pressure to change the priority list or, alternatively, to add to the priority list until it becomes
a veritable "wish list" of political goods.

Finally, it must be noted that priorities change in form, but perhaps only partly in substance, because of the perceived need to put
old priority wine into new bottles. Thus, old priorities may have to
be expressed in new ways partly to show that new things are being
tried and/or to disassociate current efforts from past failures.
Thus, an industrial policy or strategy may become a policy on "economic development," rural development evolves onto regional
policy, and a war on inflation is repackaged as the pursuit of the
"Six Percent Society." These changes are rarely just "window
dressing" because policy circumstances do in fact change over
time.

Despite periodic aspirations by governments to be more rational
about priority setting and to take a longer-term view of things,
analysis shows the episodic nature of priorities and planning. The
very nature and magnitude of the social, economic and foreign
policy challenges show that there is a need for some kind of planning both within government and between the public and private
sectors, and at the macro and micro levels. But the ideological and
normative rhetoric of Canadian politics will not allow politicians to
call it planning. It must be called something else—hence the elusive search for industrial and employment "strategies," better economic "management," "adjustment" policies and superior "consultative" forums.

Canadians must have some sympathetic understanding of the
double edged sword their politicians face in the priorities and
planning conundrum. Politicians must somehow lead (but not by
too much) and at the same time be responsive (but not be weak, too
flexible or unaware of the costs of their flexibility). Priorities in the
Trudeau era show the ebb and flow of social and then economic
leanings as domestic and international circumstances change and
as governments respond to and try to anticipate their Parliamentary opponents. Thus at a macro level the Trudeau government
has had to deal with the Nixon shocks of 1971-72, the OPEC shock
of 1973, wage and price controls in 1975, the further doubling of
energy prices in the wake of the 1979 Iranian revolution, United
States' high interest rate policies in 1981 and falling oil prices in

1982 and 1983. As we showed in detail, the internal priority-setting exercises were almost never "normal." Numerous special priority-setting exercises had to be devised to interrupt the allegedly normal one. These problems were related to and exacerbated by the inability to have general budgetary priorities and the fiscal framework coincide with expenditure priorities or with the overall priorities expressed in Throne Speeches. Over the 1970s and early 1980s there was an increased tendency to have more than one Budget Speech per year. This was in turn related to continuous opposition party and often provincial government pressure for a new budget, *now*! The magnification of these pressures by the media only adds to this "revolving door" notion of priorities. It creates greater uncertainty for many while it is promoting stability for others. The episodic nature of priorities reveals the continuous and persistent re-emergence of the dominant ideas of Canadian political life as well as the presence of uncertainty.

NOTES

For a detailed analysis of priorities and policy-making from which this chapter is partly drawn, see G. BRUCE DOERN AND RICHARD W. PHIDD, *Canadian Public Policy: Ideas, Structures and Processes* (Toronto: Methuen, 1983).

1. See DONALD CREIGHTON, *John A. Macdonald: The Old Chieftan* (Toronto: Macmillan of Canada, 1955), Chapter 6; W.L. MORTON, *The Kingdom of Canada* (Toronto: McClelland and Stewart, 1963), Chapters 18 and 19; and VERNON FOWKE, *The National Policy and the Wheat Economy* (Toronto: University of Toronto Press, 1957).

2. See DONALD SMILEY, "Canada and the Quest for a New National Policy," *Canadian Journal of Political Science*, Vol. 8 (March, 1975): 40-62; W.L. MORTON, *The Progressive Party in Canada* (Toronto: University of Toronto, 1950); and M. JANINE BRODIE, *Crisis, Challenge and Change: Party and Class in Canada* (Toronto: Methuen, 1980), Chapters 4 and 5.

3. See BLAIR NEATBY, *The Politics of Chaos: Canada in the Thirties* (Toronto: Macmillan of Canada, 1972); DAVID LEWIS, *The Good Fight* (Toronto: Macmillan of Canada, 1981), Chapters 6, 7 and 8; and REGINALD WHITAKER, *The Government Party* (Toronto: University of Toronto Press, 1977), Chapters 1 and 14.

4. ROBERT CAMPBELL, *Grand Illusions: The Keynesian Experience in Canada* (Manuscript—in press); A. ARMITAGE, *Social Welfare in Canada* (Toronto: McClelland and Stewart, 1975); L. MARSH, *Report on Social Security for Canada—1943* (Toronto: University of Toronto Press, 1975); and ROBERT

BOTHWELL, IAN DRUMMOND AND JOHN ENGLISH, *Canada Since 1945* (Toronto: University of Toronto Press, 1981), Chapters 9, 15 and 17.

5. RICHARD W. PHIDD AND G. BRUCE DOERN, *The Politics and Management of Canadian Economic Policy* (Toronto: Macmillan of Canada, 1978), Chapters 7 and 8; and BOTHWELL *et. al.*, *op. cit.*, Chapter 7.

6. GLEN WILLIAMS, "The National Tariffs: Industrial Underdevelopment Through Import Substitution," *Canadian Journal of Political Science*, Vol. 12 (1979): 333-68.

7. See WHITAKER, *op. cit.*, Chapter 5; and DONALD V. SMILEY, *Canada in Question*, 3rd ed. (Toronto: McGraw-Hill Ryerson, 1981), Chapter 6.

8. See BOTHWELL *et al.*, *op. cit.*, Chapter 27; and PETER C. NEWMAN, *Renegade in Power* (Toronto: McClelland and Stewart, 1963). See also our survey of this period in Chapter 8, How Ottawa Spends 1983.

9. See RICHARD SIMEON, *Federal-Provincial Diplomacy: The Making of Recent Policy in Canada* (Toronto: University of Toronto Press, 1982); KENNETH BRYDEN, *Old Age Pensions and Policy Making in Canada* (Montreal: McGill-Queen's University Press, 1974), Chapter 8; and MALCOLM TAYLOR, *Health Insurance and Canadian Public Policy* (Montreal: McGill-Queen's University Press, 1978).

10. See BOTHWELL *et al.*, *op. cit.*, Chapters 31 and 32; and GEORGE RADWANSKI, *Trudeau* (Toronto: Macmillan of Canada, 1978). See our review in Chapter 8, How Ottawa Spends 1983.

11. JEFFREY SIMPSON, *Discipline of Power* (Toronto: Personal Library, 1981).

12. R.M. BURNS AND L. CLOSE, *The Winter Works Program* (Toronto: Canadian Tax Foundation, 1971).

13. MICHAEL TUCKER, *Canadian Foreign Policy* (Toronto: McGraw-Hill Ryerson, 1980), Chapter 2.

14. RICHARD FRENCH, *How Ottawa Decides* (Ottawa: Canadian Institute for Economic Policy, 1980), pp. 50-4.

15. See DAVID CRANE, *Controlling Interest* (Toronto: McClelland and Stewart, 1982), pp. 68-70.

16. "Responses to the Government's Priorities," Unpublished Cabinet Discussion Paper (Ottawa: January 30, 1975): 1.

17. FRENCH, *op cit.*, p. 77.

18. Quoted in FRENCH, *op. cit.*, pp. 79-80.

19. FRENCH, *op. cit.*, pp. 83-4.

20. See SANDFORD F. BORINS, *Language of the Air* (Montreal: McGill-Queen's University Press, 1983).

21. See Canada, *The Way Ahead: A Framework for Discussion* (Ottawa: Minister of Supply and Services, 1976); and Canada, *Agenda for Cooperation* (Ottawa, Minister of Supply and Services, 1977).

22. FRENCH, *op. cit.*, Chapter 6; and G. BRUCE DOERN AND RICHARD W. PHIDD,

"Economic Management in the Government of Canada: Some Implications of the Board of Economic Development Ministers and the Lambert Report." Paper presented to Canadian Political Science Association, Saskatoon (May 1979).

23. See ALLAN MASLOVE AND EUGENE SWIMMER, *Wage Controls in Canada* (Montreal: Institute for Research on Public Policy, 1980), Chapter 1.

24. See G. BRUCE DOERN (ed.), *How Ottawa Spends Your Tax Dollars 1981* (Toronto: James Lorimer and Co., 1981), Chapter 1.

25. See G. BRUCE DOERN (ed.), *How Ottawa Spends Your Tax Dollars 1982* (Toronto: James Lorimer and Co., 1982), Chapters 1 and 2.

The Canadian Cabinet in Comparative Perspective

WILLIAM W. LAMMERS AND JOSEPH L. NYOMARKAY

The use of elite studies for systematic analyses of socioeconomic and political change has met with growing interest in recent years. Mannheim's initial suggestion that changes in elite career patterns reflect changes in underlying social structures has provided the theoretical basis for a growing body of empirical studies now encompassing most countries of the industrial world.[1] The evolution of career patterns of Canadian cabinet ministers in the years since the Second World War, with an increasingly pronounced appearance of characteristics associated with the growth of technological societies, provides an important case for assessments of social and political change. Despite the continuing impact of idiosyncratic structural and cultural forces, changes in Canadian elite careers have made several of the routes to power in Canada increasingly

Reprinted from William W. Lammers and Joseph L. Nyomarkay, "The Canadian Cabinet in Comparative Perspective," *Canadian Journal of Political Science*, Vol. XV, No. 1 (March, 1982): 29-46. By permission.

similar to those found in other advanced industrial nations. The emerging shifts in cabinet member career patterns have major implications for an understanding of both Canadian politics and the direction and sources of change occurring in the recruitment of political elites in all advanced industrial nations.

The Study of Political Elites

Elite studies can offer insights into the nature of political systems from a variety of perspectives, including: (1) representation, (2) social stratification, (3) elite behaviour, (4) policy determinants, (5) political stability and (6) systemic change. The existing literature on Canadian political elites consists of important studies in most of these areas, but with significant limitations.

An early and continuing thrust in elite studies involves assessments of the *representational characteristics* of elite groups in comparison with the general population. Education, social class, ethnic background, geographic origin and religious orientation have all been frequently included as dimensions of representational analysis. In Canadian studies, the initial analysis of the House of Commons by Norman Ward and more recent studies by Richard van Loon and William Matheson have exemplified the representational approach.[2] These studies have demonstrated that the cabinet, as a key elite group, has over-represented such occupational groups as lawyers and businessmen, along with the college educated in general, while somewhat under-representing French-speaking segments of the Canadian population. Although patterns of under-representation are characteristic of all countries in varying degrees, the same cannot be said of the view that an emphasis on the achievement of geographically-based representation has reduced the quality of cabinet members.[3]

The *social stratification* approach has focussed more specifically on social class issues than typically occurs in representationally oriented analyses and has emphasized the impact of social background on policy choices. John Porter's major work, *The Vertical Mosaic*, is a prime example of this approach.[4] That study emphasizes the overlap among economic, social and political elites in Canadian society, the circulation of individuals within the elite positions, and the extent to which the Canadian elite is able to protect its position. Although few policy issues are traced in detail, the study stresses the responsiveness of the Canadian political system to upper class interests through recruitment practices.

Analyses involving assessments of *elite attitudes and behaviour* also include important studies by Canadian scholars. Studies of the top echelons of central agencies in the federal bureaucracy by Colin Campbell and George Szablowski represent an important example of this approach and the typical emphasis on direct interview techniques.[5] A similarly thorough analysis of the interaction and lobbying activities of bureaucrats, industry leaders, and interest group representatives has been undertaken by Robert Presthus in his *Elite Accommodation in Canadian Politics*.[6] Although interview-based studies must be primarily cross-sectional in nature and are typically not concerned with long-term system change, major findings do point to the growth of technological societies in their emphasis on the importance of technical knowledge as a key resource in contemporary policy development.

A uniquely extensive effort to examine elite characteristics as *policy determinants* has been undertaken by Allan Kornberg and his colleagues.[7] This study reveals a number of problems in the measurement of both elite characteristics and policy outcomes, while stressing the importance of continued analysis of elite characteristics as policy determinants. The use of elite analysis to study the nature of *political stability* represents a broader orientation than generally occurs in assessments of policy determinants. In Canadian studies, the important work on the concept of consociational societies, such as that by Arendt Lijphart, has produced an interest in the relationship between religious backgrounds of political leaders and the potential for stability in a religiously divided nation.[8]

Finally, the *systemic change* approach employs career data to explore underlying changes in social systems. In this approach, the changing characteristics of elites are placed in a broader context than in either the representational or policy outcome studies. Changes in elite characteristics are examined here as indicators of underlying sociopolitical changes.[9] In the extensive literature on Canadian political elites, only limited attention has been paid to questions of systemic change. One indication of the absence of the systemic perspective in Canadian elite studies is the paucity of comparative studies. The comparison of Canada and Australia by Henry Albinski is only a partial exception, since his cabinet discussion is focussed primarily on issues of representation rather than on the effects of social change on elite characteristics.[10] The four-nation comparison by Colin Campbell and George Szablowski, which presently includes only the case of Canada, promises to shed light on changes in political elites in the four nations and the relationship of these changes to larger patterns of social change.[11] Finally, the important comparative study of lobbying in Canada and the United States by Robert Presthus gives an invaluable, but basically cross-sectional, assessment of key aspects of communication and interaction within key segments of the political elites in each nation.[12]

It seems clear from a review of the literature on Canadian elite studies that a systemic, cross-national analysis over time can make a useful contribution to an understanding of the meaning of the changes in Canadian elite characteristics. What patterns of change can be empirically demonstrated over the past century, and how do these patterns compare with those found in other advanced industrial nations over the same period of time? Is there increasing convergence between Canadian elite characteristics and those of other industrial nations? Are the influences of unique historical forces giving way to the impact of technology, thus making political elites increasingly similar in all advanced industrial societies?

The Research Design

It is easier to review the key manifestations of technological (or "post-industrial") societies than to develop specific measures which facilitate precise comparison. A variety of potential indicators of technological society seem promising and attractive, but on closer examination few satisfy the requisites of comparability and accessibility over substantial periods of time. Indeed, the development of useful empirical measures of social and political change stands as an increasingly critical, if difficult, challenge for students of contemporary society.

The development of comprehensive measures of shifts toward technological societies is secondary to our present purposes. We are interested in presenting a relatively simple measure which will demonstrate how selected countries compare in terms of social change over the past century. The measure we have chosen is the magnitude of government expenditures as a percentage of gross national product. This measure is admittedly an indirect indicator of social change, but besides the comparatively high degree of reliability and availability of the data for all countries for the past century, it is also the most comprehensive. The growth of government expenditures is a measure of the growth of governmental bureaucracies, and thus reflects the increasing scope of governmental activities which have been the invariable concomitant of advanced industrial development. Government expenditure data have been compiled from a variety of sources for each country. They are presented in the form of "ranges" because of the variation among major sources and the limited availability of annual data for the earlier periods. Because the four nations in this study include both federal and unitary systems, we have used data on total (instead of only central) government expenditures to satisfy the requirement of comparability.

The data presented in Table 1 show the high degree of uniformity of development among the four nations. Although Canada and the United States have consistently lagged somewhat behind the two European nations, Table 1 suggests that, since the end of the First World War, total government expenditures as percentage of GNP have risen steadily on the average by about 5 per cent per decade in each country. In terms of absolute magnitudes, all four countries were approximately at the same level before the First World War, with government expenditures generally between 10 and 15 per cent of the GNP. In the interwar period, the government expenditures of the two European nations which were most affected by the First World War jumped to the 20 and 30 percentage range, while Canada and the United States remained around the 20 per cent mark. The data for the post-Second World War decades show the effect of the Second World War on Canada and the United States, where government expenditures grew by about 10 percentage points, and ranged between 20 and 30 per cent of GNP, while the other two nations went to 30-40 per cent range. The 1960s and 1970s show a tendency toward reduced variation among the four countries, as Canada, France and the United States find themselves in the approximate range of 30 to 40-plus per cent, with only Great Britain entering the 50 per cent range. In sum, expenditure data show the relative acceleration of social change in the two European countries after the First World War, and in Canada and the United States after the Second World War. By the decade of the 1970s, with the partial exception of Great Britain, all four countries find themselves at increasingly similar levels of technological development.

The choice of countries and offices for comparison also requires specific consideration. We selected the other three countries on the basis of their comparable stage of social development as measured by government expenditures, plus the existence of liberal political institutions. We chose cabinet members as our universe representing political elites because of their institutional prominence, manageable size and availability of biographical data for the past century.[13]

TABLE 1
Total Government Expenditures as a Percentage of GNP

	Time period[a]			
	Pre-First World War	1920-1940	1941-1960	1961-1976
Canada	under 20[b]	approaching or passing 20[b]	19-28	28-41
France	13-16	17-29	high 20 to low 30[c]	34-40
Great Britain	9-15	24-30	37-42	45-55
United States	8-13	13-21	21-29	29-37

[a] Figures represent the highest and lowest estimate from a major study for any of the years included in the respective period. Because of the difficulties stemming from lack of data, particularly for the earlier periods, these figures should be viewed only as a general indication of expansions in governmental scope in the respective countries.
[b] No annual GNP data are available.
[c] No local expenditure data are available.

SOURCES: In addition to yearbooks and census documents for each country, our references have included such works as: Michael Bergeron, *Social Spending in Canada* (Ottawa: Canadian Council on Social Development, 1979); B. R. Mitchell, *European Historical Statistics 1750-1950* (New York: Columbia University Press, 1975); Frederick C. Mosher and Orville Poland, *The Costs of American Governments: Facts, Trends, and Myths* (New York: Dodd, Mead and Co., 1964); and Alan Peacock and Jack Wiseman, *The Growth of Public Expenditure in the United Kingdom* (London: Allen and Unwin, 1967).

The time period of about 100 years seemed appropriate because the years around 1870 represented the best common denominator for the beginning of a new political era in all four countries: the establishment of Canadian independence, the beginning of the Third Republic in France, the second major extension of the franchise and the consequent development of the modern mass party system in Great Britain, and the emergence of post-civil war industrialization and national political unification in the United States. The last decades of the nineteenth century represent the relatively early stages of industrialization and of mass politics in each country, thus allowing for a comparison of the manifestations of both emerging and advanced industrial political systems as reflected in changes in career patterns. The data for the period of approximately 1870 to 1980 are presented in terms of five developmental periods which proved to be more appropriate for our purposes than annual or decennial data.[14] The use of developmental periods has facilitated, in particular, the examination of a sufficiently large group of newcomers in each time period to provide a portrait of the changing requisites of entrance to cabinet careers rather than simply a review of the characteristics of those who were in office during given periods.

It is essential, finally, to consider our use of the concept of technologically-oriented societies. Technology, at the broadest conceptual level, refers to systems of rationalized control. Thus, a technological society implies an institutional order where centrally located groups of technically skilled men operating through organizational hierarchies exercise control and direction over society. Specialization, nationalization (in terms of centralization), and bureaucratization are thus the major interrelated dimensions of technological societies. The more technological a society, the more its institutions will be characterized by specialization, nationalization, and bureaucracy.[15]

Specialization is defined here in the broad sense of training appropriate to the management of political institutions. The type of specialization required will depend, therefore, on the nature of key tasks. It may be either management skills requiring a fairly high degree of general trained intelligence, or specialization of a more technical nature. Specialization will then be measured by the extent and nature of formal educational achievement: for example, the higher the percentage of cabinet members with higher educational degrees, the higher the degree of specialization; conversely, the higher the percentage of members without university degrees, the lower the degree of specialization.

The substantive orientation of professional experience will indicate the nature of major governmental tasks: in the early stages of industrial development when the tasks of governmental institutions are relatively undifferentiated, limited and oriented toward economic production and legal matters, cabinet members can be expected to come from the fields of business and law. In the later stages of advanced industrial development when the tasks of government become more extensive, differentiated, and oriented toward social as well as economic and political affairs of increasingly technical nature, the composition of cabinets can be expected to reflect these changes by an increasing number of people with the higher general educational backgrounds necessary for general managerial tasks. The increasing pervasiveness of governmental activities can be expected to bring about an increase in the number of cabinet members without any substantive private careers prior to entering politics as a full-time activity. Thus, for instance, we would expect to find a reduction in the number of persons who had pursued law as a private career, although the number of persons with law degrees may have remained the same, but with young lawyers immediately turning to public employment. The same pattern may be expected in other professional fields as well. Finally, in view of the increasing importance of communication and policy analysis skills, we expect to find an increase in the number of cabinet members coming from the field of education. These changes reflect the progression from more general and undifferentiated to more technically specific and differentiated governmental activities.

The growth of centralized institutions of control is a necessary concomitant to the development of a society based on an increasing specialization of labour. The *nationalization* of politics in the sense of a progressive subordination of local concerns to those of national politics can be expected to be reflected in an increasing importance of national career experiences and a progressive decline in the importance of local and other subnational office-holding. Thus, the degree of nationalization will be inversely indicated by the percentage of cabinet members who started their public careers at the subnational level, who had some subnational experience in executive or legislative institutions, and whose career activity was judged to be predominantly subnational.

The rise of individuals whose primary experiences lie in public administrative positions rather than elective offices represents one of the central characteristics of technological societies. Individuals in administrative positions may well develop substantial political skills, but more in the context of organizational controversies than in elective politics. While these individuals may serve for a time in legislatures, they are more apt to reflect the bureaucratic orientations stemming from their initial and primary activities. The *bureaucratic dimension*, therefore, will be measured by the proportion of cabinet members who started their careers in the administrative-executive institutions of the central government, had some administrative experience prior to their cabinet appointment, and had their dominant career activity in administrative rather than legislative activities.

It is essential to emphasize that in evaluating data on these career dimensions, one should not expect immediate, overwhelming changes in political careers as political systems adjust to greater scope and complexity. First, the average age of cabinet appointment follows by about 20 years the decisions which politically ambitious individuals typically make in seeking national government roles. Thus, unless one assumes that there is always a pool of talent with the preferred backgrounds available from which new chief executives simply choose, a lag should occur between social change and the career patterns of cabinet members. Second, it is reasonable to expect that there will be some influence on the rate of change stemming from structural and cultural characteristics. When career change is more constrained in a given country, it is reasonable to conclude that the direction of change will be in the hypothesized direction, but that the magnitude of change will be less than in systems which are less structurally constrained.

The major hypotheses of this study can thus be summarized as follows. First, with the growth of technological societies, we expect to see corresponding changes in elite career patterns toward greater specialization, nationalization and bureaucratization. Second, we expect to see a common direction of change in all countries. Third, despite some lingering impacts of structural and cultural factors, we expect to see greater uniformity in career patterns in the most recent developmental period than in earlier periods. Fourth, as a consequence of the above, we expect to find greater similarity between Canadian career patterns and those of the other three countries in the last developmental period.

Canadian Career Patterns in Comparative Perspective

The data presented in Table 2 demonstrate that following the Second World War there has been an increasingly marked shift toward greater specialization, nationalization and bureaucratization in the career patterns of cabinet members in all four countries.

Specialization

Three major patterns of change are revealed by the data on this dimension: a virtual disappearance of cabinet members without university degrees, a decline in the dominance of lawyers and a steady

TABLE 2
Cabinet Careers in Comparative Perspective[a] (percentages)

| | *Time periods* | | | | |
	I	II	III	IV	V
I. Specialization					
A. Education					
No university degree					
Canada	33	17	23	8	9
France	6	2	4	9	8
Britain	10	7	19	10	15
United States	12	13	16	14	9
University Degree					
Canada	16	20	17	32	42
France	8	16	18	15	24
Britain	46	61	45	55	56
United States	8	11	24	29	22
Law degree					
Canada	44	54	49	57	41
France	44	50	45	43	39
Britain	39	27	31	21	21
United States	78	75	49	48	45
Other professional degree					
Canada	6	10	11	4	8
France	13	9	4	8	26
Britain	0	1	1	3	3
United States	0	2	7	7	25
B. Private career					
Law					
Canada	41	49	46	49	37
France	19	22	22	20	8
Britain	37	26	31	21	17
United States	69	59	44	43	39
Business					
Canada	40	23	19	25	19
France	7	2	6	13	9
Britain	23	20	7	12	4
United States	13	18	24	38	33
Education					
Canada	3	6	7	15	12
France	10	9	12	16	14
Britain	8	13	13	14	7
United States	5	4	5	5	21

TABLE 2—*Continued*

		Time periods			
	I	II	III	IV	V

II. Nationalization

First post subnational

	I	II	III	IV	V
Canada	76	54	59	43	29
France	29	38	30	31	8
Britain	4	12	16	14	12
United States	71	45	46	48	26

No post subnational

Canada	22	44	39	60	74
France	58	44	46	50	51
Britain	82	67	67	84	83
United States	28	62	39	44	72

Dominant subnational career

Canada	33	24	23	11	5
France	10	13	4	5	2
Britain	0	2	3	3	3
United States	28	21	25	21	16

III. Bureaucratization

First post in national administration

Canada	0	1	1	8	16
France	31	31	20	27	67
Britain	14	21	17	12	9
United States	6	30	25	38	47

No post in national administration

Canada	97	92	96	64	63
France	55	53	46	54	20
Britain	22	21	29	13	16
United States	65	68	58	45	51

Dominant career in national administration

Canada	0	7	2	6	3
France	10	14	10	12	53
Britain	4	1	3	0	10
United States	6	21	13	38	30

[a] The dates for the time periods and the number of cases are as follows:

	Canada (n)	France (n)	Britain (n)	United States (n)
I	1868-1895 (63)	1870-1892 (155)	1868-1895 (72)	1868-1896 (78)
II	1896-1920 (71)	1893-1913 (108)	1896-1916 (84)	1897-1920 (56)
III	1921-1948 (94)	1914-1940 (194)	1917-1944 (94)	1921-1944 (55)
IV	1949-1963 (53)	1943-1957 (146)	1945-1963 (77)	1945-1964 (42)
V	1964-1980 (63)	1958-1978 (95)	1964-1978 (68)	1965-1978 (76)

increase of people with communication skills. Of the four countries, only Canada had a considerable proportion of cabinet appointees without university degrees in the early period under
study. With their virtual disappearance, as Canada has recently
joined the pattern of other nations, all countries now show a high
degree of uniformity on this career measure. The rise of the British figures in the third period reflects the impact of Labour cabinet
members in the 1920s.

A comparable uniformity does not emerge in the data regarding
nonlegal professionally-educated category. Substantial increases
have emerged in France and the United States, but not in Canada
and Great Britain. This may reflect at least in part the influence of
the British tradition of general education for public sector elites in
both countries. The predominance of parliament as a route to the
cabinet in Canada and Great Britain in contrast to France and the
United States provides another possible explanation for the relative paucity of individuals with nonpolitical, professional backgrounds. In addition, the questionable comparability of higher
educational degrees in the different countries may account for the
differences in the magnitude of the figures to some degree. For
example, the graduates of Ecole National d'Administration in
France were grouped in the professional category, but people with
advanced degrees from American Schools of Business Administration were not. Although we do not mean to suggest les Grandes
Ecoles are to be equated with Schools of Business Administration,
the type of training at these two institutions does have a degree of
similarity which the coding could not reflect. Thus, the figures may
have exaggerated the differences among the countries to some degree.

One of the decisive changes has been the decline in the number
of cabinet members in all four countries who have pursued law as a
private career before entering public service. The most precipitous
decline has been in the United States, with the most moderate decline in Canada.[16] Significantly, however, the proportion of cabinet
members with law degrees has not changed substantially except in
the United States, where it dropped from 78 per cent in the first
period to 45 per cent in the last period. These data suggest that in
countries with a strong and highly-developed national bureaucracy
there is apt to be a pronounced difference between the proportion
of governmental elites with law degrees and those who also had a
private law practice before entering public service. This tends to
occur in so far as legal training (often of a technical nature) be-

comes a prerequisite for entrance into the bureaucracy. In France, for example, the proportion of cabinet members with legal training has been historically between 40 and 50 per cent, but by the last period less than 10 per cent has practised law prior to entering politics. In Great Britian, the informal nature of legal training makes the distinction between legal training and the practice of law difficult to establish on the basis of the available data. In Canada and the United States, on the other hand, there is hardly any discrepancy between legal education and the private practice of law. If a prediction is in order, one might expect such a discrepancy to develop in the coming years. The decreasing importance of lawyers (as opposed to individuals trained in the law) reflects the rise of political executives for whom politics is not merely a temporary engagement preceded and followed by private professional activity, but a life-long profession. As such it may indeed be an indicator of the contemporary decline in the liberal concept of politics as an undertaking for amateurs.

Career data also bear out the increasing importance of communication and policy analysis skills for twentieth century governments. As measured by the occupational category of education, there has been a slow but steady growth in the proportion of these people in the cabinets of every country except Great Britain. As in several other areas of our analysis, the British practice of political recruitment has been comparatively more resistant to change than those of other countries.

Turning to business backgrounds, there has been a general decline in the proportion of businessmen in all countries except the United States. The Canadian record was unique in its emphasis on business backgrounds in the first period, but declined to levels more characteristic of other countries by the turn of the century. As a result, the United States has become the most business oriented in its recruitment patterns in recent decades. In part, this has occurred with the American tendency to combine business backgrounds with technical training in recent years. Among the four countries, the limited use of business backgrounds among cabinet members reflects the need for technically trained government members, including the substantial number of lawyers who enter government directly after receiving their education.

The indicators of specialization thus show the expected change toward greater specialization for all four countries in virtually all categories. At the same time, greater uniformity in absolute values has emerged in all areas except that of professional education.

Nationalization

Perhaps the most pronounced change evident in Canadian cabinet careers is the increasing importance of office-holding at the national level rather than in the provinces and municipalities. This trend has emerged in all four countries studied after allowing for the obvious impact of structural differences between federal and unitary systems. Thus the two federal systems have consistently shown a substantially greater degree of decentralized career backgrounds than the two unitary systems. The declining importance of political office-holding below the national level is therefore especially striking in federal systems which have gone from strong subnational career patterns to predominantly national ones in the course of the last one hundred years. The data show that subnational political office has not been a prerequisite for cabinet appointment in Great Britain. French political careers have included much more subnational office holding despite France's unitary structure because of the historic practice of gaining local office upon receiving appointment in Paris. This is demonstrated by the relatively low figures for individuals without subnational office (and the lack of longitudinal change on this dimension) in contrast to the relatively (for a unitary state) high figures for the other two dimensions of nationalization. Thus, the nationalization dimension shows that the careers of cabinet members of unitary countries have remained nationally based as they always had been, while careers in federal systems have become increasingly nationalized. Thus by the fifth period, substantially greater uniformity exists among the four countries.

Bureaucratization

The importance of administrative experience prior to cabinet appointment has grown sharply, especially in the last period, in every country except Great Britian. This is reflected in part by the increasing number of cabinet members who started their public careers in an administrative post. Differences among countries with dominant administrative versus legislative traditions are clearly reflected in the career data, as for example between Canada and France, but a common trend toward increasing administrative experience is evident. Thus, if one compares the first and last period, for example, the averages for the four countries show the use of first posts in the national administration increasing from 13 per cent to 35 per cent, those with dominant career activities in national administration increasing from 5 to 24 per cent, and those without any national administrative experience declining from 60 to 38 per cent. It should be emphasized, however, that the administrative backgrounds have not become more important at the expense of legislative experience. There is no indication that recent cabinet appointees have less legislative service than their predecessors. Legislative service in parliamentary systems remains a virtual precondition for career advancement even though it has become a less significant condition.

Conclusions

There has not been complete and unambiguous support for the impact of shifts toward technologically oriented societies in the cabinet career data. The relatively unchanging nature of recruitment patterns in Great Britain suggests the stability of the British parliamentary route to cabinet office. In general, however, the findings do support our hypotheses regarding both the common direction of change and the increasing similarity in the magnitude of absolute values being achieved by the last period. Of the 13 specific measures for the 4 countries (and the resulting 52 tabulations), the direction of change is in the hypothesized direction in all but 11 cases. Six of those deviant cases involve only marginal differences in the British data. Significantly, the entire bureaucratization dimension had only one negative finding, with a marginal decline in the proportion of cabinet members in Great Britain who used an administrative position as their first career step.

In terms of the shifts toward uniformity, 9 of the 13 measures show greater uniformity (less variation) in the last period. Of the 4 cases with greater variation, 2 occur with the rapid increase of administrative experience in France, while the others involve differences in professional degrees and career activities in education. When combined with our discussions of the forces behind deviations on individual measures, these data do confirm the hypotheses regarding both the direction of change and the higher degree of expected uniformity.

Several conclusions and observations are in order regarding the Canadian rates of change in relationship to the other three countries in our study, the relationship of our findings to previous Canadian studies, the impact of party differences, and the implications of our findings for studies of structural change in Canadian politics. First, changes have all been in the hypothesized direction. The changes have been most pronounced on the nationalization dimension, with all indicators showing a substantial movement toward a centralization of careers. On the dimension of specialization, the Canadian development is less dramatically indicated but the trends toward recruitment of individuals with higher levels of education and less frequent backgrounds in business are clearly indicated. Finally, on the bureaucratization dimension, Canada has been changing in the hypothesized direction, but with absolute levels still below the increasingly high levels emerging in the other three countries.

Previous Canadian studies have not explored our bureaucratization and nationalization dimensions and thus provide no basis for direct comparison. Regarding specialization, our data corroborate the findings of the more recent studies. Porter found with his pre-1960 data that the preference for recruiting lawyers had increased over time, but Matheson writing a decade later already found a declining proportion of lawyers among the incoming cabinet appointees. Regarding the circulation of cabinet members between business and government, our data also show a less extensive interchange than one might have anticipated. It seems likely that the increased specialization of career activities in both the public and private sector in recent years has reduced the opportunity for circulation between public and private sector careers.[17]

The Canadian data do show some party differences, but not at a level sufficient to alter the interpretations of social change as the underlying factor influencing change in cabinet member characteristics. In an effort to test the relationship as fully as possible, we have included all cabinet appointees through 1980, thus capturing for Canada both the brief Clark government and the newcomers in the subsequent Trudeau cabinet.[18] When compared with the norms for the Liberal appointees during the fifth period, the one substantial career difference is the greater tendency for Conservatives to have their first position at the subnational level (their figure of 21 per cent compared with 10 per cent for the Liberals). Regarding dominant subnational careers and those having no subnational experience, the Conservative appointees almost completely mirrored the averages for the Liberals. In terms of other differences, the Conservatives were slightly more likely to have had business backgrounds, and legal education, and were slightly less likely to have been teachers or journalists. These differences, however, were in the range of 2 to 5 per cent. Similarly, the bureaucratization dimension produced no significant differences. It thus seems clear that the changes occurring in cabinet career patterns cannot be attributed to major differences between political parties.

The data have interesting implications for studies of Canadian decision-making processes. Given the debate over the role of the cabinet versus the prime minister's staff and the civil service, it is appropriate to emphasize that in comparison with the levels of managerial experience and technical education reflected in the cabinet career backgrounds of the other three countries, Canadian levels have been low.[19] Notable also is the extent to which the debate over provincial autonomy, first for Quebec and then for the western provinces, has been conducted by cabinet members whose career backgrounds have been increasingly devoid of subnational political experiences. The evolution of the Federal-Provincial Relations Office as an increasingly significant body in Canadian politics might well be examined in part from this perspective. Finally and more generally, it will be important to view Canadian cabinet recruitment in the next years in the context of a continuing tension between the structural and historical forces which have in the past reduced the extent to which Canadian cabinet member careers have mirrored those of other advanced industrial nations and the increasing contemporary pressures toward bureaucratization and specialization.

NOTES

We wish to express our appreciation to the College of Letters, Arts and Sciences at the University of Southern California for the financial assistance which was provided for this project, and to Bob Sturgeon, Carol Taylor and Gene Wisnoski for their research assistance.

1. The classic analysis is found in KARL MANNHEIM, *Essays in the Sociology of Knowledge*, Paul Kecskemeti (ed.), (New York: Oxford University Press, 1952), pp. 247-8, 253.

2. The early work on representation is contained in NORMAN WARD, *The Canadian House of Commons: Representation* (Toronto: University of Toronto Press, 1950). The more recent studies include W. A. MATHESON, *The Prime Minister and the Cabinet* (Toronto: Methuen, 1976), and RICHARD VAN LOON, "The Structure and Membership of the Canadian Cabinet" (Ottawa: Royal Commission on Bilingualism and Biculturalism, 1965).

3. MATHESON, *The Prime Minister and the Cabinet*, pp. 29-30.

4. See JOHN PORTER, *The Vertical Mosaic* (Toronto: University of Toronto Press, 1965).

5. See COLIN CAMPBELL AND GEORGE SZABLOWSKI, *The Superbureaucrats: Structure and Behaviour in Central Agencies* (Toronto: Macmillan, 1979).

6. See ROBERT V. PRESTHUS, *Elite Accommodation in Canadian Politics* (Toronto: Cambridge University Press, 1973).

7. See ALLAN KORNBERG, DAVID J. FALCONE AND WILLIAM T. E. MISHLER, *Legislatures and Societal Change: The Case of Canada* (Beverly Hills: Sage, 1973).

8. The major initial work is AREND LIJPHART, *The Politics of Accommodation: Pluralism and Democracy in the Netherlands* (Berkeley: University of California Press, 1968). Canadian applications are discussed in Presthus, *Elite Accommodation*, and K. D. McRae (ed.), *Consociational Democracy: Political Accommodation in Segmented Societies* (Toronto: McClelland and Stewart, 1974).

9. Two recent books have extensively developed the systemic approach. See ROBERT D. PUTNAM, *The Comparative Study of Political Elites* (Englewood Ciffs: Prentice-Hall, 1976), pp. 165-214; and WILLIAM W. WELSH, *Leaders and Elites* (New York: Holt, Rinehart and Winston, 1959), pp. 58-96.

10. See HENRY S. ALBINSKI, *Canadian and Australian Politics in Comparative Perspective* (New York: Oxford University Press, 1973), pp. 289-304.

11. The initial study of Canada by Campbell and Szablowski, *The Superbureaucrats*, is being expanded to include the United Kingdom, the United States and Switzerland.

12. See ROBERT V. PRESTHUS, *Elites in the Policy Process* (New York: Cambridge University Press, 1974).

13. Biographical information was gathered from at least two or three sources in each country. For France, the most extensive information for each individual is in Jean Jolly (ed.), *Dictionnaire des parlementaires français, 1889-1940* (Paris: Presses universitaires de France, 1960). For the United Kingdom, the standard initial source is *Dod's Parliamentary Companion* (London: Business Dictionaries). The most extensive United States information is in Robert Sobel (ed.), *Biographical Directory of the United States Executive Branch* (Westport, Conn.: Greenwood, 1972). Canadian sources included *The Canadian Who's Who* (Toronto: Who's Who Canadian Publication), *The Dictionary of Canadian Biography* (Toronto: Macmillan, 1926), and J. K. Johnson (ed.), *Canadian Directory of Parliament 1867-1967* (Ottawa: Public Archives of Canada, 1968).

14. The basic career data have been studied with the use of several different time periods in previous papers. The differences are minor in all instances. For Canada, the periods conform to those used by Matheson with the exception of the division of the post-Second World War period. The findings in previous analyses which have used the backgrounds of all individuals who have served in a given period are generally quite similar to

those which have emerged in this analysis. We are nonetheless persuaded by such works as Phillip Buck in his *Amateurs and Professionals in British Politics, 1918-1959* (Chicago: University of Chicago Press, 1963) that an examination of newcomers represents the theoretically most justifiable approach.

15. The best known interpretation of the growth of technological societies is JACQUES ELLUL, *The Technological Society* (New York: Knopf, 1967).

16. The Canadian figures in the category of law as one's major occupational activity have also been quite constant for the House of Commons, but at a lower level than for the Cabinet. Between 1967 and 1945, the percentage of lawyers in the Commons was generally between 20 and 30. These data are presented in NORMAN WARD, *The Canadian House of Commons: Representation* (Toronto: University of Toronto Press, 1950).

17. PORTER, *The Vertical Mosaic*, pp. 209, 369.

18. We wish to express our sincere appreciation to Edward M. Hepner, the Canadian Consul in Los Angeles, for his assistance in making a set of extensive recent biographical summaries available for this project.

19. A basic introduction to the literature on this topic is provided in THOMAS A. HOCKIN, *Apex of Power: The Prime Minister and Political Leadership in Canada*, 2nd ed., (Scarborough: Prentice-Hall, 1977).

The Development, Role and Control of the Bureaucracy

S.E. FINER

The bureaucracy is the armature of the modern state; and the modern state has, everywhere, been patterned on the European model. This armature is (supposedly at least) powered by the ruler. It is also to a greater or lesser extent (sometimes not at all) checked and balanced by organs of popular control. Between the three elements—rulers, bureaucrats and popular organs—there is

Adapted from S.E. Finer, "Princes, Parliaments and the Public Service," *Parliamentary Affairs*, Vol. XXXIII, No. 4 (Autumn, 1980): 353-372. The article originally appeared in Allan Bullock (ed.), *The Faces of Europe* (Phaidon Press, 1980). By permission of Phaidon Press.

a perpetual tension. A shift in the balance is tantamount to a shift in the regime. Where the organs of popular control over the ruler and his bureaucracy are strong enough to make them answerable to the public, this is the necessary though not the sufficient condition for a democracy. Where these organs are feeble or absent, and the ruler effectively leads and commands his bureaucracy, the regime is authoritarian, possibly absolutist. Where, however, the ruler is lazy or inept and the organs of popular control equally weak, there we find bureaucracy in its original pejorative sense: the impersonal rule of anonymous and faceless officials.

It may be that the officials who head such a bureaucracy are themselves men of genius and imagination, far different from their juniors who are the more circumscribed and routine-ridden the lower their rank. The top bureaucrats may, in these circumstances, innovate in ways which their skill and dedication put beyond the capacity of the nominal rulers and in directions unhindered by the harrying of representative assemblies or the courts of law. Such an ideal—founded at present on an enthusiasm for what supposedly passes in France—is clearly desired by a number of present-day students of politics. Their view leads straight into the inescapable central dilemma of bureaucratised polities: the more the bureaucrats enjoy discretion, the less are they accountable, and the more accountable, the less they enjoy discretion. In a word— the bureaucrat can be either creative or formalistic, but never both at once. This inner tension in the bureaucratic role is an ever-recurrent theme in its long march through European history.

A thousand years ago it was "difficult to find anything like a state anywhere on the continent of Europe."[1] In the rubble of the Roman Empire only a rudimentary arrangement for maintaining public order had emerged. It was no longer based on the subjection of each individual to impersonal rule and to an abstract entity called state or republic, but was a reticulation of ties between lords and lesser lords; lords and serfs. This was the so-called feudal system—a coalescence of two tendencies, each traceable before feudalism emerged and distinct from it: a lordship-and-tenant tie prevailing over the relationship of the citizen to the community and, secondly, the determination of political role and status by the individual's relationship to the land. Consequently, the distinction between what was private and what public was everywhere effaced, whether this related to dispensing justice, to levying taxation or to maintaining defence. Private rights were the obverse of public duties and vice versa.

In this feudal system there resided, however, a contradictory, even an alien, element. This was the kingship. In the provinces his great vassals, with their vast estates, began to administer them in a similar way and they too developed their exchequers and treasuries, their chanceries and their system of courts. So equipped, they were better able to resist the constant encroachment of the Crown. Always set on a collision course over their respective rights and duties, Crown and magnates began to clash, in the late 13th and early 14th centuries, over a matter vital to the independence of either but novel in form, and contributing more in substance to the growth of bureaucracy than all the developments so far mentioned. This matter is *taxation*. So central is it that Joseph Schumpeter, in a famous essay on "the Tax State," affirmed that "without financial need the immediate cause for the creation of the modern state would have been absent."[2] That need arose, I would say, exclusively, from one cause: warfare. As *domini*, kings were entitled only to service in kind or its cash equivalent from their vassals. That and the revenues from their own private estates were all that they had for fighting their campaigns. Since it was everywhere held that a tax was an extraordinary device to be used only in emergency, and always by the consent of the freeman, so, as kings required more and more liquid cash to fight their wars, they were compelled to convene representative assemblies of taxpayers to consent to giving it. Thus as the 14th century ushered in the entrenchment and routinisation of administrative institutions, in brief of the royal bureaucracies, so it also ushered in the representative assemblies to check and control them: parliament, estates, *cortés, corts, landtag, rigsdag, Snem, Sejm*—all over Europe in numbers which run into hundreds.[3] As the prince had institutionalised his power in the bureaucracy, so did the anti-prince in these assemblies.

So began three centuries of swaying battle. The stake was crucial: absolute control of financial resources was the key to absolute control of the population. The more money a prince took from his subjects, the more soldiers he could hire to take still more money from his subjects and the less they had left to pay taxes to their own immediate overlords. The struggle for the right to tax was a zero-sum game: what one gained the other lost. Furthermore, the issue was momentous not only on the constitutional plane, but for the future of bureaucracy as such. For a tax required collectors; and it is significant that if we leap forward from the 14th century to the eve of the French Revolution we shall find that throughout

Europe between two-thirds and four-fifths of bureaucratic personnel are involved in collecting and controlling the expenditure of taxes and in activities related to these.

On the eve of the French Revolution two wholly diverse traditions had matured. England had carried her tradition into Scotland and Ireland and beyond the ocean to the thirteen American colonies where after independence the ordinary courts of law and the popularly elected organs were all-important, the rulers' authority was minutely circumscribed by them, and the paid permanent bureaucracy was tiny. On the continent of Europe it was exactly the other way around. The prince was absolute: the organs of popular control had either lost their powers or disappeared; and the bureaucracy was numerous, ubiquitous and all-powerful. In 1797 there were in Britain only 16 267 public officials of whom 12 584 (77 per cent) were Customs and Excise; 2026 (12.5 per cent) in the post office, the stamp, taxes and lottery offices, and in the treasury. Thus almost nine out of every ten officials were concerned with finance. In France on the eve of the Revolution, however, the total number of central and local officials is estimated at 300000, including—to point the contrast—gaugers of hay, salt salesmen, coal controllers, sealing-wax warmers, administrators and engineers of the roads and bridges administration and so on, all the way up to the personnel of the sovereign *Parlements*. For Prussia the best figures we have exclude local officials except for the police. Even in 1800 there were some 23 000 officials outside these categories in a population of about nine millions, as contrasted to the 16 267 British officials for a population of 16 millions. Comparatively speaking, then, there were five Prussian officials for every three British ones—and unnumbered local officials besides.

Napoleon perfected the closed bureaucratic state. The symmetrical hierarchical order he imposed on France, the mayors responding to the prefects who in turn responded to the Minister of the Interior who himself was the servant of the emperor, was to be widely copied elsewhere on the continent of Europe and in France itself has survived to this day the defeat of the imperial regime. But at the very moment of its perfection, reaction set in against it. Throughout Europe (until by 1905 even the Russian autocracy began to bend) there came the revival of organs of popular control. In Britain, on the other hand, where Parliament was never stronger or more admired, there commenced the slow accretion of a more sizeable and also a professionally qualified bureaucracy. In this fashion the two traditions of Europe began to converge. In Europe the legislature was the innovation and was grafted, at first very clumsily and often half-heartedly, on to the traditional organ of government, that is, on to the bureaucracy. In Britain, it was the other way around: here (as in the USA) the bureaucrats were the detested innovation, grafted piecemeal on to the traditional organ of authority, the legislature.

In the last thirty years of the 20th century, the assimilation between the two traditions had become rapid but the original difference still shows. In general—certainly in the larger states of western Europe—the European societies are more regulated, more tolerant of red tape, more deferential to the public official than in Britain and the USA; at the same time, the tradition of ministerial responsibility to the legislature is less salient, the anonymity, self-effacingness and political neutrality of the top bureaucracy less of a requisite and the participation of the senior officials in policy-making more overt.

We have described the development of the bureaucracy so far in terms of the rise of the prince, then (with the medieval assemblies) his limitation by the anti-prince, and then—on the continent—the renewed triumph of the prince at the head of his bureaucracy. The revival of the elected legislatures in continental Europe after 1815 did no more, at first, than revive this old antithesis: the ruler and his bureaucracy on the one side checked and balanced by the new legislature on the other. Until the very end of the century, with the solitary exception of France after 1870 (and, it is possible to argue, perhaps Italy after 1878), parliaments were not sovereign policy-making organs but simply control organs facing a self-confident, powerful and irremovable royal bureaucracy. The 19th century was liberal, not democratic. The crowned heads of the new "constitutional" monarchies of Scandinavia, Belgium and Holland, France and Savoy, let alone Germany and Austria-Hungary, did not follow the self-effacement of the British monarchy but played an active political role. Moreover the bureaucracy and armed forces were theirs, not Parliament's. This held true whatever the constitution might or might not say; but in significant cases the constitution did specifically confer this independence on the executive branches of government: the most obvious and most important example is the constitution of the German Empire (1876-1918).

Not until the collapse of the central powers in 1918 did the royal control over the bureaucracy disappear, as the new democratic constitutions of Europe proclaimed the right of the legislature to control ministers who were fully answerable to it for all the acts of omission and commission of their servants, the bureaucracy. In this way, and according to the British tradition, the bureaucracy was made vicariously responsible to the public. But this intention was frustrated, not just for the banal reason that in states such as Italy, Poland and the Baltic States and the like, the democratic constitutions were quickly subverted, but for another and fundamental one. To revert to our princely metaphor: World War I had indeed destroyed the prince, apparently leaving the field to the anti-prince, the legislature. But at the same instant that this occurred, the anti-prince was taken over by a new prince, of a wholly different type from ever before: a collective prince, a popular prince. Just at the very moment that the legislature became sovereign and not a mere counterbalance to the sovereign, so the political party took it over. Nowadays, with a possible qualification made for the Fifth Republic of France, the legislature in modern Europe is both sovereign and subject, policy-maker and critic—in a word, both anti-prince and prince. It is debatable whether the executive today is the extension of the legislature (as the theory would have it) or whether, on the contrary, the legislature is not the extension of the executive (as in practice it usually is). This self-contradiction and the corresponding retreat of legislatures from their historic mission of supervising and controlling the bureaucracy have become all the more alarming because of developments in the bureaucracy itself: its size has become unprecedentedly enormous, and it has become a self-contained and self-regulating corporation.

Within the last half-century what were often untidy and unsystematised aggregates of public servants have become self-governing, self-regulating professional organisations largely insulated from outside interference, whether popular or partisan. Recruitment had previously been made by patronage, often by party patronage, and while this still holds good for the upper echelons in some countries (Belgium, for instance), the overwhelming bulk of civil servants have for as much as a century past in certain countries (in Britain, for example) been recruited only if they possessed publicly defined qualifications. Thus in Britain, France, Belgium and Italy today the upper civil servant is recruited by competitive examinations; and in Scandinavia, Holland, Switzerland and West Germany on the basis of specified paper qualifications. In France the recruit receives a special training if he is to be retained; in Germany he will proceed to in-service training and must then pass a state examination; elsewhere recruits become probationers and are set to "learn on the job". But in all cases, qualifications are needed and an impartial board, insulated from party and personal pressures, is the body that recruits the candidates. By the same token the civil servant everywhere today enjoys an almost perfect security of tenure. This was true of most countries even in the 19th century, where only Spain, Italy and Belgium provided exceptions. Today there are no exceptions: if dismissal is to take place, it must be decided by a special and highly circumscribed disciplinary procedure. True, the security is not absolute; but whatever the reason for a dismissal—national security, impropriety or rank incompetence—it will require in some form or another the active participation and acquiescence of other members of the civil service.

In short the bureaucracy has become a professionally qualified meritocracy recruited by impersonal standards and guaranteed tenure: this insulates it from political, personal and public pressures and so do arrangements for pay and promotion. It is true that the regulations governing these can be fiddled somewhat for party advantages, but the general conditions of pay and service are usually established by a central department or council.

The obverse of such insulation is the political neutrality of the civil servant. Since he is appointed and removed on the basis of his technical capacity to serve the state, he is expected to serve it without regard to persons or to the party complexion of the government of the day. Consequently all states impose some kinds of restrictions on the political activities of civil servants. Little difficulty arises in assimilating the rights of the junior civil servants to those of the general electorate, for these are concerned in routine functions. The problem only arises for the upper 2000 or 3000 "higher" civil servants who occupy that sensitive hinge area where policy and administration merge. Britain perhaps imposes the severest limitations on the rights of the civil servant to campaign for a political party or to stand for election to Parliament, and Germany perhaps the least. In similar ways higher civil servants are usually debarred for a certain time from taking posts in private business after they have resigned or retired from the service. The degree of insulation from active politics or private business varies, as one would expect, from country to country but the general tenor is plain enough: the career is to be self-sufficient and full-time and dedicated to the impersonal "state." In practice the general rule is breached in individual cases, particularly in the sensitive highest echelon: in most of the states of the continent, some posts are regarded as "posts of confidence" where the political leanings of a civil servant are held to be relevant, as will be seen later. But, except for a few such posts at the very top, the bureaucracy in contemporary Europe is not only intended to be but is a non-partisan corps expected to serve all and any ruling parties.

At the apex of the bureaucratic pyramid the civil servant comes into direct contact with his masters, the politicians, and therefore the top 2000 or 3000 bureaucrats in any country demand special attention. All western European political systems, with a quirky qualification for the Fifth French Republic, have proceeded along English lines in relating the bureaucracy to the legislature, which is purportedly the repository of the national will and purpose, and therefore the ultimate directing and controlling authority over the bureaucracy. All the states of Europe have adopted the British practice of heading the departments by a politician—a minister— of the ruling political party, and making this minister accountable to the legislature for all acts of omission and commission by the civil servants of his department: these being deemed to be his servants and assistants, under his direction and control. This formula of "the individual responsibility of the minister for his department" is carried to greater lengths in Britain than on the continent where legislative committees have greater contact with individual civil servants who play a more open role in policy formulation. For all that, modal relationship is that the minister is the conduit between the legislature and the bureaucracy.

The top bureaucrats who come into immediate and personal contact with ministers—and with legislative committees—are wholly unrepresentative of the social make-up of their countries, even more so than the legislatures which are themselves far from being a representative cross-section. The academic training of these administrative élites differs from country to country. The British have studied in mostly literary fields—history, classics and so forth. On the continent the largest proportion of higher civil servants will have graduated in law, and a high proportion of the remainder in economics.

In Britain the doctrine of individual ministerial responsibility for the department operates nowadays as a highly impenetrable screen between the legislature and the civil service. At the same time, it is in Britain that movement between the top positions in the bureaucracy and Parliament is less, apparently, than in any other country except Denmark. Certainly in France and Germany and Norway there is a good deal of movement between the two. In the Fifth French Republic, for instance, over half the Cabinet members have been selected from the higher bureaucracy and no fewer than six Presidents or Prime Ministers have been ex-bureaucrats also. In Germany, too, the movement is easy: in the 1961-5 *Bundestag* no less than 22.3 per cent of the deputies had previously been officials and state employees.

Furthermore, the top bureaucratic posts are more highly politicised in continental Europe than in Britain. The role and influence of the senior administrator are more overt: in France, for instance, it is not uncommon for such men to write highly polemical books about their policies. Correspondingly, some of these countries have developed usages for making the top echelon of the bureaucracy more politically sympathetic to the ministers. In Germany, for instance, the head of the Chancellor's office is such a key figure that it has become the practice to move him to another place in the service, replacing him by a more politically compatible bureaucrat, when a change of government makes this seem desirable. France has developed the ministerial *cabinet*, which nowadays is mostly composed of career civil servants (and is no longer merely the personal entourage of the minister as it once was), but they are personally selected by the minister himself.

Such politicisation is not a mere matter of "jobs for the boys" as cynics might affirm. It is a mechanism for making the bureaucracy follow the lead of the ruling political parties. For, it is argued, if the political party is the expression of public opinion and if the bureaucracy is responsive to the political party, the end result will be a bureaucracy that is responsive and accountable to public opinion. And how to achieve this precise result is, today, the central dilemma of big government and big bureaucracy. The large-scale bureaucratisation of western societies has created a set of problems concerning public accountability and control which are inherent and, it would seem, intractable. The politician and the bureaucrat are very dissimilar animals: they have different outlooks, timescales and constituencies. As an elected representative the politician is partisan, passionate, responsive: as an officer appointed on merit, the civil servant is critical, remote and neutral. The first serves a cause, the second pursues a career. The time perspectives of the politicians tend to be short—MPs and, nowadays, ministers move in and out of office and, more markedly still, in and out of any particular department; the civil servant, however, looks forward to perhaps half a century in the service, and perhaps in the same department. Furthermore, in entering the service he is made to feel that he is part of a permanent and continuing corporation which will be left to pick up the pieces long after the politicians have moved out of office. Irrespective of their technical and intellectual qualifications (which are nowadays often considerable), the sufficient condition for politicians being selected is popularity. In contrast, the civil servant is chosen on the basis of publicly established criteria of intellectual or technical skill.

The bureaucracy, therefore, is regarded as the "ballast" of the democratic state, counterpoising the volatility of politicians and electorates. The combination of these two elements via the Parliament-cum-Cabinet system is regarded as the supreme achievement of the modern democratic state, blending the organ of popular direction and control with the organs of permanency and impersonality embodied in the bureaucracy.

Unfortunately this view is too bland. There is a basic inconsistency in the qualities which the public expect in their government. The most canvassed requirement is that it shall give the public what the public say they want—the representative principle. But citizens, at the same time, do not like their governments to be always chopping and changing. They demand a measure of consistency, predictability and stability in policies: this is the stability principle. Finally, they will not pardon a government which, it turns out, has lacked elementary foresight and failed to provide, in the past, for needs that have become pressing in the present; this is the futurity principle. The last two principles clash with the first. For the representative principle demands that as soon as public opinion alters, the policy should alter also, whereas the stability principle requires that it stays the same. Representativeness requires a turnover of rulers; order and stability require their permanence. Representativeness demands that these rulers respond to expressed preferences: care for the common welfare and especially for the future welfare may well require the opposite. Between the three attributes of representativeness, stability and futurity, any number of mixes is possible, but it is unlikely that any single one will satisfy all the public all the time.

That the bureaucracy has been not just coeval with the formation of the modern state but is its essential core has been the burden of this essay. Whoever says state, says bureaucracy. The benefits it has brought to populations are incalculable. But for every gain it brings, there are attendant and inescapable losses. To permit it to create freely entails that one must forgo control. To impose tight control entails that it may not innovate freely. One is the obverse of the other. As the late Levi Eshkol said, though on a different matter: "You've got the dowry—the trouble is you've got the bride as well."

NOTES

1. J. R. THAYER, *On the Mediaeval Origins of the Modern State* (Princeton, 1970), p. 15.

2. J. SCHUMPETER, "The Crisis of the Tax State" in A. T. Peacock *et al.* (eds), *International Economic Papers* (New York, 1954).

3. R. H. LORD, "Common Features of Parliament throughout Europe" (1929) in P. Spuffard (ed.), *Origins of the English Parliament* (London, 1967), p. 22.

The Deputy Ministers' Dilemma

TED HODGETTS

Recent forays into the grey frontier which separates the politicians from the most senior of our government officials—the deputy ministers—have given rise to a spate of accusations that the higher civil service has become "politicized."

While it is never quite clear what is meant by politicization, there appears to be virtual unanimity in declaring it to be A Bad Thing. There is even less certainty about who is doing what to whom, although the popular inference is that the bureaucrats, if not themselves responsible for this development, have at least brought it upon themselves by having somehow overstepped their authority. Thus, when Premier Grant Devine performed deep surgery on the upper 200 of Saskatchewan's senior public service, there was even

Adapted from Ted Hodgetts, "The Deputies' Dilemma," *Policy Options*, Vol. 4, No. 3 (May/June, 1983): 14-17. By permission of The Institute for Research on Public Policy and the author.

a murmur of support for such action from observant colleagues in other provinces to the effect that "they had it coming to them; what could they expect after such prolonged, close association with their former NDP political masters!"

If longevity of association with one political regime is taken to be the litmus test for politicization of the senior bureaucracy, then it would naturally follow that the most vulnerable group in this category would be the senior ranks of the public service in Ontario where the litmus paper has tested blue for forty years.

In Ottawa, the unusual saliency accorded by the media to the going, coming, and going of Michael Pitfield, as Clerk of the Privy Council and Secretary to the Cabinet, also conjured up the spectre of politicization, accompanied by the speculation that this not-so-grey eminence was the cause of it all.

Perplexed and affronted by what he perceived to be a gross misrepresentation of the relationship that does (or should) pertain *vis-à-vis* political minister and senior official, (the now) Senator Pitfield has embarked on an educational mission directed to audiences who could be expected to capture the nuances of the distinctions between the roles of politician and bureaucrat he is seeking to delineate.

There is, indeed, a deputy's dilemma which is superficially that of Gilbert and Sullivan's policeman: his lot today is definitely not "an 'appy one." But the source of the dilemma is to be found in the legal and functional ambiguities surrounding the office that make the deputy minister "neither fish, or flesh, nor good red herring." The ambiguity may be said to have emerged with the very choice of words to describe the office. The term "deputy minister" was in use in pre-Confederation times and since it has no progenitors in Britain nor in any of the other senior colonies of the time, it must be presumed to have indigenous origins or references.

If, indeed, the term was borrowed from the title of colonial officials deputizing for their chiefs in Whitehall (as, for example, the Deputy Postmaster General) then its very origins carry an initial ambivalence concerning the status of the office—political or administrative—that has bedeviled it ever since. The semantic confusion is enhanced in a bilingual country where *député* refers to an elected member of the legislature.

Interpreted literally, the term is a real misnomer, for the deputy cannot deputize in all instances for his minister, as for example in the performance of the minister's parliamentary functions.

For such functions the minister has been assigned a parliamentary assistant, more recently re-titled parliamentary secretary, to be employed at the discretion of the minister. Indeed, the relatively recent accretions to the one-time extremely modest personal staff of a federal cabinet minister—one private secretary—to comprise a genuine ministerial *cabinet*, ostensibly dedicated to the political, party and parliamentary responsibilities of the minister, may have compounded the confusion already present in the relationship between a deputy and his minister.

In a number of instances, presenting an ironic twist to the politicization claim, it may now be asserted that the minister's personal and political staff threaten to trespass on the administrative terrain historically and legitimately occupied by the deputy minister; that is, they are becoming "bureaucratized."

In an even more conspicuous way the same assertions can be (and have been) made about the two central agencies that serve the cabinet collectively but more importantly serve the prime minister. Thus, even as the head of the Privy Council Office is accused of politicizing his own role and that of his deputy minister colleagues, the head of the Prime Minister's Office is accused of bureaucratizing his office by trespassing on the preserves of the PCO.

In its wisdom Parliament has done its best to confirm in legislation the confusion surrounding the term and the office of "deputy minister." On the one hand, in true accord with the spirit of ministerial responsibility, when a statute creates a department of government it provides for a minister to whom is assigned the powers and duties conferred by the act, including "the care and management" of the department. One must then turn to the Statutory Interpretation Act to establish the fact that where reference is made to a minister, one can substitute deputy minister, save for the right conferred on a minister, acting individually or with his colleagues, to promulgate an order.

The exception to the deputy's capacity to deputize for the minister is presumably based on the assumption that ministerial orders are a form of subordinate legislation, and this is a power the deputy cannot share any more than he can deputize for the minister in his parliamentary functions.

Whether the deputy, in performing the functions assigned by legislation to the minister, is acting in his own right or by way of delegation from the minister may be left to those more learned in the law to debate. All the layman can point to is the common expression used by the two involved parties in describing their relationship: they will tell you that it all depends on the personal "chemistry" that evolves between them; but the deputy will be the first to say that he views his role as subordinate. In short, the minister is boss and therefore deemed responsible, even for the care and management elements of his remit.

The deputy minister now has to contend with another factor: the prime minister as the formal source of his appointment. Since the early twenties, the power to select and recommend to cabinet the candidates for deputy minister positions has been a prerogative of the prime minister.

One can speculate that this arrangement is based on the presumption that the deputy minister is there not only to serve the interests and needs of his own department and minister but also, in conjunction with his peers, to serve the interests of the collectivity personified in the prime minister as chairman of the cabinet board. Whatever the explanation, the result is that the deputy minister faces yet another cross pressure on his time and loyalties.

The deputies' dilemma is more than that of confused lines of accountability: there is also the (surprisingly unacknowledged) dilemma of the status of the office. As noted, the deputy is appointed by order in council on recommendation of the prime minister and in a legal sense has no more guarantee of security in office than his untenured political overlord, the ministerial head of his department. His tenure is essentially at pleasure of the Crown—in practice, the pleasure of the prime minister.

Excluded from the provisions of the Public Service Employment Act, he falls outside the protective writ of the Public Service Commission as guardian of the merit principle. He is clearly beyond the job protection provisions available through collective bargaining; he lacks the statutory protection against arbitrary dismissal afforded members of the judiciary. And yet—practice, now amounting to established convention, converts this apparent administrative nomad into the equivalent of *permanent head* of his department. Given the proclivity in recent times to rotate deputy ministers rather rapidly, perhaps it is more appropriate to refer to the office as a permanent career position, acknowledged as such by deputies themselves, the government and the general public.

Thus, while accession to this post entails a formal severance from the permanent public service through the instrument of order in council, in practice and perception it is viewed as the attainment of the highest position offered by the career public service. Once arrived and with salary and perquisites (e.g. chauffeur) in place, whatever subsequent postings may lie in the offing, these accoutrements of office and of status will continue.

In a remarkable confirmation of the potency of convention over legal form, for those deputies (an overwhelming majority) who have come up through the permanent career public service to their posts, there would appear to be no recognition that acceptance of the deputy ministership legally has entailed a "crossing over." Legally, the deputy is no longer a member of the permanent administrative cadre for he has now joined his political masters, ostensibly to share with them the same tenuous tenure.

How can we explain the surprisingly firm entrenchment of a tradition (convention) so at variance with the legal status of the office of deputy minister? Is it because the long, slow swings of the political pendulum at the provincial and federal level have provided so few opportunities to test the convention?

Under such conditions it has been possible for the office to develop that sense of permanency conducive to the notion of it being part of the career system and not removable.

The inviolability of the line dividing politician and permanent administrator was tested by the advent of the Diefenbaker regime in 1957, and the surprising self-restraint of a party long in the political wilderness was a remarkable testimonial to the strength of the tradition of permanency afforded the office of deputy. All the more remarkable was that self-restraint in the light of later events that saw several former deputies and senior civil servants transmuted to Liberal cabinet ministers in Mr. Pearson's government.

During his brief interlude in office, Mr. Clark displayed even more prominently an excessive "correctness" in dealing with the deputy ministers.

However, it is possible that the fragile quality of all conventions may now be beginning to show. Premier Devine's blood-letting in Saskatchewan was strictly in accord with his prerogative rights *vis-à-vis* the deputies, although questionable in reaching so far below the senior echelon to effect dismissals. His actions, together with recent denunciations of the senior bureaucracy by Mr. Clark, suggest that in future there may be less reluctance, on the occasion of a change in the party in power, to wield the undeniable prime ministerial prerogative of dismissal.

Such a development would bring fully into the open the ambiguous legal status of the office of deputy minister that calls into question the traditional assumption that it is part of the permanent career public service.

The deputy's dilemma, attributed thus far to the multiplicity of accountability lines and to the ambiguities in the legal status of the office, can be further ascribed to the ambidextrous functional roles thrust upon the incumbent. It is clear from the previous analysis that the deputy has a managerial function but, in addition, it has long been accepted that the deputy has a policy advisory role.

Are these two major functions too much for one person to bear and, even if sustainable, can one person realistically be expected to perform equally well in handling responsibilities that would appear to call for quite different and conceivably incompatible qualities?

The obvious solution, to divide the deputy's post into two positions, has not been greeted with any enthusiasm by the cadre of deputy ministers. In part, the objection is one of principle: the job is a seamless web, however schizophrenic it may appear in the demands it imposes on the incumbent. In part, the objection is that different departments call for different qualities: some are primarily policy departments, others are essentially vast managerial undertakings.

It is probable that this dilemma will best be resolved, when assigning deputies to departments, by paying more attention to matching the personal qualities and interests of the individual to the particular requirements of the department.

But the administration-policy mix in the functions of a deputy minister creates a more serious dilemma whose resolution is much more elusive than that to which reference has just been made. To state the issue carries us back full circle to the dilemma of accountability but, in this instance, regarded from the broader perspective of our understanding (or misunderstanding) of the doctrine of ministerial responsibility.

In a nutshell, the mix of functions, taken together with the other ambiguities in the office of deputy minister, seems to be precipitating a crisis in the application of the doctrine of ministerial responsibility. Moreover, because of the symbiotic relationship of the deputy to his minister there are pressures perversely contributing to the downgrading of the convention supporting a senior permanent career public service.

An important aspect of the convention is that the deputy's role is as policy *adviser*, it is the minister who accepts responsibility for taking (or rejecting) the advice and then stands up to the consequences before Parliament and the country. Should a deputy, as sometimes occurs, elect to accept responsibility for the policy itself, then both the doctrine of ministerial responsibility and the convention of a politically neutral senior civil service are impaired. Furthermore, most recent events seem to be pointing to a tendency on the part of ministers to disclaim responsibility, leaving the opposition with little recourse than to shift their criticism to the deputy who, as it is now being said, is being left out in the breeze to dangle.

If, indeed, by such action the deputy minister is willy-nilly being thrust into the public eye, perhaps it is time to re-examine for a start the ambiguities in the status and function of deputies. Otherwise we may, by our failure to grapple with the dilemma, forfeit the benefits of the tradition of a senior permanent career service and the healthy tonic of parliamentary democracy to be found in a fair application of the doctrine of ministerial responsibility.

The Politics of Patronage: James Gardiner and Federal Appointments in the West, 1935-57

NORMAN WARD

James Garfield Gardiner, one of the most redoubtable champions western Canada has ever had inside or outside Parliament, left the premiership of Saskatchewan in 1935 to become minister of agriculture in the Liberal cabinet of W.L. Mackenzie King, a post he held for twenty-two consecutive years—the national record for a single portfolio. He also served briefly as the first minister of national war services in the early forties. From 1935 to 1939 he was at King's request the minister in charge of Liberal affairs for Alberta, since the province at the time had no other. From 1935 to 1945 he was the junior minister for Saskatchewan, his senior being the prime minister, who nonetheless relied heavily on Gardiner in or-

Reprinted from *Canadian Historical Review*, Vol. LVIII, No. 3 (September, 1977): 294-310, by permission of the author and University of Toronto Press.

ganizational matters. From 1945 to 1957 Gardiner was the senior minister for Saskatchewan, serving in the cabinets of both King and Louis St Laurent.

That brief recital of Gardiner's official and unofficial positions is necessary because in each he played a different role, and each involved different kinds of patronage and different protocols governing its distribution. Gardiner went to Ottawa well schooled in many of these customs, for he had been a member of the legislative assembly from 1914 to 1935, rising to cabinet rank in 1922 to hold several portfolios, and the premiership from 1926 to 1929 and in 1934-5. From 1922 to 1926 he was one of the most important figures in the party's provincial organization, heading the great communications department of the day, Highways, and acting as the chief collector of funds for his premier, Charles Dunning. The practices for raising money were in themselves interesting, for while it was permissible for a premier to solicit funds, he rarely picked up the actual money, that duty being performed by what is now called a bagman. The bagman accounted to the party organization for the money, and the party leader was thus not in a position where he could either be accused of keeping some or of yielding to pressures from known contributors. Gardiner broke with precedent in 1926 by becoming the first premier to keep control of the Saskatchewan party in his own hands (which is one reason why the machine came to be known as the Gardiner machine, though he simply inherited it), but he generally delegated the collecting of funds, and once crossly refused a large donation because the donor wanted his name known to the leader.[1]

By 1935 Gardiner was an old hand at patronage, and had had the salutary experience of being deprived of it while in opposition from 1929 to 1934. The major posts at the provincial level were undoubtedly the cabinet portfolios themselves and below them, subject to executive appointment, was the entire public service, from the deputy ministers to the teachers chosen to mark high school examinations each summer, and from major chairmanships of boards to the suppliers of gasoline to police cars. The federal level offered new and complicating jobs: lieutenant-governors, of whom five were needed in Saskatchewan in his twenty-two years; senators, a more durable breed for which he made only four recommendations; and judges, in the appointment and promotion of which he participated at least forty times. The figures are in one way misleading, for often the holding of a vacancy, for the convenience of the party, or a constituency organization, or sometimes an individual, was more significant than the actual appointment. In any event there were hundreds of other opportunities, large and small. Gardiner's deputy in National War Services in 1940-1, chosen by him, was his lifelong friend and colleague Hon. T.C. Davis, who could have succeeded Gardiner in the premiership in 1935 but who chose instead to stay as attorney general until the bench beckoned in 1939. Besides becoming Gardiner's deputy, Davis stayed on the bench for a decade while he was simultaneously serving as a diplomatic representative abroad.[2] Gardiner's deputy in Agriculture for years was Hon. J.G. Taggart, who had served in the provincial cabinet under him and his successor for ten years, that part of his career being terminated abruptly by the election of the CCF in 1944.

Below these lofty offices the patronage fanned out in an almost bewildering number of directions. All postmasters whose office's annual revenues fell below a statutory limit ($3000 at the start) were, among others, specifically excluded from the Civil Service Act,[3] and a government member could vacate any minor postmastership in his constituency by merely asserting that the incumbent was guilty of partisan activity. In a province where the village was the most common unit of government that gave every government MP access to possibly several dozen local appointments. The patronage was increased through a practice which rarely allowed the postmaster also to hold the contract for delivering the mail from the railway station to his office, a distance in some cases of only a few feet. Christmas help in the urban post offices, labourers in the national parks, fodder inspectors for agricultural relief programmes, caretakers in buildings used by the CBC, census enumerators (and the census was used not merely to count noses, but —unofficially—Liberals, Conservatives, and others)—all were among those into whose appointment political factors entered. When in due course the Second World War created the necessity for repatriating the bodies of Canadians, the patronage began to include undertakers. Patronage even had useful negative aspects: the distribution of relief in the drought-stricken areas of Saskatchewan in the late thirties was shrewdly left to municipalities, partly because the local governments were the best informed, but partly also because it took heat off the provincial and federal authorities, both Liberal at the time. The same general rules of course applied in Alberta and Manitoba, but there a somewhat broader view was taken of the capacities of Premiers Aberhart and Bracken, neither of them Liberal, to look after themselves.

The myriads of appointments available through all these channels had a number of implications for any conscientious politician.

Gardiner more than once said that he found patronage, especially the petty varieties, a nuisance, and even the letters of congratulation he received on attaining the premiership of Saskatchewan in 1926 contained many unconcealed hints that his well-wishers would not be averse to joining the public pay-roll. Later while in charge of Alberta he found Liberals jostling each other for a senatorship while the incumbent, though unwell, was still alive. He was aware of the dangers inherent in a patronage system, for failure to satisfy an importunate worker or constituency executive could alienate votes. Even a satisfactory appointment could cause trouble by creating ingratitude among those who did not get it. The more reliable a worker, the greater the loss to the party if he was made a judge or senator, for the former could not continue to aid the party and the latter usually would not. A senator, Gardiner said roundly in 1940, was of no further use; he had reached the end of the road for the party, as well as for himself.[4] Other public servants who had been workers became of limited use on appointment, he observed in the same year, because they must in self-protection hedge against future changes of government. Besides, it was his lifetime conviction that the best party workers were those zealous souls who believed in the cause, and he continually tried to shift various segments of the organization from paid to unpaid supporters. Patronage, he also held, could be positively harmful if it distracted attention from the principles of Liberalism to the niggling consideration everywhere of who gets what and when, and it had little to do with the winning of elections anyway.[5] That depended on different aspects of the party's business altogether.

Supporters might work in the uncertain anticipation of patronage, and Gardiner followed the practice (in which he was not alone) of making no promises before an actual vacancy arose, generally keeping his recommendations secret until the last possible moment. An important part of the system was that he always did, except for appointments under the Prairie Farm Rehabilitation Act [PFRA] and the related administrations (see below), make recommendations only. While his recommendations usually had the force of a victory in an American primary in a safe seat, the actual appointment was always somebody else's or subject to somebody else's approval. Nonetheless, he got his way generally because he was of immense value as a western captain of a national party and ran a tight ship. But in 1944, for example, when asked to submit a panel of names for the lieutenant-governorship of the province, neither his first nor second choice was the winner.[6]

His authority was thus not absolute, but his influence was enormous. He was also experienced and adaptable, and he needed both those qualities when, in the absence of an Alberta minister, he supervised that province's patronage from 1935 to 1939. He had trouble with Alberta, and had the satisfaction, if such it was, of living to see most of his private predictions about the party there come true. The only way the provincial Liberals could survive, he said repeatedly in the 1930s, was by eschewing all anti-Aberhart coalitions and fighting Social Credit with straight Liberalism. They ignored his advice, and all but disappeared. The federal Liberals in the province (and it is not possible to relate this to patronage) remained stronger: they increased their victories to seven in 1940 and Gardiner, who had worked hard in Alberta from 1935 to 1939, saw James Mackinnon, who succeeded him as the minister from Alberta, get most of the credit.[7] With Manitoba he did not have even the kind of short-lived contact he had with Alberta, for from 1935 Manitoba had its own minister, T.A. Crerar, who had been in turn Liberal, Unionist, Progressive and Liberal, and was thus, if possible, even more experienced than Gardiner.

The party in Saskatchewan during Gardiner's time was to be battered by the CCF, and at the end by John Diefenbaker, but it remained alive and well. It was in Saskatchewan that his influence was greatest, for apart from his provincial career it was there that the federal policies of PFRA and the Prairie Farm Assistance Act (PFAA), by their nature, made by far the greatest impact. Gardiner used his influence on patronage in Saskatchewan with a singleness of purpose that was remarkable for many things, including its unwavering consistency. "No one should be appointed unless he is known to be a lifelong Liberal," he asserted in 1953 of a position on a public works contract,[8] and he meant what he said. He genuinely believed that the appointment of real Liberals would guarantee the best kind of merit system possible. His philosophical basis for that, clearly set forth in his voluminous papers, depended both on his upbringing in a strong Liberal family (his mother was one of those later singled out for filial attention by Mackenzie King) and his formal university education in Manitoba especially under Chester Martin and A.B. Clark, the latter a Manchester-trained economist who reportedly gave the same lectures in the year he retired as he had at the beginning. Gardiner, who similarly adhered to Liberal principles without significant change from his earliest days, believed in progress through unfettered individual effort, and did not need to be a western farmer (although he was) to be a low tariff man, or an advocate of co-operatives as against state ownership or control. Had he known of it he would have applauded a letter of 1871 in which Sir John A. Macdonald refused patronage to a Liberal: "I think that in the distribution of governmental patronage we carry out the true constitutional principle. Whenever an office is vacant it belongs to the party supporting the Government, if within that party there is to be found a person competent to perform the duties. Responsible government cannot be carried on on any other principle."[9]

Gardiner had moved west in his early twenties and watched that principle being used effectively to convey necessary services to a huge area while its population grew at an almost explosive rate after 1900. He had sound pragmatic reasons for believing that the system worked as well as any other human device was likely to, and later experience buttressed them. As a provincial premier he was early approached by what in Macdonald's day was called a "ring": a group of businessmen led by a prominent Liberal offered him generous financial support in return for a monopoly over the supply of sundry goods and services needed particularly by the Department of Highways, at prices considered reasonable by the businessmen, and he threw them out. That incident was recounted by Gardiner many times, and was large in his mind on his death-bed. It convinced him that his own reputation and security depended on keeping official business in trustworthy hands. The celebrated Gardiner machine, to him, was not a machine but the opposite, a device to ward off machines.

Its best personnel logically came from established Liberals, and when in due course PFRA began to stock up on defeated candidates (a development which did not go unnoticed by his opponents), Gardiner's view was that he was in fact relying on trustworthy and proven supporters. Who better could carry out a policy than those who had demonstrated that they believed in it? Besides, the notion that membership in a legislature, or the seeking of it, unfitted a man for subsequent public service struck him as arrant nonsense. What did not, and it tempered his whole attitude towards patronage, was the belief that no government was better than its public service.[10] Much of Gardiner's federal staff after 1935, including large numbers of temporaries employed in the summer, was of course under the same civil service rules that covered most departments, but even so he was repeatedly charged with exploiting that portion of the Civil Service Act which permitted the employment of "casuals" for six months. Allegedly he would hire people for six months, release them briefly, and then rehire them for another six months, thus keeping them temporary for years at a time. The records of the period are incomplete and such allegations, while well remembered, are difficult to document.[11]

Gardiner's employment of patronage was governed by a well-understood set of rules. These rules, as has been suggested above, tended to vary for each kind of patronage. They helped Gardiner because, once clearly established and understood (and he spent a good deal of time explaining them), they could always be cited as a reason or explanation for doing or not doing something, and complainants usually had little recourse but to accept them. They limited Gardiner because they meant that he did not have a free hand in rewarding his friends, or the deserving whether they were his friends or not. Of the several possible examples that could be used probably the most useful turn on the appointment of postmasters, because they were so minor but so frequent, and of judges, because they were the most numerous of the major appointees.

Formerly, the postmaster in rural Saskatchewan was a more politically significant figure than now. His post office was often in the village general store, or some other centrally located clearing house. Particularly in the winter, the post office was the only regular contact with the outside world, and its master was in a position to observe who was hearing from whom. He was likely to be the only political appointee in the village holding a federal position. If the citizens were predominantly non-English speaking, the postmaster's fluency in their language was important, and the outbreak of war in 1939 immensely complicated that consideration where the language was German. He mattered, in short, and in Gardiner's time his position was enhanced by the fact that the post office's traditions included seeing that the mail got through.

The appointment of the village postmasters rested in part on those sections of the Civil Service Act which exempted all those below a certain importance from its general provisions and in part on the preference given, in a defined order, to veterans of the two World Wars. The channel of communication was the local MP if he was a government supporter or, if he was not, the government's candidate in the last election or his successor if he had been chosen. If a government member retired or died, the minister's office took over for the making of a recommendation, and the postmaster general made the actual appointment.

The rules governing veterans' preference set forth a number of priorities which in effect gave first choice to persons wounded overseas, second to those returning untouched, down through those who had served but not overseas. Thereafter preference was given to mere civilians resident in the area and, finally, to complete outsiders, whose chances were roughly those of a man who had gone overseas and not come back. When a vacancy occurred, the MP was notified on a form from the postmaster general. He then, if he was Gardiner, notified his constituency executive, usually through his secretary. The executive in turn got in touch with party men in the village—sometimes a member of the executive living there, and sometimes a cell of the party covering the relevant polling division. In any event the channel was always the party. News of the vacancy was spread: openings do not often appear to have been formally advertised, partly because of the absence of any local advertising medium but partly because the best kind of advertising was a notice in the post office itself, aided by gossip. Veterans' preference was rigorously applied, and usually the local branch of the Canadian Legion, which itself would never indicate a choice between two equally qualified veterans, was in on the appointment from the start. If there was one veteran only, he obtained the job regardless of his political leanings. If there was no veteran, a civilian would be recommended by the Liberals locally, and he was not necessarily an active Liberal but a person well thought of in the village, and thus likely to enhance the party's local reputation. Occasionally the previous postmaster's widow, who had effectively assisted her husband in his duties, was the popular choice. At its simplest the system was a smooth and sensible way of staffing a small rural post office. At its most complicated, as when important villagers were not on speaking terms, it might bring in not only the constituency but the provincial executive of the party, and the provincial office of the Legion, and produce a file of telegrams and letters longer than that needed to select an ambassador. The system's workings, that is, depended on the personnel as well as the rules.[12]

The same was true of the selection of judges, but there both the type of personnel and the rules were different. Veterans' preference did not formally apply, although a man's military record might be a factor to be considered. But all judges had to be lawyers, and lawyers approved to receive government business were named on patronage lists the same as were newspapers fit to receive job printing contracts. (Gardiner once pointed out that there was no real difference between Liberals doubling as party and PFRA workers and Liberal lawyers being consulted by the Department of Justice.[13] On at least one occasion legal patronage was considered as a catalyst to soften up a law firm for the purpose of making available a future candidate who might otherwise have felt free enough to decline.) A lawyer, if he was able, was probably exceedingly valuable to Gardiner, who would accordingly be reluctant to lose him to the bench. One of the best of them, he noted regretfully towards the end of his career, was so good that he never received anything from the party.[14] A judgeship was important enough to be conspicuous, and thus for a fair share of them to be claimed by Roman Catholics, French Canadians, Ukrainians, small town and rural Liberals, Germans, and northerners and southerners.

The nice balancing of all the pressures that bore on every judgeship had to be done within a set of ground rules laid down both by the party's needs and Gardiner himself. An overzealous supplicant could hurt himself, especially if he was seeking to upset the rule which allocated the existing percentage of the appointments to Roman Catholics. In 1952 one such mounted so thorough a campaign that Gardiner, in Rome at a meeting of the United Nations Food and Agriculture Organization and incidentally being received at the Vatican, said he was surprised that the Pope did not mention him.[15] A judge could not properly sit where he had practised law, so his qualifications had to include a willingness to uproot his family. Successive appointments, or appointments close together, could not be made from the same constituency, the same town, the same religious minority, the same ethnic group, the same law firm, or the same family. The classic family case involved the Davises of Prince Albert. T.C. Davis, as noted above, was a close colleague and good friend of Gardiner, and the family consisted of loyal Liberals. Davis wanted to see his younger brother on the bench, and the latter was prepared to accept an appointment. T.C. Davis was not sitting as a judge but kept the title while on leave for a decade, and Gardiner, though favouring Davis' wish, occasionally warned him in a friendly fashion that he was wasting his time if he thought he was keeping the bench warm for his brother. The brother, in an impressively involved series of manoeuvres, finally made it, but his appointment took nearly twelve years.[16]

To the established rules which, Gardiner freely acknowledged, kept him out of a lot of trouble even if they did lock the Roman Catholics into a rigid quota and left unsettled the priorities among French, Irish, German, and other Catholics,[17] he added a few personal touches. The rules for allocating appointments on a religious basis historically went back to territorial days and Premier F.W.

Haultain and, like so many things legal, they had changed slowly. Gardiner in 1955 credited their last adaptation to W.F.A. Turgeon, who had left the attorney general's portfolio (for the bench) in 1921.[18] Operating under a partisan system which Haultain had eschewed in territorial days, Gardiner enlarged its scope. He would not recommend any Liberal whose record included flirting with coalition at any level with other parties, and he was loathe to recommend a judgeship for a constituency with a poor track record in electing Liberals. Twice, in 1949 and 1956, he expressly denied a high priority to Saskatoon, which had not returned a Liberal since 1935.[19] Gardiner also applied Macdonald's dictum of 1871 to judges: he was always concerned about the quality of the courts, and insisted that he considered only ability and service, but the service meant Liberals "first, last and all the time."[20]

The procedure in appointing judges, unlike that for postmasters, was relatively simple. It was fully recognized not only that Gardiner made merely recommendations but that others' opinions were important too. King, both as prime minister and as the member for Prince Albert from 1926 to 1945 (which made him senior to Gardiner on two counts), was naturally always a power. But despite the many influences that could enter into a judicial appointment (and it is a fair generalization that no appointments aroused wider legal, political, or economic interest), the complexity all lay in deciding on the individual to be recommended. The procedure itself began with an informal notification (sometimes apparently by telephone) from the Department of Justice to Gardiner of a vacancy which, except in cases of sudden death, everybody knew about anyway. Gardiner then considered his moves rather in the manner of a chess player, deciding whether a vacancy in square A could best be filled by moving the man in square B, which would leave a vacancy in B so that the process could be started afresh; or, unlike a chess player, he could put a new man on the board. And unlike a chess player, whatever he did would follow only after broad discussions and the consideration of minute points that only an experienced organization man would know about. In 1955, in a rare indecisive mood, Gardiner submitted a priority list of six names to the minister of justice for district court vacancies, suggesting that "providing they are capable of filling the position [they] should be given first consideration."[21] Generally he made specific recommendations, which went through the hands of the minister of justice to the desk of the prime minister. In the great majority of cases the recommendation from Gardiner was the one accepted.

The translation of Gardiner's theories and opinions into the pragmatic business of making appointments one by one on his own can be clearly seen in PFRA, which under his aegis grew from a standing start in 1935 to twelve hundred employees in its prime. PFRA, as a part of the patronage system, differed again from the rules applied to postmasters and judges. Gardiner did not inherit a system with PFRA, as he did with most other appointments, but only a skeletal legislative provision left behind by R.B. Bennett's Conservative government, for which Gardiner built his own machine and created his own traditions. The minister's powers of appointment were clearly spelled out: "The Minister may appoint such temporary, technical, professional and other officers and employees as he may deem necessary and expedient for carrying out the provisions of this Act and the salaries and expenses of such officers shall be fixed by the Governor in Council."[22]

Where postmasters and judges involved the whole province, PFRA was by its nature specifically attached to the grain-growing and ranching sections, and the strength it gave Gardiner in the south was partially offset by the weaknesses it left him in the north. With rare exceptions those segments of the Liberal organization over which Gardiner had the most trouble lay towards the northern settled areas, and no southern seats caused him the concern he had from time to time with Saskatoon and Prince Albert. Both PFRA and its sister act, PFAA, won for Gardiner repeated praises from all parties in the House of Commons, for the problems they tackled, and the expertise with which they solved them, dealt with matters dear to MPs, and not solely in the west. The chief criticisms about either focussed on the plea that while good they did not go far enough, and the application of their principles both to more cases on the prairies, and to cases beyond the prairie, was sought almost annually. PFRA and PFAA were so successful, indeed, that they led spokesmen for Quebec to complain that the west could get anything it wanted while "we cannot get anything from the Department of Agriculture for the Province of Quebec."[23] Yet the bureaucratic apparatus supporting these great good works was based on patronage: it was Gardiner's own organization, necessary after he left behind that in the province, and he always insisted it was purely federal. This description was necessary not just to free him from reliance on the provincial party, over which he had a lessening direct control from 1935, but to give him a power base at the federal level.

What made it possible, and easy, was R.B. Bennett's original assumption in 1935 that the drought on the prairies was temporary, and therefore expedients to deal with it should be ameliatory and also temporary. Certainly Bennett had no intention of providing an outspoken critic with an authoritative instrument that was to last throughout his federal career.[24] Gardiner had another stroke of luck in getting PFRA, for he did not go to Ottawa with the agricultural portfolio in mind. He wanted Finance most of all, but was prepared to settle for National Revenue, or a new Department of Colonization and Resources, at first in that order. The order was reversed when King pointed out, according to his diary, that the new department "touched all the western questions: mines, lands, forests, parks, colonization, Indians, etc. [and]. . . was a department with great patronage." Finance and National Revenue not only had little useful patronage but would have kept Gardiner in Ottawa. In any event, the juggling of personalities, regions, and portfolios that is part of every cabinet's making finally pointed to Agriculture for Gardiner, partly because T.A. Crerar had turned it down as too minor. Gardiner made one last attempt to get Trade and Commerce, because the minister of that was responsible for the wheat board, and he tried too to get the wheat board transferred to Agriculture. "The little beggar," King confided to his diary with an air of amazement, "is angling for one of the more important portfolios, and running the danger of getting out of his depth."[25]

Having settled for a department which Crerar was not alone in considering minor, and with King having already recorded his observation that Gardiner was particularly adept at organization and ambitious "to create a machine," Gardiner set about making a minor portfolio major. Bennett's 1935 legislation had appropriated $750 000 for PFRA's first year and $1 million for each of the next four. In 1937 the law was amended to remove the ceiling by providing that the administration could spend "sums not exceeding the amount appropriated by Parliament in each year" down to 1939-40. In 1939 that time limit was removed, and the minister was empowered for PFRA's purposes to enter into agreements with any or all of the prairie provinces, or with any persons, firms or corporation within them, and to purchase or rent land or equipment; any transaction over $5000 had to be approved by Order-in-Council, a limit raised to $10 000 in 1951. A year later the minister was empowered to pay "all the necessary administrative. . . travelling and living expenses incurred by officials or employees." Meanwhile, the Liberals' onslaught on prairie problems had opened a second front in 1939 with the passage of the Prairie Farm Assistance Act. Its staff too was appointed by the minister, and when in 1940 Gardiner was briefly appointed minister of National War Services he tried to get the same power over that department. Only in 1948 did PFRA receive its first classified employees when the minister was empowered to appoint a director and associate director of rehabilitation, and in 1951 those two officers obtained pension rights, while engineers, clerks and stenographers became full civil servants.[26]

The overtaking of part of PFRA by the merit system had no effect on its uses as part of a political organization because the key workers were the field men who remained the minister's choices. The work in the field—the creation of dugouts, dams and, in due course, community pastures—was almost made to order for political enterprise. By 1940, for example, the department had completed over fourteen thousand small water projects, ten thousand of which were dugouts, and that meant ten thousand contacts with individual farms. While the soil chemists and engineers who planned the dugouts were technical experts qualified to decide whether or not a particular hole would hold water, the inspectors sent around afterwards to see whether or not they did were casual appointees paid on a daily basis, frankly conceded by Gardiner to be likely to have political inclinations. In 1950 Ross Thatcher, then a member of the CCF, made a typical comment in the House of Commons: "In my opinion the PFRA is accomplishing much in the prairie provinces, yet I wonder how at every election these PFRA trucks can run around working for Liberal candidates."[27] Between elections, he might have added, the Liberal machine, at a time when for several consecutive years depression and war made both cars and gasoline hard to come by, was continually fuelled in a manner denied to other parties by the ease with which party workers could hitch rides on PFRA trucks going somewhere on their endless rounds.

The importance of such an amenity could hardly be overestimated, for when the provincial Liberals had gone into opposition in 1929 the heaviest single blow dealt the organization came from its loss of free transportation. And PFRA had other uses. In 1946, when the Saskatchewan provincial Liberal leadership was contested by E.M. Culliton and Walter Tucker, MP, the Culliton

forces alleged that Tucker won because the forces of PFRA were
thrown on his side. When in 1955 the provincial leadership was
again vacant one of the candidates was PFRA's director, L.B. Thomson, who received leave of absence for the convention, returning
to his post afterwards. When criticized for that Gardiner retorted
that any PFRA worker could receive leave to seek any party candida-
ture, and credence was soon given that when a PFAA worker in Alberta ran for Social Credit. Gardiner said it would not affect his eligibility for further assignments.[28]

That kind of undertaking in one sense helped mitigate criticism
of PFRA's political wing, but more important was the genuine popularity of PFRA among prairie MPs of all parties, and the fact that
most other MPs (that is, the vast majority of the Commons) were
not affected by it. Virtually all departments had casual workers
and the great patronage portfolios, beside which PFRA, and indeed
the whole Department of Agriculture, were small, were Public
Works and the Post Office. Agriculture was the fifth largest department in 1935, the seventh in 1957, in both years smaller than
National Revenue, Public Works, the Post Office, and Trade and
Commerce. What was unique about PFRA was its use as a minister's
personal corps. Postmasters, along with all the rest of the petty patronage, were within the orbit of every government member.
Judges were recommended to perform an important function for
the whole community, and once appointed were of no further use
to the party. The considerable patronage of Public Works and the
Post Office was scattered and unorganized. The political wing of
PFRA was an anomaly, but unquestionably the minister's own private army.

One might have argued that if it took soil men and engineers to
scoop out dugouts and build dams, it took at least equally qualified
men to inspect their work. In fact, as the record shows clearly, the
technical staff of PFRA, however frustrated many of them were at
being kept temporary, did excellent work that was repeatedly laud-
ed, and the complaints about the rest, though persistent, were remarkably mild and rarely taken far. Gardiner numerous times
checked over-zealous PFRA Liberals himself. He once warned one
executive not to use the letterhead for political business, for example, and it is not surprising that the warning was needed, for the
executive was a defeated former MP who himself thought there was
only a paper difference between administration and politics. Many
of the casual workers would have shared the indignation of one
provincially-minded elector who once complained that some

school inspectors "are more concerned with educational matters than organization"—which in this instance included school districts as well as elections.[29]

Gardiner's concern about observing the proprieties (he more than once sharply told PFRA men that they must not use PFRA money for political purposes) reflected one of the several limits inherent in the system. PFAA reflected another, for it was never as popular as PFRA, and there were more complaints about its substance, as distinct from its administration, because the difficulty of deciding which districts were entitled to relief and which were not meant an unceasing flow of dissatisfied electors to whom its provisions were not always easy to explain. Within PFRA itself the technical experts were never confused with the field men: their work was crucial. A steady production of dugouts and dams that would not hold water could have ruined Gardiner's career, among others. The experts had to be as competent as any a merit system could have found. A relevant parallel, in reverse, can be found in the brief history of the Saskatchewan provincial police from 1917 to 1928: the force scored a few triumphs but its daily routine of enforcing unpopular liquor laws did the government so much harm that it abolished the force and diverted policing under contract to the RCMP. The patronage in the provincial force, and the acknowledged usefulness of the Liberal police in reporting on opponents' activities, were simply outweighed in value by other factors.[30]

The need to pay attention to local detail points up a major weakness of the whole apparatus: quite apart from its general exclusion of all citizens who were not friends of the governing party, and the enormous advantage it gave the governing party, it was extremely time-consuming for the minister and his office. Gardiner could, and did, delegate the opening procedures in selecting a postmaster, for example, to local partisans and to an executive assistant, and he could delegate a good deal to those executives in PFRA who were trusty former Liberal MPs and MLAs. But the final responsibility in every recommendation or appointment was his, and it involved him in a vast correspondence. In his postmasters' files alone are 5481 numbered pages relating to sixty-two villages, and they do not include relevant correspondence that runs throughout his political papers.

With the outbreak of war in 1939 new and revealing problems in patronage, at first thought to be temporary, came to light. In the war effort at least the more obvious outcroppings of partisanship had to be smoothed over, and King's insistence that the Liberal government was a national government in every sense, so that no unseemly coalition with other parties (especially the Conservatives) was called for, obliged the party to change some of its ways. In 1939 a memorandum was issued to members suspending partisanship for the duration and Gardiner (who might have found it easier to suspend breathing), as a patriot as well as a partisan, had little initial difficulty accepting its terms.[31] But the day-to-day working out of a non-partisan war effort, within a system traditionally modified by a judicious attention to patronage, was to create colossal strains unforeseen by Gardiner and certainly unappreciated by the prime minister, whose work in the nerve centre of the cabinet left little time for the consideration of casualties on the political front line.

Gardiner found he had virtually no influence on temporary wartime staffs whose directors, he said in 1942, were dictators.[32] He had little influence on commissions in the armed services. His own pet projects, especially PFRA, were essentially peacetime affairs and not given a high priority in war finance. He tried to keep agricultural products away from the price controls imposed by the Wartime Prices and Trade Board, on the broad ground that farmers, especially in the west, had a lot of catching up to do where prices were concerned. He failed, and in addition began to receive complaints that the rigorous enforcement of controls and rationing was damaging the party at the electoral level. Non-partisanship, he found to his mounting irritation, was too often interpreted (and understandably so to his opponents) to mean actual coalition, and that had been anathema to Gardiner since at least the devastating election of 1917. To an organization like the Liberal party in Saskatchewan, coalition at the administrative level looked like a form of suicide.

Gardiner on the politics of coalition is a major topic in itself and cannot be even summarized here. The impact of the war on his uses of patronage is also a large subject, but more readily surveyed: the war variously challenged and sometimes destroyed the premises on which the distribution of patronage, as a normal element in the governing process, was based. For the leisurely, gossipy pace followed in selecting appointees before the war it substituted an urgency which left no time for adequate examination of all the political implications involved. For the pluralistic aims of a system seeking to satisfy a wide range of goals and claimants it substituted a singleness of purpose that made everything else irrelevant. It demanded the best in technical skills: it needed the equivalent of the soils experts and engineers in PFRA, not the happy-go-lucky inspectorial system of the field men. It is no coincidence that by 1944 so adroit a politician as the Hon. C.G. Power was concerned over Liberal MPs' disaffection with the war machine, which grew, paradoxically, precisely because the machine was so successful.[33] Most of these characteristics carried over in modified form into the post-war era, and with the growing consideration being given to collective bargaining in the public service, gradual at first but then increasingly general, the politics of patronage was by the end of Gardiner's ministerial career in 1957 vastly different from what he had learned as a freshman MLA in 1914.

In its day it had many values. It emphasized local rather than centralized considerations over an imposing list of petty appointments, and at every level involved the active participation of numbers of people. Around appointments of general interest as a matter of course a local folklore often developed, and it survives in accounts, frequently conflicting, of why or how each was made. It was part of a communications network of the most immediate value to the governing party, but also to its opponents because they responded to, and themselves reported on, the governing party's activities. It had an educational value to any newly chosen candidate on the governing side, for his plunge into constituency patronage soon told him what his constituents' needs were, as perceived by them. If he was a sensitive man, it revealed to him potential trouble spots. Sometimes it served as a welfare system for needy politicians who, in the days before MPs received pensions, had neglected their own affairs for public service. Sometimes, after an impoverished Liberal had died in harness, his widow benefitted from patronage, although in Gardiner's day the social limitations placed on careers for women made it difficult to place them. (A doctor's wife, to take a case in point, could hardly be expected to settle for a position as a waitress in a railway hotel.) The whole system was, in Gardiner's hands, as free of corruption as the public service under the merit system; and it must be reiterated that Agriculture, despite the economic implications of its policies, was a department dealing almost exclusively with rural affairs, not one which had in its purview the allocation of timber rights, hydro sites, large purchases of supplies or services, or dredging contracts. Although its expenditures multiplied by ten between 1935 and 1957, it was in the last year still taking only 1.7 per cent of Canada's total budgetary expenditures, ranking far behind those departments responsible for defence, welfare and veterans' affairs.[34]

As the war revealed, Gardiner's techniques worked better under simple majority government than under one committed to a good deal of non-partisanship. It is also relevant that his system depended on a particular technology. The original method of digging a dugout took several men, like the old pick-and-shovel way of building each mile of highway, but by the 1950s, in either kind of work, one man with a bulldozer could replace possibly dozens of men, and thus dozens of electors, most of them supporters of the party. Gardiner's own outlook involved a technology he could manage, and for that reason he disliked and distrusted television. That the end of his career coincided with Canada's first television elections was a mere historical accident, but his one-on-one approach to both campaigning and patronage could have been adapted to television by him only by a miracle he was not even interested in performing. It is not part of this essay to argue that technology has, among other things, polluted political patronage; but certainly, if Gardiner's management of federal patronage was typical, its like may not be seen again.

NOTES

This article was first presented as a paper to the annual meeting of the Canadian Political Science Association in Edmonton, 1975.

1. See Papers of Rt Hon. James G. Gardiner, Saskatchewan Archives [hereafter Gardiner Papers], Gardiner to T.C. Davis, 10 Oct. 1959, #64399; Gardiner expanded on the theme on his deathbed, when being interviewed on tape by Una Maclean (now Mrs Evans) for the Glenbow Institute, Calgary. The Gardiner Papers are closed pending the completion of a biography. The provincial Liberal machine has been described in Escott Reid, "The Saskatchewan Liberal Machine Before 1929," CJEPS, II, 1, 1936 (and frequently reprinted). The article does not take into account the several official investigations of Liberal administration undertaken by the government of Hon. J.T.M. Anderson after Anderson succeeded Gardiner in the premiership in 1929.

2. NORMAN WARD, ed., "A Prince Albertan in Peiping: The Letters of T.C. Davis," *International Journal*, Vol. XXX, No. 1 (Winter 1974-5): 24-33.

3. *Statutes of Canada*: 22 3 Geo. v, 1932, c 10, s 10.

4. See Gardiner Papers, T.H. Wood to Gardiner, 5 Oct. 1940, #45257.

5. See *ibid.*, Gardiner to L.E. Purdy, 6 April 1940, #52557; to J.P.M. Isaac, 19 Oct. 1936, #50755.

6. *Ibid.*, Gardiner to T.H. Wood, 18 Sept. 1944, #45734.

7. NORMAN WARD, "Hon. James Gardiner and the Liberal Party of Alberta,

1935-40," *Canadian Historical Review*, Vol. LVI, No. 3 (September, 1975): 303-22.

8. Gardiner Papers, Gardiner to A.K. McNeill, 2 May 1953, #54089.

9. Public Archives of Canada [PAC], Macdonald Letterbooks, Vol. 15, Macdonald to T.W. Anglin, 10 Jan. 1871.

10. Gardiner Papers, "Speech for Arm River By-Election," Oct. 1928, #11483.

11. Letter from T.C. Douglas, 14 July 1975, including statistics obtained by Mr. Douglas from the Department of Regional Economic Expansion.

12. Gardiner's main post office files are in Gardiner Papers, #35509 ff (64 files), but relevant references are throughout his papers.

13. *Ibid.*, Gardiner to R.J. Jones, 21 April 1953, #62339; A.H. McDonald to Gardiner, 7 Oct. 1955, #63034.

14. *Ibid.*, Gardiner to K. Mayhew, 27 April 1955, #62896.

15. *Ibid.*, Gardiner to T.H. Molloy, 14 Jan. 1952, #33986. The rule was (a) one Roman Catholic on each of the Appeal Court and Court of Queen's Bench, (b) a District Court Roman Catholic was replaced with another; *ibid.*, Gardiner to I. Studer, 20 Sept. 1951, #34687.

16. *Ibid.*, especially #33874 ff which cover the bulk of the files on judges.

17. *Ibid.*, Gardiner to I. Studer, 20 Sept. 1951, #34687.

18. *Ibid.*, Gardiner to Archbishop M.C. O'Neill, 9 Dec. 1955, #34772-4.

19. *Ibid.*, Gardiner to T.C. Davis, 18 April 1956, #34492, and #42378; to S. Garson, 16 Feb. 1955, #34898; to S.H. Miskiman, 1 April 1959, #34430-5.

20. *Ibid.*, Gardiner to J.E. Friesen, 19 Dec. 1955, #34225; to S.H. Miskiman, 1 April 1949, #34430-5.

21. *Ibid.*, Gardiner to S. Garson, 16 Feb. 1955, #34214; see also Gardiner to H. W. Pope, 8 July 1948, #34816.

22. *Statutes of Canada* 25-6 Geo. V, 1935, c 23, s 6.

23. For example, *Debates of the House of Commons of Canada*, 1941, 3425.

24. There was nothing unusual about temporary administrations, or even temporary administration that seemed to go on forever. The Income War Tax Act of 1917, for example, provided for a temporary bureaucracy to deal with an income tax that could be removed as soon as conditions became favourable. It is well known that the conditions have not yet arrived, and the legal framework set up in 1917 ultimately disappeared into that limbo where statutes are neither repealed nor consolidated. *See Revised Statutes of Canada*, 1952, Vol VI, No. 8.

25. PAC, King Diaries, M6, 26, J13, volume 78, 17-22 Oct. 1935, especially 764-822.

26. *See Statutes of Canada*, 25-6 Geo. V, 1935, c 23; 1 Geo. VI, 1937, c 14; 3 Geo. VI, 1939, c 7; 4-5 Geo. VI, 1940-1, c 25; 11-12 Geo. VI, 1948, c 25; 15 Geo. VI, 1951, c 58.

27. *Debates of the House of Commons of Canada*, 1950, 1995.

28. *Ibid*., 1956, 7008.

29. Gardiner Papers, G.J. Matte to R.J. Parker, #44014.

30. See FRANK W. ANDERSON, *Saskatchewan Provincial Police* (Calgary 1972). Gardiner described its espionage activities in the tapes made for the Glenbow Foundation; see note 1, supra.

31. See Gardiner Papers, "The Saskatchewan Liberal Association," 31 Oct. 1939, #56558.

32. *Ibid*., Gardiner to T.H. Wood, 30 Aug. 1942, #45535.

33. See PAC, King Papers, M 6 26, J1, volume 403, Gardiner to C.D. Howe, 18 Nov. 1946; Queen's University Archives, Power Papers, C.G. Power to W.L.M. King, 3 Jan. 1944, for representative samples of concerns over the effects of the war on the party.

34. See *Public Accounts of Canada for the Fiscal Year Ended March 31, 1957*, 37.

The Legislative Branch of Government

In the modern era, legislatures rarely make public policy. Instead, the functions of the legislative branch of government are more likely to involve representation and legitimation rather than decision-making. Such a conclusion is particularly true of British-based parliamentary systems. Only in the American presidential system, because of the separation of powers principle, does the legislature, at times, exercise substantial power in the policy process.

> The importance of Parliament does not lie in its capacity to be a centre for the detailed construction of public policy, for this capacity is meagre indeed. Parliament is, instead, a forum where the ideas and concerns of the government, the opposition, groups of MPs and individual representatives meet.[1]

The reason for such a pattern rests on the historical development of legislatures in relation to the executive branch and to the people.

> Parliaments are poised between the executive on one side and the electorate on the other. Parliament is an intermediary institution between executives and electorates. Its creation and its activities grow out of that dual relationship.[2]

The tensions produced by this dual connection in Canadian government are explored in readings twelve and thirteen.

The fundamental organizing concept of Canadian government is parliamentary sovereignty. While other principles, such as federalism and judicial review, are significant and, at times, constrain the extent of its applicability, parliamentary supremacy remains the theoretical heart of the Canadian body politic.

As so often happens, however, political developments and conventions change the ways in which principles of government actually operate. In the modern era, a crucial modification of parliamentary sovereignty has resulted from the development of mass political parties operating as unified groups within the legislature (i.e., party discipline). In reading number twelve ("Party Organization and Parliamentary Sovereignty"), Roman R. March suggests that mass parties in Canada have altered not only the role of the individual MP but also the functions of the legislature to such an extent that the principle of parliamentary sovereignty has become a myth. In effect, the executive uses an institution, the political party, which was designed to give the people some control over their government, as a tool to dominate the legislature.

The connection between the legislature and the electorate is emphasized in reading number thirteen (Ronald G. Landes, "The Legislative Defeat of the Clark Government"). An appeal to the people is the ultimate electoral connection in a parliamentary democracy. As a chamber in which confidence in the government can be tested with the power to defeat a government, the House of Commons is predicated on the principle of parliamentary supremacy, but is operated and controlled by the political parties. The analysis by Landes of the factors which led to the defeat of the Clark government emphasizes that what happens inside the legislature (passage of a nonconfidence motion) reflects, in part, the state of public opinion and the parties' expectations of success in a new election. Reading number thirteen also illustrates that the power of the legislature to make or break governments, although rarely used, can still be employed in the Canadian parliamentary system, at least in minority government situations.

While the House of Commons is a confidence chamber, the appointed Canadian Senate is not. As a result, there has been considerable confusion over the functions and usefulness of the second legislative chamber, as well as numerous proposals and suggestions for reform. One recent study even advocated abolition of the Senate and presented a detailed plan to carry such action out.[3] The latest round of proposals included then Justice Minister Mark MacGuigan's (1983) discussion paper[4] and the January, 1984 report on Senate reform prepared by the Special Joint Committee of the Senate and the House of Commons.[5] One area on which most Senate reform proposals concentrate is the appointment process, in particular, the role of party patronage as the overriding criterion for selection. In reading number fourteen ("Running for the

Red Chamber: Sam Bronfman's Senate Bid"), Peter C. Newman provides a fascinating case study of Sam Bronfman's extensive efforts to reach the promised land.

Aspects of internal legislative organization are considered by Michael Rush in reading number fifteen ("Parliamentary Committees and Parliamentary Government: The British and Canadian Experiences"). In contrast to the role of committees in the American legislative process, parliamentary committees have been not only a more recent development, but also less significant as actors in the legislative processes in Canada and Britain. As Michael Rush argues, committees have played a fundamentally different political role in presidential and parliamentary systems. In Canada and Britain, committees have neither become nor evolved towards becoming means for asserting legislative control over the executive branch of government.

Our final selection deals with public perceptions of the Canadian legislature. In reading sixteen (Ronald G. Landes, "Public Perceptions of the Canadian Parliament"), data from a previously published national Gallup poll are presented. For a polity based on the principle of parliamentary supremacy, the results are not encouraging: few individuals have very much knowledge about or appreciation for the Parliament of Canada. Of particular significance is the public's attitude towards the principle of party discipline.

NOTES

1. MICHAEL M. ATKINSON, "Parliamentary Government in Canada," in Michael S. Whittington and Glen Williams (eds.), *Canadian Politics in the 1980s* (Toronto: Methuen, 1981), p. 272.

2. DAVID M. OLSON, *The Legislative Process: A Comparative Analysis* (New York: Harper and Row, 1980), p. 6.

3. COLIN CAMPBELL, *The Canadian Senate: A Lobby from Within* (Toronto: Macmillan of Canada, 1978).

4. MARK MACGUIGAN, *Reform of the Senate: A Discussion Paper* (Ottawa: Publications Canada, 1983).

5. *Report of the Special Joint Committee of the Senate and House of Commons on Senate Reform* (Ottawa: Supply and Services, 1984).

Party Organization and Parliamentary Sovereignty

ROMAN R. MARCH

It is intended in this article to examine the nature of the Canadian parliamentary system as it has evolved since 1867. It will be argued that fundamental changes in the Canadian political system have transformed the House of Commons from a body of once relatively independent gentlemen Members of Parliament to a body dominated by the executive, which in turn is dominated by the Prime Minister. This is not to say that the independence of members has been eroded only because of a gradual change in the relationship between the Prime Minister, the cabinet, and the backbencher, for it is well known, for example, that the gradual elimination of most political patronage in the federal civil service has helped to make it a formidable enduring technocratic machine in the hands of the government. Moreover, immense social, economic and technological changes have occurred in the same period. But this study will not focus on these problems; rather it will concentrate on one very important development, the growth of modern political party machinery after 1867, and will suggest how the growth of party machines has helped to destroy the parliamentary independence of MPs.

The Price of Franchise

The process of democratization and liberalization of Canadian politics, in particular the extension of the vote to the whole adult population, and the growth of disciplined political parties, has led to profound changes within the House of Commons. The most fundamental change is the loss of independence of the ordinary MP.

While in 1867 many members were quite independent of political parties and voted free of party lines, a hundred years later, party discipline in the House has become an overriding considera-

Adapted from Roman R. March, *The Myth of Parliament* (Scarborough, Ontario: Prentice-Hall Canada, 1974), pp. 4-13. By permission of publisher.

tion. The disappearance of the loosely organized parties which dotted the political scene in 1867, and their replacement with disciplined, mass parties in the twentieth century, has led to the strengthening of the cabinet against Parliament. More recently the cabinet has been in danger of becoming the servant of the Prime Minister.

Concern about the nature of the parliamentary system is not confined to Canada. There is a substantial body of critical comment on the British Parliament itself. For example, the very titles of the commentaries and studies on this topic reveal the disquiet that exists: *What's Wrong with Parliament?*, *Can Parliament Survive?*, *Parliament in Danger!*, *Has Parliament a Future?* Critical research into the American congressional system is even more voluminous.

One of the most insightful studies, indeed a prophetic work, on the problems democratization of the political process would impose on the parliamentary system, was written by Moisei Ostrogorski, who studied the development of mass political parties in the United States and Britain in the last two decades of the nineteenth century.[1] In this major study, Ostrogorski argued that the adoption of universal suffrage would lead to oligarchic control of political parties, manipulation of the electorate, and a blurring of ideological differences between political parties. Moreover, the expansion of the suffrage would lead inevitably to a substantial decline in the political monopoly of the traditional families of aristocrats or "notables." This decline of aristocratic dominance in the House and cabinet would result in part from the structural factors associated with large-scale political organization, or party machines. That is, the very necessity to create large-scale political organizations to "get out the vote" would make most forms of independent political activity not rooted in organization utopian.

Growth of Party Organization

His prophecies have come true in Canada. Here political party power and discipline have increased in the past century, with a resulting decline in numbers of the political aristocracy who once dominated Parliament. Mass party organizations have been created in response to extensions of the suffrage. Their creation has tended to place ever greater, but not exclusive, control of nominations and election campaigns in the hands of party organizations both within and very often outside the individual constituencies. The cost of financing electoral contests has increased with the growth in the number of voters. Enormous election costs have made the individual candidate increasingly dependent on supplemental financial aid from his party. This increasing dependence on party organization has strengthened party discipline in the House of Commons so much that it has become more and more difficult for members to disobey the party line.

The basis for the social and political authority of this aristocracy was rooted in land, both in England[2] and Canada. Moreover, social and political positions were mostly honorary, carrying no salary, and were performed out of a sense of *noblesse oblige*. The aristocracy undertook, both in England and Canada, the gratuitous discharge of all the important functions of local and national government, and the administration of justice. One of the major consequences was that they cut the ground from under the feet of the lawyers in the sphere of public life. This contrasted sharply with the experience of the United States, where after the American Revolution the aristocracy was abhorred in principle and in practice. In the United States, as a multitude of studies have illustrated, the lawyers dominated these functions at all levels of government,[3] while in England, Scandinavia, and the "white" Commonwealth countries, there has been more participation by traditional elites.[4]

Apprenticeship of MPs

Since both local and federal government in Canada were controlled by members of the same aristocratic class, federal MPs tended to have served a long apprenticeship in local government. This apprenticeship tested and weeded out the less able and promoted the more talented political leaders. When the aristocratic class declined, so that its power was shared with other classes or groups, there was a parallel decline in preparation for public service.

In addition, increasing specialization of functions and offices at the local level in this century has tended to block aspirants to political office. This increase in specialization has meant that most local political and administrative offices have become full-time positions with substantial salaries.[5]

It is important to note that very often the attempts of "reform" movements to take "politics" out of local government in the name of "better government" can cut off aspirants to high political office from the valuable training so often acquired in local politics. For example, reforms of the Poor Laws have diminished the importance of the unpaid volunteer in this major area of local government. The creation of paid administrators in public (i.e. state controlled) health and other fields, with local officials controlled by other officials in remote provincial head offices, deprived the notables of still more of their scope in local public life, and of their opportunities of daily contact with the population in capacities other than purely political.[6]

To summarize the argument to this point, under an aristocratic/rural form of social/political life, the aristocracy controls almost all elective and voluntary positions and performs them gratuitously from a sense of *noblesse oblige.* Consequently, since so many of these men stand for and are elected to Parliament, MPs undergo considerable training in public service at all levels of government. But as the tasks of local government become rationalized and expand under the impact of industrialization and mass politics, and as full-time, salaried employees take over tasks formerly performed voluntarily, the dominant aristocratic class becomes cut off from its roots in local social and political life. That is, social and political life become differentiated—with predicatable consequences.

The reduction of the responsibility, independence and dignity of the men elected to the House of Commons has impaired the relationship implicit in cabinet government of the members with their party leaders. For example, members no longer revolt easily against those who lead them. The balance of authority between leaders and led, which once ensured the working of government and preserved the freedom of the House, no longer exists. This equilibrium is now destroyed in favor of the leaders. Formerly, when a substantial part of the whole House was recruited from the same social class, the leader was only *primus inter pares.* Now he is a general in command of an army. The leader now responds to what he feels the voters want, not what MPs want. The voters are loyal to the leader, not their MP. Thanks to radio, television and the press, the leader can communicate directly with the voter if challenged by a recalcitrant Commons. Elections have become personal plebiscites. MPs who don't toe the line are deprived of party support and must come to heel if they want to be re-elected.[7]

The Case for Mass Parties

A counter argument can be made. For example, it can be claimed that parties at least serve to organize and educate newly franchised groups of usually uninformed voters. The earlier type of aristocratic party or faction, based on individual representation, could not possibly do this because it lacked expertise, finance and numerous workers. The new mass parties also offer opportunities for upward mobility for members of the less favored classes. To some extent parties are able to represent choices between competing interpretations of the role of the state in social life.

The new mass political parties won their strong position partly through their psychological services in organizing and educating the newly franchised and uninformed voter. They also came to control the strategic function of nominating candidates and carried on many of the dreary election functions such as getting out the vote, licking stamps, telephoning and so on. These require hundreds of workers in each constituency for each party. Parties, at times, clarified the alternatives of policies available to governments in power, through policy conventions. Parties could secure dispensations, privileges, contracts, and assist individuals and groups in difficulties with the courts, government bureaucracies and the like. These functions were developed informally as a by-product of the parties' struggles to secure control of government power.[8]

Nor is the power of a mass party in a universal suffrage democracy necessarily unlimited. For example, if there are two strong rival party machines operating under rules which maximize the rights of others to take over legitimate sources of authoritative power, then each should be able to check any authoritarian tendency of the other party. Many scholars have raised this concept of mutual and equally balanced opposites to an almost universal principle of democratic organization.[9]

If the argument is valid that it is more functional for democratic systems to have democracy *between* parties rather than *within* them then the threat of oligarchy must take on secondary importance.

In Canada, the United Kingdom and the United States, for example, recent research on the role of mass parties reveals that they may countenance enforced legislative changes in the rules of electoral life which alter the environment in which they compete for votes, such as legislation which enforces equality of opportunity for all major parties. However, parties abhor any attempts to regulate the relationship between the elected member of a party and its leaders.[10] Consequently, any analysis of the "iron law of oligarchy" must include an analytical distinction between (1) the mass party organization, (2) the leadership of the parliamentary party, (3) the individual members of the parliamentary party and (4) the leaders of the mass organization. The many permutations and combinations of such relationships lessen the likelihood that the mass party organization would inevitably dominate the power relationships among all four groups. Robert T. McKenzie has examined only one of the many networks of relationships.[11] He suggests that the parliamentary leaders in Britain have been able to maintain much of their independence of the mass organization, but he neglects an equal if not more important relationship, that of the ordinary parliamentary members and their leaders.

Disappearance of Independents

McKenzie ignores those propositions which are crucial for any understanding of the evolution of modern parties operating under the conventions of parliamentary systems. One of the propositions was that the mass party system logically and systematically eliminates the Independent candidate and makes most official party candidates subservient to the party leaders in the House and to the regular organization. Although the chief parliamentary leaders themselves may have been able to avoid becoming subservient to the mass party organization, as McKenzie has convincingly shown, yet the ordinary member is exposed to a double form of control, that of his constituency association and the cabinet. This control can limit his ability to function as an effective MP by utilizing his initiative, expertise and talents to the full. Oligarchy exists, despite McKenzie's evidence, but it is an oligarchy of the Prime Minister and the cabinet—which he chooses himself—over the individual MP.

One other major point needs to be made. In 1867 each MP represented on the average about 750 voters. By 1967 the average MP represented 45 000 voters, and one had 190 000 constituents. It is an expensive process to win and maintain support among that number of people. The costs are far beyond the resources of all but the well-to-do. But even for a wealthy candidate who could afford to pay all his own election expenses, the task of winning and holding a seat without the support of a large political party is all but hopeless. During an election all the great communications networks, press, radio and television, focus on the major parties. Independents, wealthy or not, are ignored by the press, and don't exist as far as TV and radio are concerned. They simply cannot make themselves heard. Nor can they claim that a vote for them would help in any direct way to settle the highly publicized and artificially exciting conflict among the major parties. But it is not only the Independents who have been eclipsed in the modern electoral battle. In a sense all individual candidates, irrespective of party, have become faceless. Most experts now agree that a particular candidate, whatever his merits, rarely adds or subtracts more than 5 percent of the votes his party would win, regardless of who had been nominated.[12]

This has helped to eliminate the "notables" from the parliamentary parties. They are not needed. The mass party has come to secure close and continuous supervision over the activities of the individual member of the legislature.

NOTES

1. MOISEI OSTROGORSKI, *Democracy and the Organization of Political Parties*, 2 vols., S.M. Lipset ed. (New York: Anchor Books, Doubleday and Company, 1964).

2. OSTROGORSKI, *op cit.*, p. 2.

3. HAROLD D. LASSWELL AND M.S. McDOUGAL, "Legal Education and Public Policy," in Lasswell, *The Analysis of Political Behaviour* (London: Routledge, Kegan Paul, Ltd., 1948), p. 27: ". . .the lawyer is today. . .the one indispensable advisor of every responsible policy-maker of our society. . . ." See also, DONALD R. MATTHEWS, *The Social Background of Political Decision Makers* (New York: Random House, 1954), pp. 30-2.

4. See J.F.S. ROSS, *Parliamentary Representation*, 2nd ed. (London: 1949), for England. For Canada, see NORMAN WARD, *The Canadian House of Commons* (Toronto: University of Toronto Press, 1949).

5. AVERY LEISERSON, *Parties and Politics, An Institutional and Behavioral Approach* (New York: Alfred A. Knopf, 1958), p. 99, writes: "Elective public office is an expensive and uncertain career. . . .Full-time wage and salary employees find little opportunity to develop a political career as a sideline.. . .This rigidity, or lack of horizontal mobility, between vertical career lines is an important problem in democratic leadership recruitment, as compared with historical aristocracies in which members of the ruling class moved freely between government, church, army, business, and the professions, but cut themselves off to recruitment from below."

6. OSTROGORSKI, *op. cit.*, pp. 157-68.

7. OSTROGORSKI, *op cit.*, pp. 315-6.

8. A. LEISERSON, *op. cit.*, p. 61.

9. SEYMOUR MARTIN LIPSET, MARTIN TROW AND JAMES COLEMAN, *Union Democracy: What Makes Democracy Work in Labor Unions and Other Organizations?* (Garden City, New York: Anchor Books, Doubleday and Company, 1962).

10. V.O. KEY, JR., *Politics, Parties and Pressure Groups*, 4th ed. (New York:

Thomas Y. Crowell Company, 1958), pp. 434-95, and 531-65. BERNARD CRICK, *The Reform of Parliament* (New York: Doubleday, Anchor Edition, 1965). ROBERT T. McKENZIE, *British Political Parties* (New York: Frederick A. Praeger, Publisher, 1963).

11. McKENZIE, *op. cit.*

12. DAVID AND RICHARD ROSE, *The British General Election of 1959* (Macmillan, 1960); J. BLONDEL, *Voters, Parties and Leaders* (Penguin, 1963).

The Legislative Defeat of the Clark Government

RONALD G. LANDES

A series of largely unexpected political events between May and December 1979 resulted in the dissolution of the Canadian Parliament on 14 December and the issue of election writs for 18 February, 1980. Canada's thirty-second general election aborted the Progressive Conservative's nine-month old Government, their first taste of national power in sixteen years, and re-established a majority Liberal Government under the resurrected leadership of Pierre Trudeau.

In many respects the election was unnecessary: a series of political miscalculations by the Clark Government precipitated the February contest. Due primarily to individual and party inexperience with governing, it misread the nature of its 1979 minority electoral victory, the continuing basis of its popular support and the willingness of the opposition parties to force a new election. Singly, such miscalculations would not have proved lethal but their combination doomed the survival of that rarest of political happenings in Canadian politics—a national Conservative Administration.

The Defeat of the Government in Parliament

The significance of the parliamentary defeat of the Clark Government on the night of 13 December 1979 can only be appreciated in

Adapted from Ronald G. Landes, "The Canadian General Election of 1980," *Parliamentary Affairs*, Vol. XXXIV, No. 1 (Winter, 1981): 95-109. By permission of publisher and author.

the context of previous minority Canadian administrations. In contrast to Britain, where the "first-past-the-post" electoral system has usually produced majority governments in the postwar era, minority governments in Canada have been a common outgrowth of the confluence of the regional nature of partisan support with the plurality electoral formula. The last six federal elections have witnessed a regular alternation between minority (1965, 1972, 1979) and majority Governments (1968, 1974, 1980). In the last quarter century Canada has experienced six minority and four majority administrations.

In addition to their frequency, a second characteristic of minority Governments in Canada has been their relative stability in office: in recent decades they have rarely feared their imminent demise in Parliament. Several reinforcing factors help to explain such a pattern of behaviour. First, there is a feeling among Canadian politicians that voters do not like to be sent to the polls any more often than is absolutely necessary, particularly during the winter months. Second, throughout the 1960s and 1970s the smaller parliamentary parties (New Democratic Party and Social Credit) feared being "squeezed" between the two major parties (Liberals and Conservatives) in any attempt by either major party to turn a minority Government into a majority Administration through victory in a new election. (Thus, after supporting the Liberal minority for a year and a half, the NDP saw its parliamentary representation reduced by half in the 1974 election.) Third, several of the minority Governments in Canada have been within a few seats of an actual majority thus creating the view that they could govern "as if they had a majority." In such a situation, they could depend on the absence of some opposition members to give them a working majority in Parliament. Fourth, minority Governments have demonstrated a practical ability to stay in office until they manufactured their own defeat in Parliament (i.e., the Trudeau Liberals in 1974) or requested a dissolution from the Governor General (i.e., the Liberals in 1968). Either technique allows a governing minority Administration to return to the electorate at a time of its own choosing and with the issues calculated to enhance its prospects of electoral victory. As a result, in both 1968 and 1974 the previous minority Liberal Governments successfully returned to power with legislative majorities. These practical political factors which have made Canadian minority governments relatively stable were significantly reinforced by the outcome of the Constitutional Crisis of 1968. A minority Liberal Government, defeated on the third reading of a tax bill, managed to retain power by subsequently passing a motion that its defeat did not constitute a vote of no-confidence. Such a precedent was assumed to have altered the status of Canadian minority governments.

Given these considerations, it was not unreasonable for the new Prime Minister, Joe Clark, to announce shortly after his 1979 victory that the Conservatives intended to govern "as if they had a majority." An immediate outgrowth of this attitude was the decision not to open Parliament until autumn—a delay which was the longest in Canadian political history and one which proved to be the beginning of a series of political mistakes which would eventually bring down his Government. The delay was based on the view that having been out of power for sixteen years, time was needed for the new ministers to learn their jobs, develop specific policy proposals, and gain control of the bureaucracy and levers of power in Ottawa. However, the delay in opening Parliament helped to create an image of indecision on the part of the new Government.

A second miscalculation concerned the willingness of the Clark Government to honour its election promises and its inept handling of several initial policy problems. Finance Minister John Crosbie, at a news conference at the end of July, stated that "since the people voted against Trudeau and not for the Conservatives, according to the press, I conclude we have a free hand to do what we think is best for the country." In its first few months in office the Government became linked to an image of "flip-flops" on major policy initiatives, epitomised by the Embassy Affair. In an appeal to the Jewish voters in several marginal constituencies in Toronto during the dying days of the 1979 election campaign, Clark had promised, if elected, to move the Canadian Embassy to Jerusalem. In his first news conference after being sworn in as Prime Minister, he announced his intentions to proceed with the move immediately, although no specific dates were mentioned. The ensuing outcry from the Arab states, along with adverse editorial and public opinion, forced a postponement of the move. However, the damage had been done in that the Embassy Affair helped to generate the view of an inconsistent and incompetent Ottawa Administration.

A third set of problems for the new Government concerned the composition and structure of the Cabinet. With only two elected Members of Parliament from Quebec, Joe Clark dipped into the appointed Senate to bolster the number of his Quebec representatives in the Cabinet. While this was an acceptable Canadian practice, the lack of major Quebec spokesmen in the federal Cabinet served to undermine the perceived ability of the new Administration to deal effectively with the separatist demands of the Quebec provincial government. A further problem of Cabinet construction emerged when Joe Clark decided, on the basis of the British experience, to make a distinction between an inner and outer Cabinet. Such a distinction overloaded a number of key ministers of the inner Cabinet and left those in the outer Cabinet all too aware of their publicly acknowledged lack of influence. The distinction was a failure, for the quite simple reason that the basis of Cabinet selection in Britain differs markedly from that in Canada, where the overriding consideration from 1867 onward, has been the principle of regional and provincial representation. Yet another problem resulted from the long years the Conservative Party had spent in opposition: few members had any political-administrative experience. Moreover, a number of long-time backbenchers had been passed over for Cabinet appointments which resulted in internal caucus problems, typified when one Conservative from Alberta refused to sit in the House on crucial votes of confidence.

A fourth major problem concerned the Government's misreading of the nature of its electoral support in the 1979 election and its level of public support from May to December. It failed adequately to grasp the idea that the voters had defeated Trudeau and the Liberals rather than electing the Conservatives to implement their campaign promises. As a result, the Tories began to proceed with some unpopular policies, such as the return to the private sector of Canada's public oil company, Petro-Canada. Moreover, during the summer of 1979 the public opinion polls revealed that the new Government would have no initial "honeymoon" period with the electorate: when Parliament opened on 9 October, 1979 the Conservatives still trailed the defeated Liberals in popular support. The Clark Government seemed unwilling to accept the fact that it was a minority Administration with minority, and probably declining, popular support. Thus, as Ottawa and the country prepared for the opening of the first session of the thirty-second Parliament, the Government found itself with less public support than the opposition Liberals, with an image of "flip-flops" on major policy issues, and with problems of Cabinet composition. The party strengths in the House in October had changed only modestly since the May election. Former Prime Minister John Diefenbaker had died, while former Liberal minister Don Jamieson had returned to the provincial arena: thus two vacancies existed. One Social Credit member, Richard Janelle, had defected to the

Conservatives. The distribution of seats in October was as follows: Progressive Conservatives 136, Liberals 113, New Democratic Party 26, Social Credit 5.

Using a common practice from both previous federal and provincial minority Administrations, the Clark Government, in an attempt to redress slightly its chance of defeat in Parliament, reappointed the Liberal Speaker of the previous Parliament. Since the Speaker can only vote in case of a tie, and would be unlikely to use such a vote to bring down the Government, the total effective strength of the Liberals became 112. Likewise, the Deputy Speaker selected was also a Liberal. Being within a few seats of a majority also led the Tories to attempt to "create a majority" through defections, appointments and by-elections. Concerted attacks on the Social Credit group were evident, resulting in the conversion of Richard Janelle to the Government (and his later appointment as a Parliamentary Secretary with additional salary). Other members of the party were rumoured to be on the verge of defection. At one point Social Credit leader Fabien Roy announced that his "caucus was not for sale" and requested a Royal Canadian Mounted Police investigation of Tory attempts to raid his group membership. Senator Martial Asselin, one of the few Cabinet representatives from Quebec, announced that he would attempt to recruit both Social Credit and Liberal backbenchers from Quebec into the Tory party or open vacancies in the House by their appointment to various government jobs. Senator Asselin asserted that the Conservatives would have majority "within six months." Roch LaSalle, Minister of Supply and Services and one of two elected Conservatives from Quebec, announced after the conversion of Janelle to the Tory caucus that "the hunt continues." However, this blatant attempt to create a majority shortly before the opening of Parliament failed to produce any further miraculous conversions and certainly did little to bolster the faltering public image of the Clark Government.

The survival of the Tory Government in Parliament thus depended on its ability to gather the support of the small Social Credit group or the abstention of a handful of Liberal or New Democratic Party legislators. The likelihood of the Conservatives gaining such parliamentary support from any particular grouping varied to a considerable degree, depending on the opposition party's placement on the left-right political spectrum, past experiences of political cooperation, current policy views and expectations of public support if a new election were to be forced. As a general ideological characterisation of Canadian parties, the following placement would seem to be appropriate: the New Democratic Party, as a social-democratic party, would appear on the left; the Liberals would appear in the centre, usually on the left-of-centre but flexible enough to move to the centre-right if political conditions required it; the Progressive Conservatives as a centre-right party; and Social Credit on the right of the political spectrum.

Given this ideological positioning, the Government could expect little, if any, explicit support from the New Democratic Party. Their programmes clearly indicated fundamental disagreement on the major issues facing Canada. Moreover, the New Democratic Party's support for the minority Liberal Government of Pierre Trudeau between 1972 and 1974 still rankled among some members of the Conservative group: many felt that the Conservatives, who had been just two seats short of the Liberals after the 1972 election, had deserved a chance to govern. Thus, an adversary relationship between the two parties was to be expected. However, the New Democratic Party did fear being squeezed between the major parties in any new election: the most the Government could hope for would be abstentions by part of the NDP on important votes.

The best Tory hope for consistent support appeared to be the small Social Credit group. Although both parties occupied positions on the right of the political spectrum, Social Credit support would have less to do with ideology than with the expected political consequences of another election. Since it burst onto the federal political scene in 1962, Social Credit had usually lost ground in terms of seats won in each ensuing election, had not elected a Member of Parliament outside of Quebec since 1965, had faced leadership problems and internal dissent after the death of its former leader Réal Caouette, and had declined in the public opinion polls to such an extent that a new election might wipe out its few remaining seats in Quebec. During previous minority Administrations because of such practical considerations, Social Credit had usually supported the Government of the day, perhaps best illustrated by its vote in the Constitutional Crisis of 1968. In any election campaign it was under attack from both major parties: the Liberals wanting to recapture the Quebec seats held by Social Credit, the Conservatives hoping to acquire its constituencies as a beachhead for greater Quebec representation. Thus, fear of attack and the likely results of a new election appeared to make Social Credit amenable to supporting the Clark Government.

A major incentive that the Government held over Social Credit caucus was its ability to grant the small group official party status in the House of Commons. Such recognition would allow the party to receive research funds, additional salary for their leader, greater inclusion in the business of Parliament and its own party caucus room. However, under House rules official recognition required a party membership of twelve, although the Government of the day could make exceptions to the rule with majority support in the House. After the 1974 election Social Credit had been granted such status, even though it only had eleven members. In June, 1980 the Prime Minister, after a meeting with Social Credit leader Fabien Roy, announced that it would not be receiving official party status, a view subsequently confirmed when Social Credit was denied a position on the Committee of Selection on the opening day of Parliament (by a vote of 247 to 6). However, it was widely assumed that this was a bargaining ploy of the Tory Government, to be used later in order to ensure Social Credit support when it was most needed. This denial of status, along with the earlier defection of Janelle and the attempted raid on the remaining group, certainly did little to create a cooperative arrangement between the two parties in Parliament.

The possibility of support from the Liberal party was tenable, although likely to be indirect rather than openly declared. As the party with the largest vote in the 1979 election and in order to maintain its dominance as the leading opposition party, the Liberals could not openly back the Government without damaging their own credibility. However, it was expected that the Liberals would allow the Government to survive through Liberal absenteeism in the House. The Liberals did not want an immediate election, at least not until the question of their leadership was resolved. After having served as Prime Minister since 1968 and having fought four national election campaigns, Pierre Trudeau, now sixty years of age, was seen as the departing leader of the Liberal party. Trudeau had indicated his intention to stay on as leader until after the expected independence referendum in Quebec (contemplated for the spring of 1980). More important, the Liberals had lost crucial support in English-Canada in the 1979 election. Pundits prophesied that they could never win again with Pierre Trudeau as their leader. Internally, the Liberal group contained an important faction, composed of many members who had survived the 1979 defeat in English-Canada, which felt that a new leader was essential. Thus, it seemed logical to conclude that the Liberals would not force another election on the country.

Reinforcing such a view were statements made by the major Liberal leaders concerning the party's role in the forthcoming Parliament. In their first parliamentary group meeting after the 1979 defeat, the Liberals decided not to go all out to defeat the Clark Government. Pierre Trudeau warned against a "reactive opposition" and over the next few months they maintained an extremely low profile. Moreover, internal problems were evident in the party. Senator Jean Marchand, former Liberal Cabinet minister and confidant of Pierre Trudeau, resigned as president of the federal party in August 1979, citing internal organisational problems. A group of dissident Liberals organised a conference on the Political Process and the Liberal Party which was held in early October and to which neither Pierre Trudeau nor other major figures in the Parliamentary group were invited. This meeting was widely viewed as an initial attempt at Liberal party renewal, which could only mean an eventual challenge to the leadership of Pierre Trudeau.

The first month in the new Parliament upheld the view that none of the opposition parties really wanted an election, since on any crucial vote either Social Credit supported the Government or enough Liberals were absent to prevent the Government's defeat. After an important no-confidence motion on 7 November, on which Social Credit supported the Government, the Speaker began to recognise Social Credit members in the debates, a move which, although short of official party status, was done, according to Conservative House Leader Walter Baker, to "ensure some form of peace in the House."

The Government's position, however, became less tenable on 19 November when by-elections were held for the two vacant seats, both of which the Government lost. The defeat in Newfoundland (Burin-St. George) was expected as the Liberals had held that constituency since Newfoundland entered the Confederation in 1949. However, the loss in Saskatchewan (Prince Albert) was damaging, since the seat had been held for the Tories for 26 years by former Prime Minister John Diefenbaker. The addition of two opposition members cut the Government's possible majority with Social Credit support, to one vote. The Prime Minister indicated that these losses did not mean that his Government would call new elections: "Our policy is to govern—we'll see what the other parties do." However, election fever was evident for several days, until the sudden and unexpected decision by Pierre Trudeau on 21 November to retire as leader of the Liberal Party. Trudeau announced his intention to resign as soon as the party could choose a replacement, with a national party leadership convention suggested for March 1980. Election fever quickly dissipated: as Stanley Knowles, New Democratic Party House Leader, put it, "that clears the air— there will be no election for the next few months." Given this turn of events, it was assumed that no election would be forced by any of the opposition parties, that Social Credit had lost its bargaining power with the Clark Government, and that the Conservative Government would not force an election on the Liberals until their leadership selection process was completed. Major figures, both inside and outside of the Liberal group, began to announce publicly their intention to seek or not to seek the leadership of their party.

Within weeks, however, the Clark Government was defeated in Parliament. To explain such an event several major factors need to be considered. First, it was quickly becoming evident, particularly after the Gallup Poll on 3 December, 1979 that the Clark Government's public support was dropping rapidly—that the Government could be defeated in a new election. It showed the Liberals with 47 per cent, compared to 28 per cent for the Conservatives, 23 per cent for the New Democratic Party, and less than 2 per cent for Social Credit. The two parties which could defeat the Government in Parliament were receiving increased support in the electorate (Liberals up 7 per cent over their 1979 vote, the New Democratic Party up 5 per cent over their 1979 vote). The political will of the two main opposition parties to defeat the Government in Parliament was certainly bolstered by their expectation of possible electoral success.

A second factor which increased the will of the opposition parties resulted from their relationship with the Tories in the House. Social Credit continued to be denied party status and from the Government's view had lost its bargaining power. The New Democratic Party was still opposed on policy grounds. The Liberals were faced with the unhappy choice either of swallowing their considerable pride and allowing the Clark Government to stay in power even when they trailed the Liberals by 20 percentage points in the polls or of forcing a new election with their leadership in a state of change. The Tory treatment of the opposition parties is best illustrated by the Government's use of closure to quicken the movement of their Mortgage Deductibility Scheme through the House. The resort to closure is relatively rare in Canadian politics: its use on 10 December, 1979 clearly indicated the unwillingness of the minority Conservative Government to compromise in any way with the opposition.

One day later the Government presented its first budget: it quickly became the rallying point for election speculation and proved to be the proximate cause of the Government's defeat. Finance Minister John Crosbie described the budget as "tough," one that would ask the Canadian taxpayer to bear "short term pain for long term gain." It was certainly not designed as an election document. The budget made major and immediate increases in energy costs, exemplified by the eighteen cent a gallon excise tax on petrol. It also claimed to set Canada on a course of energy self-sufficiency by 1990. The growth of government expenditures was to be held to less than ten per cent a year, which in "real terms" meant stabilising the size of government. Major reductions in the yearly government deficits were projected over the next four years. Such a budget clearly indicated that the Conservatives were acting not only "as if they had a majority," but also as if there was no possible combination of circumstances which might coalesce the opposition parties in Parliament and bring the Government down.

The Government's apparent invulnerability was put to the test forthwith. On 12 December the Liberals introduced a motion that "this House condemns the Government for its budget which will place an unfair and unnecessary burden of higher gasoline prices, higher fuel oil prices, and higher taxes on middle and lower income Canadians." The New Democratic Party offered an amendment which added: ". . .and this House unreservedly condemns the Government for its outright betrayal of its election promises to lower interest rates, to cut taxes, and to stimulate the growth of the Canadian economy, without a mandate from the Canadian people for such a reversal." On the night of 13 December, with Social Credit abstaining and with the combined vote of the New Democratic Party and Liberals, amendment carried by a vote of 139 to 133. Perceiving the opposition parties as individually unwilling to contest an election, ignoring fairly evident danger signals (refusal of the Liberals to accept "pairing" before the crucial House vote), and unwilling to compromise in order to postpone impending defeat (i.e. the overtures from the opposition parties to delay the vote were apparently discounted), the Government convinced itself that even if it were defeated on the budget and even if it was trailing twenty percentage points in the polls, that an election would return it to office. By such gross miscalculations do Governments die.

Running for the Red Chamber: Sam Bronfman's Senate Bid

PETER C. NEWMAN

For a man whose intellect and energies had been devoted to a life-long quest for power, attempting to enter the Canadian Senate seemed an astonishing and uncharacteristic ambition. "I suppose Sam was seeking public acknowledgement for what he'd accomplished," speculates Noah Torno. "The problems of his family's early history always plagued him and he probably was trying to tell the world, 'I don't want to be lumped in with my brothers!' Plus which, there was also the question of being Jewish. He always wanted to be first."

A more likely explanation was that, shrewd as he was, Bronfman never deluded himself that becoming a senator would endow him with any real influence. Instead, what he wanted, quite simply, was the title. He felt that elevation to the Red Chamber would crown his name with the mark of legitimacy, a sure sign of acceptance into the upper strata of his country's society.

Within the international arena where he liked to operate, being able to call himself Senator Samuel Bronfman would have been something of a coup. Sam once told J.M. McAvity, "Think of what an impression it would make if I was known as Senator Bronfman in the United States." His conviction was bolstered by noting the respect that automatically accrued to his friend Senator Jacob Javits of New York, who often spoke in hushed tones of the U.S. Senate as "the most exclusive club in the world." The fact that the American and Canadian senates shared nothing except a common appellation bothered Bronfman not a whit. Who would ever know the difference if Senator Bronfman and his wife were registering at the George V in Paris or at Claridge's in London?

Having set his sights, Bronfman proceeded toward his objective in the most direct manner possible: by trying to buy a Canadian

Adapted from Peter C. Newman, *Bronfman Dynasty: The Rothschilds of the New World* (Toronto: Seal Books, McClelland and Stewart-Bantam Limited, 1979), pp. 47-60. By permission of publisher and author.

senatorship. It's difficult to calculate how much he spent in this quest, but $1.2 million is probably not an unreasonable total, because he contributed about $120 000 a year to Canadian political treasuries for more than a decade.[1] His chief agent in these transactions was Maxwell Henderson, who later became Canada's most controversial auditor-general. "As the treasurer of Seagram's, it was my lot to disburse the party funds," Henderson recalls, "and thereby hangs many a tale, because when you're donating the kind of money Mr. Sam was giving away, you expect something in return, and what he expected was to end up as a senator. That was his great goal." Ever the methodical accountant, Henderson not only kept records of all the donations but, to Sam's amazement, also actually managed to obtain signed receipts for the bank notes as they were changing hands. "I just wanted to keep the books right. So long as I had to distribute the haul money, as we called it, I wanted to know at least the name of the gentleman getting it. You don't want to have any misunderstandings later. They always signed."[2]

The politicians welcomed his cash but made no move to fulfil Mr. Sam's dream. Among others, he had Senators Donat Raymond and Armand Daigle and the well-connected Montreal lawyer Philippe Brais pushing his cause within the Liberal Party's court. At the same time, Brig. Beverley Matthews, an enormously influential Conservative corporation lawyer from Toronto, was lobbying on his behalf. C. D. Howe, then declining in authority but still a driving power in the Liberal Party, claimed to be supporting him, but he got so tired of Bronfman's assaults that he began to hint it was really Jimmy Gardiner, the all-powerful Grit ambassador from the Prairies, who was vetoing the appointment because of the Bronfmans' early exploits in Saskatchewan. Sol Kanee, a Winnipeg lawyer who was a family friend and hailed from Melville, the Saskatchewan town that sent Gardiner to Parliament, was immediately enlisted to help sway the recalcitrant Agriculture Minister. "One day I marched into Gardiner's Parliament Hill office," he recalls, "and asked Jimmy if he was really against Sam going to the Senate. When he told me he wasn't, I dialled C. D. Howe's private number and said, 'I've got Jimmy right here, and he's not opposing it.' But nothing ever happened; they were all just fooling Sam to try and get more of his money."

At one point, Bronfman became so frustrated that he confronted Howe with a direct threat: if he wasn't made a senator, he would cut off all contributions to the Liberal Party. The great C. D.

fixed Bronfman with a long, steely gaze through the foliage of his
magnificent eyebrows, then smiled a sweet smile. "It doesn't matter, Sam," he said. "We'll just raise the excise tax on liquor another
10 per cent and get it that way." Then he gently asked the distiller
to leave his office.

Sam Bronfman's main problem was that he never learned to appreciate the subtlety of the process in which he was involved. Any
number of senators had purchased their appointment by contributing to party coffers. But while senatorships might well be for
sale, they could not appear to be bought.

The idea of naming a Jew to the Canadian Senate first bubbled
up during Mackenzie King's time when Archie Freiman, founder
of the Ottawa department store, was quietly sounded out on an appointment. As soon as Bronfman heard about the approach, he
launched such a vicious counter-lobby to have himself appointed
that the Prime Minister backed off the whole idea. "If those Jews
can't make up their minds, I won't appoint any of them," King told
one associate at the time.

Louis St. Laurent, King's successor, wanted to celebrate the establishment of Israel as an independent state by announcing the
appointment of Jews to the Superior Court of Quebec and the
Quebec Court of Appeal. His choices were Harry Batshaw, a
Montreal lawyer (who was elevated to the Superior Court in 1950),
and Lazarus Phillips, who wasn't interested in a judgeship at the
time.[3] Bronfman used the occasion to renew his lobbying efforts in
Ottawa, but St. Laurent felt that Bronfman should not be named a
senator for the very reason that made the Montreal distiller want
the appointment so badly: because such a public elevation would,
once and for all, bring down the curtain on his family's early history, displaying retroactive absolution on a scale the Prime Minister
of Canada was not willing to grant.

At about this time, M. J. Coldwell, the CCF Leader, embarrassed
Bronfman by demanding in the House of Commons to know why
the Government had invited someone with his "questionable background" to a state dinner at Government House. Worst of all,
when Sam briefly tried to lobby on his own behalf by joining the
Ottawa cocktail circuit, he found himself the object of some unwanted attention. Wherever he appeared, Clifford Harvison, then
an assistant commissioner of the Royal Canadian Mounted Police
but much earlier the RCMP corporal who had arrested Bronfman
during the Montreal conspiracy proceedings of the middle thirties,
would noiselessly join any group of guests that included the distil-

ler and stand there quizzically staring at him. When Bronfman moved on, Harvison would follow and repeat the treatment.

Pressure was meanwhile building up in the Liberal Party to name Canada's first Jewish federal cabinet minister. The obvious choice was David Croll, who had followed three successful terms as mayor of Windsor by becoming Ontario's first Jewish minister in the stormy administration of Mitch Hepburn, the Liberal premier who took office in 1934. Croll resigned in 1937 in protest against the provincial government's refusal to recognize the Oshawa auto-mobile workers' union, declaring, "I would rather march with the workers than ride with General Motors." His reformist tendencies, distinguished war record and a decade as an effective member of the House of Commons seemed to make him the ideal choice. Afraid that he might be shuffled off to the Senate instead, Croll became an avid advocate of the Bronfman candidacy. But C. D. Howe once again turned out to be pivotal in the final decision. St. Laurent had granted his crusty Trade and Commerce Minister an informal power of veto over most government appointments. When Howe came out unequivocally against both Croll's becoming a member of the Cabinet and Bronfman's becoming a member of the Senate, only one solution remained: Croll would be named Canada's first Jewish senator.

Sam Bronfman and a caucus of his senior executives were con-ferring in Seagram's boardroom on the morning of July 28, 1955, when Robina Shanks, his secretary, brought in the bad news. Max Henderson, who was there, remembers Sam exploding, parading about the room in a kind of military mourner's slow march, wail-ing, "I'm the King of the Jews! It should have been mine . . . I bought it! I paid for it! Those treacherous bastards did me in!"

Trying to turn his defeat by Ottawa's Liberal establishment into only a temporary setback, Bronfman calculated that if the Liberals were willing to name one Jew to the upper chamber, they might name another. They did, but it took thirteen years of political in-fighting, and Sam was not their ultimate choice.

Out of Sam Bronfman's bizarre race for the Senate grew the most bitter feud of his life, with the man who had become one of his best friends and closest associates: Lazarus Phillips. The two had first met in 1924, when Bronfman moved his operations to Montreal. It was Phillips, then the family's chief legal adviser, who masterminded the winning court strategy against the great RCMP assault of 1935 and set up the family trusts into which Seagram's huge profits would eventually flow.

For most of three decades, Lazarus Phillips served as the Bronfmans' visible face and public voice. He was their chief go-between. He had the manners and the contacts, the social acceptability and political prestige to which the brothers could only aspire. With his brains and their money, he achieved a degree of political, legal and corporate clout unique among Canadian lawyers.

Lazarus Phillips, now in his early eighties, was the most influential Canadian Jew of his generation. His maternal uncle, Hersh Cohen, had been a great Talmudic scholar and Canada's chief orthodox rabbi, while another uncle (Lazarus Cohen) became one of the wealthiest Jews in Canada in the early years of the twentieth century (second only to Sir Mortimer Davis) by dredging much of the St. Lawrence for his friend Sir Wilfrid Laurier. Phillips inherited both these mantles and wore them with considerable pride. After serving briefly in World War I as a sergeant-major with the Canadian Expeditionary Force sent into Vladivostok to help quell the Russian Revolution, Phillips joined a small Montreal law firm started by Sam Jacobs, who not long before had entered politics and married Gertrude Stein's cousin from Baltimore. The second Jew to sit in the Canadian House of Commons,[4] Jacobs carried Montreal's Cartier riding[5] through five elections in campaigns organized by Phillips, who became Jacobs's equal partner in 1923. By the time Jacobs died in 1938, Phillips had emerged as the grey eminence of Montreal's Jewish community. He built up a miniature, subarctic Tammany Hall on Montreal Island, an organization powerful enough so that *goy* Liberals from the prime minister on down had to consult him about Jewish sensibilities and appointments whenever their policies or patronage touched the region's vital two dozen ridings. Phillips ventured out publicly himself only once, when he decided to run for Cartier in a 1943 by-election caused by the death of Peter Bercovitch, who had succeeded Jacobs. But what was supposed to be a walkaway turned into a political quagmire when David Lewis of the CCF and Fred Rose, the Communist who ultimately got elected,[6] moved in to split the Jewish vote. The night he was beaten, Mackenzie King telephoned Phillips from the Citadel in Quebec City, where he was quartered, to demand, "What do you regard as the basic cause of your defeat?"

"The basic cause of my defeat," Phillips replied, "was that Mr. Rose got more votes than I did." The terse summary so delighted the verbose King that he not only forgave his friend Laz's loss but granted him more influence than ever. It was Phillips who unfroze enough funds under export control from the grip of Graham Towers, the Governor of the Bank of Canada, to finance Seagram's wartime expansion program in the United States.

Phillips's reputation in Ottawa flowed only partly from his political clout in Montreal. His large legal practice had turned him into the country's top tax expert. "All the doors were open to Laz," Max Henderson recalls. "He was a tremendous pleader of cases. He'd walk into the tax department and just dazzle them."[7]

Typical of Phillips's high-level leverage was his involvement in rearranging Canada's vote at the United Nations sessions that preceded Israel's recognition as a state. "I remember one particular occasion," Phillips recalls, "when a high officer of the Zionist Organization asked me to submit certain representations to Brooke Claxton, who was acting Secretary of State for External Affairs in the absence of Lester Pearson. At that time the foreign ministers were meeting in Paris to deliberate on the issue of the recognition of Israel, and at that particular stage the Canadian government had decided not to support such recognition. I proceeded to Ottawa and met with Claxton, who invited me to his home that evening to dine, as I happened to be in Ottawa with my wife. After we had dinner our wives retired, and Claxton asked me to state my position, which I did. In the process I didn't realize how much time had elapsed. Close to midnight, Brooke rose and telephoned Louis St. Laurent, then Prime Minister, at his home. He apologized for waking him up, but explained the urgency of the matter in view of the meeting that was to be held in Paris the next morning. After listening to my case, the Prime Minister instructed Claxton to phone Pearson in Paris, even though it was 5 A.M. French time, and ask him to change the vote to an affirmative. Mike Pearson then spoke to me on the telephone and was less than complimentary, being in a somewhat irritable mood for my having awakened him so early. In due course he forgave me when he realized the urgency of the problem."

In the spring of 1949, when the proud and confident chieftains of the Liberal Party met in secret conclave at the Chateau Laurier to plan Louis St. Laurent's first election campaign as leader, Lazarus Phillips was there, splitting up the tasks and dividing the spoils, recruiting Paul Nathanson to make a film of the new leader, being consulted and heeded on all the fine points that in those distant days turned Liberal campaigns into royal processions. At one point in the proceedings, Jack Pickersgill, special assistant to the Prime Minister and then in the flowering of his incarnation as chief guru to the Liberal Party, waddled up to Phillips, placed a comradely arm on his shoulder, and asked him, "Are you feeling all right, Laz? We've been hanging around here for three hours and you haven't raised hell with us gentiles yet!"

How sweet it was. No Jew had ever before (or since) enjoyed such intimate access to Liberal power at its very summit. Not unnaturally, Phillips hoped to press his personal priority of becoming a senator. He saw himself blocked by a unique Catch-22 situation. The Liberals by this time had abandoned what small intention they might once have had of naming Sam Bronfman to the Red Chamber; but to tell him so would have cut off their richest party fund contributor—and the most direct way of tipping their hand would have been to appoint his friend and legal counsel, Lazarus Phillips.

"Why should Laz get it?" Sam kept asking anyone who would listen. "He was a two-bit lawyer when he started working for me, and I made him a multi-millionaire." Various middlemen, notably Sol Kanee, tried persuading Sam to give up his claim. But he wouldn't hear of it. Meanwhile, Phillips was collecting other honours that had thus far eluded Sam Bronfman: on January 14, 1954, he was named a Royal Bank director and on September 12, 1966, he was asked to join Montreal's hallowed Mount Royal Club. He'd been a director of a number of companies before joining the Royal Bank board (including Montreal Trust, Montreal Life Insurance, and Mailman Corporation, an early-day conglomerate), but the bank board was the plume on the bonnet. Other corporate rewards followed—the chairmanship of Domco Industries and directorships in Brazilian Traction, Dominion Bridge, Steinberg's, Webb & Knapp (Canada), Great Universal Stores of Canada, Foundation Company of Canada, and Trizec among them. As his reputation grew, Phillips somehow managed to fill the difficult role of being a token Jew without becoming a token. He discovered the secret of making non-Jews feel all warm and pleased with their tolerance, a way to remain Jewish and successful without appearing threatening. Very low key, intellectual, modest, deep, and virtuous, he lent his aura to business deals almost as if his presence were blessing them. He was at the centre, for example, of the complicated negotiations involved in getting construction of Place Ville Marie under way, and it was Phillips who brought E. P. Taylor and Leo Kolber together to consummate some of the early Canadian Equity transactions with Cadillac and Fairview. Two of Montreal's top real estate operators, Mac Cummings and Stan Feinberg, once cut themselves equally into a multimillion-dollar deal with only one

unwritten understanding: that all disputes would be settled by Lazarus Phillips and that his word would be final. Phillips became
chief tax consultant for the Canadian operations of Imperial Oil,
Texaco, the House of Morgan, Cominco and Du Pont, as well as
processor of the legal work for major underwritings by Dominion
Securities, Greenshields and Nesbitt, Thomson. He embodied the
very best way a Jew can prosper within the Canadian Establishment. On February 15, 1968, he attained his ultimate goal: a sum-
mons from the Prime Minister, Mike Pearson, to sit in the Senate
of Canada.

   Time had been running out on the Bronfman candidacy. By
reaching seventy-five, the upper chamber's compulsory retirement
age under legislation enacted in 1965, Sam had in March 1966
been eliminated from a contest in which he had never really been a
serious entrant. The Liberals felt it was now safe to proceed with
the elevation of Lazarus Phillips—who had only thirty-one months
left until his own seventy-fifth birthday—but there were those who
calculated that his old friend's stubbornness had cost him at least
eighteen years of public life.[8]

NOTES

1. Sam Bronfman was a Liberal. But just in case there might be a political
turn-over, he usually donated an amount equivalent to about 60 per cent
of his Liberal gifts to the Conservatives.
2. Between 1960 and 1973, Henderson served as Canada's Auditor-General. "It was a fantastic situation," he recalls. "There were certain politicians who had risen to power on Mr. Sam's money that I had handed
across the table. Now I was in Ottawa as Auditor-General, and here were
these characters who had been on the receiving end. I suppose they hoped
I'd forgotten, but being an accountant I still had the records."
3. The *Montreal Star*'s early edition of June 10, 1945, had carried a dis-
patch from the paper's Ottawa bureau reporting that Mackenzie King was
about to name Phillips to the Senate. The story vanished from later editions.
4. The first Jewish member of the Canadian House of Commons was
Henry Nathan, elected from Victoria in an 1871 by-election when British
Columbia entered Confederation.
5. It was carved out specifically to represent Montreal's Jewish vote in the
redistribution of 1919.
6. Rose was sentenced in 1946 to six years in prison as a Russian spy, following the disclosures of Igor Gouzenko. He later returned to Poland.
The prosecutor at his trial was Philippe Brais.

7. Henderson and the Phillips firm had easy access to Ottawa. Even though they were clearly representing Sam Bronfman's and Seagram's private interests, when the Department of National Health and Welfare came to draw up its food and drug regulations governing alcoholic beverages in the early fifties, Henderson and Philip Vineberg, Phillips's nephew and law partner, submitted draft clauses. Most of them were adopted without a change. On March 24, 1952, Henderson received a call from Paul Martin, then Minister of National Health and Welfare, who said, "Max, I've got my pen in hand and these food and drug regulations are going into law. Before I sign them I just want to ask you one question: Are they good regulations and are you satisfied with them?" Henderson replied, "I am, Paul." The laws governing Canada's liquor industry have not been substantially altered since.

8. When Lazarus Phillips retired from the Senate on the eve of Yom Kippur in 1970, Senator Grattan O'Leary called him "the greatest senator in the history of Canada," and his colleagues gave him a standing ovation.

Parliamentary Committees and Parliamentary Government: The British and Canadian Experiences

MICHAEL RUSH

The hopes of legislative reformers in many countries have rested heavily—some would say disproportionately so—on establishing more effective committee systems within the legislature. In cases such as the United States Congress, where the committee system is the principal focus of legislative activity and power, the stress has been on making what are already regarded as effective committees more effective. In most parliamentary systems, however, the stress has been on creating effective committees where previously there

Adapted from Michael Rush, "Parliamentary Committees and Parliamentary Government: The British and Canadian Experiences," *The Journal of Commonwealth and Comparative Politics*, Vol. XX, No. 2 (July, 1982): 138-54. By permission of Frank Cass and Company Limited.

were none; committees there may have been, but few, if any, could be described as effective: so ran the reformers' argument.

There can be little doubt that if "effective" is taken to mean such things as having a frequent and significant influence over major matters of policy, periodically denying the executive approval of or the means to carry out a particular policy, or regularly subjecting the executive and its policies to sustained and penetrating criticism, then parliamentary committees cannot generally be described as effective. It may be the case that a particular committee is widely regarded as effective in one or more of these senses—the Public Accounts Committee is commonly cited in the British case, for instance. But such examples are best regarded as exceptions that prove the general rule of committee ineffectiveness in parliamentary systems.

There is, however, a different sense in which some parliamentary committees might be described as effective, but this relates to a different purpose from that commonly subsumed in the phrase "parliamentary control." Most legislatures in parliamentary systems now use committees as a means of coping with a greater workload or dealing more expeditiously with business than can the full chamber (or both chambers in a bicameral parliament) in plenary session. For example, in 1907 the British House of Commons amended its standing orders so that bills given a second reading were referred to a standing committee for the committee stage and most bills are now dealt with in this way. Similarly, but much more recently, the Canadian House of Commons adopted the same procedure and, in addition, introduced the referral of all estimates to committees as a regular part of supply procedure. Of course, both senses of the term "effective" can be applied to such uses of committees and there is no doubt that both British and Canadian committees have proved effective in enabling the Commons to cope with an increased workload and deal more expeditiously with business, but it remains open to question whether such committees are effective in the sense of providing more effective scrutiny of legislative proposals in either country or of the estimates in Canada.

It can be argued that, whereas committees are part of the natural order of things in a congressional system based on the separation of powers, in a parliamentary system committees can be effective only as a means of coping with an increased workload and dealing with that workload more expeditiously than is otherwise possible. As a means of enforcing the constitutional responsibility of the executive to the legislature, committees could be described

as alien devices, inappropriate to parliamentary government—
doubly alien, as Lord Butler once suggested, when opposing a proposal for a Select Committee on Colonial Affairs: ". . . it smacks to
me far more of Capitol Hill and the Palais Bourbon than of the
Parliament in Westminster."[1] This is not, of course, the view of
would-be reformers, who usually vehemently deny that they wish
either to import congressional style committees or, more fundamentally, to establish a separation of powers. Moreover, the fact
remains that in both Britain and Canada reformers have, to some
extent, had their way, in that investigatory committees have been
introduced into the House of Commons in both countries.

The British Experience

The British House of Commons has made fairly extensive use of
committees since the middle of the nineteenth century but until
the 1907 session, from which date a significant proportion of public bills were dealt with by committees rather than taken in a committee of the whole house (i.e. on the floor of the house), in no
sense was there a committee system at Westminster in the strict
sense of that term. Committees were used for specific purposes on
an *ad hoc* basis and were not an integral part of the operation of the
House of Commons. Thus up to 1907 the committees used did not
constitute a system in the sense that they regularly performed tasks
peculiar to them as committees, either as investigatory bodies covering the whole or greater part of the range of governmental activities or as a procedurally integral part of the work of the legislature
in dealing with particular types of public business, such as the estimates or the committee stage of bills.

From 1907 a system of standing committees existed, but they operated and continue to operate as miniatures of the whole house,
replicating the division between government and opposition and
operating procedurally in the same way as the House of Commons. Theoretically, standing committees originally had the power
to send for persons, papers and records, to call for and to hear evidence, but the power was never used and it was eventually decided
that no such power existed. Thus, other than by normal debating
techniques, standing committees may not question the ministers
responsible for the bills with which they are dealing. Moreover,
committees are not specialised, either in terms of subject area or,
for the most part, in personnel. For each bill a new standing com-

mittee is appointed and, although some regard is given to MPs' interests and expertise in appointing committee members, the committee stages of bills in the same policy area are not necessarily dealt with by basically the same MPs. Standing committees are therefore a means of spreading the legislative burden and dealing more expeditiously with the committee stage of bills than would otherwise be the case.

It has always been possible, of course, for the House of Commons to give standing committees generally or a particular standing committee the power to take evidence on bills, while from time to time *select* committees have been set up to take the committee stage of particular bills. Investigatory committees in the form of select committees with the powers to call for persons, papers and records have a longer history than standing committees and many of the early select committees were legislative committees in that they were set up to deal with particular legislative proposals, usually to investigate whether legislation was required and, in a number of cases, to prepare a draft bill, rather than take the committee stage of a bill that had already had a second reading. Committees were also used to deal with private legislation, which in the earlier part of the nineteenth century was greater in volume than public legislation.

The demands and pressure for the creation of a fully-fledged system of investigatory committees grew during the later 1950s and early 1960s, both inside and outside parliament. The Labour Government elected in October 1964 was understandably too preoccupied with its survival to concern itself much with the question of parliamentary reform, but in the election campaign of 1966 Harold Wilson declared himself in favour of reform in general and of the establishment of more investigatory committees in particular. The massive majority won by Labour in 1966 ensured the government's survival and soon after the election the cabinet turned its attention to parliamentary reform. Wilson, with the enthusiastic backing of Richard Crossman, the newly-appointed Leader of the House, gave his full support to the creation of specialised committees, overriding objections from a number of members of the cabinet. The first steps, however, were firmly in the cautious tradition of British parliamentary reform: in 1966 two new select committees were set up, one on Science and Technology and one on Agriculture. These two committees, and others which were subsequently established, became known as the new specialist or specialised committees. Later, when their future was under review, the government claimed that these first two committees were not intended as the first instalment of a full range of investigatory committees covering the whole range of governmental responsibilities. On the contrary, the government said that both committees were experimental, one, the Science and Technology Committee, being intended as a *subject* committee and the other, the Agriculture Committee, as a *departmental* committee and that in due course it was intended that they should be *replaced* by committees covering a different subject area and a different department. While it was accepted that the committees were experimental, it was widely disputed that the government had made it clear from the beginning that, providing the experiment was reasonably successful, the committees would be replaced on some sort of rota basis.

In the event the Science and Technology Committee survived, but the Agriculture Committee offended the government, mainly over Britain's proposed membership of the EEC, and was wound up early in 1969. Prior to this, in apparent fulfilment of the government's original intentions, a Select Committee on Education and Science was set up and in 1969 two further committees were established, one on Overseas Aid and the other on Scottish Affairs. In the meantime the government had also conceded a Select Committee on Race Relations and Immigration, following the fierce criticism of its policy towards Kenyan Asians, while the establishment of the Ombudsman (the Parliamentary Commissioner for Administration—the PCA) had been accompanied by a parallel Select Committee on the PCA. It was this patchwork of committees that the Select Committee on Procedure considered in preparing its report of 1969. The Procedure Committee recommended a much more wide-ranging scrutiny of government policies, involving the abolition of a number of the existing select committees and their replacement by a Select Committee on Expenditure which would cover a wide range of government activities through a series of sub-committees.

This recommendation formed the basis of changes introduced by the newly-elected Conservative government in 1970: the Estimates Committee and the Select Committees on Education, Scottish Affairs, and Overseas Aid were abolished; a Select Committee on Expenditure, with wider terms of reference than the Estimates Committee and a large enough membership to man six sub-committees was established; and the Public Accounts Committee and the Select Committees on Nationalised Industries, Science and

Technology, Race Relations and Immigration, and the PCA were retained.[2] Subsequently the Overseas Aid Committee was revived, initially to complete an unfinished investigation, but later survived under the title of Overseas Development to embark on other en-quiries. The range of sub-committees established by the Expendi-ture Committee extended the activities of investigatory committees much more widely than ever before, notably into the areas of for-eign affairs and defence, but gaps still remained and Agriculture, and Welsh and Scottish affairs were not specifically covered.

This state of affairs prevailed until 1979, when, following a fur-ther Procedure Committee report,[3] the government decided to abolish the Expenditure Committee and establish a full range of departmental investigatory committees, of which there are four-teen, essentially covering all areas of government responsibility. This has involved the abolition of the Nationalised Industries, Sci-ence and Technology, Race Relations, and Overseas Development Committees, although the newly-established Home Affairs and Foreign Affairs Committees were given the power to set up sub-committees on Race Relations and Immigration and on Overseas Development respectively and these were set up in due course. In addition, several of the new committees were empowered to estab-lish a joint sub-committee on Nationalised Industries, but have not done so to date. The 1979 changes also involved the retention of the Select Committee on the PCA and, of course, of the Public Ac-counts Committee.

These changes have been accompanied by a growth in the ser-vices and facilities available to MPs and committees.[4] The use of outside advisers by select committees has grown considerably, al-though no committee, other than the PAC, could be said to have an extensive staff available to it.

In summary, it should be noted that the British House of Com-mons makes extensive use of committees, but that a clear distinc-tion is drawn between those which have a central procedural role —the standing committees which deal with the committee stage of legislation and to a lesser extent those that deal with delegated legislation—and those which play a procedurally peripheral role— the investigatory select committees which scrutinise the policies and activities of the government. The government exercises a closer control of standing committees because it needs them, but much less control over investigatory committees because it can ig-nore them.

The Canadian Experience

The use of committees by the Canadian House of Commons has a somewhat curious but understandable history. One of the earliest actions of the newly-elected House of Commons, following the creation of the Dominion of Canada in 1867, was to establish a fairly wide range of committees, though they could hardly be said to have constituted a committee system, in that they were not an integral part of the procedure for dealing with public business, nor did they cover the full range of governmental responsibilities. They were important, however, in dealing with private business, including the incorporation of businesses and the granting of divorces.

Before giving a brief account of the use of committees in the Canadian House of Commons, however, it is necessary to explain some differences in terminology between Westminster and Ottawa. Leaving aside committees of the whole House, used until recently in both legislatures to deal with a major part of financial business, and still used, where appropriate, for the committee stage of bills, the British House of Commons basically uses two forms of committees, standing and select, with the distinction between the two, as already noted, being that the former are miniatures of the full house in terms of procedure and are used exclusively to deal with the committee stage of legislation,[5] whereas select committees, other than those concerned with the internal operation of the house, are investigatory, operate on a non-adversarial basis, and are empowered to take evidence. In Canada, however, all committees are empowered to take evidence and the term "standing committee" is used to denote a committee established by standing orders, which may deal with any business referred to it by the house, including the committee stage of bills, consideration of the estimates and investigations. The term "sessional committee" is used to denote any similar committee established by an annual sessional order of the House and the term "special committee" (a term not used at Westminster), to denote a committee established to deal with a specific matter and disbanded once that matter has been dealt with. Canadian committees also differed in a more substantive sense from their Westminster counterparts in that from the very outset they have been *specialised*, that is to say, unlike British standing committees, which are designated by letter and which are first and foremost a replication of party support in the House with only a limited concession to the interests and expertise of MPs, Canadian committees have always been designated by *subject*. Of course, like their British counterparts, Canadian committees also replicate party support in the house, but in the Canadian case matters are referred to committees in relation to their subject areas and the membership of each committee is not redesignated for each referral.

The committees first established by the Canadian House of Commons in 1867 were re-established sessionally until 1906, when they became standing committees established by standing orders. From that date the Canadian House established only one sessional committee regularly, Railways and Shipping, although a number of special committees were set up regularly over a number of sessions and were therefore to all intents and purposes sessional committees. Of greater importance, however, is the fact that until recently the Canadian House made relatively little use of its committees in dealing with public business. A major reason for this was that the pressure of business which led to the greater use of committees to deal with the committee stage of legislation at Westminster in the early part of the century was a much later development in Ottawa, since the demands made upon the Canadian parliament were fewer than those made at Westminster, partly because Canada is a federal system so that governmental responsibilities were and are fewer and partly because the welfare state and its attendant legislation developed earlier in Britain. Moreover, Ottawa had no *procedural* incentive to use committees more extensively to deal with the committee stage of legislation, since under Canadian standing orders, even if a bill were referred to a committee, it still had to go through a committee stage on the floor of the House. Nor did referral of estimates to committees help the government, since they too had to be debated on the floor. The much earlier and regular use of the PAC and the Estimates Committee at Westminster also helped to establish investigatory committees in a limited but firm manner in British parliamentary practice, apart from the fairly widespread use of select committees for *ad hoc* enquiries, than was the case in Canada. Finally, Canadian committees tended to grow in size and become cumbersome and unwieldy bodies, often unable to secure a quorum and, although both the size and quorums of committees were later reduced, this did little to increase their use, since successive governments found it easier to keep control of business on the floor of the House than in committees. Between 1945 and 1965, for instance, one committee met in only five of the twenty-six parliamentary sessions, another in only eleven, and a third in only twelve. The average for all committees was only 61 per cent of the sessions.

Ironically, therefore, the Canadian House of Commons had a more extensive range of committees, which were specialised and which could take evidence, but which in practice played only a peripheral part in the work of the legislature, while its British counterpart had a number of non-specialised committees, unable to take evidence, which played, if not an integral, a far more important part in the work of the legislature, plus a limited but generally respected number of specialised investigatory committees.

There began in 1957, however, a process which was to lead to Canadian committees moving from the periphery to the centre of the legislative stage: a Progressive Conservative government, headed by John Diefenbaker, came to power that year with a general commitment to strengthen the position of parliament *vis-à-vis* the executive and in particular to make greater use of committees. Initially the new government lacked a parliamentary majority, but a further election in 1958 gave the Diefenbaker administration the largest majority won by any party in Canadian history, with no less than 208 Conservatives out of a total of 265 MPs. Not surprisingly it was suggested that the increased use of committees was a means of keeping the government's large number of backbenchers busy, but the changes in the use of committees should be seen mainly as a genuine attempt to improve the scrutiny of the executive and involve backbench MPs more closely in the work of the government. The Estimates Committee, which had been established only as recently as 1955, was strengthened and more estimates were referred to it or, where appropriate, to standing committees. Furthermore, more bills were referred to standing committees for their committee stage and more matters were referred to standing committees for investigation, rather than to special committees, which previous governments had tended to use in much the same way as royal commissions. Standing committees now met more frequently and regularly and for the first time since the Second World War all committees presented substantive (as distinct from procedural) reports to the house. This revival of committees was fully sustained for the first two sessions of the 1958-62 parliament, but in the third session (1960) there was a small drop in activity and a more serious one in the fourth session (1960-61), with the number of committees submitting substantive reports falling to six out of a total of eleven committees dealing with public business, and the Estimates Committee not meeting at all.

Part of the reason for this was that the Diefenbaker government was running into increasing difficulties and criticism, but of much greater importance was that without *procedural* changes committees could only be of limited use to the government and could easily become a hindrance rather than a help. The government's control of the time and business of the house has always been more limited in Canada, partly because the procedural means available were more limited in theory and in practice (more particularly in practice because recourse to closure was not accepted as a normal means of securing the passage of business) and partly because "the usual channels" were and remain less developed in Ottawa, so that cooperation among the parties, especially the government and opposition, is more limited. A more specific reason related to the committees themselves in that they had originally been established in response to regional and constituency needs, covering areas such as Agriculture and Colonisation, Marine and Fisheries, Railways, Canals and Telegraph Lines, so that there was often no appropriate committee to which business could be referred.

This experience, the increased responsibilities assumed by the federal government during and since the Second World War and the feeling among a significant number of MPs that reform was necessary, led to the setting up by the minority Liberal government elected in 1963 of a Special Committee on Procedure and Organisation. This committee and its successors in the 1965-68 parliament opened the way to extensive procedural changes, including a major reform of committees. These changes came fully into operation at the beginning of the 1968-72 parliament, although the foundations of the committee system had been laid in 1965. In particular the changes strengthened the government's control of the business of the House, though not as extensively as the government wished, and made the committees an integral part of the work of the House. With the important exception of financial legislation, the committee stage of all public bills is now referred to a standing committee, unless the House orders otherwise, which usually it does not. Estimates are no longer taken on the floor of the House, but are referred to standing committees, which must report back to the House by a date set in standing orders. In addition standing committees may conduct investigations into matters referred to them by the House. The number and

range of committees was increased to cover all government departments and, of course, committees remained specialised and retained the power to take evidence on all types of business. In 1970
a joint (i.e. with the Senate) Standing Committee on Regulations
and Other Statutory Instruments was established, bringing the
number of standing committees dealing with public business to
sixteen.[6]

From 1968 the Canadian parliament also abandoned its earlier
practice of irregular parliamentary sessions, lasting as long as the
government thought appropriate, and adopted the British practice
of a regular parliamentary session beginning and ending in the autumn, although this has not been as rigorously adhered to as at
Westminster, with, for example, longer than usual sessions being
held in 1970-72 and 1974-76. Broadly speaking, however, the two
parliaments have reached a similar stage of development in the use
of parliamentary committees, notwithstanding some important differences between the two. Perhaps the major difference that remains, especially now that the new departmental select committees
at Westminster have mostly begun to examine the appropriate sections of the government's White Paper on Expenditure, is that no
evidence is taken during the committee stage of bills in the British
case, although even here there has been some very limited experi-
mentation. In both cases it could be said that committees play a
major part in dealing with legislation and in scrutinising the actions and policies of the executive, even though they may be somewhat differently organised to play these roles.

Parliamentary Committees and Parliamentary Government

The point of development that committees have reached in both
Britain and Canada is one at which the role of committees in a parliamentary system must come increasingly to the fore. As the range
and use of committees becomes more extensive and as they become better staffed, their ability to scrutinise the actions and policies of the executive should increase. This means that however
much such a development could and should be welcomed as a
means of enforcing ministerial responsibility and generally ren-
dering governments accountable, governments have, by permitting such a development, almost certainly made life more difficult

for themselves. In response it could be said that the price has been worth paying, since the ability of governments, especially those with a majority, to secure the passage of their programmes through parliament has been scarcely, if at all, curtailed. Indeed, as far as legislation is concerned, committees have facilitated the passing of more rather than fewer bills and, what is more significant, much longer and more complex bills. Furthermore, committees generally offer a better forum for the discussion of the details of legislation and in which the government can make those changes which it feels are appropriate. In other respects committees provide a means of keeping MPs busy and feeling useful, a channel of communication for various interests outside parliament, and the evidence they take provides an increasingly useful source of information for those inside and outside parliament.

For the most part, however, committees play only a limited role in the formation of government policy. Neither British nor Canadian governments have shown any great inclination to refer matters to committees *before* policy is formed or to consult committees during the policy-forming process. In principle there is no reason why committees should not be involved in either or both of these ways in the process of policy-formation, provided the government reserved to itself the right of deciding what policy was finally presented to parliament and continued to accept responsibility for it as at present. What would be a major change would be for the government to allow committees to have *the final say*—that would constitute a substantial move towards the situation prevailing in the United States Congress and a clear departure from the principal feature of parliamentary government, the constitutional responsibility of the executive to the legislature.

To involve committees or the House of Commons at large in the initiation of policy, or, for that matter, at an earlier post-initiative stage, would almost certainly make the life of the government more difficult. Ultimately governments are in business to govern and to implement the policies they and the parties they represent have evolved and anything that lessens their ability to do this is not likely to be looked upon with favour. In short, whatever particular form of government may lie in the future, much will depend on those who form it being convinced that parliament, whether through its committees or not, should have a greater influence on how the country is governed and what policies are implemented than either the British or Canadian parliaments currently enjoy. Constitutionally this could occur within the present framework of parliamentary government, but it would require a major change in its practice and operation, a change to which thus far, in terms of *attitudes*, little more than lip service has been paid.

NOTES

1. *HC Debates*, 13 July 1959, c 42.

2. See Cmnd 450, *The Select Committees of the House of Commons* (October, 1970).

3. HC 588, 1977-78.

4. See MICHAEL RUSH AND MALCOLM SHAW (eds), *The House of Commons: Service and Facilities* (London, 1974); JANET MORGAN, "Reinforcing Parliament," 42 *PEP Broadsheet* (March, 1976); and MICHAEL RUSH (ed), "Services and Facilities for MPs, 1973-81," *Policy Studies Institute (formerly PEP) Broadsheet*, forthcoming.

5. The more recently established Standing Committees on Statutory Instruments are only a partial exception to this rule in that, while not operating on the adversary principle of other standing committees, they do not take evidence and, as their name implies, deal exclusively with delegated legislation. They are therefore essentially legislative committees.

6. For a more detailed account of these changes see Michael Rush, "The development of the committee system in the Canadian House of Commons—diagnosis and revitalisation," *The Parliamentarian* Vol. 55 (1974): 86-94, and MICHAEL RUSH, "The development of the committee system in the Canadian House of Commons—reassessment and reform," *The Parliamentarian* Vol. 55 (1974): 149-58. Accounts of the operation of the reformed committee system may be found in MICHAEL RUSH, "Committees in the Canadian House of Commons" in JOHN D. LEES AND MALCOLM SHAW (eds), *Committees in Legislatures: a Comparative Analysis* (Durham NC, 1979), pp. 191-241; JOHN B. STEWART, *The Canadian House of Commons: Procedure and Reform* (Montreal, 1977), chapters 6 and 7; and ROBERT J. JACKSON AND MICHAEL M. ATKINSON, *The Canadian Legislative System*, 2nd ed. (Toronto, 1980), chapter 6.

Public Perceptions of the Canadian Parliament

RONALD G. LANDES

In the British-styled Canadian parliamentary system, parliamentary sovereignty or supremacy, which can be defined as Parliament's unrestricted ability to enact legislation, is the centrepiece of the constitutional political process.[1] As a result, the "institution of Parliament is the heart of our system of parliamentary democracy."[2]

At least in theory, therefore, Parliament is typically perceived as crucial: "Of all Canadian political institutions, Parliament is probably the most consequential."[3] In practice, however, parliamentary supremacy has always been somewhat constrained in Canada because of the political principles of federalism and judicial review. Moreover, the rise of disciplined mass parties has undercut the effectiveness of the individual MP, as well as the significance of the body to which he or she belongs.[4]

Given the supposed centrality of Parliament, an interesting point for research is how the mass public perceives this crucial governmental institution. Although few studies have been conducted on this topic, what data are available indicate that the public has little knowledge of or appreciation for the Parliament of Canada.[5] For example, after the introduction of television coverage of the House of Commons, one study discovered that 40 percent of a national sample found the proceedings "long, boring, uninteresting, childish and rude," another 15 percent thought the parliamentary process was "comical," while an additional 9 percent evaluated the proceedings as "a waste of time."[6]

This paper presents data on how Canadians currently view their Parliament. The national sample was conducted in August, 1983 by the Gallup organization for the Canadian Study of Parliament Group.[7] Because the data are quite straightforward, comments on each table will be kept brief.

This article is based on data gathered in the Gallup National Omnibus Poll conducted for the Canadian Study of Parliament Group in August, 1983. Neither the Gallup organization nor the Canadian Study of Parliament Group bear any responsibility for the interpretations presented. By permission of John A. Holtby, Chairman, Canadian Study of Parliament Group.

The results presented in Tables 1 and 2 indicate a pattern which is, perhaps, the most negative of all for any institution of government, that is, perceived irrelevance from the perspective of the ordinary citizen. In Table 1, only 9 percent express a "great deal" of interest in the activities of Parliament, while 46 percent say "little" and 19 percent express "no interest" at all. The introduction of television coverage in 1977 has left this basic pattern unchanged (Table 2): only 13 percent "regularly" or "very often" watch the parliamentary proceedings, while 86 percent "never" or "not too often" observe the workings of Canadian parliamentary democracy. Such results would seem to show that the view "that reform of Canada's

TABLE 1
Level of Interest in the Activities of Parliament (%)

Great Deal	9
Quite A Lot	27
Little	46
None	19
Don't Know	0

TABLE 2
Frequency of Watching the House of Commons Proceedings on Television (%)

Regularly	5
Very Often	8
Not Too Often	50
Never	36
Don't Know	0

TABLE 3
The Most Important In Making Major Canadian Government Decisions (%)

Cabinet	33
Parliament	29
The Prime Minister	19
Senior Civil Servants	8
Don't Know	11

TABLE 4
How Members of Parliament Should Vote (%)

As Their Constituents Would Vote	50
As Their Party Requires	8
According to Their Own Judgment	38
Don't Know	4

TABLE 5
What Members of Parliament Consider Their First Priority to Be (%)

Passing Laws	8
Looking After the Needs of Their Constituents	38
Being a "Watchdog" Over Government Activities	14
Being Loyal to Their Party	32
Other	2
Don't Know	6

TABLE 6
What Ought to be the First Priority of Members of Parliament (%)

Passing Laws	7
Looking After the Needs of Their Constituents	62
Being a "Watchdog" Over Government Activities	18
Being Loyal to Their Party	6
Other	1
Don't Know	5

parliamentary institutions is necessary. . .if Parliament is to regain the respect and trust of the electorate"[8] must begin with a more basic change: Parliament has to first of all gain the attention of the Canadian public.

Data relevant to the role of Parliament in the decision-making process are illustrated in Table 3. Most revealing is the public perception that Parliament is more important than either the prime minister or the civil service—a view that few, if any, political scientists would accept. The lack of interest in Parliament (Tables 1 and 2) is matched by the public's misunderstanding of the role of Parliament in the political process. The myth of parliamentary supremacy is not yet dead among the mass public.

In Table 4 we see how the public conceives of the individual MPs role in Parliament. Particularly revealing is the finding that only 8 percent feel that an MP should vote as their party requires, while 50 percent think that the MP should vote as their constituents would and 38 percent prefer to leave the choice to the judgment of their MP. The partisan-basis of parliamentary organization and behaviour is not well-received by the mass public.

The differences between the public's perception of what MPs consider their priorities to be (Table 5) and what the public would like those priorities to be (Table 6) are most revealing. While 32 percent of the sample see an MPs priority as being loyal to his or her party, only 6 percent feel that there ought to be such a deference to party discipline. In contrast, the "ombudsman" role of MPs is clearly favoured by the electorate: 62 percent feel that an MPs first priority is to look after the needs of his or her constituents. The priority attached to the lawmaking function is minimal indeed (8 percent and 7 percent, respectively).

The data in Tables 1 through 6 show, in general, little understanding of or appreciation for the role of the Canadian Parliament in the political process. Few members of the public are interested in Parliament, its role in the policy process is overestimated, and its basic operating principle (party loyalty and party discipline) is not favourably perceived. Instead, Parliament is seen as an ombudsman for the individual citizen in the political process.

NOTES

1. For discussions of the role and evolution of the Canadian Parliament, consult the following works: JOHN B. STEWART, *The Canadian House of Commons: Procedure and Reform* (Montreal: McGill-Queen's University Press, 1977); ALLAN KORNBERG AND WILLIAM MISHLER, *Influence in Parliament: Canada* (Durham, North Carolina: Duke University Press, 1976); ROBERT J. JACKSON AND MICHAEL M. ATKINSON, *The Canadian Legislative System: Politicians and Policymaking* (Toronto: Macmillan of Canada, 1980), 2nd rev. ed.; COLIN CAMPBELL, *The Canadian Senate: A Lobby from Within* (Toronto: Macmillan of Canada, 1978); HAROLD D. CLARKE, COLIN CAMPBELL, F.Q. QUO AND ARTHUR GODDARD (eds.), *Parliament, Policy and Representation* (Toronto: Methuen, 1980); Michael M. Atkinson, "Parliamentary Government in Canada," in Michael S. Whittington and Glen Williams (eds.), *Canadian Politics in the 1980s* (Toronto: Methuen, 1981).

2. THOMAS D'AQUINO, G. BRUCE DOERN AND CASSANDRA BLAIR, *Parliamentary Democracy in Canada: Issues for Reform* (Toronto: Methuen, 1983), p. 18.

3. JOHN H. REDEKOP, "Canadian Political Institutions," in Redekop (ed.), *Approaches to Canadian Politics*, 2nd ed. (Scarborough, Ontario: Prentice-Hall Canada, 1983), p. 151.

4. ROMAN R. MARCH, *The Myth of Parliament* (Scarborough, Ontario: Prentice-Hall Canada, 1974). For a similar argument with respect to Britain, see Richard H.S. Crossman, *The Myths of Cabinet Government* (Cambridge, Massachusetts: Harvard University Press, 1972).

5. A similar conclusion seems applicable to provincial legislatures as well. See, for example, the data from a sample of Nova Scotian adolescents (grades 7-12) reported in JOSEPH G. JABBRA AND RONALD G. LANDES, *The Political Orientations of Canadian Adolescents: Political Socialization and Political*

Culture in Nova Scotia (Halifax, Nova Scotia: Department of Political Science, Saint Mary's University, 1976), pp. 15, 29-32.

6. RICHARD G. PRICE AND HAROLD D. CLARKE, "Television and the House of Commons," in Clarke et al., *Parliament, Policy and Representation*, p. 77.

7. For a detailed description of sample design and results, see "Gallup National Omnibus Conducted for Canadian Study of Parliament Group, August, 1983," mimeo.

8. D'AQUINO ET AL., *Parliamentary Democracy in Canada*, p. 109.

The Judicial Branch of Government

Few would likely disagree with the observation "that Canadians have little appreciation of the political significance of judicial interpretation of the constitution."[1] That significance stems from the fact that, as the late Chief Justice Bora Laskin put it, the Supreme Court is "the umpire of the Canadian constitutional system, the only umpire. . . ."[2] To buttress its role as an impartial umpire, the judicial branch of government, whether in a presidential or parliamentary system, is predicated on the principle of judicial independence (e.g., freedom from executive or legislative control). Consequently, the court system has the potential to play a significant role in the political process.

Just how important that political role should be for the umpire is a continuing and, at times, heated controversy. In reading number seventeen ("The Judiciary-Law Interpreters or Law-makers"), Mr. Chief Justice Brian Dickson of the Supreme Court of Canada points out that the real concern is not whether judges make law, because they do, but the proper limits of judicial law-making. The legislature and judiciary are seen as partners in the law-making process, even though the role of the latter is limited in Canada because of the principle of parliamentary sovereignty. As the umpire of the constitutional system, the judiciary both interprets the law and, in so doing, makes it as well.

One of the key problems that Canada's political umpire faces is that the basic components of the constitutional system are not necessarily easily compatible with each other. In readings eighteen and nineteen some of the significant rules of the game within which the umpire must decide are discussed. The potential conflict between the principles of parliamentary sovereignty and the protection of human rights—a problem which has become particularly germane since the 1982 Canadian Charter of Rights and Freedoms—is presented in Anne Bayefsky's article (reading number eighteen: "Parliamentary Sovereignty and Human Rights in Canada"). If courts are to protect human rights, then the power of judicial review of executive and legislative actions becomes fundamental. In reading nineteen ("The Origins of Judicial Review"), Jennifer Smith links the initial pattern of judicial review with possible future developments based on the Charter. While the exercise of judicial review may grow in significance and while it may modify the dominance of parliamentary sovereignty, Professor Smith concludes that the fundamental "principle of parliamentary supremacy persists." The Canadian judiciary has, historically, been conservative in its role as the umpire of a political process based on the Westminster model.

> The triumph of the doctrine of parliamentary sovereignty meant that the primary role of adapting the law to changes in social values was securely located in parliament, and the role of the courts became the subordinate one of interpreting the law.[3]

In reading number twenty ("Political Trials and the Canadian Political Tradition"), Kenneth McNaught studies the actual umpire role of the courts in two extremely significant trials in Canadian political history—those of Louis Riel and the cases growing out of the Winnipeg General Strike. As might be expected in a system of limited judicial review and judicial restraint, the courts have refused to act as agents of social and economic change. According to McNaught, the courts' overall conservative outlook has reflected "an unchanging Canadian belief in constitutionality against a backdrop of political adaptation." Such a pattern is congruent with the rules of the game within which Canada's political umpire operates.

NOTES

1. PETER H. RUSSELL, *Leading Constitutional Decisions* (Ottawa: Carleton University Press, 1982), p. 3.

2. ROBERT SHEPPARD AND MICHAEL VALPY, *The National Deal: The Fight for a Canadian Constitution* (Toronto: Fleet Books, 1982), p. 224.

3. J.R. MALLORY, "Politics by Other Means: The Courts and the Westminster Model in Australia," *The Journal of Commonwealth and Comparative Politics*, Vol. XVII, No. 1 (1979): 3.

The Judiciary—Law Interpreters or Law-makers

MR. CHIEF JUSTICE BRIAN DICKSON

For many reasons, the lines of the debate ("Do judges make the law or do they merely declare it") are more distinctly drawn in England than in Canada and the United States. The real issue in Canada is not whether judges do or should make law. It is, as I pointed out in *Harrison v. Carswell*, defining the limits of judicial law-making:

> The duty of the court, as I envisage it, is to proceed in the discharge of its adjudicative function in a reasoned way from principled decision and established concepts. I do not for a moment doubt the power of the court to act creatively—it has done so on countless occasions; But manifestly one must ask—what are the limits of the judicial function?[1]

It is a complex and difficult question and one which is of particular concern to members of the Supreme Court of Canada. Since the doctrine of *stare decisis* has fallen into desuetude at the level of final appeal, the question has become more pressing. As Chief Justice Laskin commented several years ago:

> A final court which is prepared to overrule its own precedents puts itself, institutionally, into a partnership, albeit a junior one, with the legislature.[2]

And yet, as judges, we are all sensitive to accusations of "judicial legislation." I still react with a guilty start, although I am convinced that in many instances such allegations are based on what I consider a basic misapprehension of the function of the judiciary.

Part of the difficulty lies in the term itself: "judicial legislation." Our political system is based upon the concept of the division of powers between the judiciary, executive and the legislature. The judiciary adjudicates and the legislature legislates. There is no quarrel with this. But the existence of judge-made law is not necessarily a prohibited incursion into the exclusive domain of the legis-

Adapted from Mr. Chief Justice Brian Dickson, "The Judiciary—Law Interpreters or Law-makers," *Manitoba Law Journal*, Vol. 12, No. 2 (1982): 1-8. By permission of the author.

lature. The "law" which judges make should not be confused with the "laws" which issue from Parliament. The civilian jurists with their genius for systemization speak, correctly in my view, in terms of "sources" of law. Statute law is a "source" of law; custom may be a "source" of law; and in our legal system, judicial decisions are a "source" of law. Some sources are more important or more authoritative than others, so that custom, for example, is of relatively little significance.

There have been historical examples of true "judicial legislation." In pre-revolutionary France the Courts of Appeal, the "Parlements" were given the power to enact regulations. This was a straight delegation of the legislative power of the King to the courts, a power which was used by the Parlements to challenge the authority of the King himself. For their excesses and abuse of power the Parlements incurred the wrath of the population and were almost immediately dissolved at the time of the French Revolution. The courts which took their place under the revolutionary government were totally subjugated to the legislature. Not only were they denied all power to make regulations, even the interpretation of laws was placed beyond them. An address by the court to the legislature was required in order to interpret a law.[3] A vestige of the revolutionaries' distrust of the judiciary remains to this day in article 5 of the French *Civil Code*:

> Judges are forbidden to pronounce by way of a general and rule-making disposition on the cases submitted to them.

Some eminent common law judges would adopt the very same position.

The civilian hostility to judge-made law is readily explained by history. The origins and nature of the Common Law, however, do not offer such an easy explanation for the existence of this same hostility.

The Common Law is, by definition, judge-made law. Before the conquest, as in other Germanic tribal societies, custom was the main source of law. It was transformed by the King's courts into the common law. There was, as such, no legislation as we know it today. Inspired by little other than healthy regard for the King's peace and his royal purse, Common Law courts initially ventured jurisdiction over a limited range of legal matters. That original jurisdiction was enhanced by measure. The juridical system expanded its province to accommodate new demands for remedies at law. The courts expressed creativity by first advancing, then con-

solidating, new concepts of law. Thus, the strands of the Common
Law were woven case by case in the courts of the day. In time that
body of law supported a full complement of legal principles, given
shape and cohesion by the application of like principles in alike circumstances, by an observance of precedent. Lord Wright chose an
apt analogy in speaking of the evolution of our law:

> (The judge proceeded) . . . from case to case, like the ancient Mediter-
> ranean mariners, hugging the coast from point to point and avoiding
> the dangers of the open sea . . . .[4]

Though perhaps the courts took small and carefully measured
steps the distance covered by principles of law was not insignificant. The strength of the Common Law, then as now, resides in its
resilience, its undoubted capacity for robust growth. Throughout
history, principles were devised and concepts forged anew to meet
the host of ongoing demands advanced by litigants who pursued
remedies not yet recognized and challenged the inadequacies of
rule and procedure.

If historically judges did make law how did they, according to
many eminent judges and commentators, lose this ability? L. Jaffe
in a provocative study published in 1969 quotes Lord Upjohn as
saying that "as a judge he felt that certainty in the law was of paramount importance and he saw his duty to be to declare the law as it
is; he deprecated judicial legislation."[5] "Judicial legislation" as I
have attempted to point out above, is a misnomer for judge-made
law. The Irony is that those who deprecate judge-made law revere
the great judges of the past who made it: Coke, Bacon, Holt, Mans-
field, Blackburn, Willes. The ancient powers of the judge to make
law have never formally been abrogated.

Why should judges think it better not? As in any other field of
human endeavour there is a pendulum of innovation and consoli-
dation, action and reaction. The emergence of a strict doctrine of
stare decisis towards the end of the nineteenth century marked the
onset of the pre-eminence of the view that a judge's function is
merely a declaratory one. Once a principle of law had been declared in a decision it was immutable. Those who had made it (or
"found it" as they would prefer to term the process) could not
change it. The judges forged their own shackles. Some, like Lord
Campbell, sought the justification of the rule in a principle verging
on that of papal infallibility! The law existed, and always had existed, in some Platonic ideal world and, upon his appointment to the
bench, the scales fell from a judge's eyes enabling him to see and

declare the "law." Lord Halsbury much more pragmatically based the rule on public policy, the interest of society in the finality of litigation.

There are many good arguments which may be advanced in favour of the principle of *stare decisis*: It promotes "certainty, predictability, reliability, equality, uniformity, convenience."[6]

The principle, however, has two major flaws. "Law must be stable and yet it cannot stand still."[7] Give a moment's thought to the changes in our world since 1898: automobiles to airplanes to space ships. Technology has radically altered the context within which the law operates. Can copyright law remain the same after the invention of the photocopy machine?

Secondly, judges are not infallible and the doctrine of *stare decisis* can serve to perpetuate a bad rule: inflexibly applied, "It allows the law to become a petrified forest of erroneous notions."[8] In *Binus v. The Queen*, Cartwright J. confirmed the power of the Supreme Court of Canada to depart from a previous decision.[9] The principle of *stare decisis* still applies vertically of course; decisions of the Supreme Court of Canada are still "binding" on the courts below. I would hope however that the precedents are not applied as blindly as they have been in the past.

A simplistic view of the theory of the division of powers has obscured the fact that the judiciary and the legislature are partners in the law-making process. The distinction between the judge and the legislator has been over-defined. Judges do, and must, posit rules of general applicability, the supposed preserve of the legislature. On the other hand, legislatures do pass legislation determining the rights and status of an individual, supposedly a function of the judiciary. The judiciary and the legislature both make law—but it is not the same kind of law nor is it made for the same purposes. The primary function of the judge is to decide the case before him, to *"trancher le litige"*—cut through the issue. He deals with a concrete issue and has the benefit of seeing the practical implications and repercussions of a rule of law on individual members of society. The legislature, on the other hand, is dealing with issues at a certain level of abstraction, and cannot exhaustively provide for every mutation possible. There are some areas of the law where legislative action is infinitely superior to judicial action, for example in corporate and commercial law. Those directly affected by the legislation are in close and constant communication with the legislator. They form a powerful lobby group. The law is continually being amended and updated. In Ontario, for example, there have been major revisions of both securities law and companies law in the last ten years. But the legislative process can be a slow and cumbersome one and many areas of the law which badly need reform may simply be low priority, not politically profitable. The legislative process should not be idealized out of all proportion. It is certainly not the solution to every troubled area of the law.

On the contrary, judicial law-making may be a spur to a lazy or indifferent legislature. The judiciary and the legislature do not exist in splendid isolation one from the other. They interact. But once the legislature has acted in an area at the instigation of the judiciary, do judges suddenly lose their claim to law-making authority in the area? I am firmly of the belief that they do not.

One must also I think, in a discussion such as this, have in mind the very important change effected in the jurisdiction of the Supreme Court of Canada with the enactment of section 41(1) of the Supreme Court Act in 1975. The emphasis is on legal development rather than the resolution of disputes between litigants or the correction of error in the lower courts. Leave is to be granted or not granted depending upon whether the issue raised is one of public importance, not merely of importance to the litigants. In the resolution of the legal problem presented the Court may well have to give meaning to the words of a statute or adapt the law to meet changing social conditions and, in that limited sense, perform a law-making function.

Conclusion

Judges do make law but, unlike the legislature, in a system which recognizes the doctrine of parliamentary sovereignty, their law-making power is a limited one.

> [A] judge, even when he is free, is still not wholly free. He is not to innovate at pleasure. He is not a knight-errant, roaming at will in pursuit of his own ideal of beauty or of goodness. He is to draw his inspiration from consecrated principles.[10]

I return to the question before us, namely: are members of the Judiciary law interpreters or law-makers? Provided the phrase "law-makers" is understood to mean "law developers" I would answer the question by saying that the judiciary are both interpreters and, in the limited sense I have indicated, makers of law. The role of the judiciary is not political nor executive nor administrative. It is adjudicative, but there is of necessity an element of law development in the work.

NOTES

Text of an address delivered to the mid-winter meeting of the Manitoba Bar Association. The author acknowledges the valuable research assistance of his Law Clerk, Me. Cally Jordan, in the preparation of this paper.

1. [1976] 2 *S.C.R.* 200 at 218.

2. "The Institutional Character of the Judge" [1972] 7 *Israel L.R.* 329 at 341.

3. See J.P. DAWSON, *The Oracles of the Law* (1968), pp. 375ff.

4. LORD WRIGHT, "The Study of Law" [1938] 34 *L.Q.R.* 185 at 186.

5. L. JAFFE, "Is the Great Judge Obsolete?" (Oxford, 1969), p. 28.

6. HAHLO, *The South African Legal System* (1968), p. 215.

7. ROSCOE POUND, *Interpretations of Legal History* (1923), p. 1.

8. *Supra* n. 6, p. 215.

9. [1967] *S.C.R.* 594 at 601.

10. B. CARDOZO, *The Nature of the Judicial Process* (1921), p. 141.

Parliamentary Sovereignty and Human Rights in Canada

ANNE F. BAYEFSKY

The history of human rights protection in Canada has been permeated by the influence of the doctrine of parliamentary sovereignty. Since Confederation, the doctrine has hindered the effectiveness of various attempts to increase the security of human rights. If the Canadian *Charter of Rights and Freedoms*[1] is to evoke a

Adapted from Anne F. Bayefsky, "Parliamentary Sovereignty and Human Rights in Canada: The Promise of the Canadian Charter of Rights and Freedoms," *Political Studies*, Vol. XXXI, No. 2 (June, 1983): 239-63, with *errata* published in *Political Studies*, Vol. XXXII (1984). By permission of the publisher.

new era, it will be the ramifications of this traditional principle which will have to be inhibited.

The Traditional Relationship

The doctrine of parliamentary sovereignty is thought of as the basic characteristic of the British constitution.[2] It is also the case, however, despite Canadian federalism, that the doctrine has been a fundamental tenet of the Canadian constitution.

As enunciated by A. V. Dicey the doctrine states, ". . . that Parliament . . . has, under the English constitution, the right to make or unmake any law whatever; and further that no person or body is recognized by the law of England as having a right to override or set aside the legislation of Parliament."[3]

Canadian federalism entails the distribution of legislative power between Parliament and the provinces, and the courts have assumed the power to review legislation in order to determine whether it is *intra vires* the legislative body in question. In a federal state judicial review with respect to an issue of the distribution of power is inevitable. It is true then, that legislative bodies in Canada have never been sovereign in the same sense as the Parliament of the United Kingdom.

On the other hand the Constitution Act, 1867[4] (formerly the British North America Act, 1867) provides that Canada is to have ". . . a constitution similar in principle to that of the United Kingdom"—the principle of parliamentary sovereignty being the dominant characteristic of British political institutions.[5] Applying this principle to Canada one finds the general rule that the distribution of powers between Parliament and the legislatures is exhaustive. In other words, generally speaking, the federal Parliament and provincial legislatures together have been sovereign in a similar sense to the United Kingdom Parliament or legislative powers have been exhaustively distributed among them.

This principle of exhaustiveness has been subject to qualifications. Certain specified areas of legislative competence have been withheld from both Parliament and the provincial legislatures. For instance, the power to amend the Constitution Acts 1867-1975 in such a way as to redistribute legislative power remained, until recently, with the United Kingdom Parliament.[6]

Nevertheless, for the purpose of the protection of human rights these exceptions have been few and far between. The doctrine of parliamentary sovereignty, as the view that legislative authority is not restricted as to substance, or is not subject to judicial review for the content of legislation, has been applicable to the federal and provincial legislatures of Canada, albeit each within their sphere.

The doctrine of parliamentary sovereignty has two implications for the protection of human rights. They are drawn from positivist premises. Alongside Dicey's statement of the doctrine of parliamentary sovereignty stands his contention, "the plain truth is that our tribunals uniformly act on the principle that a law alleged to be a bad law is *ex hypothesi* a law, and therefore entitled to obedience by the courts." Since a "bad law is *ex hypothesi* a law," and the law has no necessary content, there is no legal necessity that law serve to protect human rights. Secondly, the courts cannot legitimately interpret a law inimical to the security of human rights so as to avoid its clear intent. As E. C. S. Wade in his introduction to Dicey puts this, "The courts may not declare illegal what Parliament has said is law, however much it may restrict the freedom of individuals."[7]

Under the doctrine of parliamentary sovereignty therefore, emphasis in the protection of human rights is not placed on the judicial role. Reliance for the security of human rights is put on the "political sovereign," or the people, or the possibility of civil disobedience. In the words of Sir Arthur Goodhart, "it is the conviction, ingrained in the average Englishman by tradition and by education, that it is his moral duty to be free which is the only certain guarantee against arbitrary government."[8] Likewise Dicey appealed to an "external" limit on the "legal sovereign." In his words, "The external limit to the real power of a sovereign consists in the possibility or certainty that his subjects, or a large number of them, will disobey or resist his laws."[9] Protection of human rights, as a function of the threat of widespread civil disobedience or political unrest or dissatisfaction, means that security of human rights rests on the majority. Faith with respect to human rights protection is placed in the workings of democracy, in fair procedures producing legal rules with acceptable content. Thus the doctrine of parliamentary sovereignty does not turn to the judicial process for the protection of human rights or for that matter, the protection of the rights of individuals and minorities against the power of numbers.

The other side of this reliance on the political sovereign is a distrust of the judicial function. A peripheral judicial role in the protection of human rights is a consequence of a general concern to keep power with legislatures rather than with courts. This choice of emphasis may be presented, as it is within the Canadian context, in terms of the desirability of an entrenched bill of rights, one which is in a written constitution and whose amendment lies beyond ordinary legislative power. Entrenchment of a bill of rights is clearly contrary to the doctrine of parliamentary sovereignty. It alters the authority of Parliament whose legislative capacity becomes substantively limited. It alters the relationship between the legislatures and the courts since the courts are given the power to enforce substantive limitations (embodied in the constitutional document) on the legislative process.

The choice against the judicial forum as a locus for the protection of the rights of individuals and minorities is made on various grounds. Entrenchment of rights, as it transfers policy decisions from the legislatures to the courts, is undesirable because the judicial method is inadequate to define and to order human rights. The inadequacy derives from a number of facts: judicial review is sporadic or interstitial: the courts in coming to decisions take explicit account of only a limited range of facts and values, the resources available to them being limited by the practice and procedure of the Anglo-Canadian court: the judiciary themselves are insufficient in terms of background and experience for this new function, since they are generally unrepresentative of the population (selected primarily from those persons with legal practice, of middle-to-old age, conservative and male).[10] Furthermore, it is argued the kinds of human rights recognized by society and the priorities they are given are continually changing. Entrenchment of rights, because it makes amendment difficult, imposes the scope and priority of human rights of a particular time on future citizens; it allows a minority to obstruct change; it tends to bind the people to court decisions which depart from general community expectations.[11]

On the other hand, the deficiencies of the judicial system are not entirely inevitable. Judicial selection, practices and procedures can be altered, so that decisions may be better informed and more consistent with community expectations. Legislation, including human rights legislation, can be written to permit greater flexibility in the course of interpretation over time.

In theory, the question of the appropriate judicial function in the protection of human rights depends upon balancing the protection from majorities unsympathetic to the promotion of human rights which a potent judicial role offers to individuals and minorities, against the need to minimize the effects of judicial conservatism and isolation on the definition of the value system. A transfer of policy-making power to courts from legislatures by entrenchment of rights raises an impediment to the implementation of transitory prejudices. But this impediment also resists persistent demands for adjusting the status or definition of human rights. Responses thus vary to the question whether a substantive limitation on legislatures by the entrenchment of rights creates a sufficiently greater impediment to the pressures of a hostile majority, in light of the insufficiencies of the judicial system, to justify its introduction.

In fact Canadian legislative and judicial institutions have assumed a negative response and opted for the framework of the doctrine of parliamentary sovereignty. The Canadian judiciary, consequently, have adopted a particular role when confronted with questions concerning human rights protection, a role consistent with the doctrine of parliamentary sovereignty. This role has, however, meant the failure of various avenues, occasionally suggested by the courts and more recently by the legislatures, for increasing the security of human rights in Canada.

NOTES

1. Part I, *Constitution Act 1982*, Schedule B, *Canada Act 1982*, 1982, c. 11, (UK).

2. "The dominant characteristic of the British Constitution is, as . . . Dicey pointed out, the supremacy or sovereignty of Parliament." W. I. JENNINGS, *The Law and the Constitution* (London, University of London Press, 1959), p. 144.

3. A. V. DICEY, *Introduction to the Study of Law of the Constitution*, 10th ed. (London, Macmillan, 1959), p. 40.

4. *Constitution Act, 1867*, 30-1 Vict., c. 3 (UK).

5. DICEY, *Introduction to the Study of Law of the Constitution*, p. 39.

6. For a catalogue of exceptions existing prior to patriation see P. HOGG, *Constitutional Law of Canada* (Toronto, Carswell, 1977), pp. 198-200.

7. DICEY, *Introduction to the Study of Law of the Constitution*, p. cxcv; or in Dicey's words at p. 62, "There is no legal basis for the theory that judges, as exponents of morality, may overrule Acts of Parliament."

8. A. GOODHART, *English Law and the Moral Law* (London, Stevens, 1955), p. 62.

9. DICEY, *Introduction to the Study Of Law of the Constitution*, pp. 76-7.

10. See: D. SMILEY, "The Case Against the Canadian Charter of Human Rights," *Canadian Journal of Political Science*, 2 (1969): 283, 284, 285; HOGG,

Constitutional Law of Canada, pp. 46, 47; *Royal Commission Inquiry into Civil Rights* (McRuer Report), pp. 1382, 1383; D. SCHMEISER, "Disadvantages of an Entrenched Canadian Bill of Rights," *Saskatchewan Law Review*, 33 (1968): p. 250.

11. See: SMILEY, "The Case Against the Canadian Charter of Human Rights": 278, 279, 291; *Royal Commission Inquiry into Civil Rights* (McRuer Report), pp. 1566, 1567; HOGG, *Constitutional Law of Canada*, p. 44.

The Origins of Judicial Review in Canada

JENNIFER SMITH

For many years students have been taught that the practice of judicial review in Canada is less important than it is in the United States. This is because it has had less scope, and it has had less scope because until recently Canada's written constitution, unlike the American Constitution, included no bill of rights.[1] Whereas in both countries the courts, acting as "umpires" of their respective federal forms of government, have had the power to declare laws beyond the competence of the jurisdiction enacting them, the American courts have had the additional and, to many, fascinating power to enforce against governments the guarantees of the rights of citizens contained in the Bill of Rights.[2] Obviously this line of comparison is outmoded now. After a prolonged and at times bitter debate, the federal government and nine of the ten provincial governments reached agreement last year on a set of amendments to the British North America Act, among them a Charter of Rights and Freedoms.[3] As a result, the breadth of the courts' power of judicial review more closely approximates that possessed by their American counterparts. Is this development consistent with the

Adapted (and shortened) from Jennifer Smith, "The Origins of Judicial Review in Canada," *Canadian Journal of Political Science*, Vol. XVI, No. 1 (March, 1983): 114-143. By permission of the publisher and author.

nature of Canada's constitutional arrangements? Does the Charter provide the basis of the completion of an initially limited power?

A response to questions of this nature requires an examination of the origins of judicial review in Canada. Did the Fathers of Confederation intend judicial review? If they intended nothing of the sort, resort to its use offers an interesting example of an important development that was not part of the country's initial constitutional design. If they understood it differently than we do today, their understanding is of relevance for public expectations raised by the Charter. On the other hand, if they anticipated the development of judicial review as it has taken shape, the advent of the Charter may be marked by a smooth transition. These earlier opinions, by shedding light on the nature of judicial review in the Canadian setting, will help evaluate the significance of the Charter vis-à-vis our judicial tradition.

One of the most thorough studies available is B. L. Strayer's *Judicial Review of Legislation in Canada*. Strayer argues that the BNA Act, 1867 and related acts did not vest explicitly in the courts the power of judicial review. Nor can our common law inheritance be held responsible for it. Instead, judicial review is a product of the British colonial system, "implicit in the royal instructions, charters, or Imperial statutes creating the colonial legislatures."[4] Since these legislatures were bodies of limited power, the colonial charters establishing them typically included clauses prohibiting them from passing laws repugnant to Imperial statutes.[5] In his study of the pre-Confederation courts in British North America, Strayer finds no instance of their invalidating a colonial statute on the grounds of repugnancy to British laws. Yet he does discern an "awareness" of power to do just that. Other colonial courts throughout the British Empire had exercised this power. And there was also the example of the Judicial Committee of the Privy Council.

It is not surprising that Strayer looks hard at the colonial system for the roots of judicial review since he finds little evidence in the Confederation debates that the Canadian founders paid anything but minimal attention to it. The resolutions drafted at the Quebec Conference in 1864, which formed the basis of the BNA Act three years later, contained a clause enabling Parliament to establish a "General Court of Appeal for the Federated Provinces." A similar if lengthier provision was incorporated ultimately in section 101 of the Act. Neither set of resolutions absolutely required the establishment of such a court nor explicitly bestowed upon it the power of judicial review.

It might be thought that the debate on the establishment of the Supreme Court a scant eight years after Confederation would throw some light on the founders' opinions, but Strayer's interest in it is confined mainly to the controversy over the relation of the new court to the Judicial Committee. Thus he is faced with the fact that following Confederation, the Canadian courts took up the power of judicial review, and concludes that this was the result of both pre-Confederation practice and the federal character of the new constitution.

Strayer's search for an explanation of judicial review arises out of his insistence that it is not "absolute," that is, not fully guaranteed in the BNA Act. In his opinion, the relevant clauses of the Act gave Parliament and the local legislatures too much regulatory power over the courts to support such a view, power more in keeping with the principle of parliamentary as opposed to judicial supremacy. Indeed, according to W. R. Lederman, Strayer implies that an "element of judicial usurpation" figured in its establishment, an implication Lederman cannot accept. By contrast, Lederman reads into sections 96 to 100 of the Act an "intention to reproduce superior courts in the image of the English central royal courts."[6]

Lederman begins by questioning the commonly held opinion that the British Parliament possesses absolute legislative supremacy. Other principles of Britain's unwritten constitution, he suggests, serve to qualify the principle of parliamentary supremacy, among them that of the independence of the judiciary. As evidence, he traces the historical development of the autonomy of judges of the central courts of common law in such matters as tenure, removal and salaries, power to punish for contempt and personal legal immunity, demonstrating in each instance how eventually settled practice served to establish the "primary constitutional status" of these superior courts. On the question of their wide-ranging jurisdiction, he concedes that after the Settlement of 1688, the courts no longer claimed the power to review the validity of acts of Parliament. Nevertheless, they continued to review the acts of inferior governmental officials and bodies and to refuse to enforce them if the authorities exceeded their jurisdiction.

Whatever the force of their contending views, however, they clearly owe little to evidence provided by the framers' opinions. Lederman steers clear of them altogether; Strayer professes to find little of interest in those he notices. Yet a closer examination of the framers' views may throw some light on this debate.

According to the records of the Quebec Conference edited by Joseph Pope, Macdonald alluded to the need for some form of judicial review in his initial argument on the desirability of federal union. Having put the case for a strong central government, he warned the delegates not so much of the importance of provincial governments per se but of the need of the people in each "section" to feel protected, that is, secure from the reach of an overweening central authority. One way of encouraging this feeling was to provide a guarantee of the test of legality against which centralist incursions on sectional matters might be measured. Since the new constitution would take the form of a British statute, he continued, British courts could supply an answer to the question, "Is it legal or not?" The availability of some form of judicial arbitration might satisfy local partisans fearful of abandoning local autonomy to the mercies of a strong central power.[7]

The issue was raised once more towards the end of the Quebec Conference, again in connection with the extent of jurisdiction appropriate to local governments. R. B. Dickey of Nova Scotia, expressing some sympathy for the opinion of E. B. Chandler of New Brunswick that the delegates were in danger of establishing a legislative rather than a federal union by insisting on reserving all unspecified subject matters to the central government, proposed a "Supreme Court of Appeal to decide any conflict between general and state rights." He was supported by George Brown, leader of the "Grits" in Upper Canada, who suggested that provincial courts determine jurisdictional disputes, with provision for appeal to a superior court. Both men appeared to contemplate a Canadian court of last resort on constitutional questions. Jonathan McCully of Nova Scotia, however, disputed this proposal. Throughout the Conference, he had made no bones about his preference for a legislative over a federal union, although he was prepared to accept a highly centralized form of federalism.

When the time came to defend the Resolutions before the Parliament of Canada, Macdonald appeared to have changed his mind on the need for judicial arbitration. Rather than presenting it as a necessary or desirable feature of federalism, he came close to implying that it signalled a flaw in constitutional arrangements, one that the Resolutions, happily, had been designed to avoid. According to him, the Resolutions spelled out the distribution of legislative powers between Parliament and the local legislatures so clearly that conflicting jurisdictional claims were unlikely to arise. Thus there was no apparent need for a court to resolve them. The proposed scheme of union safely dispensed with the requirement of judicial arbitration. Macdonald avoided any mention of the fact that the American Constitution did provide for a general court of appeal and that, by the celebrated decision of *Marbury v. Madison* (1803) the court had reserved to itself the power of judicial review. Since he supposed the distribution of legislative powers set out in the American document so inadequate that it actually provoked jurisdictional disputes, he may have considered the American court a regrettable remedy. In any event, the possibility of a general appellate court exercising the power of judicial review certainly did not figure in his elaboration and defence of the Quebec scheme. Brown, for his part, pursued a somewhat different tack by applauding the provisions enabling Parliament to establish such a court as well as appoint judges, and by arguing that the result would be to provide a uniform system of justice throughout the union.[8]

Taken together, the views expressed at the Quebec Conference and in the debate in the Parliament of Canada suggest that no one had any illusions about the significance of judicial review, particularly as it related to the distribution of legislative powers between Parliament and the local legislatures. The point at issue was whether the type of federalism set out in the Quebec Resolutions required it. Under the Resolutions, the central government possessed the power to disallow local laws just as the British government retained the power to disallow Parliament's enactments. Disallowance not only undermined the need for judicial arbitration, whether by the Judicial Committee or a national court, it also suited partisans of parliamentary supremacy like Jonathan McCully, who clearly understood the threat to this supremacy posed by a tribunal patterned after the American Supreme Court.

Judicial Review and the Constitution Act of 1982

Viewed in the light of the older controversy, the debate culminating in the recent set of amendments contained in the Constitution Act, 1982 took a familiar turn. In the earlier contest, both opponents and partisans of judicial review focussed attention on its implications for the distribution of legislative powers so critical to the shape of the country's federalism. While some saw in it a solution to conflicts arising out of competing jurisdictional claims, others interpreted it as a direct challenge to their presumption in favour of Parliament's control of the constitution. Over a century later, the issue of judicial versus parliamentary supremacy surfaced again in connection with the proposed Charter of Rights and Freedoms. Prime Minister Pierre Trudeau, a determined champion of the notion of a charter, often defended his cause without even referring to the task it necessarily imposes on the courts. Instead, he claimed that it would "confer power on the people of Canada, power to protect themselves from abuses by public authorities."[9] A charter would liberate people by preventing governments from denying specified freedoms. On the other hand, opponents of the idea like the then premier of Saskatchewan, Allan Blakeney, attempted to counter the undeniable appeal of this claim by drawing attention to the role of the courts that it implied. According to Blakeney, including rights in a written constitution means transferring responsibility for them from duly elected legislatures, the democratic seat of governments, to nonelected tribunals. It amounts to requiring the courts to make "social judgments" in the course of interpreting a charter's clauses, judgments which, in his view, properly belong to "the voters and their representatives."[10] In the event, a Charter of Rights and Freedoms now forms part of Canada's newly amended constitution. Are we entitled to conclude, then, that acceptance of the Charter, and the increased scope for judicial review that it entails, signals a resolution of the issue of parliamentary versus judicial supremacy in favour of the latter? The answer is not quite.

It is true, as Peter Russell points out, that section 52 of the Constitution Act, 1982, by declaring the Constitution of Canada to be the "supreme law" and any law inconsistent with its provisions to be of "no force or effect," gives the courts' power to invalidate unconstitutional laws an explicit constitutional footing for the first time.[11] Further, under the provisions of the new amending formulae, the composition of the Supreme Court is protected from easy change by the stringent requirement of unanimity on the part of the Senate, the House of Commons and provincial legislative assemblies. The court is also listed under section 42(1) as an item that can be amended only in accordance with the general formula set out in section 38(1). Thus the court is constitutionally entrenched. However, neither the federal government's power to appoint Supreme Court justices nor the nonjudicial advisory task required by the reference mechanism is affected. More important still is the fact that the Charter itself, to the disappointment of its partisans, contains a provision enabling the legislative bodies of both levels of government to override some of its guarantees, namely, those dealing with fundamental freedoms, legal rights and equality rights. The provision is qualified to the extent that legislatures choosing to avail themselves of it are required to declare expressly their intention and reconsider the matter every five years, and there has been speculation about the likely effect of these qualifications on politicians' willingness to resort to the "override." Nevertheless, its very appearance in the context of the Charter strikes an incongruous note and is testimony to the strength of the lingering tradition of parliamentary supremacy. Finally, there is the first clause of the Charter which subjects its guarantees to "such reasonable limits prescribed by law as can be demonstrably justified in a free and democratic society." Ultimately it is up to the Supreme Court to stake out the "reasonable limits." In the meantime, we do know that they are held to exist, that there is thought to be something higher than, or beyond the Charter's guarantees to which appeal can be made in order to justify their denial or restriction. And the initiative in this regard is secured to governments. While the courts' power of judicial review has undoubtedly surmounted the rather narrow, partisan function envisaged for the new Supreme Court in 1875 by Macdonald, the principle of parliamentary supremacy persists.

NOTES

1. The BNA Act, 1867 did guarantee individual rights to denominational schools (section 93) and the use of the French and English languages in the debates, records and journals of Parliament and the legislative assembly of Quebec, and in the courts of Canada and Quebec (section 133).

2. See R. MACGREGOR DAWSON, *The Government of Canada*, 4th ed. (Toronto: University of Toronto Press, 1969), pp. 74-5.

3. The government of Quebec refused to sign the constitutional accord of November 5, 1981.

4. *Judicial Review of Legislation in Canada* (Toronto: University of Toronto Press, 1968), p. 3.

5. *Ibid.*, pp. 6-7.

6. "The Independence of the Judiciary," *Canadian Bar Review* 34 (1956), 805, 769-809.

7. JOSEPH POPE, *Confederation: Being a Series of Hitherto Unpublished Documents Bearing on the British North America Act* (Toronto: The Carswell Co. Ltd., 1895), p. 55.

8. *Parliamentary Debates on the Subject of the Confederation of the British North American Provinces* (Quebec: Parliamentary Printers, 1865).

9. *Statement by the Prime Minister on the Canadian Constitution* (Ottawa: Office of the Prime Minister, October 2, 1980), p. 5.

10. Notes for Remarks by Premier Allan Blakeney, Dalhousie Law Alumni Association, Halifax, October 27, 1980, p. 6.

11. *Leading Constitutional Decisions*, 3rd ed. (Ottawa: Carleton University Press, 1982), p. 4.

Political Trials and the Canadian Political Tradition

KENNETH MCNAUGHT

I suspect that a Canadian attempt to define a political trial would result in constrictive language. We have never been as ready as the Americans, for example, to view the courts as means for changing legal symbols—especially if such a process includes implementing significant social change. Thus, our courts have seldom, if ever, been used to organize movements for social and economic power and control; they have, however, very often been used in attempts to suppress such movements. It may very well be because of this Canadian tradition that attempts to politicize some trials—such as the FLQ cases, the Quebec labour leaders' trial, and the lesser cases of student anti-war and "occupation" demonstrators—seem largely to have failed, at least by comparison with the Angela Davis case, the Black Panther cases, the Ellsburg case, or the Chicago trials in Judge Hoffman's court.

Adapted from Kenneth McNaught, "Political Trials and the Canadian Political Tradition," in Martin L. Friedland (ed.), *Courts and Trials* (Toronto: University of Toronto Press, 1975). By permission of the author.

A preliminary survey of Canadian political trials strongly suggests that our judges and lawyers, supported by the press and public opinion, reject any concept of the courts as positive instruments in the political process. In Canada the positive aspects of politics seem more clearly to belong to the political parties, the legislatures, and the press. A corollary of this is that political action outside the party-parliamentary structure tends automatically to be suspect—and not least because it smacks of Americanism. This deep-grained Canadian attitude of distinguishing amongst proper and improper methods of dealing with societal organization and problems reveals us as being, to some extent, what Walter Bagehot once called a "deferential society." We have certainly shown deference to the concept of *established* authority and procedures and even to the legal idea that valid authority flows downward from the crown.

Far from being merely medieval, such attitudes have often proven more liberal in their effect than those of radical or participatory democracy. In any event, the basically British belief that both liberty and justice are impossible without order lies at the heart of the Canadian political tradition and of the manner in which our judicial process has dealt with cases of a clearly political nature.

For the purpose of hypothesizing the relation of our courts to this kind of political tradition I propose a very narrow definition of "political trial," that is, one in which there appears to be an overt confrontation between the principles or forces of social change and those of social and/or constitutional continuity. Canadian courts dealing with such cases often reveal to the historian the most basic political assumptions of our society, the nature and limits of political tolerance, change and/or continuity in the social-economic basis of the country, and how political trials can occasionally bring to a head significant issues of press freedom, religious freedom and the relation of both to established political authority.

Louis Riel

In 1885 Louis Riel dropped through the scaffold at Regina. His is by far the most complicated political trial from a historian's point of view. To lawyers it is unique for two reasons: first, Riel is the only citizen of a foreign state to have been tried for treason in Canada,[1] and second, he is the only person in Canadian history to be hanged for treason who had himself conducted a political trial resulting in execution of the accused. To the historian, Riel is unique in another respect: he led our only successful democratic rebellion.[2] However, achievement of provincial status for Manitoba in 1870 had been heavily shadowed by the execution of the Ontario Orangeman Thomas Scott. Scott was tried under "Métis law" in an ad hoc court for "insubordination" to Riel's provisional government, and Riel made the fatal mistake of permitting the death sentence to be carried out, exclaiming to Donald Smith who had pleaded for remission: "We must make Canada respect us."[3]

Although Ontario howled for Riel's blood, Macdonald allowed him to go unapprehended. Thus, when Riel was captured during his unsuccessful second rebellion there could be little doubt that, if convicted and sentenced to death, commutation would present serious political dangers. The historical significance of the trial is therefore very great indeed. It continued to focus attention on the Métis and Indian grievances by suggesting that mere suppression of the rebellion would not settle the problems created by a conflict of cultures and by governmental insouciance. Riel's own version of his defence was that the "insane" party in the case was the government of Canada, and there were many newspapers (including the Toronto *Globe*) that agreed with him. Indeed the very organization of his legal defence, supervised by L.O. David and including Wilfrid Laurier and Rodolphe LaFlamme, reads like the establishment list of French Canadian Liberalism. The trial and execution, more than the rebellion itself, brought to a head the deepest potential conflict in Canadian society; to Quebec Riel became a figure of innocence and rejected aspirations, to Ontario a figure of political criminality. The bitterness unleashed by Macdonald's refusal to have the sentence commuted became a major factor in moving Quebec from the Conservative to the Liberal party in federal politics. However, the trial itself also raises some interesting questions.

The lawyers provided for Riel by his Quebec-based defence committee were François Lemieux, Charles Fitzpatrick, and J.N. Greenshields. None of them knew anything about the west and it remains a real question whether they helped or hindered Riel during the trial. Riel was so clearly guilty of treason that the only serious question throughout was that of mitigating circumstances which might soften the eventual sentence. His lawyers, against Riel's strenuous opposition, elected to plead insanity. It seems plausible, despite a mountain of conflicting evidence as to Riel's sanity (that is, responsibility for his actions), that his own unremitting effort to *accept* responsibility is the most convincing aspect of the trial and of the lengthy post-trial period pending his execution.

Riel wrote, prior to his trial: "I desire that my trial should turn on the merits of my actions."[4] It did not. It turned on the question of his sanity, introducing such items as his prophetic pretensions and plans to resettle the discordant populations of Europe in the New World. Riel felt that gratitude prevented him from dismissing his lawyers, as he was tempted to do when he found that they could not question the crown's witnesses in the way that he knew was essential. His lawyers, he remarked, "come from Quebec, from a far province" and had to question men "with whom they are not acquainted, on circumstances which they don't know." Although Riel suggested questions, "they cannot follow the thread of all the questions that could be put to the witnesses. They lose more than three-quarters of the good opportunities." Judge Richardson was prepared to allow Riel to cross-question the witnesses, but his lawyers said they would withdraw if he were allowed to do so. Riel was forced to subside with the bitter cry: "Here I have to defend myself against the accusation of high treason, or I have to consent to the animal life of an asylum."[5] In the result he was allowed to address the jury only after his lawyers had finished. Then Riel made his essential point: "If you take the plea of the defence that I am not responsible for my acts, acquit me completely, since I have been quarreling with an insane and irresponsible Government. If you pronounce in favour of the Crown which contends that I am responsible, acquit me all the same. You are perfectly justified in declaring that having my reason and sound mind, I have acted reasonably and in self-defence, while the Government, my accuser, being irresponsible, and consequently insane, cannot but have acted wrong."[6]

When one considers that a six-man, English-speaking jury, after finding Riel guilty of treason, recommended him to "the mercy of the Crown," it is reasonable to ask whether their unadorned recommendation might not have been stronger had Riel been permitted to cross-examine the crown's witnesses. In the light of the political reactions there is little doubt about two aspects of the case. First, it confirmed the principle that if resort is had to violence, no matter how just the cause, it must be decisively condemned; and second, if an element of racial or cultural conflict enters into a political trial either a jury or a judge is likely to find reasons for compassion. In the case of Riel the jury's recommendation of mercy was overlooked only because of the Scott affair (an exceptional circumstance) and Macdonald's assessment of the political repercussions in Ontario.[7]

Winnipeg General Strike

The cases arising from the Winnipeg General Strike of 1919 also reveal racial tensions but, much more importantly, they cast a bright light on the impact of industrialization, urbanization, immigration and the continuities of regionalism in Canada.[8]

Winnipeg had grown from 42 000 in 1901 to 200 000 in 1919, and one-third of that population was foreign-born. As railway and marketing centre of the prairie wheat economy the city had developed supportive industry, especially in the metal and building trades. It had also developed a highly structured, class-conscious society. The men of power in Winnipeg, geographically isolated yet closely intertwined with central Canadian business and political organizations, were virtually all of Ontario lineage. They belonged to what John Porter designates as the principal Canadian "charter group,"[9] and they had no intention of loosening their control over government or economic life. Welcoming the new labour force supplied by the wheat boom immigration, these men vigorously resisted the claims of growing trade unions to recognition and bargaining rights. The buoyant business activity of first world war years had been preceded by a long period of increasingly bitter industrial strife.[10] As the war neared its end, organized labour in Winnipeg redoubled its efforts to secure full union recognition, anticipating serious unemployment with the return of the soldiers, while a rapidly rising cost of living sharpened concerns for the future. Undoubtedly, too, the Russian revolution, together with world-wide interest in the *method* of the general strike as the most effective way to achieve economic gains, industrial (as opposed to craft) unionism, and/or basic social change, further induced radical labour action in Winnipeg. As is evident in court cases following the strike (the largest and most nearly successful general strike in North America) the courts spoke not only for the Winnipeg establishment but also for the entire Canadian bourgeoisie as well as for most farmers.

In these cases, from the preliminary hearings through to the appeal judgments, an interpretation of the strike was promulgated which was an *esquisse* of the arguments put forth by the strike's opponents. The problem for the legal historian is to understand the relation between what "actually happened," the interpretation of what happened used by the courts in their judgments and the legal-political function of the judgments as precedents.[11]

What "actually happened" began on 15 May when a general strike vote conducted by the Winnipeg Trades and Labour Council went into effect with the declared purpose of achieving industrial union recognition and wage raises in the building and metal trades —whose unions were already on strike. Thirty-five thousand workers left their jobs,[12] including those who operated all the public utilities, and the economic life of the city remained at a standstill for six weeks. Fearing forcible suppression, the strike leaders managed to keep the immensely volatile situation almost completely non-violent. Yet the massive show of economic strength, together with the fact that a majority of the returned soldiers seemed sympathetic to the strikers, induced a condition close to hysteria in the "middle class" of Winnipeg, a class heavily influenced by lurid reports of the great Red Scare in the United States. Yet, while opposition to such a dramatic assertion of working-class demands was bound to be vigorous, the structural and ideological unity of that opposition was even more startling than the original cohesion of the working class. In a very real sense the strike's opponents planned their course of action and their frequent public statements as preparation for the ultimate resort to the courts. The politicization of the strike thus was the necessary foundation for the politicization of the trials. The point may be illustrated in many ways; a few examples must here suffice.

The case to be constructed was that the strike was an attempt to usurp constituted authority; that by its very nature it must become violent in order to achieve its end of establishing a soviet government in Winnipeg; and that it was principally the work of the much-feared, disloyal immigrants—those whose immediate deportation as "alien scum" and "bohunks" was demanded by J.W. Dafoe's *Free Press*.[13] The required violence was produced by two measures. First was the dismissal of the municipal police force (whose members had remained on duty while declaring their support of the strike) and its replacement by a force of untrained "specials" which provoked a minor riot on 11 June. The second incident of violence grew out of two similar arbitrary actions. The first of these was the arrest of eight strike leaders and four men who had no connection with the strike committee but who were foreign-born and whose names lent plausibility to fears of an alien conspiracy.[14] This truncating of the strike leadership angered the pro-strike veterans who organized a massive "silent parade" to demand of Senator Gideon Robertson (federal minister of labour) an explanation of the arrests. When the paraders refused to disperse the mayor read the Riot Act and a large contingent of Royal Northwest Mounted Police charged three times through the crowds, the third time shooting with revolvers. Two men were killed, and the centre of the city was occupied by heavily armed militiamen. A few days later the strike was called off.

No one can read the background of the 1919-20 trials, follow the evidence presented at those trials,[15] and miss the unbroken theme of a case-to-be-made. The federal cabinet, the district military commander and the RNWMP commissioner worked in the closest possible liaison with the Citizens' Committee which was organized by Winnipeg lawyers and businessmen to crush the strike and assert seditious intent. Symbolic of the interlocking arrangement was A.J. Andrews, who, as a prominent lawyer, ex-mayor, business and personal friend of Arthur Meighen (acting federal justice minister), and prominent in the Citizens' Committee, was appointed special agent of the department of justice, planned the arrests and became chief crown prosecutor in the trials. While the Citizens' Committee was trying to establish that violent revolution was the real goal of the strike, government spokesmen hammered home the same point, as when Meighen declared in the Commons that it was "essential that the greater issue raised by the assumption of Soviet authority—and it was nothing less on the part of those in control of the strike in the city of Winnipeg—should be once and for all decided and be decisively beaten down."[16] At the last moment, after the arrests, the government hesitated about bringing the leaders to trial for sedition, and Meighen wired Andrews: "Notwithstanding any doubt I have as to the technical legality of the arrests and the detention at Stony Mountain, I feel that rapid deportation is the best course now that the arrests are made, and later we can consider ratification."[17] Such a course would probably have been disastrous for the government. In the event, the decision to prosecute, which was most forcefully argued by Andrews, was accepted as the logical consummation of the whole anti-strike strategy. The eight leaders, Russell, Ivens, Queen, Bray, Armstrong, Heaps, Johns, and Pritchard were charged with seditious conspiracy. Shortly after the police-military action of 21 June, J.S. Woodsworth and F.J. Dixon were arrested on charges of seditious libel for continuing to publish the strikers' newspaper and printing critical accounts of "Bloody Saturday."

The crown's case that the economic goals of the strike were but incidental to a socialist revolutionary conspiracy which had been allegedly hatched at Calgary in the previous April was sustained by juries composed largely of farmers. The evidence, both of conspiracy and of seditious intent, consisted of the most radical socialist statements made over the preceding months by the defendants, together with their membership in organizations which advocated replacing the capitalist political-economic system with a socialist one. Yet, despite widespread police raids on labour offices and homes across the country, no evidence of preparation for, or specific advocacy of, the use of violence was produced.[18] The verdicts and sentences[19] may thus be presumed to flow from three principal conditions: the fact that the juries were composed of farmers who, as a class, were deeply hostile to the general strike; the extraordinarily circular definition of sedition in the Criminal Code;[20] and the decision by the judges to advise the juries that the prosecution had successfully proven that "force" had been threatened.[21]

Partly because opinion in Winnipeg was so deeply divided about the nature of the strike and its suppression, the sentences served further to politicize the situation. In the Manitoba election of 1920, Ivens, Queen, and Armstrong all won election to the legislature although they were still in jail and had stood on socialist platforms. F.J. Dixon topped the polls in Winnipeg while, in 1921, J. S. Woodsworth became the first federal MP to be elected by a social-democratic party. In declaring, very dubiously, an "apprehended insurrection" and by applying massive state violence, the anti-strike class had politically radicalized large numbers of Winnipeg's working class. It had also given fresh arguments to those leaders who believed that political party action (parliamentarism) must be the complement of economic action. The new condition of urban industrialism had been thoroughly, if with pronounced bias, examined by the courts for its inherent political dangers. One significant outcome was the amending of the Criminal Code in 1919 to increase the permissible sentence for sedition from two to twenty years and still further to broaden the "definition" of sedition. The revision was to prove convenient in obtaining convictions, amongst others, of J.B. McLachlan for his role in the extended industrial conflict in Nova Scotia in the early twenties and of Tim Buck for his membership in the Communist party in the thirties. As the worst of the depression passed, and with the political threat of the CCF increasingly worrisome to Mackenzie King, section 98 was finally repealed in 1937.

Conclusion

On the basis of this discussion it may be argued that our courts, in dealing with clearly political cases, have both reflected and expounded a confidence in the legitimacy of an evolving Canadian society and especially in the political-legal principles of that society. Thus they have firmly rejected the use of violence by any entity other than the state. So, too, they have resisted any effort to make them the agents of social change or to destroy the trial process by disruptive politicization. One result of these consistent attitudes has been positive encouragement of democratic party organization and, indeed, of a multi-party system which is distinctively Canadian.[22] Judicial insistence on the legitimacy of established authority, nourished by retention of the symbols and precedents of constitutional monarchy, has often, of course, worked to the advantage of social-economic elites.[23] But where this has been the case, changes in the structure of power and the distribution of wealth have been sought, often effectively, through democratic political action. Moreover, if the courts have been quick to lend support to established authority in real or alleged crisis situations and thus have appeared to be an arm of the executive, their severity has often been mitigated by executive-legislative policy—deciding, for example, who should actually be prosecuted, reprieved, or compensated.

Finally, although the courts have resisted any temptation to propound advanced ideas in social-economic policy, it would be absurd to argue that they have simply reflected a Canada that is a Lockean fragment frozen in unchanging political attitudes. What the courts *have* reflected is an unchanging Canadian belief in constitutionality against a background of political adaptation to the changing requirements of an increasingly industrial society.

NOTES

1. Riel became an American citizen while teaching school in Montana.

2. Whether one succeeds or fails at rebellion in Canada one receives a statue: Papineau, Mackenzie, Riel.

3. STANLEY, *Louis Riel* (1963), p. 114.

4. *Ibid.* p. 343.

5. *Ibid.* p. 350-1.

6. *Ibid.* p. 356.

7. In cases where strong public emotions are aroused— such as those attaching to race or freedom of the press —it may be that the defendant is well advised to conduct his own courtroom defence. Joseph Howe (Halifax, 1835) and Fred Dixon (Winnipeg, 1920) each defended himself successfully against substantial charges of politically libellous publication.

8. Accounts of the strike may be found in MASTERS, *The Winnipeg General Strike* (1950); ROBIN, *Radical Politics and Canadian Labour* (1968); MCNAUGHT, *A Prophet in Politics* (1959); and MCNAUGHT AND BERCUSON, *The Winnipeg Strike: 1919* (1974). The "racial tensions," of course, were not French-English but those which stemmed from the post-1896 immigration from east-central Europe.

9. PORTER, *The Vertical Mosaic* (1965), especially pp. 60ff.

10. For analysis of these years see BERCUSON, *Confrontation at Winnipeg* (1974).

11. The Robson Report (*Report of the Royal Commission to Enquire into and Report upon the Causes and Effects of the General Strike . . . in the City of Winnipeg . . . H.A. Robson, K.C., Commissioner, Winnipeg, 1919*), together with all the more recent studies of the strike, concludes that the "causes" were not those of a vast revolutionary conspiracy but rather the felt need for industrial unionism and higher wages to keep pace with post-war inflation.

12. Only twelve thousand of the strikers were union members, and this clear intimation of the *political* strength of the working class was a major reason for the politicization of the strike and the trials by business-legal leaders.

13. *Manitoba Free Press* (7, 11 June 1919).

14. One of the aliens, a man named Verenchuk, was picked up accidentally while looking after a friend's house. His name did not appear on the RNWMP warrant until thirty-six hours after he entered Stony Mountain Penitentiary.

15. Particularly R v. RUSSELL, (1919), 29 M.R. 511; aff'd (1920) 33 C.C.C. 1.

16. House of Commons *Debates* (1919), pp. 3039ff. The question of how far the official case was actually believed by those who constructed it is a difficult one. Certainly Gideon Robertson and Arthur Meighen gave many indications, public and private, that the main threat was to the dominance in Canada of what Robertson called "the sober leaders of organized labour in the United States." In the same debate Meighen, after conceding that the country's employers were highly organized, rejected the same degree of organization as a legitimate goal of labour: "Can any one contemplate such an event? . . . Are we to have on the one hand a concentration of employers, and on the other hand a concentration of all the labour interests of the Dominion, fighting it out for supremacy?"

17. House of Commons *Debates* (1926), pp. 4004ff. Despite frequent references to the alien threat all the strike leaders were British-born (except one who was born in Ontario) and the government had taken the precaution, during the strike, of amending the Immigration Act to permit deportation of British subjects, who were not Canadian-born, without jury trial.

18. The crown's claim that the Mounties were fired upon before drawing their own revolvers on 21 June does not stand up well against recent research; see BERCUSON AND MCNAUGHT, *The Winnipeg Strike: 1919* (1974). It now seems clear that the order to fire resulted from general stone-and-

stick harassment of the charging police and not from any shots fired from the crowd. No weapons were found on those arrested at the scene or in the later evidence-seeking raids.

19. Of the eight strike leaders arrested, Russell received two years for seditious conspiracy; Ivens, Johns, Pritchard, Queen, and Armstrong each received one year on the same charge; Bray received six months for being a "common nuisance"; Heaps won an acquittal. F.J. Dixon, charged with seditious libel, defended himself and was acquitted—after which the crown entered a *nolle prosequi* on the similar charge against J.S. Woodsworth.

20. For an interesting discussion of the definitional problem see Katz, "Some legal consequences of the Winnipeg General Strike of 1919," (1970), 4 *Manitoba L.J.* 39.

21. The propriety of this judicial comment was asserted in the Russell appeal case, especially by Cameron, JA, supra note 30, at 14-15. Despite the crown's emphasis on the "conspirators' " disloyalty to the British form of government, Cameron underlined the differences between Canadian and British law on the rights of picketing, sympathetic strikes, secondary boycotts, etc. He further commented that "the term 'sympathetic strike' may convey the idea of workmen in certain industries ceasing work voluntarily and without breach of their own contracts to express their sympathy for and moral support of other workmen already on strike. On this continent it is certainly not confined in meaning to any such peaceful demonstration . . . or to the apparently identical term 'secondary strike' in England . . . Here we have been educated to give the terms 'general' or 'sympathetic strike' much wider meanings and to so expand them as to include even the idea which underlies the significant phrase 'direct action.' " This pioneer continentalist then cited several American cases and quoted with approval an article commenting on them: "If the strike is in the nature of a boycott or sympathetic strike—that is, if it involves no trade dispute between the strikers and their employer . . . the strike cannot be justified and is therefore always an illegal one."

22. The federal multiethnic nature of the country is, of course, a primary factor, but upon this the attitude of the courts toward the legitimacy of political methods has acted as a catalyst.

23. Propriety in court procedure, on the other hand, together with a careful regard for press freedom (but not including freedom of "contempt"), have often benefited accused persons—as in the Gouzenko cases or even the FLQ cases. In Jacques Rose's third trial, for example, the judge was quick to investigate claims made by the jury that "plainclothes agents" tried to infiltrate the jury and were spying upon and "hassling" the jurors. See *Globe and Mail* (17 July 1973), p. 1.

Political Processes and Political Behaviour

In analyzing the nature of government and politics in various countries, several basic approaches can be used. In Part One we have focused on the institutional approach, with an emphasis on constitutions and the three branches of government. In Part Two we shift our attention to a concern with political processes; that is, a change of focus from political structures to political beliefs and behaviour.

As defined in the Oxford Dictionary, a process is "a series of actions or operations used in making or manufacturing or achieving something." A political process is a behaviour pattern that can occur either inside or outside a political institution. For example, passing a law (the legislative process) takes place in the legislative branch of government. However, the election process (the campaign, voting behaviour) takes place largely outside the confines of the three branches of government. While a constitution and the resulting institutions of government establish the framework for political behaviour, politics itself takes place through a series of processes (e.g., federal-provincial negotiations, elections) and non-governmental institutions (e.g., political parties, interest groups) designed to make the governmental institutions operate on a day-to-day basis. As a result, politics is more than government, even though government is, obviously, a crucial ingredient of politics.

In Part Two we analyze various components of the political process: political culture, political parties, and political behaviour. Political culture provides the context for both governmental and political processes. Political parties are a primary mechanism for acquiring control of the government and for making government work once power has been won. Electoral behaviour, such as voting or interest group participation, allows individual citizens a role in the governmental and political processes of their country.

Political Culture

The pattern of political attitudes held by leaders and citizens can be defined as a political system's political culture: "the set of political beliefs, feelings, and values that prevail in a nation at a given time."[1] In other words, Canada's political culture is composed of "what Canadians feel, think, and do politically."[2]

The values of a political culture are imbedded in a country's governmental institutions and political processes, while at the same time they help to define the rules of the game. Political legitimacy is inherently linked to political values. Political culture, thus, is a kind of perceptual filter through which we interpret the political world and, as such, usually includes various myths (e.g., parliamentary sovereignty) about the political process: "All peoples live by myth because myth is the inevitable result of any attempt to make sense of the world."[3] Finally, certain patterns of political belief (e.g., democratic values) are likely to be congruent with particular kinds of political institutions (e.g., democratic political structures, such as a competitive party system). Such a connection between political beliefs and political structures is exemplified in the following quotation:

> In an attempt to explain the Russian revolution to Lady Ottoline Morrell, Bertrand Russell once remarked that, appalling though Bolshevik despotism was, it seemed the right sort of government for Russia: "If you ask yourself how Dostoevsky's characters should be governed, you will understand."[4]

As an analytical tool, the concept of political culture can be used to describe and to compare with other countries the content of a nation's political beliefs. For example, the Canadian political culture has always been heavily influenced by the American one. Anthony Westell, in reading number twenty-one ("Our Fading Political Culture"), analyzes the impact of the United States on Canadian political values and suggests that the influx of American attitudes is fundamentally altering the "relationship between the citizen and the state" in Canada. Thus, the "Americanization" of specific political attitudes reflects the evolving pattern of Canada's political culture.

An additional important use of the political culture approach in comparative analysis is as an explanation for the patterns of political phenomena. For example, in reading number twenty-two ("Government Intervention: Canada and the United States Compared"), Sylvia Ostry explains the different patterns of government expansion, in part, by the varying attitudes (i.e., differences within the political culture) towards the role and legitimacy of government in these two North American polities. Finally, in reading number twenty-three ("Nuances of Political Culture? Definitions of Politician/Politicien"), we see some important differences in the way various systems define the role and legitimacy of the politician.

NOTES

1. MATTEI DOGAN AND DOMINIQUE PELASSY, *How to Compare Nations: Strategies in Comparative Politics* (Chatham, New Jersey: Chatham House Publishers, 1984), p. 58.

2. DAVID BELL AND LORNE TEPPERMAN, *The Roots of Disunity: A Look at Canadian Political Culture* (Toronto: McClelland and Stewart, 1979), p. 6.

3. KEITH WALDEN, *Visions of Order: The Canadian Mounties in Symbol and Myth* (Toronto: Butterworths, 1982), p. 9.

4. AILEEN KELLY, "A Complex Vision," Introduction to Isaiah Berlin, *Russian Thinkers* (Middlesex, England: Penguin Books, 1979), p. xiii.

Our Fading Political Culture

ANTHONY WESTELL

Canadians are not going to be able to invent a way of life and a system of social values much different from those of the United States. We are increasingly part of an integrated continental economy, which itself is a unit of an increasingly interdependent international system.

The sensible national goal now is not to preserve what little remains of economic sovereignty, but to own a larger chunk of North American business and the wealth it produces. The nature of our economy imposes a way of life on most Canadian workers and creates a business culture in which Canadian managers must operate. These influences are powerfully reinforced by U.S. television, which not only communicates social values but very often writes the Canadian agenda of public issues.

Canadians can probably be more active and influential in contributing to the popular culture of North America; and we can certainly preserve a national identity within the continental community, as Quebecers have preserved their identity within Confederation, the Scots within the United Kingdom, and all the member states within the European Economic Community. But, while we may never be quite like Americans, it is idle and a great waste of creative energy to go on pretending that we are going to invent a truly distinctive and independent Canadian society.

Indeed, the last remaining area of Canadian distinction, our political culture, is now giving way to the U.S. model and example. While this process is probably inevitable, it is ironic that it is being encouraged, quite unconsciously, by Canadians who think of themselves as nationalists, or at least as true-blue, true-pink or true-grit guardians of the true north strong and free.

Our political culture rests on institutions and attitudes inherited from Britain. The institutions—Crown, Cabinet government, Parliament—are still in place and unlikely to be replaced. But the attitudes they are supposed to reflect and protect are rapidly being eroded by ideas imported from the United States—adversary me-

Reprinted from Anthony Westell, "Our Fading Political Culture," *Policy Options*, Vol. 3, No. 1 (January/February, 1982): 9-11. Reprinted by permission of The Institute for Research on Public Policy.

dia, "freedom of information," the charter of rights, even division of powers.

The Fathers of Confederation were deeply conservative in their concept of the proper relationship of the state to the citizen. They viewed with distaste and even fear the revolutionary, liberal and democratic disorder of the United States. They hoped to build in Canada a more orderly and peaceful society. W.L. Morton has described the contrasting attitudes so neatly that his example has become an unavoidable cliché: The American Fathers proclaimed a revolution in the name of "life, liberty and the pursuit of happiness"; the Canadian Fathers, in the words of the British North America Act, sought "peace, order and good government."

An orderly and law-abiding society is possible only when there is respect for authority, and the Canadian system of government, copied from the British model, was intended to ensure respect. In his classic, *The English Constitution*—by coincidence, published in the year of Confederation, 1867—Walter Bagehot pointed out that the pomp and circumstance of monarchy and parliamentary government were largely a performance to impress the people while the politicians got on with the messy job of government.

Incidentally, Bagehot thought that the sturdy and independent colonials in the Americas would be able to manage their affairs without recourse to such a pantomime, but we have clung to it at least in part because it has served to distinguish us from the United States.

Canadian political conservatism was reinforced in time by Canadian socialism, which also drew upon British models. Socialism presupposes the existence of a powerful state commanding the respect and obedience of the people. While socialists were at first contemptuous of the Crown and parliamentary pageantry, they came to see the value of symbols of authority that survive the misadventures of fallible politicians.

The U.S. political tradition is completely different. The country was born in a revolution against established authority and raised on liberal ideas. The highest value is the liberty of the individual to do as he pleases with minimum interference from the state. Government is a necessary evil, and politicians, if not watched and checked, will steal your rights and rob you blind.

To sum up the difference in political cultures: in Canada the state has been viewed, by and large, as a beneficent agency, protecting the citizen and promoting the general welfare; in the United States, the state has been regarded with suspicion, as a potential threat to the liberty of the individual.

Of course, tradition is not always observed, and it is easy to think of examples that contradict the descriptions I have suggested. But I am writing here not so much of practice as of the theories, attitudes and public beliefs that constitute a political culture.

What is now happening in Canada is that U.S. attitudes are infusing political debate and changing the traditional relationship between the citizen and the state. Canadians, like Americans, are coming to see government not as friend and protector but as fool, knave and potential oppressor. The new attitude is apparent in, and much encouraged by, the media of news and commentary, which see themselves as adversaries of government.

Although the concept of the press as a Fourth Estate was first expressed in Britain, it grew to reality in the United States where it was enshrined in the famous First Amendment to the constitution. The U.S. press has always seen itself—in theory, which is not always matched by practice—as a check on government, a countervailing power.

In his recent book, *Without Fear or Favor*, Harrison Salisbury concludes that after confronting and defeating government in the battles over the Pentagon Papers and Watergate, the U.S. media, led by *The New York Times*, have finally come to their rightful place of power and influence. It does not seem to occur to him that there may be a connection between this change in the U.S. system of government and the commonly heard complaint that the system does not work as well as it used to.

The Canadian press, like the British press, was for many years content to be a party press. It could be fiercely critical of a particular politician or government, but it was respectful of the state as an institution; indeed, the owners of the press were often members of the establishment, accepting titles, honors and appointments for their services to the state.

The press eventually escaped the ties of party, claiming to have become independent critics of events. But it is only in the past ten or a dozen years that the media—TV and radio now having joined the printed press in active political journalism—have tended toward the adversarial style, consistently attacking the efficacy of government, the motives of politicians, the legitimacy of authority. It is commonplace now to hear journalists argue that government is accountable to them at news conferences, as well as to Parliament and to the electorate; to the extent that they claim a mandate from their readers and viewers to hold government accountable, they are claiming to be rivals of the elected representatives.

Many factors combined to bring about this transformation of the media, from purveyors of information and opinion to competitors for political power. The rise of TV enormously increased the importance of media in the political process. A side effect was to raise some journalists from the level of obscure, poorly paid scribblers in the service of publishers to that of public personalities, media stars with handsome incomes.

In the same period, newspapers were passing into the hands of businessmen who were interested more in profit than in political influence; they were prepared to allow journalists to write more or less what they wished provided it sold papers. In addition, new recruits to journalism were better educated, or at least more confident in their opinions, and the new journalism schools turned out graduates who often had studied U.S. models of the media and their relation to society. And then of course there was Watergate and the glory days for U.S. journalists, which set new goals for their Canadian counterparts. We suffered, as Mr. Trudeau remarked with Freud in mind, from Watergate-envy.

More recently, the rise of the West in Canadian affairs has increased the prominence of Western journalists and media. The populist inclinations of the West are more American than central Canadian in style, and it is probably no accident that the leading practitioner of adversary journalism in Canada is a Westerner, Allan Fotheringham. To Fotheringham, government is the natural enemy of the media. It used not to be that way in Ottawa.

The new attitude of the media is reflected in the campaign for "freedom of information." This idea also is copied from the United States, and it is based upon a deep mistrust of government, on the suspicion that government amounts to a conspiracy against the citizen and needs to be exposed. The idea of getting access to the files is not to provide a balanced account of the process of government; it is to find the evidence that governments are stupid and/or corrupt, that they are hardly fit to rule and certainly ought to be cut down to size.

Governments do make mistakes, act shabbily, even scandalously on occasion. But to focus exclusively on defects is to weaken public confidence, and it can be argued that "freedom of information" has led to weaker rather than better government in the United States. The interesting question is where the power has gone, and one answer might be that it has gone to the media.

The object of a Charter of Rights is to protect Canadians against their government. It is an explicit statement that government is not to be trusted, that the elected representatives of the people are not the best defenders of the people's rights and freedoms. Judges are thought to be rather more reliable than politicians, courts to be wiser than Parliament.

In the United States, the courts are one of three branches of government among which power is divided. In strengthening the courts at the expense of Parliament, we are moving toward the U.S. model, and we are tempted in other ways toward a division of powers.

A reading of the Confederation debates leaves no doubt that the Fathers intended to create a strong central government superior in almost every way to the provincial governments. The Canadian consensus now seems to be that the central government and Parliament are not to be trusted to make national policy; they must share that function with the provinces, and they are not to exercise power without provincial consent. The theory effectively divides power, but it does not explain what is to happen when Ottawa and the provinces cannot agree. The United States has a similar problem when President and Congress disagree, but surely that is not a model we need to copy.

Even within the central Parliament, there is a tendency toward a division of powers. Prime Ministers have become more presidential in style, and it is perhaps a natural reaction for backbenchers to become more Congressional, hiding themselves off in committees of the Commons in which party discipline is looser and they can enjoy the illusion of independence.

Mr. Joe Clark, when Prime Minister, proposed to make that independence less illusory by giving committees a measure of autonomy. That would have been an important break in the parliamentary tradition in which committees are creatures of the Commons, and the Commons of course is controlled by the government. Mr. Clark, it might be noted, is a Westerner, and this may explain such American inclinations.

In describing the process of Americanization of our political culture, I have neither applauded nor deplored. In truth, I have very mixed feelings. I believe that economic and cultural integration are inevitable and desirable; I don't like national borders that prevent the free movement of people, ideas and commerce, and it appears to me that nationalists usually protect private privilege rather than the public interest. On the other hand, I believe that a strong state is necessary to preserve order and promote the general welfare; I see nothing wrong in being deferential toward democratically elected authority. In a society in which economic power is largely in private hands, the state is the ordinary person's best hope of improving his or her position. So I do not like to see the erosion of the Canadian state by American ideas.

While the U.S. system of government has clear advantages over the parliamentary system in a sprawling federal union, it seems to me that we ought to be able to devise a Canadian compromise that takes the best of both systems. What I find remarkable and deplorable at present is that "progressives" of the Left, who must rely on the state to implement their ideas, and "nationalists," who wish to preserve Canadian distinctiveness, are in the forefront of those pressing the so-called reforms that are weakening the state in Canada and reproducing U.S. models.

Government Intervention: Canada and the United States Compared

SYLVIA OSTRY

It is fashionable these days to be somewhat hostile to the very size of government, and in particular, to be critical of the inefficiency of many government regulatory activities at federal, state and local levels. I regard myself neither as a dedicated proponent nor as a critic of government intervention and regulation in the market place. I share the concern of many about some of the unintended consequences of government intervention and I fully support the search for new and less costly alternatives by which to achieve society's objectives. The fabric of any society, though, requires rules, sanctions and social conventions, and these inevitably become more complex as our sights extend higher and wider.

To me, the concept of a democratic market economy is precisely what it implies—the conjoining of workable business competition

Reprinted from Sylvia Ostry, "Government Intervention: Canada and the United States Compared," *Policy Options*, Vol. 1, No. 1 (March, 1980): 26-31. Reprinted by permission of the Institute for Research on Public Policy.

and public decisions arrived at through democratic electoral processes. Within the two extremes of laissez-faire and perfect competition on the one hand, or government-legislated expenditure and allocation on the other hand, a whole range of organizational devices and instruments may bind an economy together and blend public concerns—in areas such as education, safety, health and social security—with private market processes and decisions.

The mark of a democracy is that the "big" choices that allocate scarce resources between public and private activities are ultimately made at the ballot box. How societies exercise their public and private market choices depends, in my view, largely on their state of economic development, on how wide are the disparities of economic power, how strong is the influence of various power groups, and on how inclined are the various economic actors to promote or protect themselves through initiatives in the market rather than through political action.

In coming to terms anew with the question of the role of government, we will, of course, need to look beyond the historical circumstances. Public interventions which were initially directed towards filling legitimate gaps in the economy may have little rationale in present economic circumstances. Time moves on: new technologies create new opportunities and break down old monopolies which may no longer need to be regulated. Social norms that prevail today may be obsolete tomorrow. Values and attitudes change. There is therefore a need to carefully and continually re-examine the basis for various types of government involvement.

Beyond this, it has been amply shown that there is a need to be suspect about the rate of return on many government activities, particularly when all of the longer-term and less easily measured costs are taken into consideration. Even where the return is positive, we know that it is not always the case that the least costly and most effective delivery of service is being employed.

These are some of the big and troubling questions. To flesh them out, a selective tour of North American history is useful.

The spread of eastern seaboard populations beyond the Appalachians and the Alleghenys, and further north beyond the wedge of PreCambrian forest and lakes that join Ontario and Manitoba, to abundant land beyond, meant that much of our early traditions, both east and west of the divides, were of independent farmers exchanging staple or surplus foodstuffs eastward to urban markets where trade was expedited and manufacturing undertaken.

There was local democracy, with relationships secured by social understandings—mutual responsibilities and obligations borne from hardships—or sometimes by the six-shooter. But even then some regulatory interventions were found to be necessary. One has only to remember the barbed wire and the range wars and the feuds over water holes to recognize the early necessity for systems of registering legal claims and providing for riparian rights.

In the early stages, with land abundant, the federal role was aimed largely at easing the relative scarcity of labour and capital. The U.S. 1862 Homestead Act—to Europeans an astonishing law —gave settlers 160 acres free just for the asking. Canada's Dominion Lands Act, 10 years later, required $10 for this acreage. In both countries parallel inducements encouraged other natural and mineral resources extraction. Federal and state land donations, financial grants and underwritings of foreign borrowings made possible the early canals and railways. And because citizens generally opposed direct taxation with representation almost as much as they opposed it without representation, the principal sources of federal revenue were import tariffs, which served equally as protective stimulants to industry.

In short, through a natural alliance of mercantile, agrarian and political interests, the thrust of government intervention was to attract the scarce factors of production, thereby expanding the overall domestic market and the opportunities for scale, diversification and specialization. With the "visible" and "invisible hands" thus reinforcing one another the land produced its wealth, not just in foodstuffs but in oil and coal and iron and other elements that fueled the corporate industrial expansion that followed.

Even in the early stage, though, there were important differences in approach between the United States and Canada. Canada's maturation trailed the U.S. by a generation and a half. Over the late 19th and early 20th centuries, the task of drawing the diverse elements of the young Dominion into some sort of rational and unified whole was complicated not only by barriers of distance and the inhospitality of much of the country's geography; we also had to be conscious—as the U.S. did not—of a rather overwhelming neighbour that offered a powerful counter-attraction to our efforts to build a nation in an east-west direction. The solution to these problems came to be seen in terms of a kind of partnership between the private and public sectors: working together industry and government would surmount the obstacles of distance and fend off the strong pull from south of the border.

Such thinking was enshrined as a National Policy commitment of

Canada's first Prime Minister, to build a transnational railway to link British Columbia and central Canada, to populate the lands in between and to encourage domestic manufacturing through protective tariffs. In general this National Policy of high tariffs, land settlement inducements and railway subsidies paralleled similar decisions made on a more ad hoc basis by post-civil war Republican administrations. What was different was the extent of the political commitment and the implications that Canadian governments would bail out or buy out financially troubled enterprises.

As our economies grew there emerged new sources of pressure for intervention. Luck, entrepreneurship, government influence, corruption, whatever the reason, gave market power and great economic rewards to some, often to the detriment of others. Some who suffered came to the state for elements of distributive justice. Others, who were not disadvantaged but who understood the state's power to confer economic gain, came to seek support for their ventures.

When the population is predominantly rural it is natural that many such petitions aim at protecting the incomes and savings of farmers. The early concerns of the National Grange are today entrenched in a host of agricultural adjustment, price support, commodity marketing and related programs that the U.S. federal government now administers. In Canada we have our share of federal and provincial farm income support and stabilization programs and marketing boards. Indeed, agricultural marketing legislation is a much more important phenomenon in Canada, with greater commodity coverage and generally more restrictive regulatory provisions than is the case in the United States.

Inevitably, as an economy industrializes, the countervailing calls upon government for support and assistance take many forms. Often governments are asked to be providers of last resort to bail out corporate losers, to preserve jobs or to maintain services. The larger and more diversified the economy, the more resilient and competitive its integral parts, the more indifferent governments may be to such petitions. The smaller the economy, the more fragile, the more likely an economic issue becomes a political issue.

With the passage of time Canadian governments have been heavily involved in the direct provision of goods and services, as well as in a range of industrial subsidies and incentives designed to promote economic growth. The effect has not always been as intended. Nonetheless, in broadcasting, airlines, rail and truck transport, petroleum exploration, telephone and telegraph service, even coal and iron and steel production, public enterprises are operating alongside and usually in direct competition with private enterprise. Most utility companies are publicly owned, or are highly regulated.

In the United States, intervention of this magnitude would be both unnecessary and unwelcome. Historically, it seemed to be an approach which was compatible with both Canadian concerns and Canadian sensibilities. Today, in a changed climate, there is more serious questioning of this and other kinds of intervention in Canada.

Inherent in a market economy are struggles for economic advantage and the growth of economic power. One of government's main roles is to spell out the terms and conditions governing such conflicts; to establish, as it were, the rules of the game. Both Canada and the United States accepted at an early date that the state had a responsibility to establish minimum standards of public health, education and conditions of employment and to take action to restrain the raw exercise of monopoly power. At an early date our two governments also developed basic rules to deal with a variety of fraudulent and dishonest business practices.

There were, however, some important and quite fundamental differences in the approach of Canada and the United States to the development of what we may broadly call "framework policies." While U.S. competition policy was guided from the start by an unwavering commitment to the virtues of a competitive private enterprise economy, Canadian competition policy has always reflected a good deal of ambivalence; our approach was in a sense to say, "Competition is desirable as long as it does not impede the industrialization and development of this large and relatively sparsely populated country."

So, for example, there was nothing in Canadian law to compare to the Sherman Act's clear and forthright condemnation of restrictive agreements. And whereas the United States had an effective combination of criminal and civil law, Canada's Combines Investigation Act was entirely criminal law. Recent attempts to reform and somewhat strengthen our Act have involved a long and rather intense battle, the outcome of which has not yet been completely resolved.

Labour, organized and unorganized, has long constituted a formidable political constituent. How natural then that workers should enlist government reinforcement, initially for their organizational efforts in the face of strong corporate resistance, secondly in matters of decent working conditions and, thirdly, as with other groups, to help secure the continuity of their employment and incomes.

The orchestration of government intervention legitimizing collective bargaining, and providing fair working practices for unorganized labour, has differed between the two countries. Most of the facilitating legislation in the United States has been federal, since about 70 per cent of the American work force comes under federal jurisdiction. In Canada, federal jurisdiction extends to less than 10 per cent of the work force, and the bulk of government industrial relations intervention is carried by the provinces. Moreover, the view in the United States was—and still is—that if government established an appropriate framework within which collective bargaining could occur, the system would by and large work satisfactorily on its own.

While strongly influenced by the provisions of the Wagner Act in the 1930s, the Canadian system from the start has been much more interventionist. Despite some differences between the provinces most of the legislation in Canada contains provisions for compulsory conciliation and other forms of government involvement which may appear rather curious from the U.S. perspective. Moreover, elements have been built into Canada's social security system—maternity leave, hospital and medical care, non-contributory old age pensions—that in the United States are handled in the package of fringe benefits negotiated under collective bargaining.

I might add that the labour front exemplifies the alternative choice of exercising economic and social leverage through private channels, i.e., union-management bargaining, or publicly through political intervention and government regulations. For years the major unions in both Canada and the United States have been somewhat ambivalent on how best to achieve their broader objectives, since public interventions that protect or favour unorganized workers reduce the ostensible benefits of organization. For instance, until 1919 I believe, the A.F.L. opposed minimum wage legislation in the United States; and even today in Canada some union leaders see recent federal measures to curb arbitrary dismissals and to provide grievance procedures for unorganized workers under federal jurisdiction as being anti-labour.

Government in the Postwar Economy

The most significant growth of government market intervention has occurred, of course, since World War II. This was a direct consequence of postwar reconstruction efforts and the desire of most people for government economic leadership along Keynesian lines linked to their forebearance of the heavier tax load this new role entails.

Both in Canada and the United States the federal governments undertook commitments to full employment, and their expanded tax/expenditure role in the economy gave them a fiscal leverage to counteract periodic booms and slumps in the private sector that would have been impossible a generation before. Moreover, the Keynesian approach gave a clear non-socialist rationale to unemployment insurance, social welfare and other programs that served as automatic stabilizers, as well as to the discretionary interventions intended to promote overall economic stability and growth.

This third stage in the development of our market economies has evolved into what Rostow described as "steady state maturity," and others as the consumer society. There have been more than a few differences, of course, in the routes taken by each country. Canada has been spared the heavy defence expenditures the United States has incurred—in 1975 defence took 8 per cent of the Canadian against 27 per cent of the U.S. federal budget. On the other hand, federal industrial development subsidies and investments and transfer payments have been proportionately higher in Canada—reflecting, in part, a preoccupation with regional problems. Interest payments on the national debt have also been proportionately higher in Canada. It is, however, in the broad area of social services, cultural and environmental matters, where the differences in approach between our two countries have been most pronounced.

First, however, some general comments. It seems evident that in North America and elsewhere Engel's Law applies not only to foodstuffs but to most material goods as well. There is now evidence of high income demand elasticity for services and solutions that render the quality of working and leisure activities more interesting, humane and secure. The broad stabilizing framework of monetary and fiscal levers having been established, and government's enhanced role in the economy accepted (much more so than would now appear to be the case), the emphasis had been to foster a more equitable system of real income distribution, partly through the tax system, and partly through a range of publicly financed health, education, environmental, housing, manpower, social security and related programs.

Between the mid-'50s and '70s average non-military public expenditures in OECD countries rose from 24 per cent to 37 per cent of GDP—Canada being nominally below, the U.S. considerably below, these averages.

Each country develops its own unique solutions to meet these demands and in no two countries will the role played by government be the same. Since not a few of the social requirements I have cited have formed part of fringe benefits negotiated in collective bargaining, governments' responsibilities may depend on how much of the labour force is organized. Alternatively, an industrial system, such as the Japanese, of virtually life-time employer/worker commitment with employment guarantees and family-related wage premiums including educational expenses, has resulted in that country's public health, education and welfare expenditures, as a percentage of GNP, being roughly half of North America and Western Europe. Constitutions, too, define the distribution of power between federal and state/provincial jurisdictions. Nonetheless, it seems fair to say that due largely to their taxing power and more favoured financial situation, both the federal government in Canada and the Congress and the President in the United States have played a leading role in initiating a complex range of social services. In recent years, though, there has been a significant devolution of initiative, particularly in Canada, towards the provincial governments.

Underlying the social security and regulatory systems in both countries, I believe, run the significantly differing interventionist philosophies that I alluded to earlier. Moreover, a paramount theme in Canadian politics has been that of national unity, and flowing from that concern has been the desire for the set of income security, health, education and opportunity programs to be of uniformly high standard in every part of Canada.

Indeed, during a decade commencing in the 1960s, a remarkable collection of federally-inspired programs were put into place that has had the effect of providing virtually cradle to grave basic protection and opportunity for every Canadian. Canadian federal and provincial governments put in place a *de facto* if not *de jure* guaranteed minimum income which embraced family allowances, a comprehensive social welfare program including widows and persons with disabilities, enriched unemployment insurance benefits, manpower training allowances, a greatly expanded post-secondary education program that covers about three-quarters of the real per student cost, old age pensions as a matter of right and an additional universal contributory pension program, subsidized housing and a complete hospital-medical protection program.

The principal thrust was generated through conditional grants advanced by the federal government to the provinces, reinforced by federal equalization payments to fiscally weaker provinces enabling them to bring their standards of services and institutions up to nationally acceptable levels. During this period the concept of universality was fundamental, along with a general rejection of a needs test for all but social welfare and for an old age pension supplement. Fundamental also was the view that poverty and disease and employment and income discontinuities represented personal hazards for which all Canadians shared a responsibility.

A corollary of the Canadian approach was the very heavy reliance on general revenues. Social security contributions account for about one-quarter of all government revenues in the United States, less than one-tenth in Canada. A third element of contrast was that in matters of employment, unemployment and regional economic incentives, funding and the administrative responsibility in Canada remained primarily with the federal government. Apart from a few small provincial job programs Canada's unemployment insurance benefits and her manpower training and job creation efforts are delivered through hundreds of localized offices of the federal Commission of Employment and Immigration.

In some respects our efforts have been disappointing: the education system has not been the key to greater social mobility that some initially expected; despite our progressive income tax and our comprehensive social security systems, income distribution has remained remarkably unchanged; wide regional disparities persist.

There have indeed been arguments that some government transfer and assistance programs incorporate disincentives to effort or mobility that have exacerbated the problems the programs were designed to solve. There is also considerable sympathy for the adoption of "user cost" schemes in areas such as health care. And many support the search for solutions to our problems which work through market incentives rather than legal compulsion. For many Canadians, however, I believe there is an appreciation of the high standards of income protection and medicare, and of the manpower and educational opportunities that are available across the country. The extreme financial ravages of unemployment have been eased by a scheme that covers virtually all workers—whereas less than 70 per cent of the work force in the United States is covered—and pays benefits that are probably more generous than any in the world. Again there is much criticism; serious questions are being raised, for example, about the effect of the unemployment insurance scheme on measured unemployment and work incentives.

Taking the progressivity of the tax system into account, the redistributive nature of the programs has been substantial. Recent estimates, for instance, indicate that through the combination of federal-provincial equalization payments, gains and losses from shared cost programs, transfers to individuals and unemployment insurance, the poorest regions in Canada, the Atlantic provinces, receive between 40 and 50 per cent of their provincial revenue, and Quebec about 9 per cent of its revenue, from elsewhere in Canada.

Fundamentally different approaches mark our two social security systems. Where we have emphasized national unity and uniformity, the U.S. has emphasized equal opportunity for minorities and selectivity; where we have emphasized collective responsibility and general funding from taxes, the U.S. has emphasized employment-related contributions and private savings; and where we have given preference to government initiated and delivered systems, the U.S. has tended to prefer the private competitive model, leaving the government the agency of last resort. However, the climate has changed considerably over the years, and today there is growing concern in Canada about many aspects of social security policy and about government intervention in general.

In addition to social security, there is a second area where Canadian governments have intervened more extensively than those of the United States—cultural matters. In the past, the stream of liberal thought in the United States stressed the sense of oneness of all Americans with a view to de-emphasizing separate and discriminatory ethnic identification. With the resurgence of pride among minorities this approach is now undergoing modification. More emphasis is being given to the separate histories of blacks, Indians and Spanish-speaking people. For all that, entrepreneurial initiative reinforced by a well-developed system of private patronage continues to have a major influence on the nature and development of U.S. culture. To understand the growth of cultural activities and institutions one has to look not at the role of the State, but at the strong tradition of voluntarism and the generous support that has been made available by private individuals and more recently by corporations and such vital private charitable organizations as the Carnegie, Ford and Peabody Foundations.

Canada is a relatively small nation in terms of population and it is natural that we be somewhat self-conscious and uncertain about what we can pridefully call our own. In developing our concept of national identity we embrace two official language groups each with its own traditions and each seeking equal opportunities for cultural self-determination. And as a nation of immigrants we have endeavoured to nurture multiculturalism within the broader Canadian identification and support a concept, abandoned until recently in the United States, of "a nation of nations." But superimposed on these issues is the fact of Canada's precarious status, so aptly described as that of a marginal society—English-speaking Canadians living on the margins of their British and European political heritage and their American environment, French Canadians continuing a French tradition in a setting of North American industrialism.

In the circumstances we have relied heavily on public support to encourage artistic and cultural expression in both the English and French-speaking communities and to bring to all sectors of the country a sense of Canadianism that is distinct from the American mould. The federal government, through the publicly funded Canadian Broadcasting Corporation, provides a national radio and television network that broadcasts in both languages, and Ontario and Quebec and several other provinces operate educational T.V. networks. Protective regulations and subsidies are used to promote Canadian content in the media and in book and magazine publishing, and grants are available to foster Canadian actors, musicians, dramatists and authors. The federal government through the National Film Board produces film documentaries and supports the Canadian Film Development Corporation, a public-private film venture enterprise. And the Canada Council provides support for scholarly research in social sciences and the performing arts.

All in all it amounts to an impressive level of government support for the arts—estimated at about $700 million or approximately 1.7 per cent of total federal expenditures over 1977/78; by comparison U.S. federal support for the arts through the National Endowment is under $100 million.

All democratic countries must, of course, be especially wary of excessive government control and influence over the media and the arts. The U.S. concern in this area is reflected not only by the rather limited extent of government involvement in and support for the arts, but also by the autonomy accorded regulatory boards. These sensitivities have certainly been important in shaping the nature of Canadian government participation in cultural matters. Nonetheless, Canadians traditionally have been willing to accept a more active public role than might be agreeable to their southern neighbours. Further, the institution of the independent Crown corporation, with its arm's length relationship to the government, has proved a successful device in ensuring support without political interference.

There are, of course, legitimate questions about some of our government initiatives in the cultural field. Some people are disturbed by the evidence of what they describe as chauvinism. On the whole though, I believe the federal and provincial interventions and expenditures in support of Canada's infant "culture" industry command widespread support. The popular view might perhaps be summed up by the clarion-cry—"We shall not be swamped!"

Finally, this brings me to the so-called new regulatory area of environmental and consumer-based regulations. During the 1960s and early 1970s governments in both our countries have introduced an enormous and bewildering flow of rules and regulations intended to protect us from unsafe foods and hazardous products, to make us more informed consumers, to reduce pollution, to help preserve our scarce environmental resources, and to deal wth a range of related concerns. Despite Canada's greater acceptance of government intervention, and despite a political institutional structure in Canada which is particularly well-suited to strong executive action, it is the U.S. government which has often led the way and established many of the policy directions in these newer areas. I suppose this can be partly explained by different interests and concerns. We perhaps have been more sensitive to developmental and growth objectives and reluctant to enforce policies which would impede efforts in this direction; also, in Canada clean air and water are not the scarce factors they are in many areas of the United States.

A second factor perhaps is that the American presence that worries us on the cultural side provides important external economies on the product safety and emissions control sides. Our federal/provincial food and drug experts and consumer affairs officials watch closely and benefit directly from the scientific reports and proceedings of the U.S. Food and Drug Administration, the Consumer Product Safety Commission, the Environmental Protection Agency, and other similar organizations. And since in many cases the same products are marketed on both sides of the border we benefit from the rulings the U.S. agencies lay down. Another explanation perhaps lies in the different division of legislative responsibilities in Canada and the United States. While consumer protection is a matter of overlapping responsibility in both countries, the federal trade and commerce power has been given a much broader interpretation by U.S. courts; and this has allowed central government greater scope to assume a strong leadership role.

On the environmental front in Canada, issues having to do with a province's resources fall within its legal jurisdiction and much of the legislation is at that level. In the case of forest or mineral extraction the practice in Canada is that firms obtain access to rights on a leasehold basis. Few companies own the land outright. Hence enterprise-specific environmental requirements can be written into the terms of the lease, rather than issued as a regulation or as a court decision.

I think, however, that a good deal of the explanation for the differences between our policies lies in another direction: it is related I believe to the considerably stronger and more active role of U.S. interest groups, politicians, the press and other institutions in mobilizing and articulating public opinion. Consumers and environmental groups are, of course, active in Canada; but they are frequently lacking in resources (except when these are provided by government), and they are often a pale reflection of their U.S. counterparts.

Our more closed parliamentary political system, our generally more accommodating perception of government, and our national inclination to avoid confrontation, I suppose are some aspects of the explanation for this. Our preoccupation with regional and national unity issues perhaps lowers our sensitivity to the other issues of public concern. At any rate, the result is that new issues or new conceptions of the public interest have emerged rather slowly in Canada; and indeed, often our awareness results only from the spillover effects of publicity and activism in the United States.

This conveys the impression of a strange, but perhaps desirable, set of opposing forces. In the United States the economic commitment to free market liberalism is coupled with a system of strong and aggressive politically oriented institutions. The Canadian tradition of relatively heavy public involvement coincides with a power system traditionally more accommodative and less confrontational.

Nuances of Political Culture?
Definitions of Politician/Politicien

MADELEINE ALBERT AND GARY LEVY

The agenda of the 1983 Canadian Regional Conference of the Commonwealth Parliamentary Association included a debate between a parliamentarian and a journalist on a resolution that politician is a dirty word.

It is a subject which can be approached in many ways. The opinions of scholars, both classical and contemporary, could be cited. The results of public opinion polls could be used. Even case studies focusing on particularly reputable and disreputable politicians might be relevant. The matter can also be approached more simply, but not less interestingly, by examining the standard dictionaries.

According to the unabridged *Oxford Dictionary* (1961), the term "politician" entered the English language and was used in a derogatory manner in 1588. Its definition is (1) "a political person, chiefly in a sinister sense, a schrewd schemer"; a secondary meaning is (2) "one versed in the theory or science of governing; one skilled in politics; one practically engaged in conducting the business of the state."

The United States has no equivalent to the *Oxford Dictionary* so one must look at several sources. The unabridged *Webster Dictionary* (1959) goes along with Oxford in both its primary and secondary meanings: (1) "a politic person, especially a shrewd or crafty schemer"; (2) "one versed in the art or science of government: one actively engaged in conducting the business of a government."

Another American dictionary *Funk and Wagnalls* (1954) agrees with *Webster*. It defines a politician as: (1) "one who is engaged in politics; one who seeks to subserve the interests of a political party merely; especially, one who uses politics for private advantage; a

Reprinted from Madeleine Albert and Gary Levy, "What's in a Name: Politician/ Politicien," *Canadian Parliamentary Review*, Vol. 6, No. 3 (Autumn, 1983): 41. By permission of publisher and authors.

spoilsman; a political schemer"; (2) "one versed in politics; one skilled in political science or administration; a statesman."

On the other hand the unabridged *Random House Dictionary* (1967) gives a neutral definition first: (1) "a person who is active in party politics" and only later adds (2) "a seeker or holder of public office who is more concerned about winning favour or retaining power than about maintaining principles."

In marked contrast to the British and American sources, none of the Canadian dictionaries consulted (Gage, 1983; Houghton Mifflin, 1980; or Winston, 1976) gave a pejorative sense to their primary meaning of "politician." *Gage*, for example, defined a politician as (1) "a person holding office" and (2) "a person active in politics, especially one seeking political office."

For purposes of comparison it is interesting to see what two standard French sources, Robert and Larousse, have to say about the term *politicien*. According to *Le Grand Larousse* (1976) the word has a definite pejorative connotation: "*personne qui se consacre à la politique, homme rusé et artificieux.*" *Le Grand Robert* (1966) is less categoric giving a neutral meaning but adding, "*plus couramment avec une nuance péjorative.*"

In Quebec *politicien* has traditionally been defined in a neutral way giving it a sense much closer to that of English Canada than to France. *The dictionary* by Louis-Alexandre Bélisle (1974) defines *politicien* simply as "*qui s'occupe de politique.*" Recently, however, the *Office de la langue française du Québec*, decreed that *politicien* has a derogatory connotation. The correct term is *homme politique* (or *femme politique*). The same point is made in Translation Bulletin no. 67 published by the federal Secretary of State Department.

It appears, therefore, (from the admittedly narrow perspective of the dictionary) that, "politician" (or "*politicien*") is definitely derogatory in Great Britain and France. It is pejorative by a two to one margin (with possibilities for a recount) in the United States. In Canada, however, it is not pejorative, except in Quebec, which is still undecided.

Political Parties

There is an intimate relationship between competitive political parties and liberal democracy.[1] Political parties have aided the development and maintenance of representative and responsible government in Canada and, as such, have been labelled the "touchstone of a democratic system."[2] Thus, the success or failure of a competitive party system has much to do with the viability of the larger democratic polity.

One reason that parties have such a role in a democracy is that their "*raison d'être* is to create a substantive connection between rulers and ruled."[3] A major component of that connection is party leadership. Because political parties are organized groups of individuals who seek to win and to exercise power in the political system, questions of leadership are recurring and crucial to a party's electoral fortunes.[4] The Conservatives, plagued in modern times with the reputation of being a "party of losers,"[5] have commonly tried leadership changes in hopes of party renewal. By contrast, Liberals like to change leaders while in office, so that the new party leader (e.g., John Turner in June, 1984) quickly becomes Prime Minister, without having to worry about electoral defeat.

The political recruitment process, at both the national and local levels, has an important bearing on the ability of any party to gain office. Winning may not be the only goal of parties, but it certainly is their primary one. In reading twenty-four ("Liberal Party on Forced March into Past"), Jeffrey Simpson suggests not only that the Liberal party's choice of John Turner as leader was made with the next election in mind, but also as a way of altering the relationship between the party and leader which had developed during the Trudeau years. In reading number twenty-five ("The Conservatives Choose a Leader"), Patrick Martin, Allan Gregg and George Perlin analyze the June 1983 victory of Brian Mulroney. According to this study, Mulroney has the opportunity to build a viable winning coalition both within his party and the country. Political recruitment at the local level is investigated by Marshall W. Conley and Patrick J. Smith in reading number twenty-six ("Political Recruitment in Canada and Britain"). The type and impact of incentives for party involvement are threefold: utilitarian (i.e., tangible rewards such as money), solidary (i.e., intangible rewards such as status or friendship), and purposive (i.e., intangible rewards derived from ideological or organizational claims). These factors differ between parties in the same system, as well as between the party systems in Canada and Britain.

In addition to candidate selection, parties are involved in the development of ideas and policies for the political system. However much parties may talk of policy—especially during election campaigns, it is well to keep in mind that a party in a democratic state is "not a thinking organization."[6] Political parties in Canada, especially the Conservatives and Liberals, have rarely been leaders in the evolution of new ideas and reforms. As examined in reading number twenty-seven ("Tory Party Differences in Canada and Britain"), policy is a greater concern for British than for Canadian parties.

Along with federalism and an emphasis on leadership, a lack of policy is one reason that is often cited to explain the volatile and flexible nature of partisan identification in Canada.[7] In reading number twenty-eight ("Party Identification and Party Images in Canada, Britain and the United States"), Martin P. Wattenberg compares the nature of partisan loyalties in these three democracies. Particularly useful in this analysis is the view that partisan identifications tell us not only how a citizen relates to one party, but how he also feels about the political alternatives.

Our final reading on parties ("The Mythology of the American Two-Party System") concerns the nature of two-party dominance in the United States. Theodore J. Lowi examines and rejects nine myths which support the continuation of the ascendancy of the Republican and Democratic parties. With the rise of the Social Democratic Party in Britain and the regular development of minor parties in Canada, an interesting exercise in comparative political analysis could be based on Lowi's argument: How many of these myths are applicable to the British and Canadian party systems?

NOTES

1. RONALD G. LANDES, "In Defence of Canadian Political Parties." Paper presented at the annual meeting of the Canadian Political Science Association, Guelph, Ontario, 1984, pp. 4-7.

2. HENRY B. MAYO, *An Introduction to Democratic Theory* (New York: Oxford University Press, 1960), p. 66.

3. KAY LAWSON, *Political Parties and Linkage: A Comparative Perspective* (New Haven: Yale University Press, 1980), p. 3.

4. GEORGE C. PERLIN, *The Tory Syndrome: Leadership Politics in the Progressive Conservative Party* (Montreal: McGill-Queen's University Press, 1980), and REGINALD WHITAKER, *The Government Party: Organizing and Financing the Liberal Party of Canada 1930-58* (Toronto: University of Toronto Press, 1977).

5. ALLAN FOTHERINGHAM, *Look Ma . . . No Hands: An Affectionate Look at Our Wonderful Tories* (Toronto: Key Porter Books, 1983), pp. 107-18.

6. RICHARD ROSE, *Do Parties Make A Difference?* (Chatham, New Jersey: Chatham House, 1980), p. 44.

7. HAROLD D. CLARKE, JANE JENSON, LAWRENCE LEDUC, AND JON H. PAMMETT, *Absent Mandate: The Politics of Discontent in Canada* (Toronto: Gage, 1984), pp. 55-76.

Liberal Party on Forced March into Past

JEFFREY SIMPSON

The Liberal party, the most successful national party in the Western World, has always been a party of intellectual flexibility and political agility.

To the enduring frustration of their political opponents, the Liberals have demonstrated an uncanny ability to shift with changing winds, to lean to the left or to the right as occasions require.

After 16 years of activist government under Prime Minister Pierre Trudeau, the Liberals sensed the time had come to shift to

Reprinted from Jeffrey Simpson, "Party on forced march into past," *The Globe and Mail* (June 18, 1984), p. L5. By permission.

the right. In John Turner the party found a leader anxious to trim
the activism of the past 16 years.

Mr. Turner calls himself a "mainstream Liberal," a code word
for the kind of pre-Trudeau Liberalism he admired when he entered politics in the early 1960s. Indeed, he counts among his political heroes such Liberals as Sir Wilfrid Laurier, Mackenzie King,
C.D. Howe and Lester Pearson. He most certainly does not count
Mr. Trudeau among his idols.

Seldom has the intellectual flexibility of the Liberals been more
dramatically demonstrated than in recent days. By choosing Mr.
Turner, the Liberals have opted for the candidate most committed
to altering the policies and style of the Trudeau years. By rejecting
Jean Chrétien, the Liberals have opted for change over continuity,
and maintained the tradition of alternating French- and English-
speaking leaders that began when Laurier succeeded Edward
Blake in the late 19th century.

The Turner victory presages a forced march into the past in
terms of internal party organization and broad political approach.
For decades, the Liberals have been the quintessential party of
managers, taking bold initiatives only when the time was ripe and
often borrowing their initiatives from policy proposals of their political opponents. Relentlessly pragmatic, the Liberals preferred
cautious leadership.

The coalition Laurier built has seldom been shaken. The party
dug roots into every part of Canada, especially in Quebec. From
the First World War until today, Quebec has been the Liberal bed-
rock, cracked only once—in 1958—by the Conservatives. As long
as the Liberals captured a large majority of Quebec's seats—they
now have 74 of 75—the Liberals entered every election with a lead
the Conservatives could seldom overcome in English Canada.

Until Pierre Trudeau came along, the Liberals were also a
strong presence in Western Canada. The Liberals' decline in the
West actually started under Prime Minister Pearson, but the decline became a precipitous drop under Mr. Trudeau, who never
seemed to understand what irked Westerners.

Indeed, his policies of promoting bilingualism, reasserting the
strength of the federal Government and struggling for a greater
federal share of energy revenues embittered Westerners and
turned the region fiercely against his party. In the last election, the
Liberals took only two seats west of Ontario, both in Winnipeg.

The loss of the West smashed the old Liberal coalition. At the
same time, the solid links between the party and the business com-

munity, which flourished under Mr. St. Laurent, grew increasingly feeble under Mr. Pearson and reached their nadir in the mid-1970s under Mr. Trudeau. The party compensated in part for its loss of business support—and of upper-middle class votes in Ontario—by attracting an increased share of low- and moderate-income voters. Under Mr. Trudeau, this remained the party's second most important socio-economic target group. The middle class, broadly defined, remained the party's everlasting target.

Mr. Trudeau, in addition to altering the regional and socio-economic base of the party, also changed its internal structure. Mr. Trudeau, whose motto was "reason over passion," was appalled by the lack of co-ordination inside the Pearson Cabinet and government. He resolved to impose upon the bureaucracy and party substantially greater centralized control.

This he accomplished partly by creating a network of Cabinet committees, partly by strengthening the role of his own office and the Privy Council—the Cabinet's secretariat—and partly by creating coordinating ministries which weakened the power of traditional line departments.

Under Mr. Pearson, strong ministers usually had their way without interference from their Cabinet colleagues or from the Prime Minister's office, except on matters of supreme importance. Mr. Trudeau's structures reined in Cabinet ministers, and his own powerful personality allowed him to dominate his government and the Cabinet in a way Mr. Pearson never could.

Stung by his near-defeat in 1972, Mr. Trudeau turned for his political advice to long-time party operators Senator Keith Davey and principal secretary James Coutts. As the 1970s wore on, they became more influential than many Cabinet ministers. The increasing importance of polls in Liberal decision-making furthered their influence, since they were the interpreters of those polls to the Prime Minister, the Cabinet and the caucus. In a town where information is power, Senator Davey and Mr. Coutts held one of the keys.

The power of these non-elected officials irritated MPs, ministers and the party rank-and-file. At the 1982 Liberal conference, delegates passed a resolution severely criticizing polls and patronage. No wonder all the would-be successors to Mr. Trudeau promised to open up the party, to give the rank and file more influence.

Mr. Turner, who supported that 1982 resolution, consistently pledged that he would govern without a clique of advisers. It was a promise the delegates wanted to hear.

Mr. Turner's success represented a wistful longing for a return to the governing style of the Pearson years and an inclination for the party, while changing leaders, to alter its pitch to the electorate. It was also another sign that Canadian politics has drifted to the political right.

Although Mr. Trudeau was not averse to reversing his policies, there were several constant refrains throughout his long political career. His abiding interest was obviously the role of Quebec in Canada, a role he passionately believed could be best protected by a forceful federal government with a strong coterie of French-speaking politicians, advisers and civil servants. By demonstrating that French-speakers could play a crucial role in Ottawa, he hoped to woo Quebeckers from the dream of independence.

Mr. Trudeau's departure—and the successful patriation of the Constitution—took the steam out of the constitutional issue. Neither Mr. Turner nor the other Liberal leadership candidates talked much about the Constitution or Quebec during the campaign.

The silence undoubtedly reflected a general fatigue with constitutional issues and a political judgment that economic issues will dominate the agenda for the years ahead.

Mr. Trudeau's stewardship represented several marked departures in economic policy from Liberal tradition. For most of the 20th century, the Liberals were the party favoring closer ties with the United States, a policy that meant weaker ties with Great Britain.

The Trudeau years brought the national energy program, the Foreign Investment Review Agency and a plethora of government subsidies and incentives for Canadian-owned firms. Many of these initiatives were subsequently watered down, but they were the policy heirs of the great nationalist debate within the party during the 1960s.

The forces of former finance minister Walter Gordon of Toronto lost that battle to the traditional Liberal economic managers, including another former finance minister, Mitchell Sharp, but the issues they raised were occasionally taken up by Mr. Trudeau.

Mr. Turner resolutely opposed the Gordon forces. For him, economic nationalism was an economic luxury and a political absurdity because it smacked of anti-Americanism. Although as prime minister he may be forced to make the occasional gesture to mollify nationalist sentiments in the party, his government will probably welcome all foreign investment and turn foreign policy closer to that of the United States.

Mr. Turner's profound suspicion of economic nationalism is also rooted in his conviction that the Liberal Party must revive itself in Western Canada. The West, unlike southern Ontario, has traditionally been stony ground for economic nationalism. Western resources are sold for world prices in open markets. Protectionism does not serve the region's interests well.

Mr. Turner also sent a signal to the West early in the campaign on language policy. Although he subsequently "clarified" his remarks, Mr. Turner led Westerners to believe that his government will spend less time on bilingualism and minority languages rights.

The new leader also intends to operate the byzantine world of federal-provincial relations differently. Under Mr. Trudeau, relations with the provinces were marked by repeated skirmishes and several mighty battles. The constitutional debate of 1981-82 was merely the fiercest of the rows that pitted Ottawa against most of the provinces—including all of the Western provinces.

Mr. Turner, by experience and inclination, is a deal-maker. He values his personal friendship with Western premiers, including Peter Lougheed of Alberta and William Bennett of British Columbia. All signs point to Mr. Turner trying to re-create the "co-operative federalism" of the Pearson years.

He will be aided in that effort by the relative calm prevailing in federal-provincial relations. Mr. Trudeau had to deal with assertive provincial governments in Quebec and Western Canada. Indeed, economic and fiscal clout drifted from Ottawa to the provinces until the constitutional patriation.

Mr. Trudeau reacted against this drift, and tried repeatedly to reverse it. Now the provinces are worn-out by past struggles. The energy-rich Western provinces find their coffers depleted by stagnant energy prices and their economies savaged by unemployment. The Parti Quebecois Government, having lost its referendum on sovereignty-association, finds its population supremely uninterested in constitutional fights. The provinces are, therefore, in no mood for a fight, so Mr. Turner may well be able to achieve a harmony in federal-provincial relations that Mr. Trudeau never managed.

Mr. Turner's determination to reintroduce "co-operative federalism," *à la* Mr. Pearson, jibes well with his belief in the importance of "people skills." This self-described "tactile" politician thinks federal-provincial relations—and government in general—should operate as a large club in which the members all know and trust each other, even if they may disagree on policies. This was Lester Pearson's ideal too, an ideal born of a lifetime in diplomacy. Mr. Trudeau, by contrast, was a proud individualist who spent the early years of his life defying entrenched interests. Intellectually and emotionally, he loved a fight.

Whereas Mr. Trudeau, for better or worse, shook Canadians up, engaging some, enraging others, Mr. Turner will operate in the traditional Liberal—and Canadian—political mould. He will try for consensus over confrontation, fudging over clarity, flexibility over entrenched positions. He is a Liberal in the pre-Trudeau mould. The question remains whether the country is, too.

The Conservatives Choose a Leader

PATRICK MARTIN, ALLAN GREGG AND GEORGE PERLIN

Right on the Numbers

If it had not been clear earlier, by the beginning of the fourth ballot it was a foregone conclusion—Brian Mulroney was going to be the next national leader of the Progressive Conservative party, and odds-on favourite to become the next prime minister of Canada. Of John Crosbie's supporters, 40 per cent stated before the convention that their second choice was Mulroney and only 17 per cent Clark. They had seen nothing in Ottawa to make them change their minds. Moreover, even if Crosbie had personally gone over to Clark in an effort to stop Mulroney, it is doubtful that it would have had any effect on the outcome, as 78 per cent of his supporters also claimed they would vote their own second choice rather than follow their candidate to someone else.

Clark's inability to capture the convention after leading on the first ballot was one story—a story of failed expectations, seven

Adapted from Patrick Martin, Allan Gregg, George Perlin, *Contenders: The Tory Quest for Power* (Scarborough, Ontario: Prentice-Hall Canada, 1983), pp. 195-204. By permission of the publisher.

years of acrimony, and the politics of opposition. Mulroney's victory, however, was quite another. After all, other candidates, including Clark, were seen as more likeable, more competent, and tougher than Mulroney, and were considered to have a sounder grasp of policy. More delegates even considered that John Crosbie would be better able to unite the party, and had a more appealing television image. Further, there were just as many delegates reporting they would never vote for Mulroney (21%) as were reporting they would never vote for Clark (20%). In other words, the Anyone But Mulroney sentiment was as real and large as the Anyone But Clark feelings. The major difference was that the Anyone But Mulroney camp was housed almost exclusively in the Clark delegation, while the ABC movement was spread throughout the convention.

So it would be easy to conclude that Mulroney was the choice of the majority of delegates, in the end, because he was the *only* candidate in a position to stop Clark, given his placement on the first ballot. He was that, but this kind of analysis woefully underestimates the skill, experience, and appeal of Brian Mulroney. It also seems potentially misleading inasmuch as delegates reported after the convention that in a hypothetical last ballot, with Crosbie facing Mulroney, the so-called "best candidate" Crosbie would have lost to Mulroney by 58 per cent to 42 per cent. They wanted to stop Clark and the majority wanted Mulroney.[1]

The principal reason Brian Mulroney won, despite the fact he was not seen as the "best candidate," has to do with the overriding concern of Conservatives: their quest for power. When asked how influential various factors were in their choice of a candidate, three-quarters of the delegates said finding a candidate who would best help the party win power was "very influential." No other reason figured as greatly. In 1983, the Conservatives were looking for a winner. And Brian Mulroney looked like a winner.[2]

Why did the delegates think Brian Mulroney was the best candidate to help the party win? Part of the explanation is a negative assessment of the other candidates. Joe Clark, a decent and able man, was bedevilled to the end by his image; and John Crosbie had lost credibility as a winner when he stumbled on the language issue. But to say that Mulroney did not appear to have such flaws is not enough to explain his success in relation to *all* of the candidates. How could he, a man who had no national prominence outside his party, indeed a man who even within his party was known mainly for his work in the backrooms, emerge a winner over former ministers and active members of Parliament who were portrayed almost daily in the news media as leading political figures?

The answer to this riddle lies in Mulroney's knowledge of the PC party and its membership.

Mulroney was fond of telling delegates that he had been involved with the Progressive Conservatives for 29 years. While many saw this statement as nothing more than an attempt to deflect attention away from his parliamentary inexperience, the fact is that Mulroney's 29 years of experience made him as professional a politican as anyone in Canada. Mulroney understood the enduring nature of party politics—and it showed in his networks and the lasting loyalty he was able to extract from the men and women he had met during that time. He also understood the changing nature of politics and that showed in his ability to adapt political tactics to meet these changing realities; for, across the country and especially in Quebec, only he, along with Clark, was equipped and prepared to play the game under the new rules. But, most importantly, Mulroney had a shrewder appreciation of the Progressive Conservative party than the other candidates, including Joe Clark. And that understanding showed in virtually everything he did, said, and stood for throughout the campaign.

One thing that Brian Mulroney understood was that during Joe Clark's leadership there had been a great number of Progressive Conservatives who thought of themselves as "outsiders" in the party: people who felt they had little or no influence in the direction of party affairs, or were cut off from a leader who relied too much on technical advisers. More than half of the delegates interviewed mentioned these items, saying that they believed there was an establishment in the party and that they were not part of it. And on the last ballot nearly two-thirds of those delegates voted for Brian Mulroney.

There are different reasons why many Conservatives considered themselves to be outsiders in their own party. Some party members had nursed personal grievances, because they felt their talents had not been properly recognized; others were frustrated because they had been on the losing side in most of the conflicts in the party since the battle over John Diefenbaker's leadership in 1966-1967.

At a deeper level, many party members felt themselves to be outsiders because of their social situation. Although comfortable financially, they felt insecure because they perceived themselves to be socially remote from the centre of power in Canada, which they saw as dominated by a technocratic elite operating through the bureaucratic structures of big government and big business. These individuals were proprietors of small businesses, farmers, fishermen or members of the lower middle class; they were residents of the smaller communities across the country, and/or inhabitants of one of the hinterland provinces of the Atlantic region or the West. These "social outsiders" were attracted to the Conservative party because it is both the party of opposition and a party that is conservative. The problem for many of them was that they saw the same style of technocratic power entrenching itself within the Conservative party. They looked with suspicion on the growth of the party's bureaucracy, with its commitment to the uses of the new techniques of political organization, and on the leader's dependence on this bureaucracy and these techniques.

To many outsiders in the party, John Diefenbaker was the symbol of what they stood for . . . or, rather, what they stood against. Diefenbaker's populism had been directed toward them. Thus, when Brian Mulroney constantly reminded delegates of his affection for, and connections to "The Chief," and when he won the endorsements of such prominent Diefenbaker loyalists as Alvin Hamilton and Robert Coates, he identified himself with those outsiders.

Mulroney had made the mistake in 1976 of looking too much the prisoner of technocracy. His campaign had offended people because of its slickness and sophistication. He did not make the same mistake in 1983. Mulroney was still a showman, but his campaign played in the rec rooms of the nation. He let the delegates reach him personally in homey surroundings.

And even though Brian Mulroney was the president of one large corporation, held directorships on the boards of several others, and often lunched with Conrad Black of Argus and Paul Desmarais of Power Corp., he knew enough not to flaunt such connections in the presence of delegates. Instead, he reminded them that he was "one who has worked as a labourer and truck driver and whose father was a unionized electrician." His humble beginnings included not simply a childhood in the North Shore town of Baie Comeau, but "a father who, during his entire life held down two jobs to provide for the needs of his family with neither complaint nor regret."

Mulroney's description of himself was, of course, unashamedly sentimental. Yet it appealed not just to the "social outsiders" in the party, it also identified him with the "average" Conservative delegate. Most of the Conservative delegates are people with family incomes putting them in the top 10 per cent of the population. They are high achievers in their careers, yet most of them report they came from families which were "just able to get along" or were "badly off." By portraying himself in this way Brian Mulroney was displaying his understanding of the party and its politics. And when delegates made the inevitable comparison of his roots to his current status, they saw a man who had arrived—a winner, like the one they were looking for.

There was another thing that Brian Mulroney understood about the Conservative party that was very important in his victory, and that was a change in the ideological disposition within the party.

Mulroney is as much a Tory pragmatist as Joe Clark, but he was able to capitalize on the mood of conservatism among Tories. There had been considerable shift in ideological identification within the PC party since 1976. At the convention that year only 43 per cent described themselves as being on the right of the party. By 1983, 57 per cent placed themselves on the right. As Mulroney's support grew from ballot to ballot he drew his major strength from these delegates. On the fourth ballot 75 per cent of right-wing delegates voted for Brian Mulroney.

This does not mean that his base lay exclusively among this group. Thirty per cent (30%) of the delegates who placed themselves on the left and 38 per cent of the "centre" also voted for him. Nor does it mean that Mulroney would be forced to shift the party to the right to satisfy his major constituency.

While delegates may identify themselves as being at the right end of the ideological spectrum, the positions they take on specific issues may not. For instance, while a majority said they would sell all or part of several crown corporations, 60 per cent said they believed in government ownership. And while a majority called for cuts in government spending, they didn't want them across the board: a majority called for *increased* spending on defence and high technology development as well as for education, manpower training and assistance to the disabled.

There is nothing inconsistent in this. The Conservative Party in Canada has always embraced two different traditions: the first, of social responsibility—a sense of duty towards others in society;[3] the second, of individual enterprise or self-reliance. Historically, within the party, the balance between these two traditions has fluctuated in adapting to social and economic conditions.

Responding to hard economic times in the 1980s and the resulting burden on individual taxpayers, Conservatives have placed their emphasis on individualism and self-reliance, although their attitudes on most policy issues have not changed dramatically from 1976.

Brian Mulroney understood this attitude and responded by stressing the virtues of individual enterprise while never abandoning a commitment to social responsibility or "tenderness" as he called it. His rhetoric soothed the right wing without troubling its conscience.

Although strong positions on specific issues did not form an integral part of the Mulroney campaign, he and his organization did take special steps to ensure that the candidate would not be tagged as "insubstantive" or "plastic." The book he released during the campaign, *Where I Stand*,[4] was designed precisely with this aim in mind. 3000 delegates received a free copy of the book; and those who took the trouble to read it doubtless found a view of the nation's problems and a prescription for their cure remarkably like their own. For while Mulroney's analysis of the country's problems and the necessary prescriptions to solve those problems would surely make a professional economist or public policy analyst blanch, they would almost bring a tear to the eye of a pollster or professional politician. For in those words, Mulroney and his team have captured the very essence of what makes "the average" PC delegate live and breathe. In the pollsters' parlance, they were ". . . right on the numbers."

For the PC delegates, and for Brian Mulroney as he campaigned across the country, the government which they so desperately sought to capture was neither inherently good nor evil. But it most definitely had the potential to abet or impede individual initiative. The difference, for them, was not a question of dogma, but a question of practice: whether our leaders "would quietly, gradually and surreptitiously erode our values and liberties" or whether they would allow us the "legitimate ambition to do, to build, to acquire . . ." and in so doing permit us to exercise . . . "our strength and our duties as *independent* citizens."

This view is expressed as much by the role of opposition—by acquiring the ability "to suffer defeat, sometimes with difficulty, and to start again towards new challenges"—as by the role of conservative. Few politicians in Canada are astute enough to recognize this. Caught up in the media coverage of "shifts to the right" and supply-side this and single interest that, candidates for the Progressive Conservative leadership in 1983 alternated between republican totems, socialist bogey-men and Red Tory shibboleths. Through a combination of keen political instinct and weekly polling on delegates' attitudes towards issues, the Mulroney camp was able to avoid these pitfalls.

From what started on the first ballot to be an impressive, but narrow, support base made up of Quebec delegates, Ontario youths and a smattering of senior delegates from across the country, Mulroney was able to build an impressive coalition on each successive ballot. By the last ballot, that coalition consisted of 50 per cent of all *ex officio* delegates; 82 per cent of all delegates supporting candidates other than him or Clark on the first ballot.

Brian Mulroney *was* the symbol to kick the ins out. But he also positioned himself, very deliberately over seven years, to become that symbol. Even though he may not have been seen as "the best" candidate by the majority of the delegates, he had the organization and foresight to neutralize that handicap on the first ballot.

Mulroney also was the only candidate who set out to exhibit more of those qualities a power starved party *required* of a leader, regardless of what non-partisan observers might deem to be the "best" qualities.

There is nothing paradoxical about all this. There is no conflict between the image of the hard-ball playing politican and the man with the vision from Baie Comeau. Brian Mulroney knew that the first rule for any politician is to know your constituency and secure it. That may require an adaptability that seems cynical in the eyes of those who want politicians not just to be true to principles, but always to be seen to be true to them. Brian Mulroney *did* talk about the things he believed in during the campaign; but what he was most concerned with was winning and Mulroney won because he followed the first rule of politics and shrewdly applied it to the realities of the Progressive Conservative party in 1983.

Asked what factors most motivated delegates to make the leadership choices they made, they replied: first and foremost, who was the most electable; second came the candidate's stand on issues; third, the fact the other candidates were less attractive; fourth, the personal attraction to the candidate; and fifth, personal friendship.

Probably no criteria better reflect the kind of campaign Brian Mulroney waged, and the kind of candidate he set out to portray to the PC delegates. Winning was his constant theme. Even the emphasis he constantly placed on his Quebec origins had little to do with accommodation, national unity or federal-provincial relations. It was a way of reminding conservative delegates of their successive electoral defeats and it associated his candidacy directly with these people's first concern—the quest for power. On the issues, he avoided detail, but what he did put forward fully satisfied the right-wing faction of the party, without hampering the party's electability. Through his public utterances and campaign publications, Mulroney was able to speak directly, not simply to the delegates' issue concerns, but more importantly to the unique mindset that produced those concerns.

Without ever having been elected to public office, Mulroney was also able not only to be the obvious alternative to Clark but the only alternative, given the choices offered. His business background, his fluency in both official languages, his "image" and even the altered style of campaigning he adopted, were all cultivated *in contrast* to the other candidate's attributes and not simply as desirable characteristics, unto themselves. He was the "complete candidate" . . . who developed his image as a counterpoint to all the deficiencies Conservatives traditionally associated with their leaders.

Finally, there is the question of personal friendship. Rarely has a Canadian politician understood the importance or used the influence of personal friendship in party politics more than Brian Mulroney. The team he assembled, his constant references to patronage and the cultivated charm that has become a Mulroney trademark is testimony to this fact.

In short, and in the simplest of terms, Brian Mulroney prevailed in the fourth ballot because he was the most studied and professional politician of the bunch. Like so many, his strengths are his weakness. What is seen as smoothness by some will be condemned by others as vacuousness. What is viewed as consummate organization skills from one perspective, will be seen as manipulation and guile from another. But in the final analysis, all of it is part of politics. And the politics of the Progressive Conservative party—the politics of opposition—is a unique game for which few are equipped to play. Brian Mulroney, the unelected professional politician, played that game with a vengeance.

The Party and the Leader

In his victory on the fourth ballot Brian Mulroney put together a more broadly-based coalition than either of his predecessors, Robert Stanfield or Joe Clark. He won in every province except Prince Edward Island, Nova Scotia, Quebec and Manitoba and even in these provinces he was supported by substantial minorities. His majority cut across cleavages on virtually every dimension of social identification and interest. But Mulroney's greatest strength lies in the fact that he has provided a focus for uniting groups that have been fundamentally divided for a generation—and even longer.

One uniquely important opportunity lies in the bridge he has built across the cleavage between the French and English within the party, a cleavage that has caused more disruptive conflict in party history than any other. While on the fourth ballot he did not have a majority of the Quebec French, he had very close to a majority and in the post-convention survey these delegates gave him a strong endorsement. At the same time he had a majority of the delegates who have opposed bilingualism and concessions to Quebec. He is uniquely positioned, therefore, to bring these groups together, particularly if he can provide the party with some success in Quebec. A stronger Francophone presence in the party caucus would alleviate much of the cause of the difficulties of the past because it would leaven the effect of the small minority of anti-French members and make others who have been cut off from discourse with Francophones more sensitive to French-Canadian concerns. In the interim he can count on the support of the Anglophones because most of them believe that he is going to help the party win seats in Quebec.

A second important opportunity is presented by the fact that he has the support of most of those Conservatives who have felt themselves to be outsiders in the party. Many of these people have been losers in internal party battles for nearly 20 years—since the beginning of the struggle over John Diefenbaker's leadership. It was from the ranks of these outsiders that most of the dissent came during the leadership of Stanfield and Clark. Now they are winners, positions of power and influence are open to them not as symbolic gestures to conciliate them from leaders whom they did not want, but from a leader who is leader by their choice. And, although a small majority of the *ex officio* delegates at the Convention voted against him on the fourth ballot, Mulroney will also have the loyalty of the party's established elite. While most of the Clark appointees in the key roles around the leader will be replaced by Brian Mulroney's men and women, the elite as a whole will support him because they will continue to hold their power and because they, above all, are committed to the principle of loyalty to the leader.

Mulroney, thirdly, has the opportunity to unite the party ideologically. He understands the vitally important distinction between using right-wing symbols and advocating right-wing policies. Because, in the use of symbols he captured the "conservative" mood of the party, he carried with him the vast majority of the delegates who *think* of themselves as being on the right, but because he articulated a political view that was pragmatic and emphasized the basic Progressive Conservative sense of social responsibility he appealed to their basic issue positions. Three-quarters of the delegates expect Mulroney to lead the party in a direction which is more to the right than the direction in which Joe Clark tried to lead it. But, given his positions during the campaign and his insight into what the party wants, that probably does not mean much in the way of change on basic issues of social and economic policy. However, the party under Mulroney will be more right-wing on symbolic issues and on issues that are remote from the daily concerns of Canadians such as foreign and defense policy—an area in which the party is substantially united in seeing the world in "we/they" terms.[5]

As important for Mulroney as the breadth of his base in the party is the fact that the party has the will to unite behind him. More than anything else it wants power and its members are deeply conscious of the harm internal division could do to their chances of winning power. In addition, most party members believe that despite their divisions there is a basis for consensus and accommodation within the party. Even most of those who say that there are big ideological differences in the party do not believe these differences are so big that they cannot be reconciled. A large majority of Conservatives also believe the outcome of the convention was a good thing for the party—good for its chances of uniting and good for its chances of winning. Seventy-one per cent (71%) of the delegates believe Mulroney will have greater success than Clark in uniting the caucus, while 68 per cent believe he will have greater success in uniting the party as a whole. Most importantly, 73 per cent say Mulroney's election has improved the party's chances of winning the next election.

For all of these favourable circumstances, Brian Mulroney will still have to be adept in the exercise of his leadership. The real test for him will be in the caucus. His majority is not monolithic; it is a coalition of diverse groups and individuals. Moreover, while public dissent is officially disapproved of by most party members, it has become part of the culture of the party, something that is accepted because of the Tories' individualism and because little can be done to prevent it in a party that is out of power. What makes Mulroney's task more difficult is that the party's rivals and journalists will be looking for the slightest sign of discontent because of the party's reputation for divisiveness. Internal conflict is what is expected of Conservatives. The big political question for party watchers then, is whether this time that expectation will truly be unfulfilled.

In approaching this problem Mulroney can choose from three alternative models of leadership. The first is the model of Stanfield and Clark. That is the model of conciliation through the widespread distribution of appointments and consensus-building through an attempt to engage caucus members directly in policy-making. That model didn't work—for three reasons. First, there were members so hostile to Stanfield and Clark that they were not prepared to work with the leader. Second, neither man articulated a clear vision or found a concept to articulate a clear vision around which the party could unite. In pursuing the politics of consensus they allowed the course of the process to determine the direction rather than providing a concept to give coherence to the process. Third, neither man possessed at the beginning, nor was able to develop, a strong independent popular base to sanction his authority in caucus.

The second model is the model of strong one-man leadership provided by John Diefenbaker. Diefenbaker's style worked for a time because he did have a vision and he did have a base in the country, but it ultimately failed because government is too complex for one-man leadership to work and because he included no one in his inner circle who was not completely a Diefenbaker loyalist and, therefore, had no independent channel of advice.

The third model combines elements of both of these and, judged by what the delegates say, it is a model that seems to fit what the party wants. The delegates want to share in party decisions, but they are prepared to follow a strong leader who will provide them with a sense of direction.

Brian Mulroney's life experience as a man from working-class background who is a high achiever and his attempt to express that experience in a coherent vision for Conservatives provide a basis for purposeful leadership to which most Tories can commit themselves. That gives him the opportunity to take strong stands. If he tempers strong leadership with the understanding for conciliation, the patience to seek accommodation and compromise that Stanfield and Clark brought to the leadership, he will have fulfilled two of the three requirements for achieving success. The third is to develop a base in the country and even there his prospects seem promising.

The Party and the Country

For more than six decades the Conservatives have been contenders for but seldom the holders of power in Canada. Some party members and commentators have blamed the party's minority status on its alienation of Quebec. From an historical perspective that is certainly part of the problem: the party's loss of French Canada helped precipitate the situation in which it finds itself today. Yet, for some time, the Conservative party has been a minority not just in Quebec, but in all of Canada—English as well as French.

The party's minority status is best represented by the fact that over the past 25 years the number of Canadians who have been committed Conservatives—those who have felt some sense of identification with the party—has always been less than the number who have been committed Liberals. Even at the beginning of the 1979 campaign, when the parties had about equal shares of the intended votes of the electorate, there were 10 per cent fewer people who declared an attachment to the Conservatives than to the Liberals.

Consequently in the 1980 election, when Liberal government performance was no longer an issue, and the state of the economy had been associated with the present Conservative incumbency, it was quite natural for those Canadians who considered themselves to be Liberals but voted PC in 1979, to return to their traditional partisan moorings. From this perspective, the 1979 PC victory can be seen as an aberration, only to be repeated when a sufficiently large number of "Liberals" become disenchanted enough with "their" party to vote Conservative.

The party under Joe Clark spent a considerable amount of its time grappling with the "minority party" problem. Research uncovered the fact that the Progressive Conservatives were viewed by the electorate as old-fashioned, out-of-step with the 1980s and narrow-minded; representative mainly of farmers and businessmen, while providing little room for women, "ethnic" groups and the poor. The research showed further that the perception that the party had a narrow political base prevented it from widening that base.

Canadians gravitate toward broad-based, representative organizations and avoid narrow-based, unrepresentative ones. They value compromise and seek consensus. Political parties which are seen to serve exclusively the interests of one group over another, are viewed by the electorate as politically unacceptable.

Still another problem for the Conservative party has been the popular belief that it was not as competent as the Liberal party. It was seen as a party that has been less able to manage its own internal affairs, and lacks the level of skills the Liberals possess to provide effective government.

The Conservatives who gathered in Ottawa may not have known but might have sensed intuitively that the image of their party, in relation to that of the Liberal party, had changed profoundly since their last electoral defeat in 1980.

As long ago as 1975 there was evidence in party polls that the Canadian people had begun to sense that something was wrong— that the world as they were seeing and experiencing it was becoming increasingly different from the world they wanted it to be. This feeling deepened and became more widespread as the economic crisis in the country increased in intensity. Nonetheless, people retained the basic sense of confidence in the strength of the country and in themselves. What they began to re-evaluate, was the performance of the people who were running the country. If there was nothing fundamentally wrong with Canada, then there must be something wrong with the way in which it was being managed. Thus, the difficulties in the country soon became associated with the government and, in turn, with the natural governing party, the Liberals.

Given the lasting nature of partisanship and political identification, the Liberals did not immediately fall victim to this reassessment. At first, "the blame" became highly personalized—"it was Trudeau's fault." Over time, however, as more Canadians began to associate the problems they were experiencing with the very prescriptions that were being applied by government to solve them, "the blame" began to shift away from personalities—Trudeau— and towards institutions—the Liberal party.

The PC victory in 1979 arrested this trend. While the Conservatives entered that election with 10 per cent fewer partisans than the Liberals, they were on a sounder political footing at that point than at any other time in recent history. But, by the end of the 1980 election, there were 22 per cent fewer self-confessed Conservatives in Canada than there were Liberals! By forming the government, the Progressive Conservative party—elected as an agency of change—had shifted the association of problems with the Liberal party to the association of problems with all political parties. Nothing had changed, the problems still existed, and therefore there was nothing to choose between the Liberals and the PCs. In the 1980 election the issues for the average voter once again came down to the question of "which political party is most like me?" and "which one is most for me?"—in other words, "which one do I identify with?" Given the Progressive Conservative party's chronic image problem, it was no contest.

But with the Liberals' return to power, the trend once again began to emerge and by May 1982, *for the first time ever*, the Progressive Conservatives' national polling showed that there were more Canadians who considered themselves to be Progressive Conservatives in federal politics than there were Liberals. This erosion of Liberal partisanship had been incremental, but steady and continuous with each successive poll. The implications for Progressive Conservative party fortunes, although difficult to assess, were undeniably positive. Back in 1978, after losing 13 out of 15 by-elections and trailing the Tories by 10 points in the Gallup poll, the Liberals were still seen as the most competent, practical and moderate of Canada's three major political parties. In the PCs' May 1982 poll, however, the Liberals were virtually tied with the NDP as the most incompetent, impractical and extremist. In other words, the Liberal party had lost the association with those very qualities which had made it synonymous with "government" in Canada.

Someone looking at the nation-wide Gallup poll for the 18 months preceding the Progressive Conservative leadership convention might quite naturally conclude that the decline in Liberal party fortunes would be paralleled by a rise in Progressive Conservative party fortunes. But while there can be no question that the Progressive Conservative party's image and electoral position has improved considerably since 1980, the party has yet to inherit the Liberal mantle as Canada's natural governing party. Doubts still exist, as they exist about all the political parties in Canada.[6]

Surprisingly, the Winnipeg general meeting in early 1983 did not seem to raise more doubts about the party. Instead of seeing the calling of a leadership convention as a foolish act, considering the Tories' high standing in the polls, most Canadians took the view that the party was "doing something" to clean up its' own problems, and, they hoped, those of the country as well.

In many ways Brian Mulroney is inheriting a party that has never been in a better position to cast off its minority status. For the first time in modern history more Canadians identify with the Progressive Conservatives than the Liberals. For the time being the party has put aside its leadership problems and has the opportunity to demonstrate its competence to govern by uniting behind a new leader. That does not mean that Brian Mulroney will encounter no difficulties in his quest to lead the Tories to victory.

Between 1956 and 1983 the Progressive Conservative party of Canada had three national leaders. Two—John Diefenbaker and Joe Clark—went on to become prime minister of Canada. Both were forced to contest their leadership by their own party and both failed. The other—Robert Stanfield—resigned shortly after losing his third bid for federal office in six years, undermined by his failure to impose unity on a fractious party.

When Joe Clark announced on January 31, 1983, that he was calling a leadership convention, there must have been a keen sense among some delegates that they were "doing it to themselves again."

On the following day a resounding majority voted to amend the leadership review clause in the party constitution to ensure that in future, a review vote would only occur at the first general meeting following elections when the PC party failed to form the government. To many, this amendment might have appeared to be a public declaration that the Tories had overcome their fixation on leadership. But, in fact, a mere five months later, in Ottawa, 67 per cent of these same delegates were reporting that they thought the leadership convention they were attending was a "good thing" for the party.

All of this behaviour and reported opinion is perfectly consistent . . . if you are a federal Progressive Conservative in Canada.

The fact of the matter is that for all of its recent history, the Progressive Conservative party *has* been obsessed by the so-called leadership issue. But this obsession is rooted in neither malice nor mischief.

An historian of the party wrote nearly 30 years ago that "the Conservatives have been searching for another Sir John A. Macdonald and when a new leader turned out to be an ordinary mortal he was subjected to constant criticism until he was forced to resign."[7] The standard used to measure Macdonald's successors is the standard that gives him his hero's status in the party. He was a winner. For his successors the party's failures have become the leader's failures.

This dilemma has not been eased by the Tory electoral record. Repeated defeats have manifest themselves in conflict, bitterness and acrimony which the leadership of the party has been unable to manage due to the kinds of members that the Progressive Conservative—a right-of-centre, opposition party—attracts and attempts to accommodate, and to the limited resources available for managing conflict in a party that is in perpetual opposition. This conflict, in turn, creates severe doubts among the public about the Progressive Conservative party's ability and competence to govern. When the leader of the party cannot exhibit that ability and competence by imposing his authority on the party, then the doubts expressed by the public tend to focus on the leader as well. And finally the leader becomes "the reason" for these doubts. The problem is structural but the solution is personal: change the leader.

Brian Mulroney made a point of reminding delegates that they, like him, were winners. What had made them losers were the people in charge—of the party and the country. For them, all that was required to be winners was to "recapture that spirit, that belief in ourselves."

For Progressive Conservatives it is an appealing posture. It is also one which Mulroney deliberately adopted in fashioning his leadership victory.

Now, after the convention, Brian Mulroney has what may be an unprecedented opportunity to transform the Progressive Conservative Party of Canada and, in doing so, change the entire complexion of Canadian politics. Fifty-three per cent (53%) of the voters who were interviewed for the Decima Quarterly Report in mid-June said they would be more likely to vote for the Conservative party with Mulroney as its leader. What is most important for the party is that Mulroney was most popular in central Canada where the Conservatives must develop a base if they are to become effective competitors for power.

Because Brian Mulroney was elected as "a winner" and because he understands the nature of party politics and his party so well, there is every reason to believe that he may be the very personality to alter the Progressive Conservative party's structural problems. But to do so, he must continue to win. And this is his dilemma. For to win—to convince the Canadian population that the Progressive Conservative party deserves the right to govern—Brian Mulroney and the Progressive Conservative party must overcome (or at least appear to overcome) its internal problem and appear as a governing party. To be winners they have to stop appearing as contenders; and to stop appearing as contenders the Tories must be winners. So, even though, in the final analysis Progressive Conservative leadership problems have centred on their electability, to ensure their electability, Brian Mulroney, like all Progressive Conservative leaders since Macdonald, must first contend himself with his party. Or, as Mulroney himself recognizes . . . "a condition precedent to electoral success must be tangible proof to the Canadian people that the Progressive Conservative party is genuinely united."[8]

NOTES

1. This kind of response might be dismissed as reflecting a "bandwagon effect"—an after-the-fact attempt by delegates to put themselves on the winning side—but there was no evidence of such an effect in the delegates' reporting of their real voting choices. When asked the same question pairing Crosbie and Clark, a majority of them said they would have voted for Crosbie.

2. That, too, is clear from the research. Thirty-five per cent (35%) of the delegates who said that finding a winning candidate was "very influential" voted for Mulroney on the first ballot; and, in overwhelming numbers, the rest of the delegates who cited this reason went to Mulroney as the balloting progressed. Eighty-three per cent (83%) of the delegates who said finding a candidate who could win power was a very influential reason for their first-ballot choice, and who had voted for candidates other than Clark or Mulroney on the first ballot, went with Mulroney on ballot four.

3. For a discussion of the impact of this idea (collectivism) on the Conservative party, see WILLIAM CHRISTIAN AND COLIN CAMPBELL, *Political Parties and Ideologies in Canada*, 2nd ed. (Toronto: McGraw-Hill Ryerson, 1983), pp. 85-99 *passim*.

4. BRIAN MULRONEY, *Where I Stand*, (Toronto: McClelland and Stewart, 1983).

5. The delegates wanted the country to take tough stands in dealing with the Soviet Union and to seek closer political relations with the United States.

6. In fact, in the March 1983 issue of *The Decima Quarterly Report*, it was found that 44 per cent of the Canadian population agreed with the statement . . . "None of the political parties in Canada really stand for the things I believe in" . . . Only 41 per cent disagreed.

7. JOHN R. WILLIAMS, *The Conservative Party of Canada*, (Durham, N.C.: Duke University Press, 1956), p. 42.

8. Point six of "Notes for a speech" by M. Brian Mulroney delivered to a meeting in Montreal, May 23, 1983.

Political Recruitment in Canada and Britain

MARSHALL W. CONLEY AND PATRICK J. SMITH

This research reports on the political recruitment of constituency-level party officials in England and Canada. It builds on the work of scholars in the United States and Britain. We focus on two concerns: the need to (1) identify and define role/activity functions and (2) examine alternative explanations for variations in role emphasis, especially (a) the constituency competitive position of the parties and (b) the motivational bases of party involvement.

Considerable effort has been made in previous research to identify and define role types.[1] Jacek has suggested that what is important about party organizations is the role assumed by the activists. These roles appear to give parties their distinctive character.[2] However, the major problem in identifying and defining role/activity types is that, despite frequent reference to various party functions, their identifications often remain impressionistic.[3]

Comparatively, we seek to learn whether ideological/purposive incentives are more important to English constituency party organizations and officials than to their Canadian counterparts. Many commentators have emphasized the relevance of class to politics in England and its absence in Canada.

Study Design

Three urban English constituencies that varied from "sure" to "doubtful" to "lost" were selected, all in the northeast (Middlesex/Essex) corner of Greater London.[4] Greater variety in electoral character marked the Canadian constituencies, two of which, Hamilton East and York South, were in urban Ontario, while eleven national constituencies in relatively rural Nova Scotia were also surveyed.[5]

A total population of all party officials at the constituency level

Adapted from Marshall W. Conley and Patrick J. Smith, "Political Recruitment and Party Activists: British and Canadian Comparisons," *International Political Science Review*, Vol. 4, No. 1 (1983): 48-56. By permission of publisher and authors.

was identified. In England and Ontario, personal interviews were possible; in the more complicated survey of Nova Scotia officers, mail questionnaires were used.

Motivational Differences

Regardless of how competitive their constituencies, Labour party officials in three English areas were markedly different in their motivations from their Conservative or Liberal counterparts. Even for the latter, roughly one in four activists gave purposive reasons for party involvement, while 71% of Labour officials did so. Equivalent patterns were found in Canada, with about four out of five New Democrats giving purposive reasons, while fewer than one in ten of their Liberal and Conservative counterparts did so (Table 1). In no case were these patterns affected by the constituency-competitive position of the parties. For the English data, class seems the most plausible explanation for such inter-party differences.[6] Allowing for regional variations, there are important

TABLE 1
Incentives: England, Ontario, Nova Scotia

	Utilitarian %	Solidary %	Purposive %	N
ENGLAND				
Labour	0	29	71	: 100 (44)
Liberal	3	70	27	: 100 (37)
Conservative	6	70	23	: 100 (47)
ONTARIO				
New Democrat	0	14	86	: 100 (28)
Liberal	21	73	6	: 100 (33)
PC	15	80	5	: 100 (20)
NOVA SCOTIA				
New Democrat	0	22	78	: 100 (51)
Liberal	43	43	14	: 100 (53)
PC	49	41	10	: 100 (49)

NOTE: This organizational typology as purposive, solidary, and utilitarian is adapted from J. Q. Wilson by Ron Shimizer (1972).

class differences among the local Canadian party élites also. In class terms, NDP activists are distinctive, both in Ontario and Nova Scotia.[7]

In sum, the three Constituency Labour party (CLP), two Ontario NDP, and eleven Nova Scotia NDP organizations could readily be classed as purposive; Liberals and Conservatives in both countries were essentially "non-ideological" (with utilitarian incentives somewhat more frequent in the Canadian data). These patterns were remarkably consistent over two countries and three types of constituencies.

What Triggers Recruitment?

The first point of entry into party work has been called the "trigger event." Purposive organizations were hypothesized to recruit mainly through ideological triggers, while non-purposive party associations made more personal (solidary/instrumental) appeals (Table 2). The evidence from both England and Canada supports this proposition.

TABLE 2
Initial Trigger Event Mobilizing Activists

	Ideology %	*Candidate-Leader* %	*Family-Friends* %	*Material Reasons* %	*TOTAL*
ENGLAND					
Labour	59	7	34	0	: 100 (44)
Liberal	11	46	43	0	: 100 (37)
Conservative	17	21	62	0	: 100 (47)
ONTARIO					
New Democrat	82	7	11	0	: 100 (28)
Liberal	6	24	67	3	: 100 (31)
PC	10	20	65	5	: 100 (20)
NOVA SCOTIA					
New Democrat	71	23	6	0	: 100 (58)
Liberal	12	46	32	10	: 100 (41)
PC	6	30	34	30	: 100 (44)

To what extent are activists coopted to join instead of being volunteers or self-starters? Our data support the view that voluntarism will predominate in purposive organizations, and cooptation will be the main recruitment method in non-purposive associations (Table 3). Almost 80% of the purposive English Labour officers declared that they were self-starters, compared with only 44% of the Tories and 35% of the Liberals.[8] In Ontario, too, the evidence supported the purposive-volunteer hypothesis. All (93%) but two of the New Democrats were self-starters, compared to only 9% of the Liberals and one Conservative. The Nova Scotian results were less accentuated.[9]

TABLE 3
Recruitment Method

	Volunteered %	Was Coopted %	TOTAL N
ENGLAND			
Labour	79	21	: 100 (44)
Liberal	35	65	: 100 (37)
Conservative	45	55	: 100 (47)
ONTARIO			
New Democrat	93	7	: 100 (28)
Liberal	9	91	: 100 (33)
PC	5	95	: 100 (20)
NOVA SCOTIA			
New Democrat	71	29	: 100 (51)
Liberal	63	37	: 100 (52)
PC	58	42	: 100 (49)

Motivational Change

Both Eldersveld and Jacek report that the personnel of purposive organizations tend to shift toward solidary orientations.[10] In both England and Canada, we expect to find patterns of motivational change that are higher in the purposive (namely, Labour, New

Democrat) party organizations (as activists move from ideological to associational incentives) than they are in non-purposive associations (all other English and Canadian parties) where solidary patterns should continue to predominate.

Some 70% of *all* English officers indicated their initial incentives were ideological (compared with 18% social and 12% instrumental). When present incentives were examined, only 41% said they were motivated by ideological considerations, compared to 56% by associational reasons (and 3% material). Clearly, motivations changed among English activists from point of entry to present involvement. And the direction of this change would appear to support Eldersveld's contention that initial ideologues tend to become less purposive and more social in their reasons for continuing party involvement.

Did the purposive organizations especially reflect this shift to solidary incentives? Just over one-fourth in the purposive English party organization gave different reasons for their current activity; over 70% of the Labour officers continued to explain their activism in ideological terms.

Motivational change was similarly widespread in the non-purposive organizations. One-fourth (28%) of the Tories said their motives had changed, and indeed the shift was toward solidary "rewards"—from 36% initially to just over 70% at present—a shift of 20% from purposive and a 15% decline in material reasons for involvement (Table 4). English Liberals changed similarly. Almost three-fourths (73%) expressed initial purposive incentives; two-fifths indicated that their reasons for involvement had changed.

In the Ontario parties, just over half (54%) were initially motivated by purposive considerations (37% by solidary, 9% by utilitarian). One-third of these officials (32%) said their motives had changed; ideological and associational totals were reversed (33% and 54%, respectively). Little change occurred in the more purposive NDP organizations.[11]

Unexpectedly, the rather professionalized, non-purposive Liberal party activists showed the greatest shifts in incentive patterns: 21% began party work expecting material rewards, and 21% continued party work for the same reasons. Only 45% argued that their initial motives were social, yet almost three-fourths (73%) explained their continued party association in such terms. While one-third began for ideological reasons, only two (6%) continued to stress them.

TABLE 4
Change from Initial to Present Expectations

	Initial Expectations			Present Expectations			Shift in Motives
	M %	S %	I %	M %	S %	I %	Yes
ENGLAND							
Labour	0	2	98	0	30	70	9
Liberal	14	14	73	3	70	27	41
Conservative	21	36	43	6	70	23	28
ONTARIO							
New Democrat	0	4	96	0	14	86	11
Liberal	21	46	33	21	73	6	49
PC	0	70	30	15	80	5	35
NOVA SCOTIA							
New Democrat	2	28	70	0	22	78	20
Liberal	8	59	33	43	43	14	21
PC	17	45	38	49	41	10	9

M = Material; S = Solidary; I = Ideological

There was little change among Ontario Conservatives. Social reasons had predominated initially (70%) and seem to be important currently. In Nova Scotia, the greatest shifts are away from ideological incentives and toward an increase in material reward structures among officials in the solidary organizations. While one-third of the Liberals and Tories noted initially purposive reasons for their involvement, this fell to one in ten for current motives (although few officers felt their motives had shifted). Solidary incentives remained consistent for New Democrats and Tories.

The impact of utilitarian incentives, solidary rewards for non-purposive parties, and ideological considerations for purposive organizations were clearly observable in these data. Interestingly, the majority of the initially ideologically minded activists who changed their explanations worked in the non-purposive parties—presumably because of the availability of material and solidary incentives and the frustration in sustaining an ideological orientation.

Roles and Activities

Activists in purposive party organizations should emphasize party, policy, education and ideology, while non-purposive associations should contain officers who more often stress associational and utilitarian rewards.

We found that party and policy considerations were indeed paramount among purposive party organizations in both countries: English Labour Party officers and Canadian New Democratic Party officials consistently ranked concern with public issues as more significant than their Liberal/Conservative counterparts— 84% (Labour) and 75% to 93% (NDP) compared to 30% (English Conservatives), 54% (English Liberals), 20% (Ontario PC), 46% (Ontario Liberals).

In addition, purposive activists more often thought influencing government policies was important; 66% of the Labour officers, 86% of the Ontario New Democrats, and 60% of the Nova Scotia purposive officials felt this was *very* important. Among Liberals and Conservatives in both countries, less than half of *any* of the organizations held similar attitudes.

When associational orientations were examined, these findings were reinforced. As hypothesized, solidary/utilitarian organizations stressed candidate attraction, being close to influential people, and social contacts regularly more so than their purposive "opposites."

Patterns of Activity

We hypothesized that purposive party organizations would be more "service-oriented" than utilitarian-solidary associations, in which social activity would prevail. Accordingly, we found that Labour party activists consistently stressed the importance of helping people with problems with government and with activities associated with the welfare of their constituencies. Liberals and Conservatives in the London area constituencies rated such activity as less important than their purposive colleagues; although, interestingly, the Liberals, with their particular emphasis on "community politics," ranked these constituency activities higher than did Tory officials.

This pattern repeated itself to some extent with the Ontario and Nova Scotia party officials. In Ontario, for example, the purposive party organizations helping people overcome problems with government and looking after constituents' welfare were seen as performing very important activities. While not unimportant to officials in "solidary" parties, these activities were considered much less important. Social relationships were of more significance in such organizations. For instance, in Nova Scotia only 18% of the purposive New Democrats were prepared to argue the importance of "fun." This compared with 30% of the Conservatives and 35% of the Liberals who felt that "fun" was very important.

Conclusion

Very clear differences emerged between purposive New Democrats and Labour party organizations (and officials) and non-purposive Liberal and Conservative officers/associations in England and Canada. Significantly, these differences persisted across two political systems, "sure," "doubtful," and "lost" constituencies, and urban, suburban, industrial, and rural political settings. Non-purposive party groups were found to be concerned primarily with socially oriented functions and to concentrate on personalities over ideologies. Purposive organizations were *more* concerned with questions of program, policy, and ideology; they were also more "service oriented."

NOTES

1. Past evidence is mixed (Fairlie, 1976; Jacek, 1969; Morrell, 1977; Berry, 1970; Donnison, 1954). Eldersveld (1964) reported "no major differences" between Republicans and Democrats in Wayne County, Michigan, while Ippolito (1967) noted considerable variation between Democrats and Republicans in Nassau County, New York, keyed to electoral competition. Only "majority" Republicans were electorally role oriented, while "minority" Democrats emphasized organizational activities. Whether competitive position can actually explain differences in party role orientations remains problematic.

2. H.J. JACEK, "The comparative study of party organizations in Canada and the United States." McMaster University, Hamilton, Ontario, Canada (1972), unpublished.

3. P. ABRAMS AND A. LITTLE, "The young activist in British politics," *British Journal of Sociology*, Vol. 16, No. 4 (1965); D. BERRY, *The Sociology of Grass Roots Politics* (London: Macmillan, 1970); D. KAVANAGH, *Constituency Elec-*

tioneering in Britain (London: Longmans, 1970); and J. MEISEL, "Recent changes in Canadian parties," in H. Thorburn (ed.), *Party Politics in Canada* (Scarborough: Prentice-Hall, 1967).

4. Wanstead and Woodford is our "sure" Conservative riding, represented by Winston Churchill. Edmonton, largely working class, is our "sure" Labour constituency; over one-fourth of its residents live in public housing. The "doubtful" constituency of Ilford South fell between these two in electoral, demographic and historical terms. From 1945 to 1975 it changed hands between Labour and Conservative five times in ten general elections.

5. Hamilton East has ranked as a "sure" Liberal constituency for twenty years. York South, in metropolitan Toronto, is one of the most marginal in Ontario, having changed parties eight times in 12 elections (1942-1974). The Nova Scotia data were collected later. In the ten general elections between 1957 and 1980, the Progressive Conservatives won 90 of 115 seats contested, or 78%. Except in Cape Breton Island, their major opposition was the Liberal party: only in two elections (1963 and 1980), when the Liberal party defeated an incumbent Conservative nationally, were Nova Scotia Liberals able to elect more than two (of eleven or twelve) Members of Parliament.

6. R. ROSE AND D. URWIN, "What are parties based on?" *New Society*, Vol. 15 (May 7, 1970): 774.

7. In Nova Scotia, 55% of the NDP officers characterize themselves in class terms compared to one-third of the Liberal and Conservative activists. In both Ontario and Nova Scotia, the NDP activists overwhelmingly stress purposive goals: 78% and 86%, respectively.

8. Constituency-competitive position also seems important. Voluntarism was highest in the Labour party in "sure" Edmonton and in "lost" Wanstead and Woodford, while it fell in "doubtful" Ilford South. But in non-purposive organizations the competition factor more clearly emerged: in "lost" Edmonton, 71% of the Tory activists had to be asked to join the party; in "marginal/doubtful" Ilford South this dropped to 57%; in "sure" Wanstead and Woodford almost three out of five Conservative officers had initiated their own involvement in local party work.

9. Voluntarism was somewhat higher among English activists than was found for Detroit by Eldersveld or for Canadian activists by Kornberg. Just over half of all English activists were self-starters; this compared with 64% in Nova Scotia and 37% in Ontario.

10. S. ELDERSVELD, *Political Parties: A Behavioral Analysis* (Chicago: Rand McNally, 1964); and H.J. JACEK, R. SHIMZU, AND P.J. SMITH, "Party organization and functions in the United States and Canada," American Political Science Association (1970), mimeographed.

11. All but one NDP officer (96%) explained initial involvement as ideological, and 86% gave the same reasons for their ongoing involvement.

Tory Party Differences in Canada and Britain

JEFFREY SIMPSON

A recent reproach about producing another panegyric on British Prime Minister Margaret Thatcher may have stung, but it did highlight an essential difference between British and Canadian political parties and perceptions, a difference sharply etched by the leadership traumas of Canada's Conservatives and the political success of the British Conservative Party.

Put bluntly, British parties think hard about policy both in opposition and government. An intellectual ferment exists within the parties. They debate their principles incessantly. As a result, they are better equipped to deal with the demands of power.

Canadian parties, by contrast, are often afraid of ideas and internal debate. The structure of Canadian parties and the country mitigates against hard thinking about policy. Parties take the easy and ultimately self-defeating way out: they look almost exclusively for charisma in leadership.

In Britain, parties are alive to questions about themselves. Whether one likes their approaches or not, one can only respect the amount of work that goes into crafting them.

The yearly party conferences do discuss policy issues in detail and in depth, although the Government party of the day is more chary about self-examination. As recently as 1981, however, the governing Conservatives thrashed out Mrs. Thatcher's economic policies on television.

Within the party caucuses, groups of MPs form pressure groups which issue policy statements. They try, within the confines of their party, to push the party in certain directions. Many MPs write newspaper and magazine articles, not all of them toeing the party line.

Backbenchers on all sides are especially restless. Several Conservative bills have been thwarted by backbench rebellions. During the early stages of the Falklands war, the ministry was given a worse ride from its own side than from Labor or the SDP-Liberal alliance.

Adapted from Jeffrey Simpson, "Tory difference: British build, Canadians self-destruct," *The Globe and Mail*, February 10, 1983, p. 7. By permission.

The functioning of the House of Commons illustrates the relative independence of MPs. Government MPs are given nearly half the opportunities during question period. Woe unto any Speaker who denies them. Discipline is imposed by three gradations of whips: the one-line whip leaves MPs free to abstain or vote against the party without fear of reprisal.

Numbers induce independence. With 350 members on the Government side, about 250 are free from the constraints of being a minister or parliamentary secretary. In Canada, nearly half the Government MPs are ministers or parliamentary secretaries.

The federal system also spreads out political talent. Ambitious and/or talented Canadian politicians can even aspire to make a name in municipal politics. In Britain, where mayors are not directly elected, the ambitious and/or talented all gravitate to Westminster. Of course, there are plenty of trained seals at Westminster, but there are fewer in absolute and relative terms than in Ottawa.

These institutional factors, however, do not entirely explain the weaker Canadian party tradition of thinking hard about policy. Nor is it sufficient to say British politics is more ideological.

British debates do invariably centre on distribution of income and opportunities among individuals and groups. This gives them an often sharp ideological edge.

Canadian political debates often revolve around distribution among regions, provinces and linguistic groups. There are debates about trade-offs and compromises, about keeping things together. But still the hard thinking is often missing.

Take one glaring example. Under Robert Stanfield and Joe Clark, the Conservatives resisted the Liberals' centralist approach to federalism without ever thinking hard enough about their alternative. They floundered about with a variety of formulas: two nations, co-operative federalism and community of communities.

These were admirable intentions, but good intentions may be an inadequate guide in politics. More power and tax resources for the provinces will inevitably mean more conflicts. Conflicts are at the heart of pluralist democracy and may often be healthy. But if policies open up new areas for conflict, they should also offer new ways of resolving them. Otherwise, they lack credibility.

The Conservatives have never done the hard policy work of rooting their good intentions in proposals for reforming institutions such as the Senate, the Supreme Court, the federal-provincial conference, the Commons itself. Theirs have been ideas in search of a framework.

Equally telling examples could be drawn from the Liberals, but the point remains: the framework is critical. Without the framework, or a set of coherent ideas rooted in reality, a party can lose its bearings in government or opposition.

What impresses about Mrs. Thatcher is the existence of a framework. She knows, roughly speaking, where she wants to take the Conservative Party and Britain. Like a good politician, she is willing to tack and trim to move forward, but she never loses sight of the ultimate destination. She has done the hard thinking of policy, brought the party around to her way of thinking and, if the polls are right, persuaded the largest number of voters. One does not have to accept her version to admire her tenacity and the coherence of her framework.

Better still for Britain, there are others working all the time on other frameworks: in the opposition parties and within the Conservative Party itself.

The tragedy of the recent Canadian experience has been and remains an abhorrence of frameworks. Both major parties tried hesitatingly to get straight their principles and fluffed the job.

The Liberals were just beginning the hard slog to rethinking policies after their defeat of 1979. Their re-election obliterated the tentative groping. Instead, a small group sent the party on a nationalist, mildly progressive route after the election. The party was consulted only perfunctorily, so when circumstances changed, the small group felt free to change direction again. Only in the constitutional field, where the Liberals have had a consistent framework, has the party enjoyed political success.

The Conservatives tried desperately in the run-up to the 1979 election to prove themselves fit to govern. They designed policies for every problem. But again the party was not consulted. Policies emerged from small caucus groups, from Joe Clark's advisers or from the leader's own head. None of them—Petro-Canada's privatization, mortgage deductibility, the Jerusalem Embassy, the $2-billion tax cut—were rooted in party debate.

When these promises came a cropper and the Conservatives lost the subsequent election, the party learned the wrong lesson. It resolutely fled from policy, not wishing to repeat the mistake of 1977-1979. The mistake, however, was not in designing policies, but going about it the wrong way. As a result, the party has drifted in an intellectual vacuum which led it once again into a fixation with its leadership rather than with its ideas.

How different from Britain. Here no one worries about Mrs. Thatcher's clothes or [then] Labor leader Michael Foot's unruly hair. They are mocked for their idiosyncracies but judged on their visions, their talents, their frameworks. They stand or fall in a milieu in which ideas count and the hard work of thinking about policy pays off.

Party Identification and Party Images in Canada, Britain and the United States

MARTIN P. WATTENBERG

In the brief history of cross-national survey research, few concepts have aroused as much academic discussion and controversy as that of party identification. Since its original formulation in the United States during the 1950s, political scientists have sought to investigate the extent to which stable psychological attachments to political parties exist in a wide variety of democratic systems as well as the role that they play in them. Perhaps the major reason why party identification has received so much attention is due to the great theoretical importance attributed to it in some of the earliest comparative research on the subject.[1] Party identification was postulated as functioning as a preservative or stabilizing influence on the political system.

One crucial assumption here is that party identification represents a positive sense of affect toward the party identified with. Yet it is just as plausible to argue that party identification can simply represent a rejection of the alternatives to the party which is preferred, without any positive affect toward the most preferred party. Such a possibility is especially important to recognize in systems in which only two realistic alternative governments are presented to the electorate for a choice. In multiparty systems, where there are numerous alternatives, an expressed party identification is more likely to be the result of the voter canvassing all of the possi-

Adapted from Martin P. Wattenberg, "Party Identification and Party Images: A Comparison of Britain, Canada, Australia, and the United States," *Comparative Politics*, Vol. 15, No. 1 (October, 1982): 23-40. By permission of publisher and author.

bilities and choosing the one that he or she feels most positive about.

In both multi- and two-party systems it is important to assess the attitudes that underlie partisan attachments, but in two-party systems it is apparently more crucial. This paper will examine party images in three countries in which the party system revolves primarily around two major parties—the United States, Great Britain and Canada. A close examination of party images in these societies should help in providing a better understanding of the nature of partisan identification in these democracies.

A Comparison of the Level of Party Identification in the Anglo-American Democracies

Much of the cross-national research that has been done on party identification has involved simply comparing the percentage of respondents who report a party affiliation. The data that are available on this question since 1964 are presented in Figure 1 for the three Anglo-American democracies. The most striking aspect of Figure 1 is the difference between the United States and the other two countries. In the latter set, at least 80% of each population has expressed a party identification in all the surveys that have been conducted, while in the United States the comparable figure has always been less than 80%. Furthermore, while the proportion of party identifiers has remained fairly stable in Great Britain and Canada, there has been a sharp decline throughout this period in the United States—from 77% in 1964 to only 63% in 1980.

Yet while the trend that is shown for the U.S. in Figure 1 is indicative of the changes in the American party system (i.e., partisan dealignment), the extremely high and relatively stable levels of partisan attachments in the Anglican countries have not been matched by great stability in these systems. For example, the fact that about 90% of the British electorate has consistently reported a party affiliation gives us absolutely no clue to the fact that the minor parties have grown in size and that there has been an erosion of strong support[2] for the two major parties since 1970, as is shown in Figure 2.

Finally, neither Figures 1 nor 2 would lead us to expect that party identification is substantially weaker in Canada than in the other Anglo-American countries. However, as Clarke et al. have recently argued, partisanship in Canada is much less stable than would be expected from a variable that supposedly represents a long-term force.[3] Furthermore, many Canadians hold a different identification on the provincial level from their federal party identification. And although new parties have not arisen at the Canadian federal level, at the provincial level the Parti Quebecois, which openly advocates the separation of Quebec from Canada, has been the most successful new party in the recent history of these democracies—actually gaining control of the provincial government in 1976.

In summary, simply examining the level of party identification in these democracies leaves one with an incomplete picture of how stable the party system is likely to be. If all partisan identifiers could be assumed to hold a positive attitude toward their own party and a negative attitude toward the opposition, as elites certainly do, then there would be little need to look beyond the fact of the identification itself. However, as surveys of various populations

FIGURE 1
Percent Identifying with a Political Party in the Anglo-American Democracies

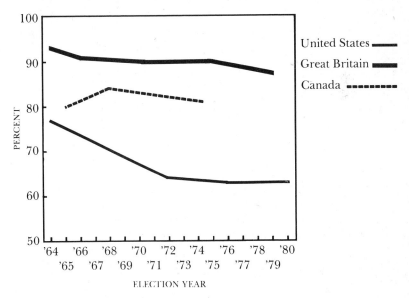

SOURCES: British Election Study Series; SRC/CPS Presidential Election Study Series; Canadian National Election Studies: 1965, 1968, 1974.

FIGURE 2
Percent Strongly Identifying with One of the Two Major
Political Parties

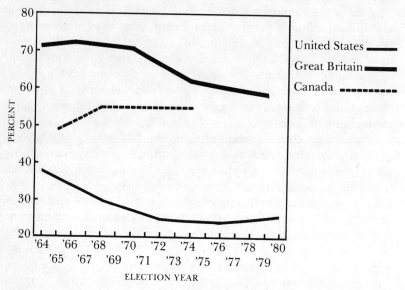

SOURCES: See Figure 1.

have shown over the years, mass attitudes rarely match those of the elites. It has already been demonstrated that there are substantial proportions of identifiers in two-party systems who are actually more negative than positive about their own party. In addition, a variety of other patterns towards the parties exist that deviate from a clear perception of one major party as good and the other as bad. By examining the nature and extent of these deviations from a clear-cut, positive-negative pattern, a more in-depth picture of the role that party identification plays in these societies should emerge.

Citizens' evaluations of the two major parties in the Anglo-American countries

In at least one national election study in each of the Anglo-American democracies, respondents have been asked in an open-ended fashion what they liked and disliked about the two major political parties—Republican and Democratic in the United States; Conservative and Labour in Great Britain; Conservative and Liberal in Canada. By simply subtracting the number of negative comments from the number of positive ones, respondents can be classified as either positive, neutral, or negative towards each of the major parties in his or her society, depending on whether the number of likes exceed, equal, or are fewer than the number of dislikes.

After collapsing the data into negative, neutral, and positive ratings on each of the two major parties, a six-fold classification representing respondents' ratings of both parties combined can be created for each country. The six categories are as follows: (1) negative-negative: those who have negative attitudes toward both major parties; (2) negative-neutral: negative ratings of one party, a neutral evaluation of the other; (3) neutral-neutral: those who are neutral with respect to both; (4) positive-negative: positive evaluation of one party, a negative evaluation of the other; (5) positive-neutral: positive towards one party and neutral towards the other; and (6) positive-positive: those who rate both parties in a positive fashion. It should be noted that in all of these categories which party the respondent feels warm, neutral, or cold to, is irrelevant. For example, some of the positive-negatives in Britain rate the Conservatives positively and Labour negatively, and some vice versa, but what is important here is that these respondents see the parties in a polarized warm-cool fashion, not which party they are positive towards.

Table 1 shows the results of this analysis for each of the three countries. In none of the three is anything very close to the idealized version of the electorate having polarized perceptions of the two major parties the actual case. This pattern is least prominent in Canada, where in 1974 only 19% of the population held a positive attitude towards one of the major parties and a negative attitude towards the other. There has been some increase in the two most negative categories in the U.S. and the U.K., but in both it is fairly small. The major shift in the U.S. is instead towards complete neutrality. In contrast, in Great Britain there has actually been an *increase* in the proportion of the population that perceives the Conservatives and Labour in a polarized, positive-negative fashion. Thus, in the United States the two parties have undergone a sharp decline in terms of their salience as attitudinal objects in the public's perception of politics, while in Britain, although there has been a similar trend away from strong identification with the major parties, the public's attitudes towards them have paradoxically shown increasing clarity and polarization.

TABLE 1
A Comparison of the Public's Evaluations of the Two Major Political Parties in the Anglo-American Countries

	Negative Negative	Negative Neutral	Neutral Neutral	Positive Negative	Positive Neutral	Positive Positive	N
GREAT BRITAIN							
1964	6.2%	16.8	16.0	37.2	20.0	4.2	1769
1966	6.5%	18.2	12.3	40.7	18.2	4.0	1874
1970	5.6%	15.0	14.9	40.5	18.7	5.3	1843
Feb. '74	9.2%	17.3	14.1	41.8	14.1	3.6	2462
Oct. '74	12.0%	16.9	7.4	46.9	12.2	4.5	2365
1979	5.9%	12.7	7.9	49.9	16.1	7.6	1893
U.S.A.							
1952	3.6%	9.7	13.0	50.1	18.1	5.5	1799
1956	2.9%	9.0	15.9	40.0	23.3	8.9	1762
1960	1.9%	7.5	16.8	41.4	24.2	8.3	1164
1964	4.4%	11.2	20.2	38.4	20.6	5.0	1571
1968	10.0%	13.8	17.3	37.5	17.4	4.1	1557
1972	7.9%	12.6	29.9	30.3	14.7	4.7	1372
1976	7.5%	11.8	31.3	31.1	13.7	4.5	2248
1980	5.0%	8.6	36.5	27.3	17.7	4.8	1614
CANADA							
1974	7.5%	20.1	25.8	19.0	22.1	5.5	2562

SOURCES: British Election Study Series; SRC/CPS Presidential Election Study Series; Canadian National Election Study: 1974.

Canada: parties without polarization

The strongest criticisms of the concept of party identification in the Anglo-American democracies have generally come from Canadian scholars. For example, John Meisel has written that "party identification has only limited applicability to Canada and seems to shift as much as the vote itself."[4] One reason why party identification apparently doesn't seem to be of much use in understanding Canadian politics is that public attitudes toward the parties are far less polarized than in the other three countries. If partisanship represents a long-term force that is resistant to short-term trends favoring a particular party, then it should involve some sense of rejection of the other major party in order to insulate partisans from shifts to the opposition. However, in Canada the positive-neutral pattern is slightly more frequent than the positive-negative. By contrast, in the other countries positive-negatives outnumber positive-neutrals by at least three to two, and in the most recent British data by about three to one.

There are several possible reasons why one might hypothesize that Canada would be somewhat different from the other two. First, there is the fact that Canada has a large French-speaking population, which may view politics differently than the English. However, there is only a slight difference between English and French Canadians, with the English being about 5% more likely to be classified as positive-negatives. Furthermore, most of this difference can probably be attributed to the Liberal party's domination of federal politics in Quebec. Within Quebec, English- and French-speaking citizens are almost equally likely to be in the positive-negative category (15.1% among the French and 15.8% among the English).

Another possible explanation is that Canadians in some regions may not consider either the Liberals or Conservatives to be one of the two major parties in their area; e.g., many commentators on the 1980 election remarked that the New Democratic Party (NDP) now appears stronger in the West than the Liberals. However, no other combination of party images (i.e., Liberal-NDP or Conservative-NDP) produces a greater degree of polarization in perceptions in any of the 10 provinces than does the Liberal-Progressive Conservative party (PC) combination.

A third possible explanation is that many Canadians, like their neighbors to the south, make their electoral choice on the basis of party leaders and local candidates rather than on party alone. This is indicated by the fact that the proportion of those neutral towards both major parties in Canada (26%) is much higher than in Britain and nearly as high as in the United States during the 1970s. Yet it does not seem to explain the lack of polarized partisans either. Those Canadians who say that party was the major influence in their voting decision are less likely to be neutral towards both parties, but only 20% can be classified as positive-negatives compared to 22% among those who say that party leaders were most important and 19% among those who mentioned local candidates.

The most plausible answer left is that Canadians do not see the two major parties in a polarized fashion because the parties do not consistently act in a manner that is conducive to the formation of such attitudes in the mass public. As Leon Epstein has written, "Not only are the major Canadian parties thought to be undoctrinal and opportunistic in their campaign appeals, but they are also said to be so in their parliamentary performance."[5] The weakness of any long-standing commitment to an ideological position in Canadian party politics is best exemplified by the Progressive-Conservative party, whose very name indicates a lack of ideology as it is hard to see how a party can programmatically be both progressive and conservative at the same time. If polarized, positive-negative attitudes toward the two major Canadian parties are to develop, it will thus first be necessary to establish a perception of long-term ideological differences between the parties. In the meantime, one can expect a high degree of volatility in Canadian voting patterns despite the fact that over 80% of the population does report a nominal party identification.

Britain: A growth in the polarization of party images

For many decades Great Britain has been pictured as a classic example of a stable two-party system. However, a number of recent trends have caused scholars to reexamine the accuracy of this description. The increasing oscillations in support for each of the two major parties indicates to many that the system is no longer as stable as was once thought.[6] Furthermore, the proportion of the electorate casting a ballot for either the Conservatives or Labour has dropped rather steadily from 80.3% in 1951 to 56.1% in October 1974 due to the decline in voter turnout and the gains made by various third parties.[7]

One cause for this, according to a number of sources, has been the decline in the percentage of the British electorate that perceives that there are major differences between the parties. From the 1955 high of 74% this figure dropped sharply to a low of 49% in February of 1974, and has since recovered only slightly to 55% in 1979. Many have interpreted this change as an indication that voters in Britain increasingly feel that whichever party is in power the outcome is likely to be disappointing.[8]

What is most interesting about this finding is that in the 1970s the degree of acrimony and conflict between the parties grew considerably. In spite of the decline in class voting the parties not only persisted with their class appeals—if anything, they increased them. Thus, nowhere in the literature is it argued that partisan dealignment in Britain has been due to any convergence between the two major parties. Instead, the prevailing interpretation seems to be that the electorate was aware of the conflict between the parties and simply rejected it. In other words the alternatives were present, but neither was well liked.

Yet as Ivor Crewe has recently noted, the process of dealignment in Britain has been relatively mild and short-lived compared to the United States, even though the British system has undergone more realignment.[9] The answer to this apparent puzzle that is offered here is that the dealigning forces in Great Britain have been of a fundamentally different nature than those in the United States, and as a consequence the major party identifiers have responded differently.

In the United States there has been a long-term decline in the salience of political parties as demonstrated by the increase in the proportion of the population expressing neutral attitudes toward both parties. Although potential realigning issues have been present, they have been associated in the voters' minds increasingly with presidential candidates rather than with the parties.[10]

One might hypothesize a similar trend in Britain as a result of the decline in the perception of differences between the parties. However, this is not a very likely possibility due to the crucial role that political parties play in the British system. As Richard Rose has written, "British government is party government."[11] Certainly the electorate is well aware of this fact, as evidenced by the results of a 1976 survey that showed that 86% of the British population agreed with the statement that political parties are "essential to our form of national government."[12] The centrality of the major parties in the voters' minds is also shown in Table 1 by the consistently low percentage in the neutral-neutral category. Between the 1964 election and that of February 1974, this figure fluctuated in the 12-16% range, and has since dropped to less than 8%.

Thus, in Britain it is far more plausible than in the United States to argue that partisan decomposition has been a result of specific political events rather than due to long-term processes of change. It is not very difficult to speculate on what sort of events might be responsible—Britain has suffered a severe blow to its international prestige in recent years and has been faced with a chronically (some might even go so far as to say terminally) ill economy.

Conclusion

Perhaps the most general analytic point that can be drawn from this analysis is that to fully understand the role that party identification plays in any given society, it is necessary to investigate how respondents feel about the major alternatives from which they must choose. Party identification is fundamentally a statement of how the voter feels about the political alternatives. One limitation of the measurement of party identification is that one can only assess which party the respondent generally prefers and how strongly—it does not necessarily imply how positive, neutral, or negative people feel about the parties. In order to interpret what party identifications are likely to mean for the system, it is essential to know the evaluative nature of the attitudes on which they are based; i.e., how each of the major alternatives is perceived.

NOTES

1. See, in particular, PHILIP E. CONVERSE AND GEORGES DUPEUX, "Politicalization of the Electorate in France and the United States" in ANGUS CAMPBELL ET AL., *Elections and the Political Order* (New York: Wiley, 1966); and PHILIP E. CONVERSE, "Of Time and Partisan Stability," *Comparative Political Studies*, Vol. 2 (July, 1969): 139-71.

2. In the Anglican countries strong support is defined as being either a "very strong" or "fairly strong" identifier.

3. See HAROLD D. CLARKE, JANE JENSON, LAWRENCE LEDUC AND JON H. PAMMETT, *Political Choice in Canada*, abridged ed. (Toronto: McGraw-Hill Ryerson Limited, 1980).

4. JOHN MEISEL, *Working Papers on Canadian Politics*, 2nd enlarged ed. (Montreal: McGill-Queen's University Press, 1975), p. 67.

5. LEON EPSTEIN, "A Comparative Study of Canadian Parties," *American Political Science Review*, Vol. 59 (March, 1965): 58.

6. See IVOR CREWE, "Party Identification Theory and Political Change in Britain" in Ian Budge et al.

7. IVOR CREWE, BO SARLVIK, AND JAMES ALT, "Partisan Dealignment in Britain: 1964-1974," *British Journal of Political Science*, Vol. 7 (April, 1977): 129-90.

8. See S.E. FINER, *The Changing British Party System, 1945-1979* (Washington, D.C.: American Enterprise Institute, 1980).

9. IVOR CREWE, "Prospects for Party Realignment: An Anglo-American Comparison," *Comparative Politics*, Vol. 12 (July, 1980): 379-400.

10. See MARTIN P. WATTENBERG, "The Decline of Political Partisanship in

the United States: Negativity or Neutrality?," *American Political Science Review*, Vol. 75 (December, 1981): 941-50.

11. RICHARD ROSE, *Politics in England*, 3rd ed. (Boston: Little, Brown and Co., 1980), p. 249.

12. See S.E. FINER, *The Changing British Party System, 1945-1979* (Washington, D.C.: American Enterprise Institute, 1980), p. 130.

The Mythology of the American Two-Party System

THEODORE J. LOWI

On Myths

A myth is a statement about reality. It is not a falsehood. A myth may be true or based on the truth; the closer the myth is to the truth, the more durable it is likely to be. Nevertheless, myths are accepted for reasons other than evidence and argument. This is the main distinction between mythology and science. Anything can be a myth. Even this year's scientific truth can be next year's myth by rote learning and habitual acceptance. Surely one of the great preventives against mythology in science is the stress on disproof.

Politics is obviously a myth-infested universe. The Greeks were probably the first to recognize the difference between myth and science; Plato was probably the first thinker to imagine inventing myths self-consciously for the purpose of maintaining a republic. From Plato through Hitler to the present, myths have been an important component of all systems of government. Sometimes the myths are deliberate inventions. Sometimes the myths emerge out of habit and tradition, in which case not even the top leadership may recognize them as myths.

Adapted from Theodore J. Lowi, "Toward a More Responsible Three-Party System: The Mythology of the Two-Party System and the Prospects for Reform," *PS*, Vol. XVI, No. 4 (Fall, 1983): 699-706. By permission of the author and the American Political Science Association.

Party systems, like governments, are to a large extent built on myths. And as with government myths, party system myths are a powerful defense against criticism and change. The paradigm may stand steadfastly as the hypotheses are disconfirmed. During the past 20 years or more, the reality of the American party system has deviated so far from the ideal image that the myths supporting it should have been exposed for what they are. But myths die hard, as long as high priests in academe and journalism rise to their defense. Nothing is likely to invite more personal criticism than a proposal for a new party, leading to a three-party system. Fear of such criticism undoubtedly contributed to the great reluctance of John Anderson in 1980 to declare himself the leader of a third party. As forthright as Anderson was on all of the issues—as combative as he was to become an independent presidential candidate —his courage evidently melted away in face of the American idea of the two-party system. Questions about whether he planned to form a new political party were dealt with vaguely and tentatively. In the spring of 1983, Anderson came forth with a plan to try to form a new political party. Perhaps this is a sign that reality is beginning to catch up with the mythology.

Without any great difficulty I have identified nine of the myths comprising the myth-system about the two-party system and its virtues. These nine myths are far from an exhaustive inventory. And they are not intended to be sufficient to make a case for a three-party system. They are intended only to weaken the arguments of the self-appointed defenders of the two-party system who stomp around so destructively with their big flat feet on any questions raised about it.

Nine Easy-to-Spot Myths About the Two-Party System

1. The first myth is truly a supermyth, the one from which many of the others logically flow: "American democracy is based on the two-party system, and we have been operating continuously under a two-party system for almost our entire history. American democracy is inconceivable without it."

True, the two-party system goes back a very long way in American history. One can say it goes all the way back to 1800. However, its golden age was the nineteenth century. Around 1896, the great two-party system of the nineteenth century died. The southern states became exclusively one-party systems dominated by the Democrats; and to a lesser degree the northern states became one-party systems dominated by the Republicans. And in some of the important states where the two parties competed directly against one another, in reality one of the parties was overwhelmingly dominant in one part of the state while the other party was overwhelmingly dominant in another part of the state. Therefore, while nationally, the two-party system seemed to dominate, in actuality we were governed by two competing one-party systems.

This system of two competing one-party systems prevailed at the national level and within many states from 1896 virtually until the 1950s. After 1956, thanks to the efforts of President Eisenhower, the Republican party began making inroads into the Democratic south. But by that time, the two political parties were internally so weak that the two-party system Eisenhower helped reintroduce was hardly a shadow of its nineteenth century ancestor. During the 50 or 60 years of one-party dominance, both parties weakened progressively until neither was able to enact serious legislation without the crutch of presidential power. In order to adjust to this state of affairs, the defenders of the two-party system helped rewrite democratic theory in order to put the presidency at its center although in actual fact the presidency is both a cause and a reflection of the *decline* of the two-party democracy.

2. Myth #2 provides the basis for the faith: "The two-party system must be defended at all cost because, as with competing enterprises in a market economy, the competition between the two major parties yields great though unintended public benefits. These include: increased voter turnout and other forms of participation; automatic majorities, so that Congress and the President can get on with the job of governing after the election is over; greater effectiveness and decisiveness in government, where there is continuity extending all the way from the voter to the highest councils; therefore, more legitimacy of government because of the continuous connection between the electorate and the important policies."

If all this were true, a person would be a real subversive to support anything other than a two-party system. But a closer examination reveals the nonsense of attributing so much good to the two-party system. In the first place, two-party competition has not had an appreciable regular positive effect on voter turnout since the late nineteenth century. Moreover, the reintroduction of two-party competition in many states following 1956 did not contribute to an increase in political participation. Two-party competition cannot even explain the dramatic increase in the political participation of blacks. In the South, blacks were effectively enfranchised by laws passed with nonpartisan northern majorities, imposed upon southern states. And one of the most dramatic instances of increased political participation in recent years has been in the city of Chicago, not a famous case of two-party system competition.

As for the provision of automatic majorities, the defenders of the two-party system argue this in face of the fact that Congress for the entire twentieth century has consisted of coalitions among voting blocs. Except for an occasional honeymoon, such as Reagan's in 1981, there has been almost no party cohesion in recent decades; for every major legislative campaign, a coalition of voting blocs and their respective interest group supporters must be developed virtually from scratch. Party leaders in Congress do help make the legislative merry-go-round go around. But the important work they do would in no way be eliminated by the mere presence of members of a third party.

What of legitimacy? Over the past decade, dozens of studies by reputable and disinterested social scientists have documented a very significant decline of political legitimacy in the United States. Some call it the decline of trust, others call it the decline of confidence, but it all adds up to the troubling conclusion that American attitudes toward government and public life have been negligibly or negatively affected by political parties. The dramatic increase in the percentage of voters who refer to themselves as independents —during the very two decades in which two-party competition was restored to many of the states—ought to bring at least some discomfort to the defenders of the two-party myth.

3. Myth #3 steps behind the first two: "The two-party system is natural, it is American, it is the only system consonant with America's historic electoral system—the single-member district system."

This proposition holds up no better than the previous two. In the first place, if a two-party system is so natural, why are there so many rules and laws defending it? In the second place, the single-member district system itself is not so historic. There have always been significant numbers of *multiple*-member districts. In 1955, over half (58.3 percent) of the districts of the 48 state legislatures then existing (each house of representatives plus Nebraska's unicameral legislature) were multiple-member districts. By the mid-seventies most districts (92.8 percent of the senate and 80.5 percent of house districts) were single-member. Even so, 42 percent of house members were elected from multi-member districts. In 1912, when the forty-eighth state entered the Union, multiple-member districts were numerically dominant in at least half the states.

This was true for even more than half of the original 13 states. This was true also for congressional districts. In 1842, Vermont was the only state, among 26, where all representatives were chosen one to a district. In all other states, all or most members of Congress represented multiple-member districts. Although Congress attempted to change this in the 1870s with laws requiring single districts, the multi-member practice was slow to disappear from congressional districts and has persisted in state legislative districts.

Although it is true that the two countries with the most widespread practice of single-member district representation—United States and Great Britain—have had the most extensive experience with two-party systems, their experiences are not nearly as confirming as has been believed. In the United States, *one*-party systems spread all over the southern states and many of the northern states despite the single-member district system. And Great Britain has operated under a *three*-party system for perhaps most of the twentieth century. This gives rise to still another question, whether the famous single-member district system itself is hiding behind a myth system in need of examination. But that is another story.

4-5. These two myths are taken together because they give contradictory arguments against supporting a third party: 4. "A vote for a third party candidate is a wasted vote." 5. "A vote for a third party candidate is a mischievous vote, more powerful than a vote for one of the major party candidates, because it helps elect the worst of the two major candidates."

This proves that myths need not be consistent to be effective. Nevertheless, though the two taken together seem to exhaust all the possibilities, neither withstands close inspection. Take #5 first. It operates on the assumption that one of the major candidates is clearly better than the other. But what are voters to do if they have concluded that *both* major candidates are worst? Vote for the least worst? Such voters, recognizing the absurdity, tend to become non-voters. Since non-voting is stigmatized, non-voters are usually quiet—depriving their non-vote of the influence it can and should have. Non-voting, when done loudly, is an important form of participation. But by the same logic, so is a vote for a candidate for a third party.

The short answer to myth #4 is that a vote for a third-party candidate is never wasted. If the vote is for a candidate of a dissident party, it is a protest vote which can instill considerable anxiety in the leadership of the major parties. If the vote is for a candidate of a programmatic third party, a more substantive message is sent; and history shows that these messages are almost always received by leaders of the major parties. How could a vote for Populists in the late nineteenth century be considered wasted if it transformed the programmatic position of the Democratic Party? Major third parties in the past have disappeared because of their *success*. How can that be considered a wasted vote?

There is still another type of third party, and a vote for it would be the most effective—if a party of that sort were made available. This is an *electorally* based third party—a third party just as pragmatic and just as concerned with winning elections in local districts as are the two major parties. This has not been tried seriously on a national scale since the Progressives tried it in 1912. As shall be shown below, the very presence of such a third party could be so directly influential that not even the most ardent myth maker could consider a vote for it a wasted vote. An undesirable or unwanted vote, yes, but a wasted vote, no.

6. Myth #6 is a correlative of myth #2: "If some third party candidates got elected to Congress, there would be havoc. Their presence would foul up the allocation of committee assignments, and all during the session their presence would remove from the more important two parties the automatic majority that makes decisive legislatures possible. There would be resort to bloc voting and balance of power politics."

All of this is of course nonsense, because most of what has been described in the proposition already exists within a Congress controlled by the two parties. While the presence of third-party members in Congress would complicate the allocation of committee assignment surely the task is not impossible. And once Congress got itself organized with these people in their assigned committees, why should three blocs calling themselves by a party name complicate congressional coalition-building any more than the present multiple-bloc structure complicates it? The presence of a significant third-party delegation in Congress might very well ease the burden of legislative leadership inasmuch as the conferences and caucuses of the two major parties could more readily and clearly develop and maintain policy positions. This could produce a form of collective responsibility that the United States Congress has rarely had. Many party leaders cultivate the two-party system mythology precisely because they want to avoid collective responsibility.

7. Myth #7 moves the same argument another step higher: "If a third party elected some members of Congress and *also* received some electoral votes in a close presidential election, then there could be a real calamity—a constitutional crisis where the lack of an absolute majority for one candidate would require selection among the top three candidates by the House of Representatives, with each state having one vote regardless of its size."

One of the strange beliefs of the defenders of the present system —a myth of very considerable convenience—is that American democracy is so fragile that the very slightest constitutional jolt will have an apocalyptic effect. Thus, presumably we would fall apart if President Nixon were impeached. We would fall apart if President Nixon were not pardoned. We would fall apart if FDR were elected to a third term. We would fall apart if the Supreme Court seriously implemented *Brown vs. Board of Education.* The defenders of the status quo will always invoke the spector of constitutional crisis when in fact constitutional crisis is contemplated by the Constitution itself.

The prospect of a constitutional crisis over the election of the president turns out to be one of the best arguments *in favor* of a three-party system. Almost everyone now agrees that the presidency has gotten too big. The last two presidents won by running against the big presidency and the big government for which it is responsible. Most people now agree that the presidency is too directly exposed to a mass public, too heavily burdened by having been made personally responsible for putting the whole world to rights. The aggrandizement of the presidency surely helps to explain why the last four presidents ended their careers in political disgrace, having failed to meet the impossible expectations of the mass public. The presence of an important third party capable of obtaining seats in the House of Representatives and a few electoral votes would hardly throw each presidential election into the House of Representatives; however, such a presence would force each of the candidates for the nominations of the two major parties to look to the House of Representatives as the place where the real election *might take place.* This would transform the presidency to the extent that Congress would become the president's direct constituency. That is precisely the relationship embodied in the original plan of the Constitution before the two-party system captured the Electoral College. During the era of real two-party democracy in the nineteenth century, it was probably very good that the presidency had an independent, democratic popular base in the United States. But all that changes when the president's base is no longer a party base but a loose mass base. A president with a direct constituency in Congress would bring the presidency back to human scale and provide the basis for real collective responsibility.

8. Myth #8 supplements myth #7: "Even if the presence of an important third party did not have an apocalyptic effect, it would hold a balance of power position which could give a small third party a disproportionate influence on the president and on the policies of the national government."

Once again, the problem posed by the defenders of the two-party system disappears on closer examination. In the event that no candidate received an absolute majority of the electoral votes and the decision went to the House, it is true that the two major candidates would have to do some very serious bargaining with the opposition, and it is true that the bargaining could lead to some serious compromises with the platform as adopted the previous July or August and developed during the October campaign. But why should this necessarily give the third party such a disproportionate influence? What is to stop the candidates of the two major parties from compromising with each other? This ability to compromise "across the aisle" is often identified as one of the virtues of American practical politics. There is no reason to assume this virtue would disappear in the presence of a third party. Quite the contrary, the presence of an important third party with some electoral votes and some congressional seats can be viewed as having an entirely beneficial effect. Either way, it could hardly become the tail that wags the dog.

The Ninth Myth and the Prospects for a New Reality

Myth #9 turns out to be a myth from the past that is becoming a scientifically validated reality of the future: "Without his own party base, the President would not be able to govern."

As long as presidents had a party base, they had a fair chance of being able to govern. But during our own epoch, when presidents are expected really to govern, the major parties are no longer there to help them do so. This has to be part of the reason why recent presidents have ended their careers in political disgrace.

Thus, nothing about the present party system warrants our deep respect. Presidents need a party and have none. Voters need choices and have none. Congress needs cohesive policies and has none. The presence of a real third party with a real electoral base and a real presence in state legislatures, in Congress and in the Electoral College, could clarify the policies, programs and accountability of the two major parties by reducing their need to appear to be all things to all people. The scale of their coverage and their access could be narrowed. And, perhaps most importantly, it would no longer be necessary for presidential candidates to appear omnicompetent. Parties could present real choices, especially once everyone recognizes that compromises would take place after the election in the legislature. And the policies produced in this manner are much more likely ones to which the victorious party or party coalition could be held accountable.

A three-party system will seem alien on American soil only as long as the two-party system is taken as the true and only American way to govern. But in our epoch, that is almost the same as saying that the sun's daily crossing of the sky is a heavenly chariot of fire drawn by two giant horses. It is the two-party system that has become the alien phenomenon. Although almost everyone recognizes that party organizations in the United States have virtually disappeared, most people nevertheless assume that this is nothing other than a momentary exception to the historic truth, that the two-party system is the American way. But this moment is now two or three or four decades in duration. The fact is that modern, big, programmatic governments are not hospitable to two-party systems—anywhere in the world. A two-party system simply cannot grapple with the complex alternatives facing big, programmatic governments in a manner that is meaningful to large electorates.

Electoral and Political Behaviour

Even in an era of participatory politics, the typical role of the average citizen in a democratic polity is centred primarily on the election process. This "most important governmental innovation of the modern era," that is, elections, has given citizens some say in the political affairs of their country: "Since the nineteenth century, governments have ruled through electoral mechanisms even when they sometimes have been ruled by them."[1] The major distinction between democratic and nondemocratic politics rests on the nature of the electoral process: in a democratic system there is an open, competitive battle for power, while in other systems the contest is closed and noncompetitive.[2] As a result voting is the crucial ingredient of democratic political participation.

Aspects of Canadian voting behaviour and involvement are discussed in readings thirty and thirty-one. Lawrence LeDuc and his associates investigate voting trends in Quebec ("Trends in Political Support in Quebec"), particularly the support basis for the Parti Quebecois. The 1976 and 1981 provincial election victories for the Parti Quebecois, combined with their desire for sovereignty-association, makes the continuing support basis for that party a highly significant variable in the operation of both provincial and national politics. As LeDuc and his colleagues point out, support for the Parti Quebecois and the independence option are inversely related. Thus, if the party runs the next election campaign on the independence theme, as it has promised to do, its electoral support will be put to a severe test indeed.

While most Canadians only participate through voting in general election campaigns, other avenues for involvement are sometimes made available. One such mechanism—the referendum—is discussed by Agar Adamson in reading number thirty-one ("We

Were Here Before: The Referendum in Canadian Experience"). While rarely used in national politics, the referendum technique has been more widely experimented with at the provincial level. The practice of referendums and other related devices raise an important theoretical question: How can the notion of popular sovereignty be reconciled with the doctrine of parliamentary sovereignty?

In readings number thirty-two ("Voting Turnout: An International Comparison"), and thirty-three ("Converging Electoral Currents in British and American Politics"), our focus shifts from Canadian voting patterns to an international perspective. One of the usual comparisons made between political systems concerns the rate at which people participate in the political process. While clearly written from an American point of view, reading thirty-two provides an excellent example of comparative political analysis, as well as some interesting comparative data on voter participation in Western democracies. The impact of the relationship between politics and economics on the electoral process is the subject of reading number thirty-three. Everett Ladd, pinpoints some emerging similarities in the electoral patterns of Britain and the United States. In both countries a pattern of partisan dealignment has occurred, along with a growth in ambivalent perceptions about the role of government. Such developments have provided the bases for a Conservative partisan revival. Whether such trends will continue in Britain and the United States will likely be revealed by the next general election in each country.

In addition to voting behaviour, a modern technique by which citizens increasingly seek to influence their government is through the development of interest groups. Sometimes referred to as pressure groups or lobbies, interest groups are "organizations which make demands on political authorities for specific policy outputs."[3]

The behaviour of interest groups is heavily influenced by the political culture and institutional structure of the political system.[4] For example, in a federal system interest groups are forced to operate and deal with more numerous governmental units than in a unitary system. Moreover, a parliamentary system focuses interest group attention on the political executive, while in a presidential system, because of the separation of powers principle, such groups may concentrate on the legislative process directly. The resulting concentration of interest group efforts on the federal political executive in Canada is clearly seen in readings thirty-four ("Anatomy of a Letter-Perfect Lobby") and thirty-five ("Pressuring the Executive"). The case study presented by Sandy Fife in reading thirty-four also demonstrates some of the factors which help an interest group to be successful in the Canadian context. The comments by former Canadian cabinet minister J. Hugh Faulkner in reading thirty-five are particularly interesting because they present the viewpoint and reaction of a member of the executive to his interaction with pressure groups.

NOTES

1. BENJAMIN GINSBERG, *The Consequences of Consent: Elections, Citizen Control and Popular Acquiescence* (Reading, Massachusetts: Addison-Wesley, 1982), pp. 2, 7.

2. DAVID BUTLER, HOWARD R. PENNIMAN AND AUSTIN RANNEY, *Democracy At the Polls: A Comparative Study of Competitive National Elections* (Washington, D.C.: American Enterprise Institute for Public Policy Research, 1981), pp. 1-3.

3. JOHN MCMENEMY, *The Language of Canadian Politics* (Toronto: John Wiley and Sons, 1980), p. 138.

4. JEFFREY M. BERRY, *The Interest Group Society* (Boston: Little, Brown and Company, 1984); ALLAN J. CIGLER AND BURDETT A. LOOMIS (eds.), *Interest Group Politics* (Washington, D.C.: Congressional Quarterly Inc., 1983); ROBERT PRESTHUS, *Elites in the Policy Process* (Toronto: Macmillan of Canada, 1974); and A. PAUL PROSS (ed.), *Pressure Group Behaviour in Canadian Politics* (Toronto: McGraw-Hill Ryerson, 1975).

Trends in Political Support in Quebec

LAWRENCE LEDUC, HAROLD D. CLARKE, JANE JENSON AND JON H. PAMMETT

The reelection on April 13th, 1981 of Premier René Lévesque and his Parti Québécois government demonstrated conclusively that the PQ is far from a spent force in Quebec politics. Only eleven months earlier, in the May 1980 referendum, the Quebec electorate had decisively rejected (by a 6 to 4 margin) the party's request for a mandate to negotiate sovereignty-association with the rest of Canada. When its referendum question was defeated, many observers expected that the PQ, clearly identified with the rejected constitutional option, would likely lose the subsequent provincial election. But less than a year later, the party won a stunning victory, taking 49% of the popular vote and 80 of the 122 seats in the Quebec National Assembly. The swift post-referendum recovery of Péquiste electoral fortunes poses some obvious but very important questions — about the balance of long- and short-term forces in Quebec politics, the stability of the present political alignment, and the future of the PQ itself, with its vision of an independent or quasi-independent Quebec.

In this paper we will argue that both the rejection of the Parti Québécois' sovereignty-association proposal in the referendum and the party's subsequent electoral victory can be understood in terms of the extent and nature of the party's support in the Quebec electorate. Specifically, the reorientation of the Quebec party system that has occurred during the past 15 years has given the PQ a large and durable base of partisan support. This base both is a product of and is limited by the proportion of the electorate which has accepted the party's vision of a sovereign Quebec. To date, only a minority (albeit a substantial one) has done so. Until and unless this situation changes, only in instances such as the April 1981 provincial election when the issue of sovereignty is not on the polit-

Adapted from Lawrence LeDuc, Harold D. Clarke, Jane Jenson and Jon H. Pammett, "Sovereignty Association 'Non'—Parti Québécois 'Oui': Trends in Political Support in Quebec," *The American Review of Canadian Studies*, Vol. XII, No. 3 (Fall, 1982): 61-71. By permission of the publisher.

ical agenda can the party expect to achieve success at the polls. In such situations, however, the party has an opportunity to build on the large and solid foundation provided by its ideologically committed partisans to construct a winning coalition. The size and stability of the PQ's electoral base strongly indicates that the party will be a major force on the Quebec political scene in the coming decade. The fact that a majority of Quebecers have deeply divided and ambivalent attitudes toward the Canadian political community but have not accepted the constitutional alternative proposed by the PQ ensures that this period will be one of uncertainty — for the party, Quebec and Canada as a whole.

Data: The analysis presented in this paper focuses on trends in public opinion in Quebec during the 1976-81 period, paying particular attention to the period surrounding the referendum and subsequent provincial election. For this purpose we employ a series of *panel* studies of the Quebec electorate which we initiated in 1974, and continued with successive waves of interviewing in 1979, early 1980, and at the time of the referendum.[1] Supplementing the above are the results of several cross-sectional surveys conducted by private polling firms in Quebec over the past decade.[2]

Partisan Realignment and the Referendum

The PQ emerged as a major force in Quebec politics during the 1970-73 period, only a few short years after it had been created as an electoral rallying point for several disparate groups advocating the independence of Quebec. Virtually since its inception, the party has been associated with the policy of "sovereignty-association," meaning political independence for Quebec in conjunction with an economic association with the rest of Canada. However, the 1976 election that brought the Parti Québécois to power generally is interpreted not as a popular endorsement of the cause of Quebec independence but rather as a decisive rejection of the incumbent Liberal regime, to which the PQ had emerged as the principal opposition.[3] While the Parti Québécois was without doubt the beneficiary of powerful short-term forces acting against the Liberals in 1976, it is important to recognize that the party's growth also reflects a major partisan and ideological realignment in Quebec politics. During its initial five-year incumbency, the party's popular base continued to broaden, and the 1981 provincial election indicates that it was not permanently damaged by the referendum defeat.

Although the Parti Québécois is not yet the "natural majority" party in Quebec, the 1981 election demonstrated that it possesses a large enough base to win a provincial election whenever a sufficient number of short-term factors work in its favor. Support for this proposition may be seen in data on Quebecers' partisan attachments in provincial politics (Table 1). These data dramatically illustrate that the province now has reverted to a two-party system, polarized between the alternative political agendas advocated by the Liberals and the Péquistes. Identification with the Union Nationale (which held power in Quebec City as late as 1970) has all but disappeared; a demise which was confirmed in the 1981 provincial election by the UN's meagre 4% of the popular vote and failure to win a single Assembly seat. In all, only 8% of all respondents in our May 1980 referendum survey reported neither a PQ nor Liberal identification.

Yet another indication of the polarization of the Quebec electorate is provided by our repeated interviews between 1974 and 1980 with a *panel* of voters. These show that during the 1970s the PQ and, to a lesser extent, the Liberals had considerable success in retaining the loyalties of their identifiers, and that substantial numbers of persons previously identified with other parties migrated to either the Liberals or the PQ. The 1974-79 panel data illustrate these patterns of partisan realignment (Table 2). In this panel, fully 88% of the 1974 Péquistes and 77% of 1974 Liberals reported PQ and Liberal identifications five years later. In sharp contrast, less than half (41%) of those identifying with other parties in 1974 reported the same partisan ties in 1979. Similarly, less than one-third of 1974 non-identifiers refused a party label five years later. Large proportions of these latter two groups (34% and 63% of "other"- and non-identifiers respectively) had shifted to either the Liberals or the PQ by 1979. Similar analyses (not shown in tabular form) of the 1970–80 panels show a continuation of these patterns of realignment.[4]

As a result of the partisan realignment that occurred in the past decade the PQ now has a sufficiently large group of committed adherents to make it a major force in Quebec politics for many years. In fact, our cross-sectional surveys show that the proportion of voters identifying with the PQ increased throughout the 1970s and accelerated somewhat in the year or two preceding the referendum. By the spring of 1980, slightly over two-fifths of the electorate (41%) were PQ identifiers (Table 1). Moreover, from its inception to the present, the strongest support for the party has come from younger persons. At the time of the referendum in May 1980, no fewer than 71% of francophone respondents under the age of 30 in our survey were PQ identifiers. Because the party's greatest strength always has been among younger voters, it is quite possible that patterns of population replacement will continue to favor the Parti Québécois at the expense of other parties, and thereby further solidify and extend the realignment that has taken

TABLE 1
Distributions of Provincial Party Identification in Quebec, 1974-1980

Provincial Party Identification	1974	1979	Feb. 1980	May 1980
Liberal	59%	51%	54%	52%
Parti Quebecois	18	32	36	41
Creditiste	9	3	1	1
Union Nationale	4	6	3	1
Other	——	——	——	1
No Identification	10	9	5	5
(N =)	(664)	(753)	(498)	(327)

TABLE 2
Changes in Provincial Party Identification as Measured by 1974-1979 Panel Studies

1979 Party Identification	1974 Party Identification			
	Liberal	Parti Québécois	Other	No Identification
Liberal	77%	4%	15%	40%
Parti Quebecois	13	88	19	23
Other	6	6	41	6
No Identification	4	2	15	30
(N =)	(210)	(62)	(55)	(37)

place in the last decade. On the other hand, it is also possible that the large influx of young Péquistes into the electorate in the 1970s represents a "period" effect linked to the political maturation of a particular generation — something that may not necessarily continue as more new voters reach the age of majority in the years ahead.[5] In either case, however, the party's strength among the present generation of young Québécois and the very low rates of erosion in PQ partisanship documented in our panel data suggest that the party will be a major presence on the provincial political scene in the foreseeable future.

As for the effects of the referendum, by focusing attention on two obviously different, albeit poorly defined, visions of a new Quebec, the referendum campaign likely contributed to and possibly accelerated the provincial political realignment that had been in progress for some time. In this respect, the vast majority of "yes" voters in the referendum were PQ identifiers and virtually all PQ identifiers supported the "yes" side in the referendum (Table 3a). The stability of this alignment is suggested in that only 7% of those voting in the referendum shifted their position during the campaign (Table 3b). It also is undoubtedly true that an overwhelming proportion of PQ identifiers supported their party's candidates in the subsequent 1981 provincial election. As the referendum clearly demonstrated, the PQ-sovereignty-association group does not yet constitute a majority of the Quebec electorate. As noted, however, the large minority which comprised the "yes" vote is not likely to

TABLE 3
Voting Behavior in the Quebec Referendum, May 1980

A. Party Identification and Referendum Vote			B. Referendum Vote Intention (Feb. 1980) and Actual Referendum Vote (May 1980)		
	% Voting 'YES'	(N)		Feb. Vote Intention	
				YES	NO
Liberal	9	(147)			
PQ	96	(118)	May	45	1
All other*	41	(12)	Vote	6	48/100%
	$V = .85$				
				$0 = .86 *$	
				$(N = 261)*$	

*Includes non-identifiers	*Feb. and May 1980 panel respondents

vanish quickly, and may well grow in the future if the PQ is able to maintain its strength among newly eligible voters and younger members of the electorate more generally. The "yes" side in the referendum and the Parti Québécois therefore represent essentially the same force in Quebec politics — a highly cohesive minority which can challenge for power successfully in instances where various short-term advantages can be effectively combined with its already firm base of support. The referendum question was defeated essentially because it was interpreted as presenting a choice between two political communities, Quebec and Canada, even though it was not worded in these terms, rather than as a choice between leaders, parties, or finely nuanced constitutional options.[6] In situations such as the ensuing provincial election where the choice is not so perceived, a different outcome is possible, even with the present distributions of partisanship and opinion on Quebec's constitutional options — distributions which place the PQ and its sovereignty-association proposal in the minority.

The 1981 Election

Similar to the situation in 1976, the PQ was aided in its 1981 election victory by a number of short-term forces working in its favor. In both cases, the party apparently profited substantially from its "good government" image. For example, on the eve of the latter contest, fully two-thirds of the respondents in a SORECOM poll indicated that they were satisfied with the PQ government.[7] Leadership effects also operated in the party's favor. In both the April 1981 SORECOM poll and one conducted under the same auspices a few weeks earlier, Premier Lévesque was selected as the "best leader" by margins of approximately two to one over his Liberal rival, Claude Ryan. Additionally, the poll data show that many voters were satisfied with the PQ's handling of important issues (Table 4). Positive evaluations of the party's handling of the Quebec economy, satisfaction with the results of its initially controversial language legislation (Bill 101), and the aforementioned reputation for honest, efficient government were among the factors that worked in the party's favor in 1981.

As the referendum result testified, issues related to sovereignty-association or independence had great potential to adversely affect Péquiste electoral fortunes. Thus, in retrospect, the party's campaign promise not to hold a second sovereignty-association refer-

TABLE 4

Satisfaction with PQ Government's Performance on Selected Issues, April 11, 1981*

	Labour Rela- tions	Legis- iation (Bill 101)	Consti- tutional Problems	Honesty in Govern- ment	Negotia- tions With Federal Govern- ment	Manag- ing the Econ- omy	Attract- ing New Invest- ments
satisfied	50%	64%	42%	63%	48%	52%	47%
dissatisfied	38	28	37	23	39	37	39
undecided	12	8	21	13	12	11	15

*SOURCE: *Montreal Gazette-Le Soleil* Poll, conducted by SORECOM Inc. between March 30-April 5, 1981 (N = 766), results reported in the *Gazette*, April 11, 1981.

endum was perhaps particularly important. By detaching itself at least temporarily from this highly-charged issue where it was in a minority position, the PQ was able to take advantage of the popularity of its leader, Mr. Lévesque, and the widespread popular satisfaction with its performance on economic and other salient issues documented above. To some extent also, the PQ victory was a product of the failure of the Liberal election campaign. The Liberals did not attempt to make the election a second referendum on sovereignty-association, and disarmed (or disarming themselves) on this issue, they failed to marshal any other issues that might have helped them to offset the general impression that the PQ had governed effectively.[8]

The Future

What then do the referendum and election tell us about the likely future of the Parti Québécois and its vision of a sovereign Quebec? Both PQ partisanship and referendum voting are related very strongly to opinions regarding possible constitutional options for Quebec (Table 5). At least some of the latter, in turn, are strongly correlated with basic ethno-linguistic divisions in the province— favorable attitudes toward sovereignty-association and outright independence being largely confined to francophones. In contrast, substantial majorities of anglophones and francophones favor re-

TABLE 5

Attitudes Toward Four Constitutional Options for Quebec, 1979 and 1980 by Language, Partisanship and Referendum Voting

	Independence		Sovereignty Association		Renewed Federalism		Status Quo	
	1979	1980	1979	1980	1979	1980	1979	1980
% favorable	18	25	38	47	60	67	36	29
% francophones favorable	19	29	42	53	58	62	34	26
% anglophones favorable	6	5	19	15	76	92	39	42
% of favorable group identifying with PQ	87	90	72	77	21	25	18	12
% of favorable group voting 'Yes' in referendum		90		76		24		13
(N =)	(684)	(322)	(529)	(319)	(473)	(309)	(691)	(318)

newed federalism, and majorities of both of these linguistic communities reject the status quo. These patterns of opinion within and between major societal groups in Quebec have served as powerful forces shaping the contemporary party system and narrowing the choice of constitutional options to some variation of the sovereignty-association theme around which the referendum was framed and the renewed federalism advocated by the Liberals. In this regard, it is significant that complete independence never has had wide support in Quebec, and the proportion who favor it now is not substantially greater than it has been in the past. Thus, the most basic division of opinion in contemporary Quebec is that concerning the desirability of moderate versus extreme constitutional change. This cleavage reflects, to a considerable extent, the division between the Liberals and the Parti Québécois, opinions on renewed federalism and sovereignty association, and the actual result of the referendum itself.

Relatedly, both the 1981 election and that which initially brought the PQ to power in 1976 can be interpreted as indicating that the electoral success of the party and the salience of sovereignty-association are *inversely* related. The PQ's two election victories have occurred in circumstances where it has explicitly ruled out the issue of constitutional change in relations between Quebec and Canada. In the one instance (i.e., the referendum) when the subject was voted on, the party was defeated decisively.[9] It would appear, then, that the PQ will do no better in a future constitutional referendum unless it can generate significant *new* support for its sovereignty-association option. More generally, unless that support is forthcoming, the party will risk the prospect of defeat at the polls whenever the province's constitutional status becomes an important issue.

This battle between competing visions of a future Quebec will likely continue in various forms in the foreseeable future, despite the referendum result and Mr. Lévesque's campaign commitment not to hold a second referendum during his new term of office. Neither the referendum nor the recent election have finally resolved the matter of Quebec's future.

Since a choice between sovereignty-association and a federal option is always likely to represent, in at least a symbolic sense, the need to choose between alternative political communities (Canada and Quebec), and since many Quebecers currently have deeply divided and ambivalent attitudes toward these communities, it may be several years before the future of the province is finally decided. Until it is, the political future of Canada itself will continue to be one of uncertainty.

NOTES

1. The data reported here are part of the Canadian National Election and Panel Studies of 1974, 1979 and 1980 which were conducted by the authors. At the time of the Quebec Referendum (May 1980), respondents in the Quebec portion of the panel were contacted again by telephone and questioned regarding referendum vote, attitudes toward parties and leaders and opinions on various constitutional issues. All four studies were funded by the Social Sciences and Humanities Research Council of Canada. All analyses and interpretations presented here are the responsibility of the authors.

2. With the exception of surveys conducted during the April 1981 provincial election campaign, the results of these polls are contained in HÉLÈNE ROBILLARD-FRAYNE AND CLAUDE GAUTHIER, *Les Québécois et La Campagne Référendaire* (Montreal: Radio-Canada, le 9 mai, 1980). The results of polls conducted during the election campaign itself are reported in the Montreal *Gazette* and *Le Soleil*, March 28 and April 11, 1981.

3. See MAURICE PINARD AND RICHARD HAMILTON, "The Parti Québécois Comes to Power: An Analysis of the 1976 Quebec Election," *Canadian Journal of Political Science*, Vol. 11 (1978): 739–776.

4. A more detailed study of the dynamics of party identification in Quebec over the 1974–1980 period may be found in HAROLD D. CLARKE, "The Parti Québécois and Sources of Partisan Realignment in Contemporary Quebec," *Journal of Politics*, Vol. 45 (1983). A more general analysis of party identification in Canada is contained in HAROLD D. CLARKE, JANE JENSON, LAWRENCE LEDUC AND JON PAMMETT, *Political Choice in Canada* (Toronto: McGraw-Hill Ryerson, 1979), ch. 5.

5. There is scattered evidence in recent polls to suggest that the PQ was not as strong among the 18-22 year old group of voters entering the electorate for the first time in this election as it was among the 23-29 year old group who cast their first provincial vote in 1976. Regarding the strength of the PQ among younger Québécois at the time of the referendum see MAURICE PINARD AND RICHARD HAMILTON, "Les Québécois Votent 'Non:' Les assises de l'appui au regime et de son rejet," paper presented at the "Political Support in Canada: The Crisis Years" conference, Duke University, Durham, N.C., November 21-22, 1980. On the importance of support by younger, well-educated Québécois for the growth and electoral success of the PQ more generally see HAROLD D. CLARKE, "Partisanship and the Parti Québécois: The Impact of the Independence Issue," *American Review of Canadian Studies*, Vol. 8 (1978): 28-47.

6. This argument is developed in JON PAMMETT, HAROLD D. CLARKE, JANE JENSON AND LAWRENCE LEDUC, "Political Support and Voting Behaviour in the Quebec Referendum," in Allan Kornberg and Harold D. Clarke (eds.), *Political Support in Canada: The Crisis Years* (Durham, N.C.: Duke University Press, 1983), ch. 12.

7. Although analytically, the PQ's "good government" image should be considered a "short-term" force, evidence suggests it is hardly ephemeral. For example, in 1980, a month prior to the referendum, a CROP/Radio-Canada poll found 67% of its respondents "very" or "fairly" satisfied with the PQ government — this despite the fact that the party's sovereignty-association proposal was about to be soundly defeated. Also, there is evidence that the PQ's image of probity was a factor in helping it to defeat the Liberals in 1976. See MAURICE PINARD AND RICHARD HAMILTON, "The Parti Québécois Comes to Power," pp. 763, 772.

8. Regarding the Liberals' failure to inject the sovereignty-association issue into the 1981 campaign, it is noteworthy that the April 11th *Gazette-Le Soleil* pre-election poll showed that 45% of the respondents believed Prime Minister Trudeau had misled Quebecers during the referendum campaign with his promise of a "renewed federalism." (An additional 15% were undecided.) In the face of such sentiment, the Liberals may have decided that there were substantial risks in bringing sovereignty-association into the campaign in that the issue might backfire and harm the party's

electoral prospects. Moreover, were the Liberals to lose the election for whatever reason, it was important that the PQ not be able to claim that a Péquiste electoral victory constituted its long-sought after mandate to negotiate sovereignty-association with the federal government.

9. Also, the PQ was soundly defeated in the 1973 provincial election — a contest in which Quebec independence was a highly salient issue. The importance of this issue for mobilizing a majority of voters against the PQ in that election is argued in MAURICE PINARD AND RICHARD HAMILTON, "The Independence Issue and the Polarization of the Electorate: The 1973 Quebec Election," *Canadian Journal of Political Science*, Vol. 10 (1977): 215-60.

We Were Here Before: The Referendum in Canadian Experience

AGAR ADAMSON

The Quebec government's referendum on "sovereignty-association" reintroduces to the Canadian political scene the issue of the usefulness and relevance of direct legislation. It is not as new an issue as is often supposed. The Quebec Referendum Act, known as Bill 92, is not the first such piece of legislation adopted by a province, but the fifth. Manitoba, Saskatchewan, British Columbia, and Alberta all adopted such legislation at one time or another between 1913 and 1936. Newfoundland, prior to 1949, held three referendums, two of them on the issue of uniting with Canada.

The concept of direct democracy is to some extent back in vogue in several western nations, including Denmark, France, Sweden, the United Kingdom and the United States. Before reviewing the Canadian situation, it may be helpful to offer some definitions.

Direct democracy is a term that derives from the Greek City States

Reprinted from Agar Adamson, "We Were Here Before: The Referendum in Canadian Experience," *Policy Options*, Vol. 1, No. 1 (March, 1980): 50-54. Reprinted by permission of The Institute for Research on Public Policy.

and their concept of direct rule with all the eligible citizens partici-
pating in the decision-making process directly, rather than
through elected representatives. *Direct legislation* is a partial form
of direct democracy in that it transfers some part of the legislative
process from the democratically elected representative assemblies
to the electorate itself. It has three recognized expressions, "the initiative," "the recall" and "the referendum," of which the last is the
most important.

The referendum requires that, on the petition of a certain number
of voters, a particular piece of legislation (or a constitutional
amendment in Australia and Switzerland) is not operative until the
whole electorate has voted to accept or reject the law in question.
Thus, the result of a referendum is binding on the legislative assembly. Until quite recently, this was the accepted definition of a
referendum. Strictly speaking, the Quebec vote is not a referendum at all. In stricter language, it is a *plebiscite*, by which a government obtains an expression of popular opinion on a particular issue. Unlike a referendum, the results of a plebiscite require
legislation to place the wishes of the majority into the statute
books. The responsibility remains with the elected representatives
to determine the specific legislative action consequential on the
plebiscite result.

If one accepted the Quebec vote as being properly defined as a
referendum, then so is every municipal vote concerning local option on the sale of liquor, the fluoridation of the water supply, the
borrowing of money or Sunday sport. The list of Canadian referendums would be very much longer than that given in Table 1.
Only those votes the results of which are binding on the legislature
should be considered to be true referendums, and the Quebec vote
of 1980 is not a referendum but a plebiscite. The same is true of
Bill C-40 introduced in the House of Commons on April 3, 1978
and reintroduced, but never adopted, in the fourth session of that
Parliament. The compromise terminology is to talk about plebiscites or "consultative" referendums.

Direct legislation, including the referendum, was an American
import into Canada. The forty-ninth parallel is not a geo-cultural
boundary. The same socio-economic problems that faced Canadians living in the West also beset their American counterparts. The
issues had arisen earlier in the United States because it was more
advanced industrially and socially, and it was natural that Canadians would look south for the answer to their plight. The solution
they sought, and attempted to apply to Canadian federalism and

the British Parliamentary system, was derived primarily from the Populist and Progressive parties, the American protest movements.

However, there were other influences which fueled the fires for reform in the West. One of these was the impact of immigration, particularly from Great Britain and, in the case of Alberta, the United States. Another was the defeat of reciprocity and the election of the Conservative government of Robert Borden in 1911. The West lost faith in the existing parties, and two lines of thought emerged. One was the need for a third party which might be able to hold the balance of power in the House of Commons and therefore be in a position to bargain for better conditions for the West. The second was direct legislation. At first these were separate ideas, but in time they merged together so that third parties such as the Progressives and United Farmers arrived on the national scene demanding direct legislation.

The case for direct legislation and how it would help to lessen the handicap of the West was ably stated by R.C. Henders, president of the Manitoba Grain Growers Association, in 1912:

> ...the sovereign people have, . . . no direct efficient control. They are sovereign *de jure* but not *de facto*, except at election times. The actual powers experienced by the people consist chiefly in the periodic choice of another set of masters who make laws to suit themselves and enforce them until their term of office expires, regardless of the will of the people. We are governed by an elective aristocracy of wealth. Behind the government and the legislatures are the corporations and the trusts . . . behind the political monopolists are the industrial monopolists . . . the principal remedy is direct legislation.

Generally speaking, the concept of direct legislation appealed to those who had a special case to advance — a class interest, a moral reform such as temperance, or a "grand idea" to remedy the West's problems. The Canadian advocates of referendum politics today are in many respects the rightful heirs of the devotees of direct legislation in 1911.

In Manitoba there was considerable agitation for direct legislation, particularly for the initiative and referendum. Initially, this demand was rejected by the Conservative Government of Sir Rodmond P. Roblin on the grounds that direct legislation was not compatible with the British parliamentary system. He denounced direct legislation "as a denial of responsible government and a form of degenerate republicanism." The Liberal party under T.C. Norris included direct legislation in their platform for the 1914 election; and though they lost then, a year later they defeated the scandal-rocked Roblin government.

At the session of 1916 the Legislature was unanimous in passing the Initiative and Referendum Act: or, to give it its full title, "An Act to enable electors to initiate laws, and relating to the submission to the electors of Acts of the Legislative Assembly."

The bill was given Royal Assent on March 10, 1916. However, the enthusiasm with which it was passed soon disappeared and the Norris Government decided to refer the Act to the courts to test its constitutionality. It was upheld by the Chief Justice of the Court of Kings Bench for Manitoba. However, the Manitoba Court of Appeal reversed this decision in 1917. In turn, this decision was appealed to the Judicial Committee of the Imperial Privy Council. The Privy Council, in a 1919 decision given by Lord Haldane, upheld the Manitoba Court of Appeal and concurred in that court's argument that the Initiative and Referendum Act was *ultra vires* of the Manitoba Legislature.

The argument of the two Appeal Courts centred around the Office of Lieutenant-Governor. Section 92(1) of the British North America Act of 1867 denies to the province the right to amend its constitution in respect to the office of Lieutenant-Governor. Both the Court of Appeal and the Privy Council found that the Manitoba Act of 1916 clashed with section 92(1) of the B.N.A. Act. Lord Haldane, in his decision, said in part:

> Their Lordships are of opinion that the language of the Act cannot be construed otherwise than as intended seriously to affect the position of the Lieutenant-Governor as an integral part of the Legislature, and to detract from rights which are important in the legal theory of that position. For if the Act is valid it compels him to submit a proposed law to a body of voters totally distinct from the Legislature of which he is the constitutional head, and renders him powerless to prevent its becoming an actual law if approved by a majority of these voters.

This decision by the Judicial Committee of the Privy Council remains the key judgment with respect to referendums in the provinces. It is the reason why Quebec's Bill 92 talks of consultation rather than of ratification on the question of "Sovereignty-Association."

The Norris Government made no effort to introduce a new Act which might have been acceptable to the courts. There was little public demand for constitutional changes which would have permitted a new Act to withstand appeal.

TABLE 1
Consultative Referendums or Plebiscites Held in Canada

Canada	29 September, 1898	—Prohibition of liquor
	27 April, 1942	—To release the government from the 1940 promise of no conscription for overseas service
Newfoundland	November 1915	—Prohibition of liquor
	3 June, 1948	—1. Responsible Government 2. Join Canada 3. Stay under Commission Government
	22 July, 1948	—Join Canada, not responsible self government
Alberta	21 July, 1915	—Prohibition of liquor
	25 October, 1920	—Prohibition of liquor
	5 November, 1923	—Temperance Act
	17 August, 1948	—Ownership of power companies
	30 October, 1957	—Additional outlets for sale of liquor
	23 May, 1967	—Daylight saving time
	30 August, 1971	—Daylight saving time
British Columbia	25 November, 1909	—Liquor
	14 September, 1916	—Women's suffrage
	14 September, 1916	—Liquor prohibition
	20 October, 1920	—Liquor temperance
	20 June, 1924	—Sale of beer by the glass
	1 June, 1937	—Public Health Insurance
	12 June, 1952	—Daylight saving time
	12 June, 1952	—Regulation of the sale of liquor
Manitoba	23 July, 1892	—Prohibition of liquor
	2 April, 1902	—Prohibition of liquor
	13 March, 1916	—Temperance Act
	22 June, 1923	—Government control of liquor sales
	11 July, 1923	—Amendments to Temperance Act
	28 June, 1927	—Three questions on the sale of beer
	24 November, 1952	—Marketing of coarse grains

Nova Scotia	15 March, 1894	—Prohibition of liquor
	25 October, 1920	—Regulation of liquor sales
	31 October, 1929	—Temperance Act
Ontario	1 January, 1894	—Control of liquor
	14 October, 1902	—Prohibition of liquor
	20 October, 1919	—Temperance Act
	18 April, 1921	—Control of inter-provincial trade re: liquor
	23 October, 1924	—Government control over the sale of liquor
Prince Edward Island	13 December, 1893	—Sale of liquor
	28 June, 1948	—New Temperance Act
Quebec	10 April, 1919	—Sale of beer and wine
	20 May, 1980	—Sovereignty-Association
Saskatchewan	November, 1913	—Direct Legislation Act
	11 December, 1916	—Abolish liquor stores
	21 October, 1920	—Importation of liquor by export houses
	16 July, 1924	—Government liquor control
	19 June, 1934	—Sale of beer by the glass
	October, 1956	—Daylight saving time
New Brunswick	Nil	

As for the recall of members of the legislature, no effort was ever made in Manitoba to legalize or formalize in any way this aspect of direct democracy. Undoubtedly, some members of the Legislature did sign some type of recall statement. However, like those signed by the Progressives elected to the House of Commons in 1921, these were unofficial and had no legal standing if they were ever presented to the Speaker of the Legislature.

The concept of direct democracy was popular in Saskatchewan, and both the Liberal and the Conservative parties supported direct legislation. At the 1912-1913 session of the Legislature, the Liberal government of Premier Walter Scott introduced "An Act to provide for the initiation or approval of legislation by the electors." It won quick support and was given Royal Assent on January 11th, 1913.

The Act was to become operative upon its ratification by 30% of the electorate. This rather novel method of ratification was prescribed by the Legislature in a separate "Act to submit to the electors the question of the Direct Legislation Act."

There was no mention of the recall in the Saskatchewan legislation; it was confined strictly to the initiative and referendums. The Act permitted a percentage (under normal circumstances 5%) of the electorate to initiate or recommend action to the House and also allowed the voters to approve or reject action taken by the Legislature.

There is a distinct possibility that the Saskatchewan Act would have suffered the same fate as the Manitoba Act and for the same reasons. A reading of the Saskatchewan Act leaves one with the distinct impression that it too would have been an infringement on the constitutional position of the Office of the Lieutenant-Governor.

However, that issue was never tested. In the referendum, the Act failed to win the support of the required 30% of the electorate. Thus it never came into force and was repealed in 1913. With that, there was an end to public agitation to make the initiative and referendum a part of the law of Saskatchewan.

The prairie revolt against the political system and the consequential demand for direct legislation crossed the Rockies into British Columbia. This province was not dominated by agriculture, nor at this time was it prone to political radicalism. Nevertheless, at the 1919 session, the Legislature passed "An Act to provide for the Initiation and approval to Legislation by the electors," assented to on March 29, 1919. The Act stated that an initiative or a referendum must be requested by 25% of the voters in 75% of the electoral districts and that 10% of the electors in these electoral districts must have signed the petition.

No money bill could be initiated by the public. The Speaker was to rule on the acceptability of a petition; if he so desired, he could request a judge of the British Columbia Supreme Court to inquire into the petition's validity. Similarly, the Attorney General had the authority to request the Supreme Court to advise him on the constitutionality of the proposed law.

The initiative and referendum elections were normally to take place at the same time as a provincial election. A special vote could be held if so stated in the petition, but it would then need the signatures of 30% of the electors. A law approved by an initiated vote would be passed by the next session of the Legislature.

The Direct Legislation Bill was proposed by the Government, and on second reading was approved by 21 votes to eight. There was no vote on third reading.

Nevertheless, the Act was never implemented. Article 40 stated: "This Act shall come into operation on a date to be fixed by the Lieutenant-Governor by his Proclamation." It is listed in the *Statutes of British Columbia* from 1919 to 1923. It is not listed in the *Revised Statutes of British Columbia, 1924*, except for a note that it was never in force.

The reasons are not clear, but one may presume that, as the Act was passed prior to the Judicial Committee of the Privy Councils' decision in the Manitoba case, the government of British Columbia wished to be prudent and await Lord Haldane's pronouncement.

Alberta, however, is a province unlike the others. It shaped its own political ideals and had both direct legislation and the recall. Both were implemented by Acts of the Legislature.

Between 1919 and 1924 many members of the United Farmers of Alberta, which formed the government from 1921 to 1935, favoured the recall; but the zeal died away and a motion calling for the legalizing of the recall was defeated at the 1924 party convention.

The recall was not an issue again in Alberta until the victory of Social Credit under the leadership of William Aberhart in 1935. During the election campaign, Aberhart pledged to introduce legislation providing for the recall of any member of the legislature, and in April 1936 the Alberta Legislature passed "An Act providing for the recall of members of the Legislative Assembly." This Legislative Assembly Recall Act was the only Canadian legislation that made recall a legal possibility. Evidence had to be submitted to the provincial chief justice, and recall was to be effective upon the affirmative report of the chief justice which was to be delivered to the speaker. Any member recalled could stand for re-election and only one motion could be made against a member every legislative term.

The statute's existence was, however, brief. The only known attempt to recall a member was made in 1937, in the electoral district of Okotoks — High River, with Aberhart himself the intended victim. The Premier struck back quickly. In October 1937, the Legislature repealed the Legislative Assembly Recall Act retroactive to April 3, 1936, the day the original Act had received Royal Assent. All pending proceedings in connection with the recall of any member were declared to be null and void. With this, the principle of the recall vanished from Alberta and from Canadian politics.

In Alberta, however, unlike the other western provinces, direct legislation was not only enacted but became operative and remained on the statute books; it was not repealed until 1958. The Alberta Direct Legislation Act 1913 was introduced by the Liberal government of A.L. Sifton and supported by the opposition Conservatives. The Act required that a referendum petition must be supported by 10% of the voters polled in the preceding general election; in 85% of the electoral districts, at least 8% of the vote must be represented. The initiative petition called for 20% with the same limitations as the referendum. No money bills could be initiated by petition and the Attorney General had to certify all petitions as being within the legislative jurisdiction of the province.

In 1916 the Act was amended to permit women to vote, and to allow them to take part in any request for action as prescribed by the 1913 statute. It was amended again in 1923 by a U.F.A.-dominated House. This amendment permitted the government to submit questions on proposed statutes to the voters for their opinion and to guide the government in their deliberations. The Alberta government was thus given essentially the same authority that is provided for in the current Quebec legislation and which would have been given to the government of Canada by the now dead Bill C-40.

In 1931 the Alberta Act was further amended to allow the Lieutenant-Governor in Council to refer questions of law in respect to requests for an advisory opinion, before the taking of any legislative or electoral action.

The Act of 1913 was used in 1915 by the Sifton Government to obtain the views of the electorate on the question of prohibition. In this vote, which was officially called a referendum, but which had some of the markings of a plebiscite within its terms of reference, the electors voted heavily in favour of prohibition. In 1916 the Alberta Legislature enacted legislation to implement the wishes of the voters. As the Alberta electors did not approve an Act already passed by the Legislature, but only stated their view on the subject in order to guide the government on what action to take, the constitutional position of the Lieutenant-Governor was not affected.

The Alberta Direct Legislation Act, 1913, like the British Columbia Act, called for action by the Legislature after any referendum. It was used again in 1920, for another liquor vote, but not thereafter. The initiative and referendum in effect disappeared with the

1923 amendment, under which a so-called referendum was conducted that year but it was truly a plebiscite. The people were asked to choose one of four alternatives: prohibition; licensed sale of beer; government sale of beer; government sale of all liquors.

The amendment of 1923 was tested in the courts but only indirectly. As a result of the 1923 vote, the Alberta Liquor Act was enacted. The Judicial Committee of the Privy Council upheld the legality of the Liquor Act, with the implication — though it was not the issue — that the Direct Legislation Act, as amended in 1923, was valid.

The plebiscite — or, to use the less exact expression, advisory referendum — is a means by which an electorate may express its collective opinion on issues of the day. Unlike the referendums proposed in the four western provinces, the result is not binding upon the government concerned and the government is under no legal or constitutional obligation whatsoever to enforce the verdict

TABLE 2
Direct Legislation Acts in Canada

Manitoba	1916	Initiative and Referendum Act	Never proclaimed. Declared *Ultra Vires* in 1919.
Saskatchewan	1912-1913	Direct Legislation Act	Never operative. Failed to gain required percentage in prescribed referendum.
British Columbia	1919	Direct Legislation Act	Never proclaimed.
Alberta	1913	Direct Legislation Act	Proclaimed. Amended in 1923 to permit the holding of consultative referendums. Repealed in 1958.
	1936	Legislative Assembly Recall Act	Repealed in 1937 when attempt made to recall Premier Aberhart.

of the electorate by enacting legislation. It may, of course, be under strong moral and political obligation.

The major drawback to plebiscites is that they may allow a government to shirk its duties on controversial issues. On a relatively uncomplicated matter such as "Sunday Shopping" this action, or rather inaction, by the government is not too serious a point; the issue is one which can be easily explained to the electorate. However, when a government proposes that a plebiscite be held on issues like nuclear power, abortion, capital punishment, sovereignty-association or fluoridation, all of which are extremely complicated, emotional and technical and thus difficult to explain to the voters, then a government may well be negligent in its duties to its electorate.

Such an avoidance of a controversial issue was taken by the Government of Ontario during the premiership of the late Leslie M. Frost, when it brought forward legislation permitting municipalities to hold plebiscites on the question of the fluoridation of the local water supply. In many of these Ontario plebiscites the real issue was clouded by the fact that those opposed to fluoridation had used such tactics as calling it a communist plot, a cause of cancer, rat poisoning, and a source of heart disease. It is very difficult to campaign on the other side with reasoned scientific evidence, and little wonder that plebiscites have turned down fluoridation in many municipalities. One can imagine with horror a plebiscite campaign on the issue of capital punishment.

The referendum, particularly in the United States, and more recently in Switzerland, has frequently permitted a minority to rule because of the often confusing questions on the ballot. These complexities often force the confused voter to mark the ballot incorrectly or not to vote at all. Similar criticisms may be made of the plebiscite, as anyone who has voted in a certain style of plebiscite held under the Ontario Temperance Act has discovered. In these elections, those in favour of the sale and consumption of liquor must vote "no," while those opposed must vote "yes."

However, the evidence in Canada and elsewhere is that plebiscites and referendums are again gaining in popularity and public acceptance. The problem therefore is to define limits within which the use of this tool of direct democracy may be acceptable within the Canadian context.

For the time being at least, the Judicial Committee's decision in the Manitoba Initiative and Referendum Act rules out the possibility of the introduction of the initiative and referendum in the strict sense, at the provincial level. Quite possibly, the same arguments could be made at the federal level concerning the Governor-General and the exercise of the Royal Prerogative. These legal obstacles could be overcome by amending the pertinent sections of the Constitution Act 1867.

During the discussions leading to the formulation of the Fulton-Favreau Formula, some consideration was given to the use of referendums in the constitutional amendment process. But enthusiasm was not strong then, and it must be further dampened by the impact of Proposition 13 in California in 1978. Initiative referendums can indeed have a drastic effect on a political system. They may keep the politicians in check, but is the price the polity must pay worth it? It is hard to see either politicians or the public service in Canada thinking so.

It is, therefore, the plebiscite or advisory referendum that is currently at issue. This is the consultative process used in Britain in March 1979 on the question of devolution for Scotland and Wales, and in June 1975 on the issue of continued membership in the European Economic Community. The latter prompted S.E. Finer to write: "The referendum is the Pontius Pilate of British politics. It permits and was intended to permit a party to take two wholly incompatible views and in the meantime allow government to stand back and wash its hands of the entire issue."

Another adverse description might be that of the "Trojan Horse." The Parti Quebecois very effectively used the promise of a consultative referendum when gaining power in 1976, and then in office devoted much of their time and energy to preparing the electorate for this vote at the expense of other public issues.

The nature of modern election campaigns makes it difficult to say whether the successful party has been given a clear mandate for even the most conspicuous points in its program. A plebiscite may bypass that aspect of the mandate issue, but does it do more than move the issue on to another plane? The difficulty about plebiscites, which increases greatly the more they are used, is that the turn-out may drop off to the point that a committed minority has a distinctly disproportionate influence. In Britain in 1975 only 64.5% of the electorate voted and in 1979 the turnout was even lower. Swiss experience shows that, to obtain a significant turnout, a referendum must be held simultaneously with an election.

These doubts in no way challenge the desirability of the plebiscite or consultative referendum on some "local option" issues. The citizens of a relatively small area can well say directly how they wish to observe Sunday and whether they want liquor outlets. But in complex issues, such as nuclear power or capital punishment, which must be decided on a national or provincial basis, it may well be questioned whether parliamentary government and plebiscitarian democracy can co-exist effectively. The results of the 1942 consultative referendum on conscription — when the turn out was 71.3% and of those voting 63.7% in total voted yes but in Quebec only 29% — vividly illustrated the difficulties of a national vote on a divisive issue in a bilingual country. In simpler circumstances, the reformers of the Canadian West discovered that direct democracy is not so much a panacea as a *pinata* filled with problems for the unwary electorate.

Voter Turnout: An International Comparison

DAVID GLASS, PEVERILL SQUIRE AND RAYMOND WOLFINGER

Everyone knows that Americans vote less than citizens of other democratic countries. There are several explanations offered for this disparity. One theory is that low American turnout reflects alienation or mistrust that can discourage voting. We have concluded that this is not true. Another possibility is that calculating turnout percentages on different bases affects comparisons of the United States and other democracies. We conclude that this is indeed the case; when the base used is people who are registered, American turnout measures up very well against other countries.

Some election specialists recognize that the United States computes turnout differently from other countries: the percentage of the American *voting-age population* who vote is contrasted with the turnout rate of *registered persons* elsewhere. The latter figure includes only those people who are legally qualified to vote in the

Reprinted from David Glass, Peverill Squire and Raymond Wolfinger, "Voter Turnout: An International Comparison," *Public Opinion*, Vol. 6, No. 6 (December/ January, 1984): 49-55. By permission of the American Enterprise Institute for Public Policy Research.

current election. The voting-age population includes a great many people who could not possibly vote: millions of aliens, who are categorically ineligible to vote; over a million citizens who are ineligible in most states — ex-felons and inmates of prisons and mental hospitals; and, most numerous, citizens who would be eligible if they had taken the step of establishing that eligibility by registering. This apples-and-oranges international comparison inevitably casts American voting performance in the most unfavorable light. To the best of our knowledge, no one has compared turnout in the United States and in other countries on both percentage bases: as a percentage of the voting-age population and as a percentage of registered voters.[1] How would American turnout stack up if the same yardstick were used for all countries?

Table 1 compares turnout in the most recent national election in the United States and a number of other countries for which we could obtain data. The left column in Table 1 presents the data in the customary way, with American turnout as a percentage of the voting-age population and other countries' turnout as a percentage of registered voters. This produces the familiar picture: at 52.6 percent, the United States places twenty-third among the two dozen nations. Only Switzerland (48.3 percent) has lower turnout. At the top of the list, five countries have voting rates above 90 percent (see Table 1).

The right column in Table 1 provides a common base for all countries: the number of votes cast divided by the voting-age population. This is a fairer comparison, but it does not make the United States look any more like a nation of voters. Of the twenty-one nations for which we could obtain data, the United States ranked twentieth, with Switzerland again the only country lagging behind. The gap between the United States and the top-ranked country is the same as in the first column. In short, ranking turnout by the American standard does little to dispute the traditional finding that fewer Americans vote than do the citizens of any other democratic country (except, of course, Switzerland). Now that we have established that Americans do indeed vote less, our task is to explain why.

Alienation's Not the Answer

One plausible — and certainly popular — hypothesis about low American turnout is that it is caused by alienation from the political system. Commentaries deploring the state of American politics often link low turnout to public disaffection. Yet, repeated cross-sectional analyses have shown that the relationship between alienation and turnout is weak or non-existent.[2] Our concern, though, is with levels of alienation in the United States compared with those in other countries. Data on this point are scarce. None of the handful of comparative studies includes most of the countries in which we are interested, but together they give some clues about relationships between alienation and turnout across national boundaries.

We begin with a 1959 survey, which asked respondents in the United States and three European democracies about aspects of

TABLE 1
Ranking of Countries by Turnout in their Most Recent National Election[a]

Traditional Measure of Turnout[b]		Vote as a Percentage of Voting-Age Population[c]	
1. Belgium	94.6	1. Italy	94.0
2. Australia	94.5	2. Austria	89.3
3. Austria	91.6	3. Belgium	88.7
4. Sweden	90.7	4. Sweden	86.8
5. Italy	90.4	5. Portugal	85.9
6. Iceland	89.3	6. Greece	84.9
7. New Zealand	89.0	7. Netherlands	84.7
8. Luxembourg	88.9	8. Australia	83.1
9. Germany	88.6	9. Denmark	82.1
10. Netherlands	87.0	10. Norway	81.8
11. France	85.9	11. Germany	81.1
12. Portugal	84.2	12. New Zealand	78.5
13. Denmark	83.2	13. France	78.0
14. Norway	82.0	14. United Kingdom	76.0
15. Greece	78.6	15. Japan	74.4
16. Israel	78.5	16. Spain	73.0
17. United Kingdom	76.3	17. Canada	67.4
18. Japan	74.5	18. Finland	63.0
19. Canada	69.3	19. Ireland	62.3
20. Spain	68.1	20. United States	52.6
21. Finland	64.3	21. Switzerland	39.4
22. Ireland	62.2		
23. United States	52.6		
24. Switzerland	48.3		

348 Political Processes and Political Behaviour

NOTE:
a. Most recent as of 1981.
b. In the "Traditional Measure of Turnout." U.S. turnout is calculated as the percentage of the voting-age population, while turnout elsewhere is calculated as the percentage of registered voters.
c. An anomaly exists between the right and left columns in table 1 (as well as between table 1 and table 2) for five countries: Greece, Ireland, Italy, Portugal and Spain. In each of these cases the vote as a percentage of voting-age population is higher than the vote as a percentage of registered voters. This is because there is a separate source for calculating the voting-age population. The less trustworthy number is the voting-age population figure. This often had to be estimated from old census data for present-day populations. For example, the Italian and Spanish numbers had to be projected from 1971 and 1970 census figures on the percentage of the population over 18.

SOURCE: The figures for the United States are from the *Statistical Abstract of the United States* 1982-83. The data for all other countries for the number of voters and the number of persons registered are from *The International Almanac of Electoral History*. 2d ed. by Thomas T. Mackie and Richard Pose. The voting-age population was derived from the countries' Year Books. It was occasionally necessary to extrapolate the present age breakdown on the basis of the last census.

their countries in which they took pride. Fully 85 percent of the Americans said they were proud of their political institutions, compared to 46 percent of the Britons, 7 percent of the West Germans, and 3 percent of the Italians.[3] The question about pride seems not to have been asked in Europe since 1959. At that time, when the turnout gap was only slightly smaller than at present, Americans clearly were far prouder of their political institutions than were Europeans.

More recent European data are available on a closely related topic, citizens' satisfaction with their political system. *Euro-Barometre* regularly asks Europeans, "On the whole, are you very satisfied, fairly satisfied, not very satisfied, or not at all satisfied with the way democracy works in [your country]?" The 1980 National Election Study asked Americans "how good a job you feel [the federal government] is doing for the country as a whole" on a scale from 0 ("very poor job") to 8 ("very good job"). These two questions are not identical. The European question asks respondents to judge "democracy" as part of their assessment of their government's performance. The NES item has no such cosmic implications and seems more likely to evoke partisan answers. Thus, the NES question invites more critical responses than does the European one. Fifty-nine percent of American respondents gave answers ranging from "fair job" to "very good job"; the mean for ten European countries was 51 percent. Respondents in Luxembourg (77 percent), West Germany (73 percent), and Denmark (60 percent) were more satisfied than Americans; people were less satisfied in Belgium, France, Greece, Ireland, Italy, Holland and Great Britain.[4]

Americans may vote less than citizens in other democracies, but they also seem less alienated. Ireland and Switzerland, the two countries that resemble the United States in their anemic turnout, also exhibit high levels of confidence and support for the system. In 1973, the only year for which we could find data about Switzerland, the Swiss ranked first (67 percent) in satisfaction with how democracy worked in their country, and the Irish were in third place. Residents of the two countries with highest turnout, Belgium and Italy, ranked second (62 percent) and last (27 percent), respectively.[5]

Finally, we have the results of an eleven-nation survey conducted by the Gallup Organization in 1981, reported in *The Confidence Gap* by Seymour Martin Lipset and William Schneider. Gallup asked about the respondents' degree of confidence in

> the armed forces, the legal system, the educational system, the churches or organized religion, the press, labor unions, major companies, the civil service, and the parliament or Congress . . . The overall level of confidence turned out to be higher in the United States than in any other country surveyed except Ireland. After Ireland and the United States came Britain, Denmark, Spain, West Germany, Belgium, Holland, France, Japan, and Italy, in that order.

Whatever the reasons for Americans' lower turnout, dissatisfaction with their political system is not one of them.

Americans also surpass Europeans in other attitudes that seem conducive to voting, such as a belief in their ability to influence political developments. In 1982 *Euro-Barometre* asked respondents in ten nations, "Do you think that if things are not going well [in this country] people like yourself can help to bring about a change for the better or not?" The 1980 National Election Study solicited agreement or disagreement with this statement: "People like me don't have any say about what the government does." Fifty-nine percent of the American respondents disagreed with this statement; that is, they expressed feelings of political efficacy. An efficacious response to the *Euro-Barometre* question was given by 62 percent of Greeks and 56 percent of Danes. Luxembourg and Great Britain followed at 42 percent; all other countries had even fewer citizens who expressed efficacious feelings.

Americans are also more likely to engage in all forms of political participation other than voting. A mid-1970s comparative survey asked Americans and Europeans about their participation in both conventional activities like discussing politics, attending political rallies, and the like, *and* unconventional or protest behavior, such as signing petitions and going to lawful demonstrations. The levels of participation were higher in the United States than in Austria, the Netherlands, West Germany and Great Britain.[6]

Using the European Denominator

If activity, optimism and self-confidence about political participation determined turnout, Americans would lead the world. But there are some important steps between impulse and action, when the action is voting. Enthusiasm is not enough; in order to vote in this country, one's name must appear on a register of those whose qualifications have been established. What happens if American, as well as foreign, turnout is measured as a percentage of these registered voters who go to the polls?

The decentralization of election administration in the United States makes it difficult to tell exactly how many people register, and how many of those vote. No one source is completely satisfactory. Of those available, we have most confidence in the Vote Validation Study conducted as part of the Michigan 1980 National Election Study, in which interviewers inspected voting records to establish whether each of their survey respondents had registered and voted.[7] The major drawback of this source is the somewhat upscale character of the Michigan sample, which underrepresents some underprivileged elements of society, particularly uneducated young men. Doubtless this is why the vote-validated Michigan sample shows a 1980 turnout rate of 60 percent. While this surely exaggerates turnout, it should be noted that the Census Bureau's 52.6 percent figure understates it.[8]

Eighty-seven percent of the registered respondents in the Michigan sample voted in 1980. The 1980 Voter Supplement of the Census Bureau's Current Population Survey, based on unverified responses from a sample of more than 90 000, yields an estimate that 88.6 percent of those registered voted. Both figures are very respectable rates in the international rankings of turnout. If the basis of comparison with other countries uses the American denominator — the percentage of the voting-age population who vote — the United States looks bad. If the yardstick is the measure used elsewhere in the world — the percentage of those registered who vote — then the United States looks pretty good, as Table 2 shows. Using this European denominator, the United States ranks eleventh among the twenty-four countries, more than 38 percentage points ahead of last place Switzerland, and at least ten percentage points higher than Greece, Israel, Great Britain, Japan, Canada, Spain, Finland and Ireland. Moreover, the gap between the United States and top-ranked Belgium is not very wide — only

TABLE 2
Turnout of Those Who Are Registered

Vote as a Percentage of Registered Voters		*Compulsion Penalties*	*Automatic Registration*
1. Belgium	94.6	Yes	Yes
2. Australia	94.5	Yes	No
3. Austria	91.6	No (some)[a]	Yes
4. Sweden	90.7	No	Yes
5. Italy	90.4	Yes	Yes
6. Iceland	89.3	n.a.	n.a.
7. New Zealand	89.0	No (some)[a]	No
8. Luxembourg	88.9	n.a.	n.a.
9. W. Germany	88.6	No	Yes
10. Netherlands	87.0	No	Yes
11. United States	86.8	No	No
12. France	85.9	No (some)[a]	No
13. Portugal	84.2	n.a.	n.a.
14. Denmark	83.2	No	Yes
15. Norway	82.0	No	Yes
16. Greece	78.6	Yes	Yes
17. Israel	78.5	No	Yes
18. United Kingdom	76.3	No	Yes
19. Japan	74.5	No	Yes
20. Canada	69.3	No	Yes
21. Spain	68.1	Yes	Yes
22. Finland	64.3	No	Yes
23. Ireland	62.2	No	Yes
24. Switzerland	48.3	No (some)[a]	Yes

NOTE:

a. Penalties apply only to small portions of the country or certain types of elections.

SOURCE: See table 1. Compulsion penalty and automatic registration information are from G. Bingham Powell, "Voting Turnout in Thirty Democracies: Partisan, Legal, and Socio-Economic Influences," table 2. p. 10, except for Canada and Spain. The information on these two countries is in Inter-Parliamentary Union, ed., *Parliaments of the World* (New York: De Gruyter, 1976).

eight points in Table 2 instead of the 42 percentage points in Table 1. By this measure the United States looks better than most countries and nearly as good as any country.

The Impediments

Two aspects of the election laws in different countries seem to be particularly important in explaining international variations in turnout. One of these is "compulsory voting" (actually penalties for nonvoting) present in five countries: Belgium, Australia, Italy, Spain, and Greece. Political scientist G. Bingham Powell's analysis revealed that such provisions are associated with about a 10 percent increase in turnout. The rather substantial impact of these laws seems to be achieved through moral suasion rather than actual sanctions. British political scientist Ivor Crewe confirms that "both convictions and sanctions against nonvoters appear to be negligible. . . ." Nevertheless, their impact is substantial; mean turnout in the Netherlands dropped 11 percentage points after that country abandoned compulsory voting. The most formidable sanctions may be in Italy, which does not formally require its citizens to vote, but whose constitution declares that voting is a duty; Italians who fail to vote have "DID NOT VOTE" stamped on their identification papers. What prudent Italian would risk blighting his chances of favorable consideration by a government official?

The second source of variation in turnout, and one that is much more important for the United States, is the location of responsibility for registration. In most countries, voter registration is automatic, a by-product of government-maintained records of every citizen's name and location. In a few countries, voter registration is a separate step, but one that the government initiates through a systematic canvass, either by public officials or payments to party workers. Great Britain and Canada, which register by canvass, have lower turnout than continental nations that make use of more automatic procedures. The United States is the only country where the entire burden of registration falls on the individual rather than the government.

Registration requirements make voting in the United States more troublesome than in any other country. The need to register — and the difficulty of doing so — impedes Americans' relatively strong impulse to participate, helping to produce a relatively low rate of voting. In most American states, registration is separated from voting by both time and geography. Registration usually does not provide the emotional gratification that voting does. Election day is the climax to a widely publicized and hotly contested competition. In contrast, the deadline for registration is as obscure as the registration requirements and procedures themselves. What is more, almost anyone who moves must register all over again; and in any given year one-sixth of the population moves.

The deterrent effect of American registration procedures can be tested by examining turnout in those states whose registration laws pose the smallest obstacles to voters. The most important legal provision in this respect is the closing date for registration; all other factors held constant, the closer to election day one can register, the greater the likelihood of voting. Four states permit election-day registration (Maine, Minnesota, Oregon and Wisconsin), and one requires no registration (North Dakota). How does turnout in these five states compare with that in other countries?

Table 3 shows that the five states allowing election-day registration or requiring no registration had considerably higher turnout

TABLE 3
Turnout in States With Election-Day Registration (1980)

State	Percent of the Voting-Age Population Who Voted	Where to Register
Minnesota	70.1%	At polls on election day, City Hall, City Clerk, County Auditor
Wisconsin	67.2	Election day at polls with Identification, Municipal Clerk or Board of Election Commissioners in countries where registration is required
North Dakota	64.8	No registration
Maine	64.6	Registrar of Voters, Board of Registration, Justice of Peace, Notary Public
Oregon	61.5	County Clerk
All U.S.	52.6	

than did the United States as a whole. The national percentage of the voting-age population who voted was 52.6 percent; for the five states, it ranges from a low of 61.5 percent (Oregon) to 70.1 percent (Minnesota). By comparing Tables 3 and 1, we see that even our most permissive states do not match most other countries in turnout, although they come close to a few. All but Oregon exceed Finland and Ireland. Minnesota does better than Canada as well.

If the difficulty of registration accounts for much of the poor American turnout, why is there still such a gap between the permissive states and Europe? One reason is that the measures of turnout are still not equal. The numerator of the turnout percentage, the "number of votes cast," is some millions less than the number of all voters in the United States, because it excludes spoiled ballots, people who go to the polls but do not vote for a presidential candidate, and those whose write-in votes are not counted. According to Ivor Crewe, turnout elsewhere "includes invalid and blank votes (a more than negligible proportion in a few countries).. . . " These differences account for one to two percentage points of the turnout gap.

A second explanation is that election-day registration as practiced in some states is not equivalent to automatic registration. In Maine and Oregon, the voter must make two trips — one to register and one to vote. Oregon voters must first register with the county clerk, which may mean quite a trek for people in small towns and on farms. Another impediment may be that people are unaware how easy it is to vote. One-third of the nonvoting respondents in North Dakota — the best example, since it has no registration requirement — said they could not vote because they had not registered.

Finally, the sheer number of elections that confront Americans in a year may result in low turnout figures. The only evidence on this point is fragmentary but fascinating. Richard Boyd found that the number of residents in a Connecticut town who voted *at some time* during the year was considerably higher than the number who participated in any single election.[9] In short, voters may simply grow weary of voting.

One explanation that we have found unsatisfactory is that political choices in this country are not defined sharply enough to mobilize people to vote. There is no left-wing party, for example, to represent the workers' interests. Clearly, this notion cannot account for most of the gap between turnout in the United States and, say, France. Turnout in France is 15 percentage points higher than in the United States, but only three to five points higher than in Wisconsin or Minnesota. Since it is difficult to believe that either the class basis of the political parties or the character of partisan competition in these high-turnout states is different from that in states with average turnout (say California or Colorado), this line of thought has its limitations as an explanation of American turnout.

The Registration Obstacle

Analyses of group differences in turnout usually emphasize that impediments to voting are greater for some than for others. In fact, this applies to registration far more than it does to actual voting. Tables 4 and 5 provide strong confirmation for our hypothesis that registration is the critical hurdle. Table 4, for example, contrasts the relative difficulty for those of different ages and at different levels of education. Only 51 percent of people with a grammar school education managed to vote in the 1980 election, compared to 84 percent of those with a college degree or more — a gap of 33 percentage points. This is a familiar story. The gap, however, narrows to 17 percentage points when the comparison shifts to *registered respondents*. In other words, the less educated act much more like the better educated once they have crossed the crucial barrier of registration.

The same pattern also appears among age groups and those with different levels of political interest. The gap in turnout between the young and old, and between the least and most interested, narrows significantly when the comparison is among those who have registered. It is especially striking among different age groups. Young Americans are notoriously light voters. Only 42 percent of those aged 18 to 24 made it to the polls in 1980, far behind the 69 percent turnout rate of those 65 and older. Yet, among young people who managed to register, 86 percent voted, compared to 90 percent of those aged 35 to 64. The gap between various age groups all but disappears among those who registered; the young vote at the same rate as the old once they pass the registration hurdle.

Even those least likely to vote — the uneducated, young and politically uninterested — vote at fairly impressive rates if they are registered. Seventy-nine percent of people with only a grammar school education who were registered, for example, managed to

TABLE 4
Turnout and Registration (1980) by Age and Education

	Percent of All Respondents Who Voted	Percent of Respondents Registered to Vote	Percent of Registered Respondents Who Voted
BY AGE:			
18-24 years	42%	49%	86%
25-34	57	65	88
35-64	69	77	90
65 and over	69	82	85
BY EDUCATION:			
0-8 years	51	65	79
9-12	53	64	84
1-4 college	68	75	90
5 or more college	84	87	96
All U.S.	60	69	87

SOURCE: The Vote Validation Study of the University of Michigan Center for Political Studies. *The American National Election Study, 1980.*

vote. Comparing this with the data in Table 2, we see that this group would rank sixteenth; higher than Greece, Israel and Great Britain, and just below Norway and Denmark. The youngest group in Table 4, with an 86 percent turnout, would rank much higher. Even people who were "hardly at all interested" in politics turned out at a rate of 74 percent (see Table 5).

Remedies

Once we understand that the basic cause of our low voting rate is the registration requirement, we can see where major efforts to raise turnout should be directed. If we were to institute the European model of automatic registration, turnout would increase dramatically. This would be the surest method, but it goes strongly against the grain of American political culture. Far more than people elsewhere, Americans seem possessed by a desire to guard individual privacy from governmental intrusion. In fact, there are no records of all inhabitants in any American locality, and Americans have shown a genuine aversion to establishing them in the past.

Short of making it automatic, what might be done to ease the burden of registration? One impediment to voting is a closing date far in advance of election day. The closer the deadline to the election, the more people will vote. Many states could shorten their 30-day closing dates to a week or two before the election, without any apparent sacrifice of convenience or procedural safeguards. Potent interest groups oppose this step. County election officials often plead their need for a full month to consolidate records and then distribute them to precincts in time, although those states with shorter deadlines seem to get the job done in less time. Another interesting source of opposition to shorter closing dates is candidates for office, many of whom spend most of their campaign budgets on direct mailings in the last two or three weeks before the election; an early closing date permits them to use an up-to-date set of addresses. With a deadline just before the election, candidates would have to use lists from the primary election, which would be missing recent immigrants to their district and also would include people who had moved away. In addition to these procedural opponents, shorter closing dates, like other reforms, are often opposed by conservatives who believe that they would

TABLE 5
Interest in Politics, Turnout, and Registration in 1980

Follow politics[a]	*Percent of All Respondents Who Voted*	*Percent of Respondents Registered to Vote*	*Percent of Registered Respondents Who Voted*
Hardly at all	38%	51%	74%
Only now and then	54	64	84
Some of the time	70	76	92
Most of the time	75	83	91

NOTE:

a. The question (variable 974): "Some people seem to follow what's going on in government and public affairs most of the time, whether there's an election going on or not. Others aren't that interested. Would you say you follow what's going on in government and public affairs most of the time, some of the time, only now and then, or hardly at all?"

SOURCE: The Vote Validation Study of the University of Michigan Center for Political Studies, *The American National Election Study, 1980.*

strengthen liberals; the evidence shows that more permissive registration procedures would increase the number of voters but not change their political character.

Election-day registration carries to a logical extreme the goal of shortening closing dates. While this provision unquestionably increases turnout, it has some potential for serious voting fraud. The brief experience in Minnesota and Wisconsin has not produced any scandals, but this may reflect the clean politics culture of those states more than the presence of adequate safeguards. One study of the two states concluded that election-day registration was an "honor system" without adequate procedural protection. Moreover, this seems to be an idea whose time has come and gone; Congress easily defeated President Carter's proposal for a nationwide system in 1977, and since then the provision has made very little progress.

Two more modest proposals occur to us. One concerns the possibility that some Americans refrain from registering because they fear that doing so will make them liable to jury duty. Voter registration lists are used almost everywhere as a basis (sometimes the only one) for selecting jury panels, and serving on juries is a form of civic participation that many Americans wish to avoid. There is no hard evidence on this point, but there is a wealth of anecdotes from precinct workers and local election officials. If states were to use other sources in addition to registration rolls for selecting juries, such as lists of people who have registered their cars or obtained drivers' licenses, and then publicized the policy, people might be less motivated to avoid jury duty by refusing to register to vote.

The burden of registration is most likely to deter two kinds of people: those whose interest or clerical skill is insufficient to get them over this threshold, and people who, having moved, need to re-register. Movers do eventually get around to registering, but their registration rate takes approximately five years to catch up with those who have stayed put. Movers take their time about registering, but they cannot be so casual about telephone service, electric power connections, and similar arrangements that are made on arriving at a new home. Concerted efforts to include registration by mail forms with the paperwork required by utility companies might boost registration in those states that perm' it (some 60 percent of the population). Some of these organizations are accustomed to including civic-minded material in their monthly mailings.

Post office change-of-address notices are an even more interesting possibility. If these were filled out in duplicate, the second copy could be mailed to the relevant secretary of state. In the case of intra-state moves by those who are already registered (83 percent of moves are within the same state), the secretary of state might be able to transfer the registration to the new address. Mail registration forms could be sent to the unregistered. Pilot programs to try these suggestions in limited areas are feasible, and would be appropriate subjects for financial support by foundations or a federal grant program.

If almost everyone who is registered votes, measures such as holding elections on Sunday, making election day a holiday, or extending the hours that polls are open would do little to improve turnout. All these are designed to encourage those who are already very likely to vote. Money, energy and political capital should be reserved for actions that have more potential — getting people to register, on the amply documented assumption that once people register, they vote.

NOTES

We are grateful for advice and comments from Jack Citrin, Seymour M. Lipset, Thomas E. Mann, Nelson W. Polsby, G. Bingham Powell, Austin Ranney, Eric R.A.N. Smith, Dick Verheyen, Mark C. Westlye, and Harold L. Wilensky. The survey data we analyzed are part of the holdings of the State Data Program of the University of California. They were gathered by the National Election Studies of the University of Michigan's Center for Political Studies and were made available by the Inter-University Consortium for Political and Social Research. The data were collected under a grant from the National Science Foundation. Neither the NES nor the ICPSR has any responsibility for our analyses or interpretations.

1. The only exception of which we are aware is in NELSON W. POLSBY AND AARON WILDAVSKY, *Presidential Elections*, 5th ed. (New York: Charles Scribner's Sons, 1980), p. 241. Great Britain, the U.S., and Idaho are compared. Idaho compares favorably on both measures, and the U.S. exceeds Great Britain in the proportion of the registered who go to the polls.

2. See JACK CITRIN, "The Alienated Voter," *Taxing and Spending* (October, 1978): 1-7 and AUSTIN RANNEY, "Nonvoting is Not a Social Disease," *Public Opinion* (October/November, 1983): 16-19.

3. GABRIEL A. ALMOND AND SIDNEY VERBA, *The Civic Culture* (Princeton, N.J.: Princeton University Press, 1963), p. 102.

4. The *Euro-Barometre* data appeared in *Public Opinion* (June/July, 1981): 38.

5. DUSAN SIDJANSKI, "The Swiss and Their Politics," *Government and Opposition*, Vol. 11 (1976): 294-321.

6. SAMUEL H. BARNES ET AL., *Political Action* (Beverly Hills, California: Sage Publishing Co., 1979), p. 169.

7. For a variety of reasons, information on the registration status or voting could not be gathered for 177 of the 1614 respondents. We have deleted them from our analysis.

8. For an explanation, see RAYMOND E. WOLFINGER AND STEVEN J. ROSENSTONE, *Who Votes?* (New Haven: Yale University Press, 1980), pp. 115-7.

9. RICHARD W. BOYD, "Decline of U.S. Voter Turnout: Structural Explanations," *American Politics Quarterly*, Vol. 9 (April, 1981).

Converging Electoral Currents in British and American Politics

EVERETT CARLL LADD

The British General Election of June 9, 1983 gives us a fresh opportunity to examine whether Great Britain and the United States are becoming more alike. The notion that the politics of industrial democracies are growing ever more similar — the theory of convergence — has three major elements.

The first of these is that industrial democracies have become much wealthier over the last three decades. In the process they have increased substantially the protections and guarantees accorded to all segments of their populations, especially those who

Adapted from Everett Carll Ladd, "Converging Currents in British and American Politics," *Public Opinion*, Vol. 6, No. 3 (June/July, 1983): 4-6, 55-56. By permission of publisher: American Enterprise Institute for Public Policy Research.

are the least well off. Social class, in both its traditional forms and political effects, has been greatly altered by growing affluence.

The second element in discussions of convergence is the retreat throughout the industrial world of many particularistic sources of political attachments. Ethnic group, trade union and neighborhood associations, and political parties — to name only a few — have yielded influence to the nationalizing messages and "universalist appeals" of the media and the university-trained, idea-generating groups that manage them.

The third element involves the political domination of advanced technology and its repercussions. Populations who are less receptive to class appeals, who have a larger stake in the society, and who draw information from universalistic media, confront similar problems that are at once broad and technical, and that defy answers offered by older, particularistic ideologies. Agreement on *ends* is assumed. Finding the appropriate *means* is what preoccupies democracies today. And, for many of them, the older class-based ideological formulas do not provide helpful guides.

If these observations about convergence are correct, we should be able to see the effects in electoral politics, particularly in countries like Britain and the United States, which have common roots in political institutions and values.

Popular Ambivalence about the State

The most important change in American political attitudes of the past 15 years has come in the full flowering of highly ambivalent assessments of government. This development owed little to the old political philosophies and their contrasting views of the state — New Deal liberalism *for*, conservatism, *against* — and much to the practical lessons the public drew from contemporary experience. The key precipitant of the public's rising criticism of government was sustained high inflation. Gradually over the 1970s, the public came to see inflation as the most unsettling feature of the modern political economy — and to believe that government was the source of the problem.

The public had no desire, though, to put the knife to governmental programs and services. The things government did domestically had come to be seen as important parts of the entitlements of modern life — and most Americans no more wanted cuts here than in consumer goods. Much this same mix took place in British political attitudes — although it occurred in the United Kingdom against the backdrop of a considerably less affluent and somewhat less individualistic society that had accepted a larger governmental presence.

For all the talk — which many Labour party leaders still find so appealing — of the "two Britains," one a deprived working class, the other a traditional upper class and *haute bourgeosie*, the fact is that it is the *lower middle class* that has been growing in the postwar United Kingdom. Perhaps the most revealing measure of this is the steady rise in the proportion of all housing that is owner-occupied. From just 10 percent in 1914, the proportion owner-occupied in England and Wales climbed to 31 percent in 1939, 47 percent by 1966, reached 50 percent for the first time in 1970, and stood at almost 60 percent in 1983. Owning one's home is a powerful stake in society, and since 1970 a majority of British citizens have had it. (Earlier in this century, the United States had far more owner-occupied housing than Britain, but this gap has narrowed dramatically. The figures for the United States — percentage of all housing owner-occupied — are 46 percent in 1920, 44 percent in 1940, 62 percent in 1960, 63 percent in 1970, and 66 percent in 1980.)

Given this movement in Britain toward the American pattern of class make-up, it would have been surprising if British voters had not responded to the rampant inflation of the 1970s much the same as Americans did. And so they did. When asked by Harris interviewers, in a poll taken for the *London Observer* on May 26-27 — when 3.2 million British workers were unemployed — "which matters most to you and your family, reducing unemployment or keeping down inflation?" — 56 percent nationally said "keeping down inflation," compared to just 38 percent "reducing unemployment." The Thatcher government had, of course, made a long-term campaign against inflation the cornerstone of its domestic economic program.

Partisan Responses to the Electorate's Ambivalence

In both Great Britain and the United States, decisive majorities had come by the late 1970s to feel that there were structural problems inhering to their national governments that needed correcting. It is evident from poll data and actual political behavior alike that many had in fact come to believe that the difficulties were basic and deep-rooted. From this perception sprung a willingness to bear some considerable short-term discomfort to see government launched securely along a new path. In both countries, then, there was a popular impulse to "stay the course" long before any such campaign slogans appeared.

As noted, this did not mean that the electorate wanted to see the welfare state dismantled or even substantially cut back. The public had become ambivalent about government, not hostile to it. Had the Thatcher or Reagan governments proceeded to do what their critics accused them of attempting, and what some of their supporters really wanted — namely, cut back radically on governmental programs and services — their partisan opponents would almost certainly have rapidly revived. In fact, no major surgery on the welfare state was seriously pursued in either country.

It was the parties of the left that seemed to resist the mixed appeals of ambivalent electorates — the Democrats in the United States and, far more so, the Labour party in the United Kingdom. Both the Democrats and Labour were burdened by the popular perception that they were unwilling or unable, given their interest group make-up, to rein in government — the chief symbol of which was bringing inflation under control and keeping it there.

Popular ambivalence is not confined to attitudes toward government. It is also evident in public thinking on foreign policy and defense questions, and on various social issues. In Britain and in the United States, controlling majorities of the electorate want a strong national defense and an active assertion of national interests in foreign affairs — but not policies that smack of stridency or bellicosity. Similarly, they favor greater emphasis on older social norms and values — but without anything like a return to social relations of the past. To win majority backing, appeals on these issues must somehow capture the electorate's contradictory impulses. Both the Thatcher and Reagan governments have been vulnerable to the charge that they give too much emphasis to one side: that they are too inclined to cut the welfare state, too hawkish, and too conservative on social issues. And yet their Labour and Democratic opponents have been having even greater difficulty in striking the balance that the electorate's ambivalent feelings require.

Comparison of the Conservatives' approach under Thatcher to that of the Republicans and Reagan comes easily because the two obviously have much in common. Comparisons of Labour and the Democrats is far more strained, however, because Labour's position is much more extreme — and hence politically weaker. Labour's subservience to the union hierarchies, and its policies with regard, for example, to Europe, NATO, and national defense, were unpalatable enough to broad segments of the public and to the right wing of the party's own leadership to prompt four senior Labour politicians — Roy Jenkins, David Owen, Shirley Williams, and William Rogers, the "gang of four" — to establish the Social Democrats as a rival left-of-center party in 1981. In the June 9 balloting, the SDP and the Liberal party, working together as the Alliance, received 7.8 million votes, or 24.6 percent of the total, just 685 000 fewer votes than Labour.

Yet for all of their real differences, Labour and the Democrats have shared over the last two decades a common difficulty in fashioning a clear majoritarian appeal. Since 1964, the Democrats have won the presidency only once, in 1976. Even then, with the Republicans reeling from the shocks of Watergate, the Democrats succeeded only by a whisker. And since 1966, Labour has seen its share of the popular vote drop a full 20 percentage points — from 47.9 percent in 1966 to 27.6 percent in 1983. Its vote proportion has fallen in every succeeding election since its big 1966 victory, save for the second national election in 1974 (the October balloting) when it rose slightly. The Democrats' problem with the presidency and Labour's deteriorating position are too persistent to be dismissed as idiosyncratic results arising from special circumstances.

Electoral Dealignment

The electorates of Great Britain and the United States, despite their different political, philosophic and cultural backgrounds, share a diminished inclination to support faithfully "my party," come what may. With more formal education and more diverse sources of information; with exposure to the fluid, personality-centered view of televised politics; and turned off by the old class-based ideologies, growing numbers are prepared to decide each election on their assessments of what party leaders are *currently* saying and doing. An electorate could be said to be fully "dealigned" if every voter approached every contest as an electoral free market, in which he decides which party (or candidate) best serves his own and the nation's needs (in whatever mix), wholly unencumbered by persisting partisan loyalties or particularistic group attachments. By this standard, British and American voters still are a long way from pure dealignment — and the former are somewhat further away from it than the latter — but both have been dealigning steadily over the past fifteen or so years.

One key result of dealignment is the cutting off of political parties from the once-reliable bases of social group support. In the United States, for example, the ethnic and regional loyalties that were so important to the Republicans and the Democrats over most of their histories have become greatly attenuated. A group such as white southerners, so securely and instinctively Democratic for so long, is now truly up for grabs each election. The 1980 presidential election saw this facet of electoral dealignment advance further than ever before.

Similarly, in the June 9 British election, the unraveling of group identities and partisan loyalties was strikingly apparent. The British party system has been strongly class based — and for this reason dealignment has expressed itself most dramatically in the erosion of the old class differences and strongholds. Ivor Crewe notes that in 1959 manual workers were 40 percentage points more for Labour than non-manual workers; by 1979, however, the gap had shrunk to 27 percent and in 1983 to just 21 points. In the June 9 balloting, for the first time in a half century, Labour failed to win the backing of a majority of the working class. Among all blue-collar workers, Labour had just a 5 percentage point margin over the Conservatives — and among skilled manual workers it actually trailed the Conservatives by 4 points. In the big Tory victory of 1959, 62 percent of manual workers had remained loyal to Labour; in 1983 the proportion was just 38 percent.

According to the large poll taken June 8 and 9 by British Gallup for the BBC, only 39 percent of trade union members themselves backed the Labour party, compared to 32 percent for the Conservatives and 28 percent for the Alliance. When a political party established by the labor movement and constitutionally tied to the trade unions can muster the support of fewer than two union members in every five — in an election where an incumbent Conservative government refused to offer even a faint hope that unemployment, already at 3.2 million, would not for a time continue to rise — one sees just how far dealignment has proceeded.

Another characteristic of voters with weak party ties is that they jump back and forth among the parties from one election to the next. In the June voting the British electorate displayed an extraordinary amount of this partisan mobility. Ivor Crewe observes that because Labour had a bad election in 1979, it might be expected that those who stayed with it that year would constitute a loyal core. Thirty percent of its 1979 supporters switched parties, however, in 1983, while another 7 percent did not vote. Seventeen percent of those who backed the Conservatives in the previous election switched this year, and another 6 percent stayed home. Twenty-three percent of 1979 Liberals changed parties in 1983, while 5 percent abstained.

Just as in the United States, dealignment has been accompanied in the United Kingdom by the growth of so-called "negative voting." The BBC/Gallup survey showed 55 percent of Conservative, 62 percent of Labour, and 63 percent of Alliance voters saying their dislike of the other parties was more influential in their voting decision than their positive feelings for the party they wound up supporting. Such findings are, of course, inevitable given dealignment — which means a decrease in positive attachments to political parties.

Thatcher and Reagan

The striking similarities in British and American electoral politics — such as the strength of voters' backing of new approaches to political economy and a reining-in of government, the persisting problems that the parties of the left are encountering, and the weakening of partisan attachments — seem clearly to be responses to the many common structural conditions of advanced industrial society. The final parallel I want to discuss also owes much to social-structural experience, but it cannot be wholly explained as such. There is always a place for chance — and chance plays some part in the intriguing similarities of political style and philosophy of the British Prime Minister and the American President.

Margaret Thatcher and Ronald Reagan are both the second generation leaders of their countries' populist conservatism. British journalist Peregrine Worsthorne calls Thatcherism "Mark II Powellism," acknowledging the aborted first thrust of Tory orator Enoch Powell. And in much the same sense, Reaganism is "Mark II Goldwaterism." Neither Powell nor Senator Barry Goldwater had the right political personality or found the right political formula, but each led the first charge.

Thatcher and Reagan have much the same political roots and

heroes. Their economic philosophies can be traced to the work of economic theorist Milton Friedman, and less directly to economic philosopher Friedrich Hayek. If John Maynard Keynes was the guru of the New Deal and Butskellism, Friedman and Hayek played that role for Thatcher-Reaganism.

Both Margaret Thatcher and Ronald Reagan emerged as their nations' leaders much underestimated. Both were thought by most of their countries' political commentators to be insufficiently sophisticated, and neither was at first recognized for her (his) ability to mobilize national majorities and maintain them over the arduous course of governing. While Reagan was quickly dubbed "the Great Communicator," Thatcher as well became an effective speaker and — in a respectable sense — television performer. Both are strong personalities and share a high measure of confidence in the rightness of the course they have chosen to follow.

Margaret Thatcher and Ronald Reagan are nationalists in the Hamiltonian sense of that term. Reagan's addiction to the "doctrine of American exceptionalism" is well understood by American audiences. But Thatcher has an equally lively sense of her country's history and special role.

Thatcher and Reagan have often been depicted as right wing ideologues. And yet in power both have behaved consistently as highly pragmatic politicians, bending and trimming as necessary to stay the course on a few broad goals. Only their rhetoric at times merits the label "extreme."

Finally and perhaps importantly, Margaret Thatcher and Ronald Reagan have retained the public backing needed to govern, even in the face of economic dissatisfaction, not through being loved but rather through being thought necessary. This sense that Thatcher and Reagan are attempting necessary corrections has been shared, the polls tell us, by majorities of their countries' electorates. This is why, when confronted with recession and a surge of unemployment, their popular standing bent but did not break. Polls in the United Kingdom and the United States keep showing an otherwise curious tension between the public's substantial opposition to many specific policies, and its simultaneous endorsement of the overall direction of policy change. When asked whether the effort will make Britain [or the United States] better in the long run, majorities in both countries have consistently answered "yes." The much celebrated patience of British and American voters is not that at all, but rather a cautious mandate to proceed, however haltingly, along a new course.

Envoi

It would be senseless to claim that British and American politics are in any sense becoming identical. But they do now share some impressive similarities — and certainly far more than in 1800, 1900, or even 1950. This electoral convergence seems not to be happenstance but rather the result of deep-seeded social and institutional developments accruing from advanced industrialism. The capacity of the latter to override vast historic differences of class and culture is a major dimension of contemporary politics.

Anatomy of a Letter-Perfect Lobby

SANDY FIFE

It wasn't until August, 1982, that Norman Stewart read the new definition of a letter proposed by Canada Post Corp. in the July 3 issue of the Canada Gazette. But it didn't take him long to grasp its implications.

Stewart is a staff lawyer for General Motors of Canada Ltd. in Oshawa, Ont. By his reckoning, Canada Post's attempt to define and enshrine its monopoly on the delivery of letters would cost his employer $3 million or more annually, thanks mainly to its proposed restrictions on the bulking of interoffice mail carried by private couriers.

Across the country, meanwhile, other executives just back from holidays were being similarly alerted to the damage that could be done if the new crown corporation's proposals were accepted by the federal cabinet.

Thus were planted the seeds of the "ad hoc business/consumer group," an unlikely alliance of 16 major organizations from every sector of the economy, formed to negotiate a more flexible definition of the post office's monopoly. Membership ranged from the Consumers Association of Canada and the Canadian Manufactur-

Reprinted from Sandy Fife, "Anatomy of a letter-perfect lobby," *Financial Times of Canada* (August 8, 1983), p. 17. By permission of publisher.

ers' Association, to the Conseil du Patronat du Quebec and the Toronto Stock Exchange.

Persuading the Feds

With Stewart at the helm, the group ultimately persuaded the federal cabinet to reject the proposed regulation, and Canada Post to amend it to reflect the alliance's concerns.

The group proved that by co-operating to achieve maximum economic and political clout, making the most of the party system and the media, and taking a positive approach to issues, business interests can positively influence the seemingly remote lawyers and bureaucrats who make the rules.

Peter McInenly, a Canada Post lawyer who dealt with the lobby, believes that while the media and political pressure exerted by the group "can't be discounted," its success was mainly due to a "mature, reasoned approach to a sensitive issue. An element of good faith developed (during discussions of the proposed definition) and was built upon."

But good faith seemed to be lacking initially when GM's Stewart helped draft a Canadian Manufacturers' Association position paper on the definition, addressed to Canada Post and Andre Ouellet, minister of consumer and corporate affairs. "There was no response," Stewart says. "And because time was of the essence, we (Stewart and GM's government relations department) started calling other companies and organizations that might be affected to see if they shared our concerns."

Sense of Urgency

Ironically, part of Stewart's sense of urgency stemmed from a misunderstanding of the regulatory process. Along with many others, he believed Sept. 3 was the deadline for amendments to the proposed definition, after which it would automatically pass to cabinet. The date, in fact, was merely the deadline for public submissions to Canada Post regarding the definition. Cabinet, Stewart learned, was not scheduled to consider the proposal until late November, giving the intervenors several months to persuade Canada Post to alter its definitions.

Stewart and his colleagues, mainly contacts through the CMA, rounded up 16 interested parties to form the ad hoc group, which held its first meeting in early October. The worried participants exchanged what information they had on the regulatory process and discussed the definition's impact on the users of Canada Post and its competitors' services.

At a second meeting, on Oct. 18, the lobbyists agreed on their goal: to gain time and support for "constructive dialogue" between users and Canada Post before the new regulations were approved. They agreed to concentrate on trying to change a few key points of the proposals: to narrow the post office's broad definition of a "letter," to ease its suggested restrictions on the bulking of mail, and to provide more freedom for the use of private couriers.

According to Stewart, who was elected chairman of the ad hoc group's steering committee, the coalition wasn't looking for a fight or trying to embarrass Canada Post. "We tried not to be negative. We wanted to be able to discuss and work with officials rather than alienate them."

The committee considered hiring a professional lobbyist to carry its message to Ottawa, but decided against it, because of both the expense and the possible damage to the group's image.

In dividing up the work, members of the committee simply looked at their respective talents and resources. Having already demonstrated his ability to muster support, Stewart was put in charge of taking their concerns to the public via the media. Jim Bennett, then director of national affairs for the Canadian Federation of Independent Business, was to take the case to the bureaucrats and politicians in Ottawa. Bennett, now executive director of the Canadian Wine Institute, had spent 10 years working for the federal government — two of them in a minister's office — and had valuable contacts and savvy.

Other committee members acted as liaisons with the organizations in the ad hoc group, which were consistently encouraged to continue their own efforts to change the definition. The Toronto Stock Exchange, for instance, asked individuals associated with it to write to Canada Post and Ouellet about their concerns.

Stewart's media campaign, meanwhile, was intended to generate new support for the lobby among small companies and independent businessmen.

His approach to publicity was unsophisticated but effective. He quickly put together an information package on the lobby, and gave it to the Toronto papers, along with the reasons he felt it was newsworthy. "Then the story was picked up by Canada AM (a

CTV public affairs program), and after that it mushroomed," he says.

Coverage of the ad hoc group's activities generated interest from other organizations and companies, which in turn led to more stories. Support for the lobby grew continuously, Stewart says, and members of the public and the business community began writing Ottawa protest letters of their own.

Contact with key government officials was the other crucial element in the group's success. Bennett knew that, to obtain a regulatory reprieve, meetings with departmental policy advisors would be more effective than with ministers. All departments which would be concerned with the economic impact of the proposed definition of a letter were canvassed, from the Treasury Board and finance to industry, trade and commerce.

Events were so compressed due to the impending regulatory deadline that Stewart's appearance on Canada AM, and his and Bennett's meetings with various bureaucrats, selected opposition members, and Ouellet all took place on one day, Nov. 1. Ideally, Stewart and Bennett agree, they would have met Ouellet first and given him a chance to react before approaching other officials.

Still, the relentless badgering, by mail, telephone and the press, imposed cumulative pressure on the Liberals that was too great to ignore. "The government knew what they had to lose if they allowed the regulation to be rushed through," says Bennett. "They had to balance their own image against (Canada Post president Michael) Warren's loss of face. And it wasn't an issue where delay meant millions of dollars of lost revenue."

Visible Results

The results of the pressure were soon visible. In late November, Canada Post announced it was working on amendments to the definition, to be considered by Cabinet after the original's approval. In fact, the Crown corporation's officials had already begun meeting with groups that had made submissions regarding the regulation, including members of the ad hoc lobby.

But the group, unsatisfied, continued to apply pressure. "Canada Post's position was 'let's push this thing through and then amend it'," says Bennett. "Nobody in his right mind was buying that."

Fresh stories were fed to the media, telegrams were despatched to members of parliament, and information packages were sent to Liberal caucus members as the deadline drew nearer. Finally, on Nov. 23, the cabinet announced it had rejected the definition.

Amend Proposal

Canada Post was directed to amend its proposal and resubmit it for regulatory approval within a few month's time. Consultations began in earnest. As the group began to feel it was playing an active role in producing a satisfactory regulation, it relaxed its media campaign and sent letters of support to corporation officials.

Finally, a new version of the definition was published in the Gazette in February, 1983, and it was one with which the business community could live.

"It's the first time something like this has been done," says Stewart, summing up. "We've affected the regulatory process, and made it more consultative."

Although the ad hoc group has disbanded, he believes its spirit should live on. He would like to see a "clearing-house" or independent forum established through which companies could regularly share information and concerns about government.

Canada Post's McInenly agrees that business's common front aided the postal negotiations. "It's useful when a bunch of essentially different groups get together to debate common interests and discard what's unimportant. It saved us time to meet with these organizations on an umbrella basis."

"Not everything was sweetness and light," he adds, "but we think we've opened a big door."

Pressuring the Executive

J. HUGH FAULKNER

In discussing how, why and where groups apply pressure to the executive, and how the executive responds to that pressure, I shall be duly cautious. I shall try to convey my understanding of what distinguishes group-executive relations; how the policy system works; the problems we face within it; and what we can do about those problems. My approach will not be a theoretical one, however. I shall discuss these developments and issues from the point of view of the practitioner — an ex-member of the executive. I shall try to show how we viewed pressure and the interaction between the executive and interest groups. My comments will not be researched and organized comments; they will be my recollections — highly selective and difficult to document.

Characterizing Executive-Group Relations

What characterizes the relationship between cabinet, and public servants and large and established interest groups? My view is that that relationship is essentially characterized by a high level of interdependence.

An interest group that is related to his portfolio is, for any cabinet minister, a primary constituency: the bankers for the Minister of Finance; the Indian associations for the Minister of Indian Affairs; the Canadian Legion for the Minister of Veterans Affairs. These are primary constituencies. Their backing is often essential to maintaining ministerial clout within cabinet, even to surviving in the job. Their support in the implementation of programs and policies is usually important. A minister who loses the confidence of his primary constituency is in trouble. You can quickly read in the political columns the impending political mortality of a minister who has lost that support.

The primary constituency is also a minister's principle alternative source of information for his department. Any minister who

Adapted from J. Hugh Faulkner, "Pressuring the Executive," *Canadian Public Administration*, Vol. 25, No. 2 (Summer, 1982): 240-253. By permission of publisher and author.

decides he can run a department on the basis of the advice he gets from his bureaucrats is bound to be in trouble. Not because the advice from bureaucrats is mischievous or malevolent or badly thought out, but because it represents a particular point of view; and in a world where the public agenda is increasingly broad, a single source of information, a single point of view, can no longer be relied upon. Furthermore, deputy ministers and their supporting policy advisors have no particular monopoly on wisdom and they can as easily become victims of myopia or tunnel-vision as anyone else. The primary constituency, on the other hand, provides a minister with grass-roots feed-back on issues and the concerns of its membership. So political heads of agencies need very good communications with that primary constituency to provide intelligence on what programs are working and on how they are working. They need their views on what policies should be changed. In short, they depend on the primary constituency as a source of policy countervail to departmental advice.

Likewise, those primary constituencies, those interest groups, very much need the politician. From the interest group's point of view, the cabinet minister directly responsible for their interest is their single most important ally. None of the issues of concern to them will make it through the decision-making system without the assiduous attention and support of their minister. I have yet to see an interest group get a proposal through cabinet without it being strongly supported by the relevant minister.

Despite the fact that most groups recognize this, few make any effort to provide the public and political support that would ensure or reinforce their cause. This is because the relationship is perceived to be adversarial in nature. Leaders of interest groups seem compelled to posture as fighters, not negotiators. If they appear too supportive of the minister, they risk losing their credibility as negotiators. The dynamic of the interaction reflects the lack of maturity and sophistication in many Canadian interest groups and their leadership. The transition from participation in an adversarial system to a new one that is broadly consultative in nature, is one of the major changes that interest groups and politicians must undertake over the next few years.

The aim of interest groups is to maximize support for their interests within the system. Influences are highly dispersed both horizontally and vertically. Cabinet ministers are, in general, enormously over-extended and do not have adequate time to devote to any single special interest, unless it happens to be central to the management of the portfolio, such as the chartered banks for the Minister of Finance, or the Canadian Labour Congress for the Minister of Labour. The best way to influence the executive is to influence the advice the executive receives. A minister who is over-extended when confronted with a request from an interest group, is more likely to accede to that request if it is supported by the departmental officials he invariably consults. To influence that advice it is important to identify the individuals within the department or the minister's office who have a responsibility or an interest in the subject matter. When those individuals are identified and contact is made, the group's best strategy is to see that the goals of the interest group correspond as much as possible with their thinking. It is unlikely that an interest group will make progress with an idea that would correspond in no particular way to the thinking of those advising the minister. The rare exception would be on an issue where the minister personally shares the view of the interest group and generally feels the department to be out of touch or ill-informed. These circumstances arise from time to time but tend to be very much the exception. This being so, more time is usually spent persuading the officials and the members of the minister's office on a policy or an interest issue than with the minister. This may not be as insidious as it appears. A minister must manage his time; if he is any good, he will force the parties to sort it out, and retain the authority to accept or reject the result. In short, a minister cannot afford to spend much time on a particular issue — his task is to ensure the issue gets the ablest and most broadly based consideration possible and then apply his judgment to shaping the final product. The reverse is only true when the departmental officials are clearly opposed to the request of the interest group, and are determined to obstruct it, and/or when it is clear that his advisors have lost the trust and confidence of a primary constituency.

This suggests that the relationship between the primary constituency and the bureaucracy is as interdependent as that between the minister and the constituency, and it is. However, because contact with the bureaucracy is multifaceted, and usually private, the relationship is more diffuse. To secure the support of this group necessitates understanding the dynamics of the process at work. Because the bureaucracy has various protective devices, negotiations are often confused by arguments about who said or promised what to whom, or by the need to consult the minister and probably officials of other departments. It is important to recognize that senior civil servants are career people, most often talented, intelligent and committed to the public service. They work within a system which has its own peer-group pressures, a system of rewards and punishment and an internal value system. Most civil servants are professionally disposed to push or recommend policy that is likely to achieve political support both at the cabinet level and within the civil service.

Working in a Dispersed Power System

Power is the authority to influence policy. The federal government's ultimate power appears highly concentrated. In practice, it is widely dispersed. It is perfectly true that the Prime Minister and the Minister of Finance can decide that what this country needs is a system of wage and price controls. But for them to proceed with that sort of policy without the support of cabinet, without the support of caucus and without an astute sense of where the public is at, would be foolhardy. Decision-making is highly dispersed and becoming more so. The exercise of power in the federal government is a collegial operation incorporating most of the principal elements of the system: cabinet, caucus, civil servants, interest groups (primary constituencies) and the public. The degree of participation and influence of each of these depends on the issue and the circumstances.

Since the late 1960s many structural and procedural changes have contributed to this dispersion. One of the most important has been the creation of a number of new ministries with specific mandates. This has provided identifiable interests at the cabinet level for a wider range of primary constituencies. At the same time, it has further dispersed power. For example, an interest group that has secured the support of its minister has not secured the agreement of cabinet. That would not have been as true of cabinet in the 1950s. Cabinet has its own internal set of interests, not least of these is a collegial interest in retaining substantial public support for the overall performance of the government. As well, each minister has a political career, a political following of some dimension and a specific geographic area to attend to. All of these predispose ministers to take a collegial view of departmental proposals, and they force interest groups to cultivate ministers other than their own.

The new policy and expenditure management system also ensures that ministers must process any initiative that involves expenditures (which includes tax expenditures), through their cabinet colleagues. This process integrates policy decisions into the government priorities framework, tightens up decision-making by juxtaposing policy options and expenditures, and strengthens the pattern of collegial authority over policy development and expenditure management. The effect is to limit the capacity of an individual minister to respond to interest groups. To take an initiative in one area means that another area is going to be affected. Trade-offs will be required, so that other area has to be massaged as well. Consequently, interest groups must now be prepared to deal with the whole range of cabinet, including the cabinet committees, the membership of which has only recently become public information.

The attempt to focus on cabinet in its entirety means that interest groups can no longer ignore the Privy Council Office and the Prime Minister's Office. These agencies are an important factor in the dispersed decision-making system, yet they tend to constantly understate their role in the process. But it is an important role, as ministers in line departments are aware; therefore they have to be dealt with. But it is difficult for groups to reach PCO and PMO officials. Because they understate their role they do not see the relevance of meeting with interest groups, and avoid doing so.

Another factor in the dispersed power model is, of course, the dispersed staff. As I have suggested, the civil servants are obviously of key importance and they are a target group that most successful interest groups understand has to be dealt with. When an interest group is trying to pressure the executive it starts with the officials; it works proposals up from the bottom, and by the time they get to the minister, he generally agrees to what has been worked out between the two.

Nor do successful groups ignore those parts of the public service that operate outside the usual departmental machinery. Regulatory bodies often have to be attended to, for example, the recent decision of the National Energy Board to delay by two years the commencement of the Norman Wells pipeline is eloquent testimony to the capacity of interest groups to influence them. The recent rate award of the Canadian Radio and Telecommunications Commission to Bell Canada clearly bears the imprint of consumer interest representation. Ministerial staff also are often important. They develop the minister's agenda, monitor access to him or her and offer advice gathered from a variety of informal channels.

Individual members of Parliament and caucus can be influential if they participate prior to the issue getting to the House of Commons. I give more credence to the role of the MP's than most, and certainly more than the official literature on the subject. Parliamentarians can be enormously important before a bill becomes government policy. Caucus can be effective if it is mobilized. In my judgment the Quebec caucus has been the single most important influence in maintaining the Quebec textile industry, despite the government's policy of opening up trade with the Third World. The Quebec caucus has managed to keep that industry alive and well through the sheer force of numbers and spelling out what the political consequences are of closing it down. In this group, as well, one must include senators, some of whom are quite openly engaged in pursuing certain interests, even to the point of accepting retainers from clients. Others are free of any conflicts of interest and exercise influence through much the same channels as the MP's.

It will be clear from this short outline that the dispersed power system that has developed in Canada is not easy to work in, or to work with. Furthermore, it poses some problems for those of us who are concerned about the preservation of democratic parliamentary government. At the same time, it has many valuable features and it is capable of reinforcing, rather than undermining, the legitimacy of the policy process. In the following paragraphs, I shall look at one of the most effective groups that I have seen at work in the system and one which might be said to represent its best aspects. I shall also look at some recent changes in executive-group relations and discuss their promising potential for the future.

An interest group at work

The most significant adaptation interest groups have made to this changing, increasingly dispersed power system has been a trend toward better management. This does not necessarily mean that the bigger, more affluent groups are more likely to have things all their own way. On the contrary, one of the ironies of the contemporary pressure group scene is that the influential interest groups today seem to be less satisfied with the results of their efforts than some of the less powerful. The critical factor in both success and failure is, more often than not, the quality of management.

Let me take one interest group to illustrate my point — the Canadian Arctic Resources Committee (CARC). It is infinitely more successful than most big, powerful, well-financed groups. I observed CARC as a minister; they used to give me hell. More recently I have observed them as an interested citizen, watching progress in Lancaster Sound and Norman Wells. A recent survey of opinion among the interested public in government, industry, academic and northern circles found a high degree of respect for CARC's constructive role in the public policy process, even among the committee's adversaries. CARC is a good example of how a small group of citizens with a relatively small budget can have an impact well beyond the level of dollars spent and the size of the organization.

In 1978 CARC intervened in an environmental hearing that was examining the application of Norlands Petroleum to drill for oil and gas in the centre of Lancaster Sound. For the rest of Canada that was a non-event. Few had ever heard of Norlands and most certainly did not know where Lancaster Sound was. Lancaster Sound is the eastern entrance to the Northwest Passage. It has been described as an Arctic oasis, one of the places in the North where a combination of currents and temperatures have made it an area of unusual biological productivity.

CARC's intervention argued that before the government approved the authority to drill, it should look at two things: first, the substance of the application and second, the process by which a decision would be made on the substance. No decision to drill a single well in Lancaster Sound should be made until the government had an understanding of the competing and conflicting demands which would be placed on the Lancaster Sound region in the future, with an accompanying acceptable set of principles and guidelines as to how these competing interests might be satisfied. The environmental panel accepted CARC's argument. The government launched the Lancaster Sound Green Paper which some described as a regional planning exercise. That was something that we really had not had in mind. All we were doing there originally was drilling — innocently drilling to see if there was anything there; and suddenly, because of the effective intervention of CARC, we found ourselves into a regional planning exercise, looking at the alternative uses for the area and the impact of oil on the alternative resources there.

CARC did not stop there. It followed up with a scientific workshop and publication, funded by Petro-Canada, which brought together many of the competing interests in Lancaster Sound to attempt to achieve a consensus, independently of the government process. The consensus was achieved and the CARC publication became the focal point for public meetings held on the Green Paper in the North and in Ottawa at the beginning of the summer. At the initial hearing CARC also dealt with the review process itself. It criticized the environmental assessment review process for its lack of rigour and for procedures which did not meet minimum standards of fairness. It initiated a research project to make recommendations for reform of the Environment Assessment Review process. CARC continued to lobby for this reform and is now preparing new legislation for the EARP. CARC did all of that in a period of three years, operating with two or three people and a modest budget.

CARC's influence is not based on friends in high places or special knowledge of the secret latch in government which opens all doors. Their success seems to be based on four simple rules which can work for any interest group.

First, their information is as good as the government's. That is critical. They do not appear before the executive or the environmental review panels or any other agencies of government with half-baked information. They spend an enormous amount of time on the quality of their research and they know a great deal about government and industry activity in the North. One reviewer of their work has said: "If you want to find out what the government as a whole is up to in the North, you're better to ask CARC than any agency in government." One of the keys to CARC's success is their ability to bridge all the interests — to deal with the oil and gas industry, to work with all departments of government at the every day working level, and to somehow consistently maintain the confidence of native organizations across the north, and with people in the communities.

The second thing that typifies CARC is its credibility. It sets high standards for any work that it publishes and attempts to be accurate in the use of information. Even where there is disagreement, a debate is always more productive if parties are dealing from an accurate and credible information base.

Any organization seeking to influence public policy must be prepared to come back again and again at whatever level of government is dealing with an issue. In other words, the group must have tenacity. What many interest groups do not realize is that the upper management of government and the politicians are only a part of the picture. CARC works at that level, but it does so only as a part of its total approach, which involves the public service right down to the seemingly mundane day-to-day working level. Its people never let up. They never step back from an issue satisfied they have achieved their objectives. Thus they start off dealing with a single well in Lancaster Sound and they work from there so that they end up changing the whole environmental review process.

Finally, CARC is usually more interested in having an impact on the decision rather than getting attention in the media for its own point of view. Their interventions are made to be useful to the hearing panel or bureaucrat who is faced with making a decision. Interventions which demonstrate an understanding of the pressures upon the decision-maker and which are directed towards a practical solution will always get a better hearing. Interest groups suffer enormous temptations to go after the bureaucrats. The risks of that sort of politics are much greater than the advantages. CARC has always been fairly careful and by only rarely and selectively attacking bureaucracies — and even then in terms which are measured — has been able to retain its links with the Department of Indian Affairs and others who can give them the information they need to maintain their credibility.

In short, CARC is a model of the kind of pressure group which can survive and be very effective in today's dispersed power system. It is institutionalized, but it is not fat. Its strength lies in the quality and range of its information, its credibility, its tenacity and in its understanding of the norms of the system. These are capacities within the grasp of any reasonably funded interest group, but to attain them the group must have its act together — it must know what it wants — and it must submit to good management.

Some recent changes

The enormous proliferation of interest groups in the 1960s and 1970s has broadened the agenda of issues that come before government. Thus far, our experience with this proliferation suggests that our political system needs to design new ways to cope with these interests. They reflect the wide-ranging changes within the country associated with broader educational opportunities, with more information about domestic and global patterns and with the increasing involvement of people previously excluded from the responsibility of political choice. All of this is the maturing aftermath of participatory democracy. The resulting challenge facing the executive is one of managing the demand for access from these interests and of adjudicating between them with equity, fairness and an eye to the general good and not simply the particular interest, so that the system itself remains a credible instrument for making political choices. This must be accomplished without overloading the system or unnecessarily delaying decision-making. In the following paragraphs I shall review the progress I think we have made towards meeting that challenge.

Basically my thesis is that adaptations have been quite incremental on the government's side and equally incremental on the special interest group side. In fact, the only major change on the latter side is a change toward better management. In my comments on CARC I have tried to show how important this trend can be.

On the government side, adaptation has focused on providing greater access. This has been approached from three directions: through the use of consultative devices; by providing financial assistance to groups; and by creating or enhancing consultative structures.

The development of consultative devices has produced a number of new mechanisms designed to provide public notice of government thinking and to give the general public and interest groups opportunities to react. White papers and green papers in particular have served this purpose admirably, as examination of the major policy debates of the 1970s will clearly show. Public discussions of tax reform, Indian policy, developments in telecommunication, competition policy, to name only a few, were promoted by publication of these documents.

One of the greatest innovations initiated by government in this field was the decision to permit public funding of interest groups. A variety of interest groups have been receiving money from the federal government since the 1960s. Consumers and native people have been the principal beneficiaries. The capacity of the people to intervene before the National Energy Board on the Norman Wells pipeline, for example, was a result of federal funding over the years. Government core funding has allowed groups to participate in the political process who up to that time had been unable to be effective for lack of money. That public funding achieved that end is evident in the results of the Berger inquiry, where $1.2 million was granted to Indian organizations to make representations. Another $540 000 assisted a coalition of interests, including the Canadian Arctic Resources Committee, the regional associations of municipalities and the Métis Federation.

Funding is particularly important for regulatory agencies. Without funding, the full range of interests will not be heard. Regulatory agencies have their own proceedings, schedules, requirements and bureaucracy — and are every bit as complex as a line department of government. To effectively penetrate these agencies, an interest group needs expensive legal and expert help. A good illustration of the levels of funding needed for this sort of participation is found in the decision of the Beaufort Environmental Assessment Panel to provide $250 000 in 1981-82 for public intervenors wishing to make representations on the commercial exploitation of the Beaufort Sea. A further $150 000 was set aside for the 1982-1983 fiscal year. Among the groups seeking support for this work were the Canadian Arctic Resource Committee, the Nature Federation, Energy Probe, the Yukon Conservation Authority and the Arctic International Wildlife Range. The money was to be allocated by a committee chaired by the senior scientific advisor to the Department of the Environment and composed of distinguished individuals from both within government and from outside.

Despite the positive aspects of public funding, it does raise some thorny issues. Practically everyone seems to agree on the principle; practically no one agrees on the modalities. It has not been decided who should be eligible for how much, or from whom. Even the recent parliamentary task force on regulation reform could not offer anything more definitive than to suggest that there be further study of the most appropriate means of funding special interest groups and that such studies should look at the possibilities of using tax incentives and other nongovernmental methods of increasing financial support for these groups.

This last point reflects another issue associated with public funding of interest groups: the notion that governments, through public funding, are manipulating interest groups. Of course, both governments and groups are manipulating each other on a daily basis, at the operational level. But I find very little evidence that, even with public funding, the basic purposes of groups are being distorted. As Minister of Indian Affairs I never had the sense that the Indian constituency was co-opted by those millions of dollars of core funding. Every train that arrives in Ottawa with all those thousands of protestors; every visit to the Queen; every demonstration and every sit-in testifies that that is not a group that is being manipulated by federal funds.

The third type of governmental adaptation to interest group proliferation has taken the form of elaborating the structures through which the executive and groups can talk to one another. There has, for example, been an increased use of advisory boards and commissions with direct links to ministers and their departments. There can be little doubt that these initiatives for consultation have broadened the base of advice to government and have tended to provide views other than those of special interest groups. The key to their longer-term usefulness will be determined by the quality of the appointments and the time and attention the minister gives to their views. The field is quick to note whether or not an advisory board has the ear of the minister.

At the level of the department, joint committees can be very useful. That was my experience with a joint committee of the Department of Indian and Northern Affairs and the mining interests of the Northwest Territories and the Yukon. In 1977 and 1978 I was having enormous troubles with these interests. I had initiated studies to establish some parks in the Northwest Territories; land claims negotiations in the Mackenzie Valley were moving ahead rapidly and the mining industry suddenly foresaw great tracts of the NWT being alienated from any exploration or development. Their initial reaction was to have a senior executive write an open letter to me condemning what I was doing as mindless and thoughtless and obviously insensitive to the needs of the industry. It then became an open battle between us and it soon became obvious that this was going nowhere either for them or for me. So I established a joint committee. Half the committee was from the mining industry and half from the northern program, working under joint chairmen.

The committee started off with both sides very far apart. The mining interests were convinced that park sites were chosen with a view to pre-empting exploration and development. Land claims were seen as a most esoteric process that had nothing to do with the real world and was based on no principles that were discernable to them. But suddenly they had to sit down with my departmental people and deal with substantive issues. The result was that both sides had to start examining issues from the perspective of the other participants. When the representatives of the mining industry saw the departmental rationale for land claims, or heard the civil servant from the National Parks program explain the reasons why certain areas of the Yukon and Northwest Territories were being suggested for a park preserve, they grew to understand and respect the integrity of both those interests and the process of decision-making. Likewise, the civil servants grew to understand the objectives of the mining industry. The committee was ably served by a retired mining executive; he acted as the liaison between the two sides, and was probably instrumental in forcing the participants to try to understand the objectives and motivation of the other side of the table. Ultimately both sides were capable of agreeing to a report that represented a consensus amongst the members of the committee. Conservation interests that were not involved in the committee subsequently had reservations about that consensus. However, there is no doubt that whatever its short-comings, the consensus represented a substantial adjustment in previously strongly held positions. As important was the emergence of a shared understanding on some of the broader objectives and implications of both mining and conservation.

Potentially, the most important initiatives in fostering communication between government and industry have come at the parliamentary level. The existing parliamentary committees and their variations have never proved satisfactory as either instruments for hearing interest groups on proposed legislation or as instruments for studying potential policy areas. In practice, they have been usually crippled by partisanship, floating membership, conflicts with other matters and other parliamentary duties. Too often they are *pro forma* affairs lacking both style and substance. One can think of exceptions to this generalization, but they are exceptions. However, they still serve as a useful source of contact for interest groups. During the first session of the Thirty-second Parliament, for example, 631 witnesses appeared before special committees, 2370 witnesses before standing committees, and 325 witnesses before sub-committees. Some of these were public servants or politicians, but a large proportion were private citizens representing individual or group points of view. Clearly for these people, Parliament is still an important listening post for government.

In May 1980, the government decided to build on this activity by appointing seven special committees to act as parliamentary task forces. They differed from standing committees in several important aspects. Their membership was limited to seven MP's; continuity of attendance was assured by requiring committee approval to changes in membership; they were provided with budgets to hire staff; and they were allowed to travel. They also had the right to make their report public. The subject matters covered by the seven were alternative energy and oil substitution, the disabled and the handicapped, employment opportunities for the 1980s, federal-provincial fiscal arrangements, north-south relations, national trading corporations and regulation reform.

These task forces heard 2500 witnesses and had 796 interest groups appear before them. They also visited communities across Canada to hear representations or invited individuals to Ottawa. In the case of the Task Force on Regulatory Reform, four thousand invitations to appear or comment were sent out and a comprehensive discussion paper was prepared to help focus the issues. They operated relatively unhindered by partisanship. They were free to select witnesses and were unhampered by the normal restrictions of party discipline in writing their report. In large part, this was possible because they were outside the area of developed government policy. The possible exception to this was the Task Force on the National Trading Company where there was no government policy, but the responsible minister, the Minister of State for Trade, had well-publicized and developed personal views.

These committees are a significant step in the direction of reform of the parliamentary committee system. They provide an opportunity for early access for public and special interest groups. In this way they overcome the limitations associated with influencing policy after it has become government policy. It should be noted that the Prime Minister personally chose and mandated the committee chairmen — each one a bright and ambitious MP — so there is some discreet element of discipline. Even so, the committees provided a politically broadly based forum which was popularly elected and had direct access to Parliament and the public to hear and respond to the concerns of private and public interests. The longer-term usefulness of this device can best be measured against the serious concerns for system overload at the executive and bureaucratic level. The fact that these committees can hire their own staff gives them additional opportunity for fresh and considered insights in policy questions.

Conclusion

In any political system there has to be a legitimate process for defining the public interest in an on-going manner. But what is the public interest? Who is to define it? Who is to decide, for example, whether the activity of an interest group serves the public interest? In reality there is no absolute definition of the public interest, at least not one to which ordinary citizens in a democracy will respond if enjoined. When a majority of members of Parliament decided to resist a majority of public opinion and abolish capital punishment, where did the public interest lie? Who was right? In practice, the public interest on any question appears to be what a majority of Parliament declares it to be. If they are wrong or if they are wrong too often, they risk being thrown out of office.

So, short of an ideal definition of what is the public interest, it becomes necessary to find a legitimate process for defining it in an on-going manner. That is clearly the role of Parliament and the executive. For them to fill this role effectively, they in turn have to enjoy widespread legitimacy as the final arbiters of the public interest. The process of accommodation and adjustment requires that the political act of initiation, leadership and arbitration must proceed from sources that command political legitimacy. The present Canadian context demonstrates the risks and dangers to the system when that is not present. The system of decision-making that I have referred to here is excessively dispersed. It leaves many Canadians confused and uncertain about how public policy is made; it increasingly puts a premium on group interaction — generally well-organized interaction — with the political and bureaucratic executive, and it leads many to conclude that the heart of the system, Parliament, has become weak and futile. All of these undermine the legitimacy of the policy-making process and they should command our concern.

Fortunately our condition is not without hope. I do not believe that the system's legitimacy has been compromised, so far, by these developments. In fact, political experience with interest groups since the 1970s does not offer much evidence to suggest that the integrity of the political system has been compromised or that distortions of public policy have been achieved by the powerful, wealthy and well-organized. This is probably due to the enormous increase in government activity and the simultaneous dispersal of power amongst a variety of new government departments and agencies. We have begun to develop effective adaptations to the changing system which, with luck and application, will resolve this issue of legitimacy.

At heart, the issue is not the substance of policy, it is the process. The key to the process is Parliament and the key area for change in that process is the parliamentary committee. And the key to the parliamentary committee, if we are not to change to a congressional system, is to give those committees a variety of things — resources, independent chairpeople, continuity of membership, capacity to travel, ability to produce a report that does not have to be approved by the members of the government. Consequently, to me, the development of the special parliamentary task forces is the most promising innovation that we have yet undertaken. If these committees can continue to have the kind of resources I have spoken of, if they can continue to move across the country and elicit across-the-board opinion, and if they can continue to deal with issues before they become government policy, then I think we will have gone a long way to deal with the problems of access and so with the ultimate problems of legitimacy.

Subject Index